Linguistics

Introducing Linguistics

This outstanding series is an indispensable resource for students and teachers – a concise and engaging introduction to the central subjects of contemporary linguistics. Presupposing no prior knowledge on the part of the reader, each volume sets out the fundamental skills and knowledge of the field, and so provides the ideal educational platform for further study in linguistics.

1	Andrew Spencer	*Phonology*
2	John I. Saeed	*Semantics*, Third Edition
3	Barbara Johnstone	*Discourse Analysis*, Second Edition
4	Andrew Carnie	*Syntax*, Second Edition
5	Anne Baker and Kees Hengeveld	*Linguistics*

Linguistics

Edited by

Anne E. Baker & Kees Hengeveld

A John Wiley & Sons, Ltd., Publication

This edition first published 2012

Blackwell Publishing was acquired by John Wiley & Sons in February 2007. Blackwell's publishing program has been merged with Wiley's global Scientific, Technical, and Medical business to form Wiley-Blackwell.

Registered Office
John Wiley & Sons Ltd, The Atrium, Southern Gate, Chichester, West Sussex, PO19 8SQ, UK

Editorial Offices
350 Main Street, Malden, MA 02148-5020, USA
9600 Garsington Road, Oxford, OX4 2DQ, UK
The Atrium, Southern Gate, Chichester, West Sussex, PO19 8SQ, UK

For details of our global editorial offices, for customer services, and for information about how to apply for permission to reuse the copyright material in this book please see our web site at www.wiley.com/wiley-blackwell.

Library of Congress Cataloging-in-Publication Data

Linguistics / edited by Anne E. Baker & Kees Hengeveld.
p. cm.
Includes bibliographical references and index.
ISBN 978-0-631-23035-9 (cloth) – ISBN 978-0-631-23036-6 (pbk.)
1. Linguistics. I. Baker, Anne, linguistics professor 1948–. II. Hengeveld, Kees, linguistics professor 1957–
P121.L568 2012
410–dc23 2011036309

A catalogue record for this book is available from the British Library.

Typeset in 10/12pt Palatino by Aptara Inc., New Delhi, India

Printed in Singapore by Ho Printing Singapore Pte Ltd

2 2013

Contents

List of Figures and Tables

Figures

Tables

Preface

This introduction to the field of Linguistics offers a broad survey of the discipline. The book is intended first of all for students of language, but it is also suitable for others who want to know more about modern linguistics. It testifies to the enormous richness of natural languages and shows this richness with illustrations from a great many different languages.

Linguistics is intended in the first place for use in education. To this end, the most important linguistic terms are given in bold when they first occur in the text. These terms have also been included in the index, and are repeated in the summaries at the end of each chapter. Each summary is followed by a range of assignments suitable for developing further the subject studied in the chapter. After these assignments students can test themselves to see whether they have sufficiently mastered the key concepts and principles in the chapter. At the end of each chapter, sources of information, examples and other materials are acknowledged, and suggestions for further reading given.

Linguistics is the product of a team of linguists working in the Department of Linguistics of the University of Amsterdam. The book is a revision and English adaptation of Appel *et al.* (eds) (2002), which itself incorporated parts of Appel *et al.* (1992). Appel *et al.* (1992) was edited by René Appel, Simon Dik and Pieter Muysken, while Appel *et al.* (eds) (2002) was edited by René Appel, Anne Baker, Kees Hengeveld, Folkert Kuiken and Pieter Muysken. We edited the current version of the book on the basis of a translation by Reinier Salverda. The responsibility for the various chapters shifted over the two editions mentioned above. The table below indicates which authors wrote the earlier versions of the various chapters.

Chapter	**1992 author**	**2002 author**
1. From Language to Linguistics	Simon Dik, Pieter Muysken	Anne Baker
2. The Language User	Rob Schoonen	Ron Prins, Rob Schoonen
3. Language Acquisition	Anne Baker, René Appel	Folkert Kuiken
4. Discourse	René Appel	Sies de Haan
5. Speech Acts	René Appel	Sies de Haan
6. Constituents and Word Classes	Simon Dik, Pieter Muysken	Kees Hengeveld
7. Simple Sentences	Simon Dik	Kees Hengeveld

Chapter	1992 author	2002 author
8. Complex Sentences	–	Kees Hengeveld
9. Constituent Order	–	Kees Hengeveld
10. Sentence Meaning	Pieter Muysken	Sies de Haan
11. Lexicon	Pieter Muysken	Casper de Groot
12. Word Formation	Pieter Muysken	Casper de Groot
13. Compounds and Idiomatic Expressions	–	Casper de Groot
14. Speaking and Understanding – Speech Sounds	Norval Smith	Louis Pols
15. Sound Systems and Phonological Processes	Norval Smith	Norval Smith
16. Syllables, Stress and Intonation	Norval Smith	Norval Smith
17. Differences and Similarities between Languages	René Appel	Pieter Muysken
18. Language Variation	René Appel	Pieter Muysken
19. Language Change	René Appel, Pieter Muysken	Pieter Muysken
20. Bilingualism	René Appel	Pieter Muysken

A great many readers and users sent us their comments on the earlier versions, and we greatly benefited from these for the current edition. We thank them all very much. We are also very grateful to the anonymous reviewers who provided us with many helpful comments on the pre-final version of this book. Specifically we wish to thank a number of colleagues for their checking of examples: Titia Benders, Ying Lin, Bibi Janssen and Wim Honselaar. Finally we are indebted to Gerdien Kerssies and Kirsten Smorenberg for their contribution to the technical production of the book.

Amsterdam, November 2011
Anne Baker, Kees Hengeveld

Language and the Language Faculty

Humans generally communicate with each other by means of language. In this respect they are very different from other animals. Human language has a number of specific properties that set it apart from other communication systems. Chapter 1 of this book, *From Language to Linguistics*, discusses these properties of human language, explains how they are studied in linguistics, and what sort of phenomena will be covered in this book.

When we say that humans know a language, this means effectively that they have mentally stored a large amount of knowledge about the language and how it is used. Operating as speakers and hearers, they can employ their language faculty in actual language use. In Chapter 2, *The Language User*, we will discuss how this works and review the mental processes that play a role here.

But the knowledge of a language is not present from the beginning. Children have to acquire their first language and adults also sometimes learn one or more other languages later. This is the theme of Chapter 3, *Language Acquisition.*

chapter 1

From Language to Linguistics

1.1 Introduction

Every person knows a language; many people know more than one. But what do we really know about the language we use every day? What could we say, for example, about the five following sentences:

(1) Impossible a was job it
(2) I am hungry
(3) Why you left wanted to know
(4) Marilyn Monroe wants to become President of Great Britain
(5) The tlint was beert

Everybody will probably agree that (1), (3) and (5) are not good, in contrast to sentences (2) and (4), which are at least well formed. In (1) the order of words is not correct; in (3) there is a word missing; and (5) contains two elements that are clearly not words of English. On what grounds can we make statements like these? Is our knowledge of language simply a collection of all the words and sentences we have ever heard? Could we say, for example, that (1) is not

Linguistics, First Edition. Edited by Anne E. Baker and Kees Hengeveld.

good because we contrast it with the sentence *It was an impossible job*? Have we perhaps once heard this last sentence and still remember it as a 'correct English sentence'? This is very unlikely, as we can demonstrate with example (4). Sentence (4) is good English, even though it is not true. We know that this is a well-formed English sentence, even though we probably have never heard it before. Language users are capable of deciding whether a sentence is good or not, not just on the basis of memory, but also on the basis of their knowledge of language. This knowledge of language is not conscious; it is rather abstract and often couched in general rules. As a consequence we may not find it easy to explain why a particular sentence is good or not.

What do we mean when we speak of 'abstract knowledge' here? This can be explained with help from the following example. Suppose somebody shows us an unknown object and calls it a *pewt*. What would we say if there were two of these objects? Most probably we would say *two pewts*. Speakers of English do not need time to think about this; they just know that the form *pewten* would not sound right, even though there are a few English plurals that take *-en*, such as *oxen* and *children*. We learn the basic rules for plural noun formation as children, at a very early age: *cat–cats*, *dog–dogs*, *house–houses*, *goose–geese* and *ox–oxen*. But although we have this knowledge, many people may not be able to say why *pewts* is better than *pewten*. Knowing a language for most language users means that they can understand and produce it, but not necessarily that they can explain how the system works. For this reason we say that this knowledge is abstract and unconscious.

In this introductory chapter we will discuss the phenomenon of 'language' and the ways in which it is studied in the discipline of linguistics. In Section 1.2 we will review a number of important properties of language. 'Language' is here taken to mean natural language, that is, languages that are spoken by humans, and that have developed in a natural way in the course of history, probably from some primitive communication system used by our ancestors. There are also, however, other kinds of language, such as the languages used for writing computer programs. These other kinds of languages, and the way they differ from human language, will be discussed in Section 1.3. In Section 1.4 we will consider the variation that exists within the natural languages, including the difference between sign languages and spoken languages. The ways in which language is studied in linguistics will be discussed in Section 1.5. An important aim of linguistics is to try and make explicit, often in the form of a grammar, the unconscious, abstract knowledge that people have of the languages they speak. Section 1.6 will consider the various different types of grammar we may distinguish, such as, for example, a grammar which describes the history of a language versus a grammar that aims to describe the current situation of that language. Finally, Section 1.7 presents an overview of the various subfields within linguistics. This section also serves as an introduction to the rest of the book.

1.2 Languages

In this section we will consider natural, human languages such as English, Hindi, Turkish, Swahili, etc. What is so special about language as a phenomenon? We can get an idea by looking at the properties of such languages.

Every language is used for general communication. Using a natural language, humans can in principle communicate with each other about anything in their world, from talking about the weather to writing or reading a scientific article about global warming. Depending on the subject a different jargon may be used – when talking about football, people in a café use words that are quite different from those used in a parliamentary debate about health insurance costs. These different jargons are, however, part of the language as a whole. Also, to a very large extent, they employ the same grammar.

As we said in the introduction, languages have a certain structure. We can establish the rules that the sentences of a language need to satisfy. The sum total of those rules is the grammar of that language. The sentence *Tomorrow I will travel to Manchester* is correct, but *I tomorrow will travel to Manchester* is not. This is not to say that the first sentence is the only option we have in English when we want to say this, for we can also say *I will travel to Manchester tomorrow* and *I will tomorrow travel to Manchester*. There are quite subtle differences in meaning between the three correct sentences we have here, though for the moment we will ignore such differences. The key point is that the grammar of English allows for three different word order patterns in which to present the elements of this sentence, and does not allow other orders.

It is a well-known fact that languages may differ from each other in the rules their sentences have to satisfy. Sometimes the difference is only a small one. Compare, for example, the Dutch and German examples below, in (6) and (7) respectively, both meaning 'The publisher had the book translated'.

Dutch

(6)	De	uitgever	heeft	het	boek	laten	vertalen.
	The	publisher	has	the	book	let	translate

'The publisher had the book translated.'

German

(7)	Der	Verlag	hat	das	Buch	übersetzen	lassen.
	The	publisher	has	the	book	translate	let

'The publisher had the book translated.'

The relative order of the two infinitives ('let translate') at the end in Dutch is the reverse of that in German ('translate let'). Spanish is different again, as is illustrated by (8), where the verbs are not placed at the end but in the middle.

Spanish
(8) La editorial hizo traducir el libro.
The publisher made translate the book
'The publisher had the book translated.'

There are other languages that are even more different, as we can see in the following examples from Japanese and Irish.

Japanese
(9) Taro wa Hanako ni tagami o kai ta.
Taro *topic* Hanako *to* letter *object* write *past tense*
'Taro wrote Hanako a letter.'

Irish
(10) Tà carr nua seo liom.
Is car new that with+me
'I own that new car.'

We will just take a detour here to describe how we will present language examples in this book using sentences (9) and (10). The first line presents the example in the foreign language written in Latin script; the second line offers an almost literal rendition of every individual element it contains into English. When there is no equivalent English word, we will give the category to which this element belongs in the other language. Thus, *topic* in (9) means that Taro is the person about whom something is being said (see also Chapter 10); the word *o* indicates that *tagami* is the direct object of the verb; and *-ta* is tagged onto *kai* to mark it as a past tense-form. Labels such as *topic* will be given in italics. The third line of (9) gives a free translation of the Japanese example into an English sentence. In (10) the elements meaning 'with' and 'me' are fused in one form and this is indicated by using a '+'. Other symbols (diacritics) have to be fused to reproduce the correct spelling of a word such as 'tà' in Irish. Some languages also use falling and rising intonation on a word to distinguish meaning. In Mandarin Chinese, for example, the word *ma* has at least four different meanings according to the tone used, so the tone has to be indicated as below:

mā (level) means 'mother'
má (rising) means 'torpid'
mǎ (fall-rise) means 'horse'
mà (falling) means 'scold'

Let us now take a closer look at (9) and (10) from the point of view of structure. They reveal considerable differences between English and other languages. Japanese (9) has no prepositions but only 'postpositions', so *ni* only appears after *Hanako*. Also, the verb *kai* takes up the final position in the sentence. The insertion of *wa* to mark *Taro* as the topic is another typical feature of Japanese. Irish is quite different again. From (10) we see that the verb is in first position, the noun 'car' is followed by the adjective 'new' and the expression 'to own' is expressed quite differently from English by locating the object with the person.

So, languages can be quite diverse in structure. Nevertheless, linguists have been operating for centuries on the idea that the languages of the world must have a common basis. As Roger Bacon wrote in the thirteenth century:

> *Grammar is substantially one and the same in all languages, despite its accidental variations.*

Another anonymous writer a century earlier had already written:

> *He who knows the grammar in one language, also knows it in another, as far as the essentials are concerned.*

Which aspects of grammar or structure could constitute these essentials? In (11) we give some examples of universal properties of language.

(11) a. All languages consist of small elements. In spoken languages these elements are the speech sounds, and in sign languages they are, amongst other things, hand shapes (see Section 1.3). From these small elements all larger units, words, or signs, are built. And these in turn are combined to make sentences.
b. All spoken languages have vowels and consonants.
c. In all languages the users can express a negative statement, ask a question, issue an order.
d. All languages have words for BLACK and WHITE or DARK and LIGHT. (The capitals indicate that these are concepts and not words.)

These properties, which are shared by all languages, are known as **universals**. They are discussed in more detail in Chapter 17, where we will consider differences and similarities between languages.

Of particular interest here is the property mentioned in (11a) above, since this feature is a specific characteristic of human languages. It is known as the **compositionality** of language. A word on its own has a particular meaning but it is at the same time composed of combinations of sounds that help distinguish meaning, so 'boy' is different from *toy* on the basis of the two sounds *b* and *t*. This will be talked about further in Chapter 14. Words when combined with other words can also form a complex message. And these messages may vary depending on the order in which the words are presented. For example, sentences (12) and (13) consist of exactly the same five words, each with their own meaning. Yet (12) and (13) clearly have different meanings.

(12) The lifeguard saved the girl.
(13) The girl saved the lifeguard.

An important further property of human languages is illustrated in (14).

(14) the dog [of the man [with the hat [without a feather]]]

In this example we see how the phrase *without a feather* forms part of the phrase *with the hat without a feather*. These two phrases are of the same type because they both start with a preposition, *without* in the first case and *with* in the second. The prepositional phrase *with the hat without a feather* forms in turn part of the prepositional phrase *of the man with the hat without a feather*. This phenomenon, where a linguistic unit of a certain type contains another linguistic unit of that same type, is known as **recursion**.

Recursion is also found when we embed a sentence within another sentence, as in example (15).

(15) Sheila assumes [that Peter knows [that Ahmed thinks [that he is a liar]]].

As the brackets show, the sentence *that he is a liar* is contained within the sentence *that Ahmed thinks that he is a liar*, which itself forms part of the sentence *that Peter knows that Ahmed thinks that he is a liar*, which is itself contained in the sentence *Sheila assumes that Peter knows that Ahmed thinks that he is a liar*.

In principle, recursion can go on infinitely. Recursion can be exploited for amusement as in the nursery rhyme *The house that Jack built* (16).

(16) This is the farmer sowing the corn,
That kept the cock that crowed in the morn
That waked the priest all shaven and shorn,
That married the man all tattered and torn,
That kissed the maid all forlorn,
That milked the cow with the crumpled horn,
That tossed the dog,
That worried the cat,
That killed the rat,
That ate the malt,
That lay in the house that Jack built.

A question on a different level is whether only humans can express themselves in a human language. Could animals perhaps also learn to use human language? Here it is more or less natural to think first of certain birds, such as parrots and cockatoos, that can imitate human speech. These birds, however, have no clue as to what they are 'saying'. But what about the great apes? They are, after all, our closest evolutionary relatives and share a large amount of our DNA. None of the great apes has, however, developed a speech organ with which it could produce a wide variety of sounds. Experiments to teach the great apes to do this have failed. One chimpanzee, Vicki, could articulate no more than four words: *mama*, *papa*, *cup* and *up*, and this only after endless practice and then still with great difficulty.

However, could it be that the great apes can learn language, but not in the form of human speech? There have been many experiments with great apes to try and teach them a language using plastic buttons or computer symbols. Also, because great apes use their hands to make gestures, experiments have been done using a sign language for the deaf, American Sign Language. The results of these experiments are rather contentious. Some researchers claim that the great apes learn enough to be able to combine symbols and gesture signs, that is that they have learnt the syntax of the language in question. American researchers carried out such an experiment with the chimpanzee Nim Chimpsky. In (17) we give some of the most frequent combinations of gestures made by Nim.

(17)	PLAY ME	PLAY ME NIM
	TICKLE ME	TICKLE ME NIM
	EAT NIM	EAT GRAPEFRUIT NIM

What can these gesture combinations tell us about the grammar underlying the 'sign language' of Nim? The combinations of three gestures in the first two examples in (17) amount to no more than a relatively redundant extension of the combination of two gestures. After all, NIM and ME refer to the same person, or rather, ape. Also, the combinations remain very restricted. Many of the longer utterances merely consist of repetitions of earlier gestures. A later experiment with a bonobo, Kanzi, showed that the ape could apparently understand many spoken words and sentences without having the explicit training that Nim had received in the earlier research. His production in a symbol system on a board was however quite limited. The spontaneity and creativity that are so characteristic of humans when they are using language is difficult to find in apes. It is claimed that they do transmit some words to others of their kind – but the extent of this is in no way comparable to human adults passing on their language to their children. This last point brings us to another typical feature of natural, human languages: that they are acquired (by children) through interaction with their environment, and thus handed down from one generation to the next.

1.3 Other Languages

Natural languages, as we have mentioned above, are used by humans to communicate with each other. There are, however, other languages and communication systems, and the question is in what ways these are different from, or similar to, natural languages. Below, we will discuss in more detail some

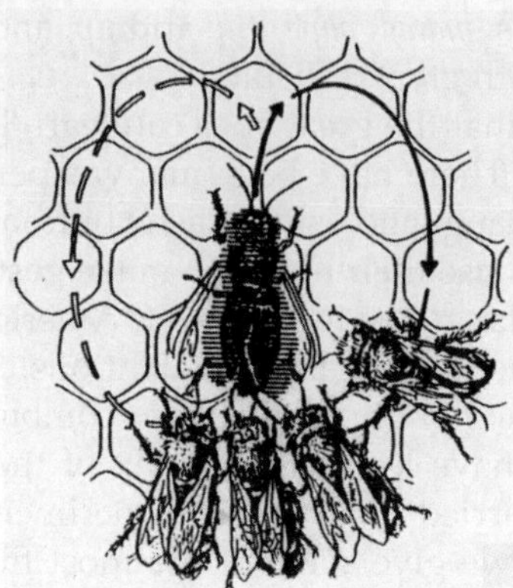

Figure 1.1 The 'wiggle' dance of bees, according to Frisch (1923). Frisch, K. von (1923) Über die 'Sprache' der Bienen, Jena: Gustav Fischer Verlag.

of these 'other languages'. At the same time, we will use this discussion to highlight the special character of natural languages.

Humans are not the only ones who communicate with each other. Various kinds of animals do this too, and use a communication system or a language for this purpose. Birds, for example, can signal with their call or song that there is an enemy nearby, or that they have taken possession of a certain area, etc. But the range of possible messages they can convey is very limited. This is a key difference with human language. We can see this clearly by looking at an animal language of which the structure has been investigated, that is the language of bees. By executing different dance patterns on the side of the beehive, one bee can signal to another where it can find flowers with the basic ingredients needed to make honey. As the Austrian biologist, Karl von Frisch, discovered early in the twentieth century, Italian and Austrian bees do not speak exactly the same 'language'. The Italian honeybee, for example, knows three dances. The 'round dance' is used to indicate food sources located less than ten metres away from the beehive. By dancing with varying degrees of energy, the bee can indicate how large the food source is. The 'sickle' dance is used when food sources are located at a distance of between ten and hundred meters from the beehive. In addition, the bee can signal the direction of the food source. In the 'wiggle' dance, the intensity of the bee's movement and the number of repetitions signal the size of the food source, and how far away it is. In Figure 1.1 we see a drawing of the 'wiggle' dance.

In an experiment, a computer-controlled artificial bee was used to give messages to other bees. After some initial hesitation, the real bees dutifully flew out to the food source that had been indicated. You might imagine that bees are able to communicate about many more things than just food sources, but the content of their communication seems to remain restricted to this one subject. In another experiment, a bee was made to walk rather than fly to the food source. Upon its return the dance of this bee signalled a distance that was far too great, because it could only indicate the time it had taken. Its communication system could not be used to tell the other bees that it had not flown but walked.

This example of bee communication shows how their system is rather limited. This holds true for the communication systems of other animals as well. These systems contain far fewer elements, such as movements or sounds, than there are words in human language. But the most important point appears to be that in animal communication these elements cannot be combined to produce new expressions. Neither bee language nor the language of other animals has **creativity**, one of the characteristic features of human language. With 'creativity' we do not mean 'artistic creativity'. In the context of language, creativity means that humans, with the rules at their disposal, can always make new, and possibly unique, sentences. The sentence you just read may well have been such a 'unique sentence'.

In what other ways is the language of bees different from human language? First of all, language use in humans is a matter of 'cooperative behaviour'. People adapt their use of language to that of their conversation partners, who in turn react to what others say, etc. There is interaction. Bees, on the other hand, dance their dances regardless of the response they get from other bees.

Secondly, human language is spontaneous. That is, there does not have to be a direct prompt or stimulus. In principle, at any given moment anyone can talk about anything, and some people actually do. With bees this is quite different. They only do their dance after they have found the flower – the stimulus, in this case – and have returned to the beehive. A bee will never 'just' do a little dance, in the way people can 'just' say anything about any subject they like. Human language is completely independent of the here and now. Bees are also different from humans since they can only tell the truth – and nothing but the truth, for they cannot lie – about what is the case at that particular moment. A bee utterance such as 'Well you know, yesterday I found some honey in that direction over there' is therefore impossible.

Finally, human language, but not that of bees, is largely arbitrary as far as form and meaning are concerned. In English, for example, there is no relation whatsoever between the form of words like *north*, *east*, *south* and *west*, and the various directions denoted by these words. In contrast, we find that in bee language the angle between the axis of the sickle dance and the vertical axis of the beehive corresponds exactly with the angle between sun, beehive and food source. So, the relation between form and content of the message is here not arbitrary, on the contrary. There are, nevertheless, a few exceptions to the rule of arbitrariness in human language, for example in **onomatopoeia**, where the sound shape of the word imitates the sound it denotes, as in *cock-a-doodle-doo*, *miaow*, *barking*, *sneezing* and *whinnying*. In sign languages, too, the relation between the form of a sign and its meaning is not always arbitrary, as we will discuss in Section 1.4. Finally, however, we should note that in many forms of animal language – such as birdsong – the relation between form and meaning is in fact also arbitrary. So, it is not the case that the difference between human and animal languages coincides with that between arbitrary and non-arbitrary elements.

Very different types of languages are the so-called **constructed languages**, which we shall discuss here only briefly. Constructed languages are languages that have been consciously and deliberately designed by humans. Historically, a range of different constructed languages has been developed in order to solve the practical problems of international communication, or even to further the ideological cause of bringing the many different nations of the world closer to each other. Over the centuries there have been scores of such languages, often with beautiful names like Mundolingue or Interglossa. These often did not last very long. The best known of these is Esperanto, designed in the 1880s by the Polish eye doctor Ludwik Zamenhof, and currently spoken and written by hundreds of thousands of people around the world.

Esperanto makes considerable use of Latin words that function as a kind of lexical stem. New words can be formed by systematically attaching prefixes and suffixes to these stems. For example, *san*, meaning 'healthy', can receive the prefix *mal*, meaning 'opposite of', to give the new word *malsan*, for 'ill'. The suffix *-ul* denotes the person who has the property expressed by the preceding stem, so *malsanul* means 'sick person'. Esperanto's grammar is equally transparent. Questions are formed simply by putting *cu* in front of a statement, a process adopted from Polish, as shown in (18) and (19).

Esperanto

(18) Petro legas revuon.
Peter read journal
'Peter reads a journal.'

(19) Cu Petro legas revuon.
question Peter read journal
'Does Peter read a journal?'

Constructed languages share a number of properties with natural, human languages, such as their compositionality and the arbitrariness of their units. But in at least two respects they are quite different from natural languages. First of all, constructed languages generally do not change over time, whereas natural languages constantly do. The English language in the twenty-first century is different from the English of around 1900. But Esperanto, like constructed languages in general, has a deliberately constructed form that changes relatively little. The second difference has to do with the fact, mentioned before, that natural languages are acquired by children from birth and through direct interaction with their environment. This is not the case in constructed languages, although to some extent this may be different for Esperanto. Children who grow up in a family where both parents are speakers of Esperanto sometimes learn this language in the same way as other children may acquire English as their mother tongue.

A third type of language we need to discuss here are **computer languages**, that is languages used for writing computer programs and for giving instructions to computers. Just like constructed languages, they have not evolved slowly over the millennia through natural interaction between humans, but have been constructed by somebody for a specific purpose. Among the computer languages we find programming languages such as Prolog and Java, operating languages like DOS, and languages such as SQL that can be used to question databases. Other languages that are similar to computer languages are the formal languages of algebra, mathematics and logic.

The most noticeable feature of computer languages is that there is a fixed, one-to-one relation between form and meaning. In a natural language like English on the other hand, words and sentences can easily carry various different meanings at the same time. In a newspaper headline HOUSE DEFEATS BILL nobody thinks that the house refers to a building; clearly a government body is meant. It is also highly unlikely that a person Bill has been defeated; more probably a government paper is referred to. The same goes for jokes, which often depend on utterances being ambiguous. In formal languages, however, utterances always have one, and only one, meaning. For example, the basic rule of arithmetic that multiplication takes precedence over addition ensures that the outcome of (20) is always 23 and cannot be 35 as well.

(20) $3 + 4 \times 5 = 23$

Another, though less noticeable, difference between natural and formal languages is that users of natural languages often omit things which they can assume their listeners will fill in on the basis of their knowledge of the matter under discussion. Thus, during a soccer match somebody may say:

(21) ... and then in the same move he headed it in.

Here the listener, assuming of course he or she is familiar with the sport of soccer, will normally be able to fill in who *he* refers to since they will know the players, to tell that *it* refers to the ball, and that *in* means 'into the goal of the opposite team'. In formal languages it is impossible as a matter of principle to omit such things, for computers do not have the knowledge of the world they would need to fill in the missing information.

On the other hand, ordinary language users, especially in spontaneous conversation, may well produce a lot of 'redundant noise' in their utterances. A speaker who produces (22) could probably have limited himself to (23).

(22) I am inclined to agree with most of what the last speaker just said.
(23) I think so too.

Note, however, that the elaborate construction of (22) does have an effect, in that it expresses a certain reservation the speaker may have in supporting the previous speaker. In formal languages there is no room for such nuances. Everything written in a formal language is taken literally, and cannot be interpreted as nuance, colouring, flavouring, innuendo or spin. It remains a great challenge to write programs for computers in such formal languages that can interpret or produce human natural languages.

A fourth type of language we shall discuss here is that of non-verbal communication, that is, language without words. In oral communication humans often make use of non-verbal and non-language means such as gestures, body position, and facial expressions. When two humans are talking to each other, the distance between them may be an indication of their intimacy, or lack of it. In other words, the distance between speakers may carry meaning: the closer you stand, the more intimate or personal your relation. In different cultures there may be different rules for such distances. Arabs generally stand much closer to each other than people from the western world. In the trains on the London Underground, on the other hand, the convention is that people first sit down as far apart as possible from each other.

Non-verbal communication is more limited than ordinary language. Certain gestures, such as the abusive gesture of pointing to your forehead in Britain or Germany, have only one meaning in that specific culture. The gesture cannot be broken down into smaller parts, and is thus not compositional. The vocabulary, that is the repertoire of gestures and other non-verbal elements, is also fairly restricted. Combining such gestures into a message with a completely different meaning is generally not possible. Of course, you can combine gestures, for example pointing at someone and then pointing to your forehead, but the order in which this is done is irrelevant. That is, in non-verbal communication, unlike in natural, human languages, there is no grammar or fixed structure.

Languages are systems of symbols that represent something. This is an aspect of language that we also find in pictograms such as the signs used in railway stations and airports to indicate the exit, the baggage lockers, etc. Traffic signs constitute a comparable sign system. They all differ considerably from natural, human language. There is no compositionality possible. And, again, there is no interaction. Apart from the notion of representation, none of the other features of natural, human languages applies.

The term 'language' is often used metaphorically, for anything used by humans to transmit meaning. Thus, for example, we speak of the 'language of fashion'. When a woman wears a smart two-piece suit, she sends out a different message from when she is dressed in jeans and a T-shirt. Similarly, the term 'language of architecture' is used to indicate that an architect may be aiming to express an idea or make a statement with a building he or she has designed. The expression 'Let the music do the talking' as used in the title of the song by Aerosmith also reflects this metaphor. In these various cases the term 'language' is used not literally, but in a figurative sense, as a metaphor. Music or clothes are not 'real languages', in the sense in which we consider natural, human languages as 'real'.

We can summarise the features of natural, human languages and their use, as discussed in Section 1.2 and Section 1.3, as follows:

- Languages have structure; utterances are formed according to certain rules.
- An important distinguishing property of languages is that of compositionality.
- Languages are acquired by children via interaction with their environment, and they are transmitted from one generation to the next.
- Creativity is a property of the human language faculty.
- Human language use is a form of 'acting together' or interaction.
- Language use is not bound to the here and now, that is, language use does not have to be directly linked to present experiences and circumstances.
- In language there is often an arbitrary relation between the form of the language symbol and the meaning of that symbol.
- Many utterances have more than one meaning, but with the help of the context it is usually possible to establish what the intended meaning is.

1.4 DIFFERENCES

We have seen that languages have much in common. But they can also be quite different, especially in structure, as we mentioned in Section 1.2. A first distinction to be made is between **spoken languages** and **sign languages**. A spoken language is produced by using the tongue, the lips and the vocal chords, and is heard through the ear. A sign language uses a different **modality**, which is visual. Sign languages are *seen*, and signers use above all their hands. The linguistic universals mentioned above in (11) apply equally to spoken and sign languages. But the use of a particular modality, for example the visual modality in the case of signs, can affect the form of a language. In (24) we see examples of signs from three different sign languages: American Sign Language (ASL), British Sign Language (BSL) and Sign Language of the Netherlands (NGT). What do they mean? In (24c) we can probably guess that the sign means 'baby'. Examples (24a) and (24b) are more difficult. The ASL sign in (24a) means 'to know'. The place where the sign is made is related to the fact that knowing is a mental activity. The ASL signs for 'to dream' and 'to plan' are also made near the head. The BSL sign in (24b) means 'cruel'. Here there is no clear relationship between the meaning of the sign and the form. There does seem to be such a relationship in (24a) and (24c); this is called the iconicity of signs. Certainly it is not the case that the relationship between the form and the content is iconic in all cases, but the visual mode in the case of signs seems to promote iconicity. In this respect, a number of signs can be compared to the onomatopoetic words we discussed earlier, such as *cock-a-doodle-doo*, *miaow* and *cuckoo*, which imitate the sound of certain animals.

(24)

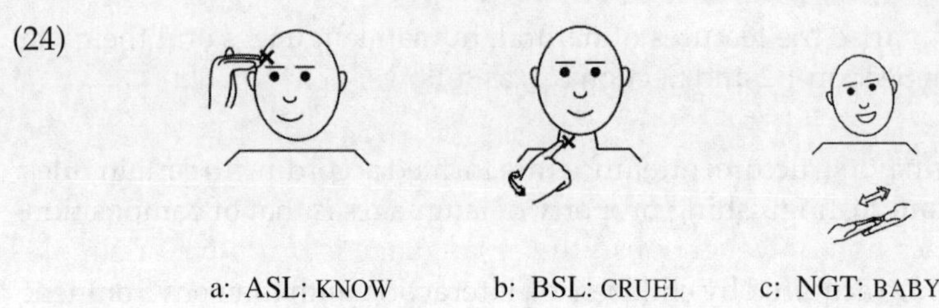

a: ASL: KNOW b: BSL: CRUEL c: NGT: BABY

When hearing people see two deaf people communicating in a sign language, BSL, for example, they will find it probably impossible to follow the conversation. The same holds true for a deaf person who communicates in a different sign language, like Italian Sign Language. This person would not be able to understand a BSL conversation. The number of iconic signs with a very clear relation between form and meaning is really rather limited. In many other respects, sign languages are completely comparable to other natural, human languages. For example, sign languages have structure or grammar. Also, deaf children acquire their sign language in interaction with other sign language users. And in sign language, too, in principle anything can be said, asked, requested, etc. at anytime, about anything.

A completely different type of distinction is that between languages that are only spoken, and those that are also written. Writing is a fairly recent invention. Humans have been speaking for tens of thousands of years, but the oldest known form of writing is only about 5,000 to 8,000 years old. Children can speak long before they can write, and writing is always related to speaking. The written form of a language is based on its spoken form, and therefore a secondary form of language. Writing turns a language into a visual and much more permanent phenomenon. Writing makes it possible to store information without burdening our memory. It enables a society to record its culture and history. Still, there are many societies in the world that do not use a writing system for their language; in such cases cultural transmission takes place via an extensive oral tradition. There is a great deal of variation in the forms used in writing. Some writing systems use one symbol for one word; others use one symbol per syllable; others have one symbol per speech sound. We will come back to this in Chapter 15.

Languages that have no written form are often spoken in communities that are less developed technologically or economically. For this reason they are often called 'primitive' languages. Is this correct? Can we indeed make a distinction between primitive and more developed languages? In linguistics, the general assumption is that there are no primitive languages. Each language can in principle express all the meanings that can be expressed in other languages. But the means used in different languages to express these meanings can vary significantly, as will become clear in the course of this book.

Some languages may have a limited vocabulary in a particular field, though, usually when this field is not very important for the language community in question. Kwaza, for example, an American Indian language spoken in the Amazonian area, does not have any words for *word processor*, *life insurance* or *disco* – as you might expect. Having a less extensive vocabulary in a particular field does not, however, mean that a language is primitive or simple. New concepts can always be expressed by circumscribing them with existing words. A good example of this comes from the North American Indian language Comanche. When the previously unknown lemon was introduced to the Comanche, it was called 'sour little brother of the orange'. Another option is to 'borrow' words from a different language, as we can see in many languages of the world, where numerous concepts that are to do with the computer have been borrowed from English, just as English has coined most of its scientific vocabulary on the basis of Greek and Latin.

The last major difference between languages that we want to discuss here is that between complex and simple languages. Is there such a difference? Second language learners often find one language harder to learn than another, but this is more related to the fact that their first language is more or less similar to the second language. In linguistics we are cautious about assuming that there is such a difference in complexity. Every language has both relatively simple rules as well as rules and features that are quite difficult or complex, and it is rather problematic to 'weigh' these up against one another. Some people insist, however, that we really can make a distinction between simple and complex languages. English is often held up as an example of simplicity in comparison with Chinese or Russian. On the other hand, many Russian and Chinese speakers find the English language extremely hard. The notoriously low scores and achievements in English of many people from the Far East is a case in point. On the other hand, children can learn any language and have no more difficulty learning one than another. Aspects of Chinese that may present an insuperable difficulty for a native speaker of English, for example, are picked up effortlessly by little Chinese children.

1.5 LINGUISTICS

Language is essential in order to function as a human being. To understand humans, we also need to understand the phenomenon of language. As Noam Chomsky, one of the most important linguists of the twentieth century, wrote in 1972:

When we study human languages, we are approaching what some might call 'the human essence', the distinctive qualities of the mind, that are, as far as we know, unique to man.

In linguistics, we usually begin by describing a language, or rather languages. The question then is, how are languages organised, and what are their rules? A simple rule of English grammar, for example, could be written down as follows:

(25) In English an adjective always precedes the noun it is describing.

According to this rule, *He bought a similar book yesterday* is a correct sentence in English. But it is also possible to say *the book is similar*. So, could we perhaps rephrase (25) in a more general way, as for example (26)?

(26) In English an adjective precedes the noun it is describing unless it occurs after the verb *to be*.

The answer to this question is 'no'. Rule (26) is too general, since it excludes perfectly acceptable English sentences like *the book appears similar* and *He bought a book similar to mine*. So, rule (26) – and for that matter (25) – will have to be reformulated, if we want to do justice to the facts of English. It is an important principle of linguistics that we always aim for maximum generalisation. We could, of course, give a separate description of where the adjective would be placed for each individual sentence type, but, when writing linguistic rules, we generally aim to formulate them in such a way that they will apply to as many cases as possible.

Within linguistics we try, among other things, to write rules that can 'predict' what a possible correct sentence of the language in question will be. This may seem easy, but we will see that this is often quite hard. Also, in linguistics we not only deal with the form of sentences, but also describe other aspects of language. Take, for example, the formation of plural nouns in English. As we saw in Section 1.1, the plural of the nonsense word *pewt* will naturally be *pewts*, and a linguist who wants to describe this will have to draw up a satisfactory rule. The rule in (27) seems plausible.

(27) English nouns form the plural by adding -s to the singular form.

Many well-known words illustrate that this rule is right: *maps, tasks, hats*. But what about *buses, fishes* and *bosses*? These words do not follow rule (27), since they form the plural by adding *-es*. In fact the situation is even more complicated than this. So if we want to account for English plural formation in nouns, we will need either to amend rule (27) or to add some other rules.

In Section 1.1 we highlighted the unconscious and abstract character of the knowledge that language users have of their language. This knowledge is represented by the rules linguists draw up, for example the rule of plural noun formation just mentioned. The central aim of linguistics is to make explicit, in a grammar of the language, what knowledge of that language its users have 'in their heads'. In the first instance, we do so by studying the individual grammars of individual languages, but – following Bacon's lead – at the same time we also aim to elucidate the general principles of language, stating these in terms of the linguistic universals we discussed earlier in Section 1.2. These general principles can then be taken as an explanation of the way languages are organised.

This may seem to suggest that all linguists are looking for one particular kind of grammar. But this is not the case. Linguistics, even when it is dealing with the problem of grammar, is a vast and diverse domain of study and investigation, as we will see this in the next section.

1.6 Different Kinds of Grammar

What should we think of the sentences *Oh you're awful warm* or *Did you post all them letters?* Are these wrong or not? Or were they, perhaps, once wrong in the past, but not anymore? The question of what is wrong in a particular language and what is not is a difficult one, and has to do, essentially, with change. Look at the following sentences. Can we decide whether these are correct or not?

(28) Me and Jody had a contest for the ugliest pictures
(29) They were by the pub what we stayed in
(30) *She already live London two year

Most speakers of English will probably say that (30) is wrong, although many non-native speakers learning English actually produce such sentences. Nevertheless, (30) is not an acceptable structure in English. Linguists mark such sentences with an asterisk, which means that they are incorrect or ungrammatical. In other words, the rules of English grammar predict that this sentence is not amongst the possible sentences of English. The other two sentences, (28) and (29), are judged differently by native speakers; they often say something like 'I might say this, but you can't use it in writing', or 'You'll often hear this, but it isn't really correct English'. Sentence (28), for example, uses a construction (*Me and Jody*) that is becoming more frequent in the spoken language. Sentence (29) uses *what* in a way that occurs only in certain dialects of English.

The job of the linguist is to describe the language forms produced by native speakers, and, if possible, to indicate the variety of language they belong to. A grammar as written by a linguist represents, at least in theory, the knowledge all native speakers have of the rules of their language. In principle, this so-called **descriptive grammar** describes the rules for all varieties of the language. No variant is considered to be intrinsically better or worse than the others, though the description usually only covers those variants that are more or less systematic in character. That is, if a single individual native speaker of English were to say *Those jobs has got to be done*, this variant would not normally appear in a descriptive grammar of English. Since quite large numbers of English speakers now use the construction with *me* instead of *I*, as in (28), then this needs to be described in such a grammar.

Of course, a descriptive grammar may report whether a certain form is part of the standard language, whether it is more common in spoken English, or whether it only occurs in certain well-defined regions. Nevertheless, many linguists restrict their descriptions to the standard language or to the variety that is in general use, and ignore the many different dialect forms that may also occur.

Quite different from a descriptive grammar is a **prescriptive** grammar. This is a grammar that does not describe, but prescribes which forms of a language are good and which are not. In this kind of grammar, change may be regarded as a threat to the 'pure' form of the language. This purist view of language goes back a long way, in fact all the way to Classical Antiquity, when Latin was the dominant language in Europe. The purist view was especially dominant in the 18th and 19th centuries. But language is living and continually changing, and the process of change cannot be stopped. In a complete descriptive grammar, a linguist describes what the speakers of a language actually do and say in all their varieties. A real prescriptive linguist will dictate what they should say and write according to the linguistic norms prevalent at the time. For second language learners a grammar describing the standard variant is, however, often very useful and such grammars fall between the two types, as we will see.

So far, we have spoken about language as it is at a given moment in time, the language of today. But, as we have just seen, languages change. When we describe a language from the perspective of change, we are giving a **diachronic** description. In (31) we see two sentences that are variants of the same meaning: (31a) is formed according to the rules of the fifteenth century and (31b) is the modern variant.

(31) a. For to dihyte a swan, tak & vndo hym & wasch hem.
b. To prepare a swan open him up and wash him.

The diachronic description must cover the fact that *for to* is no longer used and now just *to*, although interestingly the *for to* variant survives in some dialects such as Irish English. Diachronic description is also known as historical grammar. The opposite of a diachronic description is a **synchronic** one, which offers a representation of a language at a particular moment in time (with considerable leeway in defining the limits of the notion 'particular moment').

Almost everyone who has learned or is learning a foreign language in school or at university will one day come across a grammar of the language, often as part of a coursebook that also deals with other aspects of the language. In general, such a grammar does not have scientific or scholarly aims. This type of grammar is known as a **pedagogical** grammar, or learner's grammar. It explains the rules of a language for the purpose of teaching and learning.

Sometimes this is done by giving a number of examples to illustrate a particular rule of grammar. The following passage, for example, comes from a learner's grammar of German for secondary schools:

The comparative and superlative in German:

klein	*klein*er	*klein*st
lieb	*lieb*er	*lieb*st
schon	*schön*er	*schön*st

Note special forms such as am schönsten, am kleinsten, *etc, where English has* the most beautiful, the smallest, *etc.*
German also has irregular comparatives, for example:

gut	*besser*	*best*
viel	*mehr*	*meist*

Note that after the comparative, German has als *(where English has* than*):* kleiner als, mehr als, reicher als, besser als.

Following this explanation, there would normally be a series of exercises, to practice the rules just given. Often this involves translations and comparisons with the mother tongue of the learners, as for example when German *am schönsten* is compared to its English equivalent *the most beautiful*. Very often, pedagogical grammars have a prescriptive character. They will not refer to the variation in forms used, so for example in an English grammar for speakers of other languages in the section on the use of pronouns the form *me* in the construction *Me and Jody* would not be mentioned.

There are quite a number of important differences between pedagogic and scientific descriptive grammars. As we have just mentioned, pedagogical grammars are often prescriptive, whereas scientific grammars are not. The most important difference is the ground covered. A scientific grammar contains much more information than a pedagogic grammar; it is also much more explicit in stating rules and exceptions. Learner grammars may only cover some ten per cent of this. They may also present the grammatical information concerning a particular issue in a number of different chapters or sections, because learners have to work their way through these step by step. The German coursebook mentioned above, for example, returns to the comparative in the following chapter, where it is explained that adjectives ending in *d, t, s, sch* or *sz* form the superlative by adding *-est* instead of *-st*, as in *laut–lautest (loud–loudest), weiss–weissest (white–whitest), rasch–raschest (quick–quickest).*

1.7 The Contents of this Book and the Subfields of Linguistics

There are, broadly speaking, two different perspectives or approaches you can take when studying language. The first is a thematic approach, where you explore language from the point of view of a certain theme, for example the way in which the human language faculty operates. In the second perspective you start from the language itself and study its different parts or levels, for example the level of speech sounds or that of sentences and sentence construction. Each of these two different approaches will be adopted in the various parts of this book.

Part I, *Language and Language Faculty*, which includes the present chapter, is thematic in character. Several times in the preceding sections we have mentioned that people have the rules of language 'in their heads'. This is what is also known as the 'language faculty'. In Chapter 2, *The Language User*, we will explore the way in which this language faculty operates in actual usage. How is it that language users are able to put the vocabulary and the rules they (unconsciously) know to use when producing and understanding language? 'Language' is a uniquely human property, which is acquired by children at a very early age. The way in which their language acquisition works, and the processes involved, will be discussed in Chapter 3, *Language Acquisition*. In this chapter we will also discuss the acquisition of a language other than a first language, that is, second language acquisition, and how this often does not proceed as smoothly and easily as mother tongue acquisition.

The next four parts of the book are not thematic but structural, and are organised on the basis of the linguistic levels or units of analysis.

In Part II the focus is on *Language and Interaction*. The main function of language is that humans can talk to each other and can produce longer stretches of text, that is, coherent series of sentences. This forms the largest unit of analysis. Both in texts and in conversations there is a certain system. Conversations have a certain structure, and the people taking part in them expect their conversation partners to react and not talk at cross-purposes. Chapter 4, *Discourse*, will discuss a number of characteristic systematic properties of conversations and of longer texts or monologues. The next issue we will discuss is how humans use language in order to transmit meanings. Thus, they 'do' something with language. In verbal interaction, utterances function as speech acts. For example, when someone says 'I have a pit-bull terrier', they may actually be issuing a warning. In other words, this utterance functions as the speech act 'warning'. In Chapter 5, *Speech Acts*, we will consider in more detail this aspect of language utterances and explore the systematic phenomena we can observe in this domain. The subfield of linguistics dealt with in Chapters 4 and 5 is usually referred to as **pragmatics**.

In Part III of the book, *Sentences and Their Meaning*, the focus is on the sentence as the unit of analysis, and we will consider in particular how sentences are constructed and what meanings we can attach to them. In Chapter 6, *Constituents and Word Classes,* we will discuss the building blocks of sentences. The notion of 'constituent' refers to the units, often consisting of more than one word, that sentences are made up of. Put simply, in *The man is doing nothing, the* and *man* together form one constituent. Many people will be familiar – from school or from a pedagogical grammar – with notions like 'subject' and 'direct object'. These notions refer to constituents that serve a particular function in the sentence. Chapter 7, *Simple Sentences,* is largely concerned with this type of function, though from a scientific, and not a pedagogical, point of view. The way in which complex sentences are formed will be the subject of Chapter 8, *Complex Sentences.* When discussing the first example in this book – (1) to (5) in Section 1.1 – we indicated that sentences have a certain structure, by which we mean that its constituents will have to be placed in a certain order. Word Order and the form of sentences will be the subject of Chapter 9, *Constituent Order*. Chapters 6 through 9 are concerned with the subfield of linguistics that is usually referred to as **syntax**. But sentences have more than just a particular form; they also have meaning. How, for example, do we know that in a sentence such as *He got the ball, but didn't want to give it away,* the *it* refers to *ball*? Language users again need rules that enable them to come to such an interpretation. Chapter 10 will explore the domain of *Sentence Meaning*. The subfield of linguistics that is concerned with the rules for assigning meaning is known as **semantics**.

Semantics will also be discussed in the first chapter of Part IV, *Words and Their Meaning*. In Chapter 11, *Lexicon,* we will discuss the collection of words that make up a language. Words are not immutable units, as we can see when we compare a verb like *to work* with the forms *worked* and *working* that have been derived from it, as in for example *She worked* and *He was working*. Such derivations, and other processes through which words can change, will be discussed in Chapter 12, *Word Formation*. The subfield of linguistics that is concerned with processes such as these is known as **morphology**. Part IV closes with a chapter on *Compounds and Idiomatic Expressions*. Here we will discuss compounds like *road map* and *homework,* as well as expressions like *beavering away* (for 'working very hard'). Note that Chapter 13 cannot be placed within any one specific subfield of linguistics. The information it presents is relevant for both syntax and semantics, as well as morphology.

In Part V we reach the 'lowest' level of language and the smallest units of analysis, that of *Speech Sounds*. In Chapter 14 the (physical) process of *Speaking and Listening* will be studied from the point of view of **phonetics**. How do humans form sounds, and how can they hear and interpret them? The role of individual sounds in the words of a language, that is, the linguistic significance of these sounds, will be discussed in Chapter 15, *Sound Systems and Phonological Processes*. In this chapter we will also take a look at differences between languages in the domain of sound. Chapter 16 is devoted to larger units than individual speech sounds, in particular *Syllables, Stress and Intonation*. Together,

Chapters 15 and 16 cover the main topics in the subfield of **phonology**, which can be seen as the linguistic twin of phonetics.

Finally, Part VI, entitled *Languages and Communities*, is, like Part I, thematic in character. Part VI is not concerned with one particular linguistic level, but concentrates rather on a number of themes that involve a range of different levels of analysis. In Chapter 17 we will come back to a subject that has been mentioned briefly in this introductory chapter, that is *Differences and Similarities between Languages*. Here we will discuss issues to do with 'language families', the investigation of earlier forms of languages, and the relation between language and culture. Chapter 18, *Language Variation*, looks at the variation that occurs within a language. There is, for example, not one single language English or Turkish or Chinese that is spoken by everybody in the corresponding language community, as very often people are speaking different dialects of that language. Also, languages are not only 'varied', they are variable as well. The English or French language of today is not the same as the English or French of two hundred years ago, as we will discuss in Chapter 19, *Language Change*. Here, too, we will explore the different kinds of change that may occur inside a language, for example at the level of sounds or sentence structure, as well as changes that may be occur between social groups. So far, we have mostly dealt with single, individual languages, but in fact in nearly all communities and societies around the world more than one language is being used, and very often these different languages do influence each other. Such *Bilingualism* will be discussed in the final chapter of the book.

At the end of each chapter there will be a *Summary*, a number of *Assignments*, an opportunity to *Test Yourself*, and a short list of *Acknowledgments and Further Reading* suggestions. The summary will revisit all the main concepts (printed in **bold**) covered in the chapter. The aim of the assignments is to work through the chapter's subject matter and take it further, for example by applying certain ideas to phenomena from a different language, or by finding and analysing examples that are characteristic of a particular linguistic phenomenon. By answering the questions in *Test Yourself*, you can check whether you have a reasonable grasp of the subject matter of that chapter. The questions here are asking for a reproduction of parts of the subject matter that has been presented. In the *Acknowledgments* section, finally, we provide the details of the sources used, and refer the reader to other, mostly introductory, books or articles on the different topics.

Summary

Human knowledge about language is unconscious. It is not the knowledge of a list of utterances, but of an abstract system. Languages have a specific structure, and may be quite different from each other in this respect. Some properties are shared by all languages; these are the linguistic **universals**. A characteristic feature of human language is that of **compositionality**, which holds that, while the words of a language each have their own meaning, they are made up of smaller elements that distinguish meaning and combine to make different meanings in sentences. Another important characteristic is **recursion**, that is, where one linguistic unit is contained within another of the same type. Animal languages are very different from human languages in that they are far more restricted. This holds true for the languages that some great apes have been taught in experiments as well as for bee language. These languages also lack the property of **creativity**, another characteristic of human language. The possibility of using a limited number of symbols or signs (words or gestures) and a limited number of rules (the grammar) to produce an unlimited number of new, and possibly unique, utterances is not available to animal languages. Human languages are to a very large extent arbitrary, though in the case of **onomatopoeia** there is a definite link between form and meaning.

Constructed languages such as Esperanto constitute a different type of language, though they are for the most part similar to natural languages. **Computer languages**, used to write computer programs, are generally very different from natural, human languages. The term 'language' is also used for other systems with which humans transmit meaning, as in the term 'body language' for the system of non-verbal communication, but in general they are not comparable to natural, human languages.

Languages can be produced in different **modalities**. There are **spoken languages** and **sign languages**. In sign languages, the relationship between form and meaning is closer than in spoken languages; but on the whole it is arbitrary. Languages can also be written, and they can differ from one another in the type of writing used. Written language is based on spoken language, and therefore secondary. From a scientific linguistic perspective it is impossible to distinguish between 'primitive' languages and more developed or 'advanced' languages. Equally, there are within linguistics no grounds for distinguishing between 'simple' and 'more complex' languages.

The aim of linguistics is to make explicit the unconscious knowledge people have of the language they speak. To this end, linguists study how languages are organised as systems, with a view to describing and explaining their grammars. In a **descriptive grammar** all forms of a language are accounted for, not just the standard form. **Prescriptive grammars** do not describe, but prescribe the rules for 'correct usage'. Changes in language are the subject of a **diachronic grammar**. In contrast, a **synchronic grammar** describes the rules of a language at a given moment in time. **Pedagogical grammars** describe the rules of grammar in order to help learners of the language in question.

A grammar of a language contains different subparts, which will be discussed in this book: the construction of sentences in **syntax**; meaning (**semantics**); the way language use is organised in interaction and in longer texts (**pragmatics**); the sounds (**phonetics and phonology**); and word formation (**morphology**). These various aspects are also known as 'linguistic levels'. Linguistics furthermore investigates a number of topics: the way in which humans use their language faculty in comprehension and production; the way in which language is acquired; and the way languages function in their communities. These various topics will also be discussed in this book.

ASSIGNMENTS

1. Put an asterisk (*) before the sentences that are ungrammatical. Can you explain why they are ungrammatical?
   (a) There walks the woman in the street.
   (b) Mary said that I should wash himself.
   (c) I haven't heard the postman yet.
   (d) John has studied.
   (e) Bill has murdered.
2. Discuss why the rules for forming the English comparative (for example *lovely* → *lovelier*, *good* → *better*) can be considered a form of unconscious, abstract knowledge.
3. In examples (12) and (13) in the text we find the same words, but in a different order, hence the meaning is different. Can this principle also be applied to sounds?
4. Suppose you could teach a dog a hundred different commands, such as *Go, fetch the newspaper* or *Sit, Bobby, sit*. Does this mean the dog now knows English? Give arguments to support your view.
5. In what way could you call a hairstyle or way of wearing your hair a 'language' in the figurative sense? In what way would this 'language' be different from human, natural languages?
6. In mime, hands are used to make gestures, just as in sign languages. Explain the difference between mime gestures and the sign languages of deaf communities.
7. British Sign Language (BSL) is one of many sign languages in the world, as are Sign Language of the Netherlands (NGT) and Italian Sign Language (LIS). Compare the following sentences:
   (a) BSL: MAN HELP WOMAN
   (b) NGT: MAN WOMAN HELP
   (c) LIS: MAN WOMAN HELP
   What conclusion can you draw from these examples about differences and diversity amongst sign languages?
8. Traditional grammar lessons often consisted of exercises in 'parsing' and naming sentence parts and word categories. What is the difference between this 'parsing' and the scientific approach to language structure in linguistics?
9. Assignment (1.2) involved a discussion of the English comparative. In what subfield of linguistics is this subject located?

Test Yourself

1. How do we know that our knowledge of language is not a list of utterances that is stored in our memory?
2. What is the technical term for those properties that are shared by all languages?
3. Explain what is involved in the phenomenon of compositionality?
4. Does the language of bees, like human language, have creativity, in the sense that one can always construct new 'messages' in it?
5. What is onomatopoeia?
6. What are constructed languages? Are they very different from natural human languages?
7. Can you identify some differences between human languages and computer languages?
8. Can sign languages be compared to other human languages?
9. Is it possible to make a clear distinction between complex languages and simple languages?
10. Leaving aside the writing system, are there any other differences between languages that have a written form and those that do not?
11. What is the difference between a prescriptive and a descriptive grammar?
12. What is a linguist doing when he or she studies language from a diachronic perspective?
13. Can you name the linguistic terms for the study of the following aspects of human language:
    (a) the sound system;
    (b) the structure of words;
    (c) the structure of sentences;
    (d) meaning;
    (e) language use in interaction.

Acknowledgments and Further Reading

Miller (1991) and Pinker (1994) are interesting books about language. A highly readable book about animal communication is by Bright (1990). The picture of the 'wiggle' dance of bees in Figure 1.1 is from Frisch (1923). Savage-Rumbaugh and Lewin (1994) present their work with Kanzi but it is important to also look at the criticism as in Wray (2000). Sign languages of the deaf are discussed in general terms in Sacks (1989) and an introduction to sign linguistics is provided in Baker *et al.* (in preparation), from which the examples in this chapter are taken. Other books consider specific sign languages such as British Sign Language (Sutton-Spence and Woll, 1999) or Australian Sign Language (Johnston and Schembri, 2007). The quotes from Roger Bacon and Anonymous come from Lyons (1968:15–16). The quote from Chomsky is taken from Chomsky (1972:100).

chapter 2

The Language User

2.1 INTRODUCTION

(1) Waiter: Madam? Can I help you? Have you decided what to order?
Woman: I feel like having duck, but my plane is leaving in an hour.
Waiter: In that case you might want to consider something else, Madam.

The short dialogue in (1) may at first sight strike you as slightly incoherent. But when we consider that the waiter is working in an airport restaurant, and the woman wants to have a quick meal before her flight, the conversation begins to appear a lot more normal. The woman does not ask explicitly how long it takes to prepare duck to help her work out if she can still have it before her plane leaves, but the waiter does take her remark as a question to that effect. He does not give a specific answer though, but proffers some well-intentioned advice. This enables the woman to deduce that preparing duck will take too long for her to be able to catch her plane.

Conversations that leave a lot of things unsaid – as in (1) – are very common. Language users take part effortlessly in such conversations and information is exchanged at high speed. But when we take a closer look at a dialogue like that in (1), it becomes harder to understand how this kind of conversation can be so easy. This short dialogue could not have lasted more than ten seconds, and

Linguistics, First Edition. Edited by Anne E. Baker and Kees Hengeveld.

in this very short time the woman has had to process some seventy sounds produced by the waiter. From this sequence of sounds she has recognised the words and at the same time sought, and apparently found, their meanings from her own memory. In addition she has produced a sentence of her own, consisting of thirteen words. Now consider that for the production of just one sound the speaker already needs to use about a hundred muscles. So the speed alone at which this whole process operates is astonishing. But that is not all. It is even more astonishing to see how much is left unsaid, and that what is actually meant is left implicit. Nevertheless, language users usually know immediately how to deduce the meaning or the communicative message from the utterance they are hearing, and they can also, without great effort, establish the connection between the time it takes to prepare duck and the departure time of an airplane. How do they do all this? What sort of knowledge and abilities do they need? In other words: which cognitive processes underlie the production and comprehension of language? This is the subject of the present chapter.

In the next section, 2.2, we will first discuss in general the system that enables humans to produce and understand language, focusing in particular on the way human linguistic knowledge is implemented. This system must be located somewhere in the brain, but which areas are involved, and what happens when these are damaged? These questions will be discussed in Section 2.3. In Section 2.4 we will discuss the processes involved in understanding language, and in Section 2.5 we will look at the other side of the coin, namely the production of language.

2.2 Knowledge and Ability: The Cognitive System

Consider the example in (2).

(1) This is the story of which Anna said that Tom had heard that Janet had told Bill how much she liked it.

Sentence (2), although not elegant, is constructed according to the rules of the English language system. It can easily be extended further, both to the left, by prefacing it with *Richard believed that this was the story etc...*, and to the right, by adding *...compared to the story about which Margaret had said that William felt that it was really not very interesting*. But although sentence (2) is grammatically correct, many people will find it hard to understand and would not be very likely to say it themselves. Yet, at least in principle, adult language users have the knowledge of the language system that is necessary to understand or produce sentences like these. This knowledge of the language system is known as **linguistic competence**. It is the abstract and largely unconscious knowledge of the language system that we first discussed in Chapter 1.

In addition to this linguistic competence, there is the actual use that is made of it in **performance**. As we noted above, sentence (2) can always be extended further and further, simply by following the rules of the language. However, there are limitations on performance, because, for example, human memory is not capable of processing sentences that are too long. By the end of the sentence the language user has forgotten the beginning. But we can study such sentences and establish, with the help of our linguistic competence, whether they are correct in principle. In this sense, performance imposes more limitations on what we can produce than would be possible according to linguistic competence. Another difference between the two is that people by no means always speak in flawless and grammatically correct sentences. Repetitions and hesitations are common, as we can see in examples (3) and (4).

(3) He said he would do it he said.
(4) With. . .eh, with that story, of. . .eh Anna's, I. . .eh. . .I don't know. . .eh. . .what to make of that story.

In short, the rules of competence are not always applied correctly. Everyday language – as anyone who listens carefully can confirm – contains very many ungrammatical, slightly incorrect or incomplete sentences.

Now, in order to produce and understand language, do humans need only linguistic competence? What about, for example, sentence (5)?

(5) The right back tricked the player he was marking into running offside.

Someone who does not know anything about the sport of soccer will find it hard to interpret this sentence. In order to understand (5) it is not enough to know the meaning of the words; you also have to know the role of a right back in the team, what marking means in the context of soccer, and also the offside rule. Knowledge of the language system is therefore not enough for a full understanding of (5); language users also need **knowledge of the world**.

In addition, to function properly in their language, humans need at least one further kind of knowledge. This third kind of knowledge pertains to language use, as we can see from example (6).

(6) Give me stamps.

It is quite easy to understand (6); you do not really need extensive knowledge of the language or the world. The problem with (6) is that it is an unusual and rather rude way of asking for stamps in an English post office, newsagent's or supermarket. Anyone who uses (6), perhaps because English is not their mother tongue, will be perceived as rude or ill-mannered. What is lacking here is a third type of knowledge, known as **communicative competence**, that is, the knowledge of how to use your language in different situations.

Thus, there are at least three different, large domains of knowledge that a language user draws upon while speaking and understanding language. This

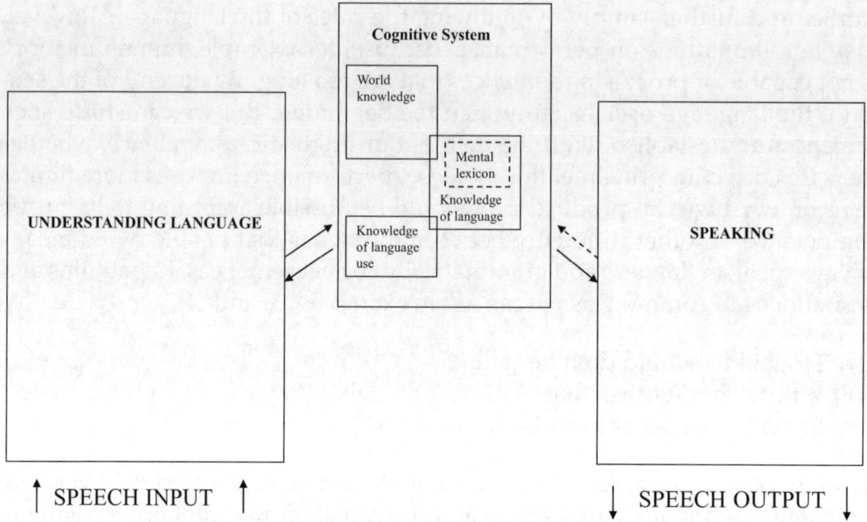

Figure 2.1 Three kinds of knowledge within the cognitive system involved in speaking and understanding.

is graphically represented in the middle block of Figure 2.1, where the box labelled 'cognitive system' contains three elements:

1. knowledge of the language system (linguistic competence);
2. knowledge of the world; and
3. knowledge of how to use language in different situations (communicative competence).

These various kinds of knowledge are all put to use in the process of speaking and understanding language. This is represented by the various arrows in Figure 2.1, leading from the cognitive system to the boxes for understanding and speaking. These two abilities will be further discussed in Section 2.4 and Section 2.5, together with some remarks on reading and writing. Sign languages will also be discussed and where here we talk of speaking, signing can usually be substituted.

The cognitive system is constantly being refreshed and updated by the processes of understanding language and, to a lesser extent, speaking. That is why there are also arrows in Figure 2.1 from the two side boxes to the central cognitive system.

The interface between our knowledge of the world and our linguistic knowledge is our knowledge of vocabulary. Through language use we constantly learn new words and our existing knowledge of the words of the language is constantly evolving. So far, when we discussed 'knowledge of language', we

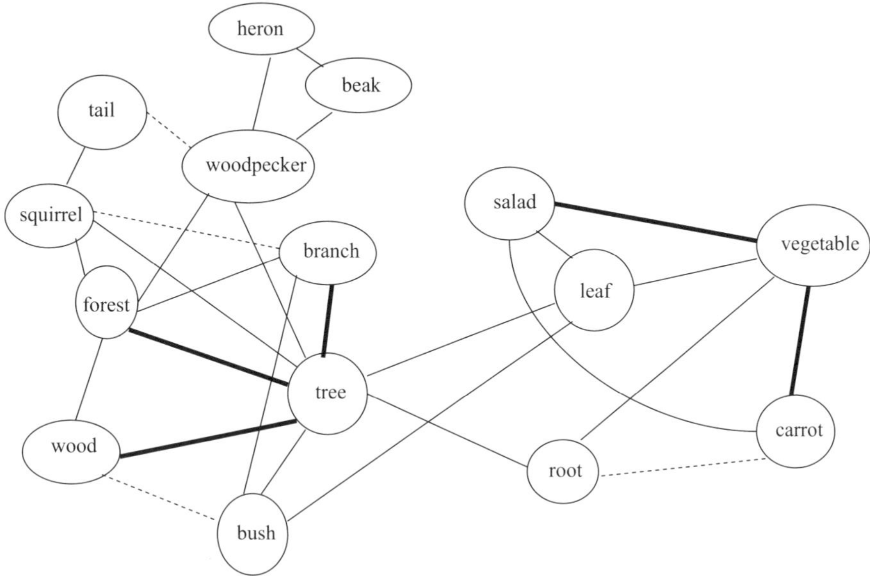

Figure 2.2 A fragment of a possible network of connections within the mental lexicon based on meaning. (Bold lines represent stronger connections, dotted lines weaker links.)

were mostly concerned with the rules of how to form sentences, words and speech sounds. But 'knowledge of language' also includes, as an important part, our knowledge of words. Adult language users have at their disposal an enormous vocabulary of, on average, an estimated 60,000 words. This knowledge of words, which is closely connected to our knowledge of the world, is our **mental lexicon**. The mental lexicon is quite unlike an alphabetical dictionary; it is rather more comparable to a network of 'nodes' and 'strings'. In Figure 2.2, connections based on meaning have been drawn. The nodes are the words, and the strings connect words that are related in meaning. There are also connections based on aspects of words other than meaning. Sound correspondences also connect words to each other, for example the word *wood* is related to *would*, *weed*, *wide*, *wade* and *woad* based on sound, but not meaning.

When people are reading, listening, speaking or writing, they constantly draw upon their mental lexicon. In speaking and writing this may involve finding the right word forms for the concepts they want to express. In listening and reading, on the other hand, it involves finding the right meaning for the word forms they hear and see. When using the mental lexicon, we say that this knowledge is being **activated**. When language users hear a word, that word form plus its meaning is activated. This activation will fan out to surrounding word forms that are closely connected. This is known as **activation**

spreading or **spreading activation**. When, for example, the word *tree* from Figure 2.2 is activated, connected words like *branch* and *wood* will also be activated or primed. Due to this activation, these latter words will be relatively easily recognised if presented in the following sentence. This gain in recognition speed is known as the semantic **priming effect**, *tree* being the prime. Priming effects are used to study the mental lexicon and language understanding processes (see Section 2.4).

The language user does not only need all these various kinds of knowledge, but also needs to be able to function cognitively. We will not develop this further here, but simply assume that speakers have normal mental faculties, have a sufficient memory capacity and attention span, etc. and do not suffer from any physical impediment related to language. The various cognitive functions also belong in the middle block of Figure 2.1, though they have not been represented separately. All these various types of knowledge and ability we shall from now on refer to as the **cognitive system**.

2.3 Language and the Brain

A term like mental lexicon implies that our knowledge of the language system, our linguistic competence, is 'somewhere in our head'. But where? Can we identify specific areas in our brain where language is localised? We can look for an answer to this question using different methods. One way is to study the kind of language problems that can occur after certain brain areas have been damaged.

In example (7) an adult male (A), in answer to the interviewer's questions (I), is telling her something about his hometown. Dots (. . .) represent pauses or hesitations.

(7) A: . . .Stratford. . .upon Avon. And er. . .beautiful. . .er. . .I. . .nice. . . walk.
I: Yes. . .yes where?
A: Where? Er. . .Stratford upon Avon.
I: You walk all through it?
A: No. . .cycle or no, er. . .er. . .car er. . .shopping.

It is immediately noticeable that the man speaks with difficulty and that it is almost impossible for him to produce grammatical sentences. He has some damage to the front part of his brain, in Broca's area (see Figure 2.3), named after the nineteenth-century French neurologist Paul Broca. Damage to this part of the brain will mostly affect his speaking, whereas his comprehension remains relatively intact. Such patients will speak slowly and with difficulty; they use no or almost no words with a grammatical function, such as articles or prepositions (see Section 6.9). Since these words are usually also left out in telegrams, this kind of language use is known as 'telegraphic speech'.

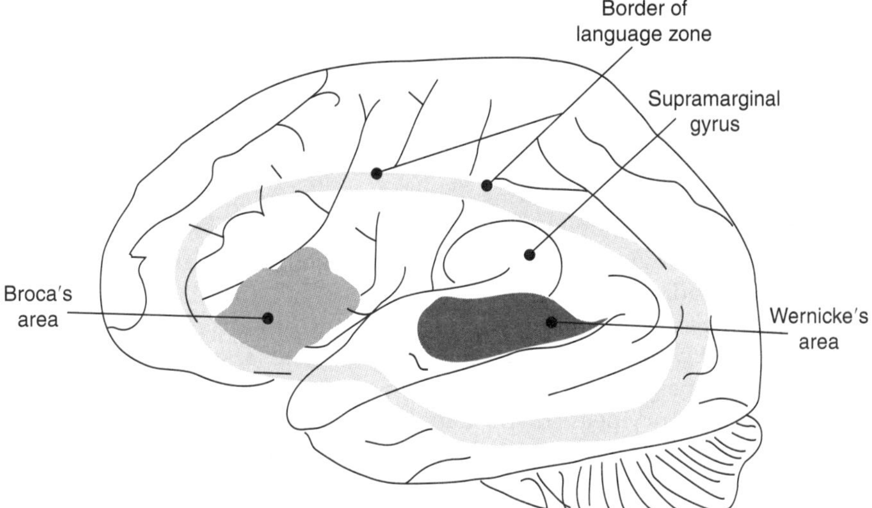

Figure 2.3 Language areas in the left hemisphere.

Damage to more posterior areas of the brain will have different consequences. Damage to Wernicke's area, named after a nineteenth-century Austrian neurologist and also indicated in Figure 2.3, will lead to problems in language comprehension. The language production of patients with damage to Wernicke's area is normal in speed and sentence length, but when they speak, they may replace one speech sound with another, for example *putter* instead of *butter*, or they may exchange words with similar meanings, saying *boy* instead of *girl*, or *fork* instead of *knife*. In serious cases such speech errors – of which the patient is usually not aware – may lead to meaningless 'jargon'. Later in this chapter, in fragment (29) of Section 2.5, we will see a transcription of spoken language that is in part no longer comprehensible.

These examples demonstrate that different areas in the human brain can be connected to different functions involved in language. Language dysfunctions that are caused by damage to the brain, for example as the result of a stroke or an accident, are known as **aphasia**. About 95% of all aphasia cases are caused by damage to the left hemisphere of the brain, since in most humans this hemisphere is specialised for language. A small minority, mostly left-handed people, however, have language localised in the right hemisphere of the brain. With a lesion in Broca's area it is mostly processing and understanding of syntactic information that is affected. For example, in a sentence like *The lion was bitten by the tiger*, Broca patients often do not understand who is doing the biting and who is being bitten; they usually think that it is the lion who is doing the biting. Wernicke's area turns out to play an important role in processing phonological and semantic information (speech sounds and word meanings).

Evidence from aphasic signers of a sign language confirms this picture. Signers who have suffered left hemisphere damage to Broca's or Wernicke's area also show similar symptoms in their signing. But damage to the left hemisphere does not always lead to aphasia. Aphasia only occurs if certain specific areas in the brain have been damaged.

Damage to areas other than those discovered by Broca and Wernicke may also cause language dysfunctions. For example, damage to the area of the supramarginal gyrus may cause very serious word-finding difficulties, both in spontaneous language and when objects have to be named, as well as difficulties in reading and writing.

Language dysfunction in humans with damaged brains is not the only evidence we have when tackling the question of where language is localised in the brain. In the past few years new scanning techniques have been developed for investigating and measuring brain activity in healthy subjects too. Using these techniques, such as functional Magnetic Resonance Imaging (fMRI), we are now able to see which brain areas are active when certain language tasks are carried out. As a result, we now know that Broca's area is not only involved in speaking, but to some extent in comprehension as well. The fMRI pictures in Figure 2.4 show the brain activity (indicated by light areas) in the

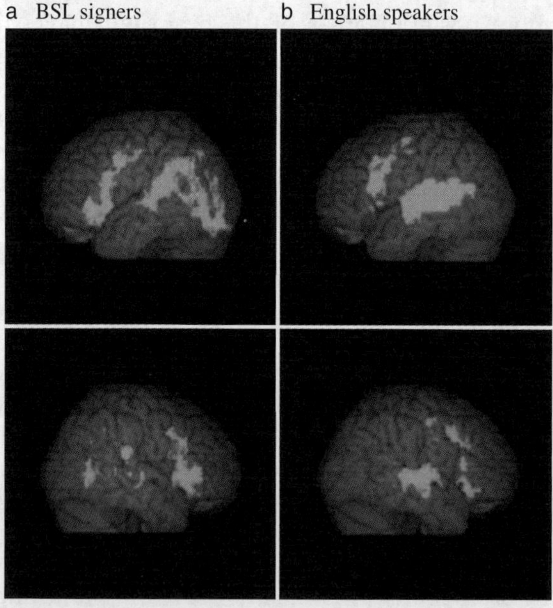

Figure 2.4 fMRI scan of left (top) and right (bottom) hemispheres of (a) British Sign Language signers presented with BSL and (b) English speakers presented with spoken English. Brain activity is indicated by the light areas. MacSweeney, M., Woll, B., Campbell, R. *et al.* (2002) Neural systems underlying British Sign Language and audio-visual English processing in native users, *Brain* 125, 1583–93.

left hemisphere (top picture) and the right hemisphere (bottom picture). In the right-hand column we see the images of the brains of English speakers presented with sentences such as *I will send you the date and time* or *The woman handed the boy a cup*. The left hemisphere (top) shows much more activation than the right hemisphere, although the right hemisphere (bottom) is involved to some extent.

The same scans done with signers of British Sign Language (Figure 2.4, left column) show very similar patterns of activation, indicating that the language areas are active for language in general and not just for a spoken language.

A different technique, based on electrical activity in the brain (Event Related Potentials or ERP), is used to indicate how, and especially how fast, language users respond to features of language input. For example, do language users react to grammatical features of the language input or just to semantic features? Studies have shown that language users do in fact react to syntactic violations such as those in 8(a or b) below. This reaction, known as the P600 effect, is in the form of specific brain activity occurring about 600 milliseconds after the violation is presented. This does not occur in grammatically correct sentences such as (8c). However, a sentence such as (9a), that contains a semantic violation, triggers an effect about 400 milliseconds after exposure to the italicised critical word (the N400 effect), whereas (9b) does not. Such evidence is support for the types of distinctions that linguists make in their descriptions of language, that is, between grammar and meaning and between incorrect and correct.

(8) a. Where do a boy like to play?
b. Where a boy like to play?
c. Where does a boy like to play?

(9) a. Where does a *chair* like to play?
b. Where does a boy like to play?

As we have seen, the ability to use language depends on the way certain areas in the brain function. These areas each contribute to the use of language. The timing of reactions in the brain also reflects the different status of grammatical and semantic information. The question remains as to what (cognitive) steps the language user has to take in order to interpret and produce language.

2.4 Language Comprehension

As a rule, language comprehension takes place very quickly and automatically, and the language user can barely influence it. At the same time, it is a very complex process. Below, we will give a short description of the sub-processes involved in comprehension. We will start with the recognition of sounds, then we will discuss the recognition of words, the comprehension of sentences and the interpretation of utterances, in particular as regards their communicative intentions. At the end of the section we will draw these various sub-processes together.

2.4.1 Speech Recognition

Which sentence do you think is being pronounced in (10)?

(10) Idunnowatsaytim

Utterance (10) is a fairly realistic representation of the way the sentence *I don't know what to say to him* is often pronounced in fast speech. In actual speech there are fluent transitions from one speech sound to the next, and no clear breaks between words. The spoken utterance is a continuous stretch of sound. This is quite obvious when we are listening to a language we do not know. The spoken utterances come in one long sound stream, and the individual words, and even individual sounds, are often hard to distinguish. In technical terms we say that speech sounds form a **continuous signal**.

Another feature of (10) is that many sounds have been 'omitted'. If the utterance were pronounced more slowly, the *t* of *don't* would probably be heard. One and the same speech sound, word or sentence will never be pronounced in exactly the same way, even by the same speaker, let alone different speakers. Pronunciation will vary depending on the different circumstances under which speech is produced – whether the speaker has a cold, is chewing gum, is speaking fast or slowly, is whispering or screaming. Moreover, the pronunciation of a particular speech sound will be influenced by the surrounding speech sounds. The actual *k* sound of *kill* is different from the *k* of *cool, kale, cot, teak* and *tick*. The pronunciation of *k* is influenced both by the sounds that precede it and by those that follow. This is known as **co-articulation**. As a result of the variation in speakers and circumstances, and also because of the phenomenon of co-articulation, the sounds we produce while speaking are in many ways **variable**.

If the actual sound shape of language is continuous and variable, how is it possible, therefore, that listeners in everyday life have little difficulty in understanding spoken language? This has been studied in language experiments. For example, people were asked to listen to the following sentences:

(11) a. *It was found that the #eel was on the* axle.
b. *It was found that the #eel was on the* shoe.
c. *It was found that the #eel was on the* orange.
d. *It was found that the #eel was on the* table.

In each of these examples the italicised part sounds exactly the same, but the # is realised as a sort of cough. But what do the listeners think they hear? In

(11) it is *wheel*, in (11b) it is *heel*, in (11c) *peel*, and (11d) *meal*. Listeners are unaware of the fact that they fill in the missing sound; they think they hear complete information, because on the basis of the context of the sentence and their knowledge of the world they make sense of the sentence.

The importance of the context for our understanding of the speech signal is confirmed by a different experiment, in which individual words extracted from the speech stream were presented to listeners. The words were no longer in their original conversational context. So, for example, the word *cake* was identified only 45% of the time when taken out of the context of sentence (12).

(12) The baker had forgotten to let the *cake* cool.

In the whole experiment listeners could identify no more than 50% of these isolated words, whereas they easily managed a score of 100% when the same words were presented in their original conversational context. The context evidently is of crucial importance when we try to understand spoken language.

The examples above clearly demonstrate that understanding speech is not a process in which we identify each individual speech sound within the sound signal and then combine these into a word (**bottom-up processing**). Speech recognition is evidently influenced by our knowledge, expectations and higher levels of processing, such as constructing an interpretation that makes sense (**top-down processing**).

The next higher level in the process of language comprehension is that of word recognition.

2.4.2 Word Recognition

In conversation a speaker will, on average, produce some 150 words per minute. This means that a listener will have to 'look up' about two or three words per second in his or her extensive mental lexicon, as has been shown using the ERP techniques described in Section 2.3. How is this possible? How do language users do this? How do they manage to recognise the words they hear so quickly?

According to most investigators, listeners already begin to consult their mental lexicon as soon as the first speech sounds of a word have been heard. For example, when hearing an initial *b-*, this activates all words in the mental lexicon that begin with this sound (*bath, baker, big, book, blossom, blot, blog*, etc.). When the next few sounds of the word are perceived, for example *-lo-*, the first selection is reduced to the set of words that begin with *blo-* (in this example *blossom, blot, blog*). Now when the next sound is an s, the listener can already decide that the word must be *blossom* (or perhaps a related word like *blossoming* or *blossoms*). A set of words that is activated at a certain stage in the process of word recognition is known as a **cohort**. The model of word recognition we have just sketched is known as the **cohort model**.

The same model applies when words are read rather than heard. The resulting cohort in written language can be different from the cohort in spoken language, depending on the spelling rules of the individual language. Thus if the letter *c*- was presented in the written form, then the set *cat*, *city*, *chat*, etc. could be activated). In the spoken form of course the letter *c* is pronounced differently in these words. Interestingly mobile telephones and computers make use of the cohort model in their typing or spelling aids. Using special software they can offer a few options for the word to be used as the letters are typed in. Such programs also record individual users' most frequent choices and are much more restricted than the activated cohort in the listening or reading process.

We usually hear words in context. In sentence (13) the listener hears the word *blossom*.

(13) In a vase on the table stood some beautiful cherry blossom.

Here it is highly likely that the listener, having processed the first part of the sentence, *In a vase on the table*, already has an idea of what might be in the vase. This contextual information will definitely facilitate the recognition of the word *blossom*. In this example, upon hearing *blo*... the listener hardly needs the rest of the word to be able to eliminate the other candidates from the cohort, such as *blot* or *blog*. Even if *blossom* was mispronounced as *blisson*, the listener would probably still recognise the word that was intended.

In sentence (14) we have a different context for the word *blossom*. What would be the effect of this context?

(14) This afternoon I saw some blossom.

Clearly, the context in (13), which mentions a vase, is much more specific than that in (14). In (13) the context helps to build up an expectation in the listener which may lead to faster recognition. This is known as the **context effect**. And in fact, as a result of this effect, *blossom* is recognised more quickly in (13) than in (14).

When a word (form) is recognised, this does not automatically mean that just one meaning is activated; some words are ambiguous, that is they have multiple meanings (see Section 11.8). For example *bank* can mean a financial institution or the side of a river, or *bug* can mean an insect or an illness. It turns out that when speakers are presented with such an ambiguous word, they react more quickly to other words related in meaning to *both* possible meanings. Thus hearing *bank* would mean that *money* and *cheque*, and *water* and *boat*, would all be primed. In other words, both meanings of the ambiguous word show a priming effect. This means that both meanings of ambiguous words are activated, although the most frequent meaning shows a stronger activation than the less frequent. This happens whether or not the meanings would both fit in that sentence, though the meaning that does not fit is quickly eliminated on the basis of context. The ultimate goal is still to make sense of what you hear.

2.4.3 Understanding Sentences

(15) a. The Prime Minister has decided on the high-speed train.
b. It is the high-speed train the Prime Minister has decided on.
c. It is on the high-speed train that the Prime Minister has decided.

The sentence in (15a) is ambiguous. The ambiguity is not caused by a single word, but by the way in which the words have been grouped, as (15b) and (15c) illustrate. The word *on* can be combined either with *decided*, or with *the high-speed train* marking a location. In interpreting a sentence we have to do more than just process the words and their meanings. The words have to be properly grouped together and the listener has to analyse or parse the sentence correctly.

The process of **parsing** starts right away. Just as the cohort model illustrates this at the word level, at the sentence level, too, the listener cannot afford the time to wait until the whole sentence has been heard. Of course, this immediate parsing increases the risk of errors; different solutions lead to different interpretations, as is illustrated by (15b) and (15c). The following newspaper heading illustrates again this process of sentence comprehension:

KILLER SENTENCED
TO DIE FOR SECOND TIME
IN 10 YEARS

The sentence is not ungrammatical but its structure tempts the reader to make an analysis that is initially not intended. At first reading *for second time* may be combined with *to die*. It is when the reader realises that you only live once that it becomes quite clear that this first analysis is not what is intended. The reader has to go back and try again, ending up with the intended analysis that it was the fact that the killer was sentenced for the second time. Such sentences show that listeners have a preference for a simple parsing, in this case relating *for second time* to the nearest verb. In other cases, such a **syntactic strategy** may not work and might lead the listener up the garden path. Such sentences are in fact called 'garden path' sentences. In written form they are processed from left to right, right to left or from top to bottom, depending on the writing system in the individual language. Eye-tracking experiments show how in reading sentences the reader's eyes move forwards but sometimes back to check the analysis. The more complicated the sentence is, the more the reader has to check back. The listener or reader certainly does not wait until the end of the sentence before starting to analyse it.

That the first analysis is not always correct is shown in the now classic garden-path sentence shown in (16).

(16) The horse raced past the barn fell.

It is only when the verb *fell* is perceived, at the end of the sentence, that you realise your initial analysis may have been wrong. The word *raced* cannot be the main verb connected to the subject *the horse*, so it must be a past participle in the phrase 'raced past the barn'. Hence, the proper paraphrase of (16) is (17).

(17) The horse that was raced past the barn fell.

The difficulty in processing sentence (16) is due to a syntactic strategy that is often adopted by people listening to English. The first group of words containing a noun (*the horse*) is assigned the role of subject of the sentence and the first inflected verb (*raced*) the role of predicate. In many cases this works, but not in (16).

Sentence (18) is another example of a garden path sentence. The reader may easily go wrong.

(18) Assuming they have the parcel arrives today.

Many people initially combine *have* with *the parcel* as a result of a syntactic strategy to relate new words to the current group of words instead of starting a new group, the so-called 'late closure' strategy. Only when they get as far as *arrives* do they realise that there is something wrong. To prevent this erroneous interpretation, the written text could have a comma after *have*, just as in the spoken version there will be a very short break after *have*.

The application of such **syntactic strategies** can be best demonstrated when things go wrong, as in the examples above. However, the strategies allow the language user to start the parsing of an utterance from the very start and thus to uncover the structure and meaning of the sentence as quickly as possible and, in practice, with a great chance of success.

Do language users only use syntactic strategies? To answer this question, let us first look at sentence (19). How difficult is this to understand?

(19) The cat is being chased by the mouse.

It may take a moment to grasp that it is the mouse that is chasing the cat. Our natural tendency is to interpret this sentence as the cat chasing the mouse. This is the result of a different kind of strategy, a general **semantic strategy**, that is to identify the content words in the sentence, and then on that basis to construct an interpretation that makes sense. This explains why sentences like (19), that have an improbable meaning, are often misinterpreted in the first instance. In many cases the listener's knowledge of the words and of the world – that is, their semantic strategy – will suffice to produce an interpretation, and in that case the syntactic strategies are not that important. For people who are learning English as a second language, sentence (19) may cause even more difficulties. Their command of grammar may be less good and so they may rely more heavily on a semantic strategy.

2.4.4 *Interpretation of Utterances*

(20) Once again the year has come full circle, and for me there can be no greater privilege, and honour, than to that to which it is my lot to have befallen this evening. There can be no finer honour than to welcome into our midst tonight a guest who has not only done only more than not anyone for our Society, but nonetheless has only done more. (Monty Python, 'Grandstand').

The text in (20) is a satire on making an after-dinner speech. The sentences in (20) are deviant in syntax and semantics, but we still manage to understand what is meant. Listeners first of all listen for meaning when they are processing language. When this meaning is unclear or difficult to recover from the utterance, they will persist in their attempt to assign a global meaning to the sentence. In all cases the language user will try to make a 'mental model' of what is said and meant and to integrate the new information into what he or she already knows.

Sentence (21) is not deviant in any way, but what does the speaker really mean?

(21) Can you pass the salt?

This utterance is usually interpreted as a request. It is not a question, that is, the speaker is not interested in finding out whether the listener is physically capable of passing the salt; the speaker wants the request fulfilled. Example (21) shows how the literal meaning of an utterance may well be different from the communicative intent of the speaker. This communicative intent can only be understood by listeners when they, in addition to their knowledge of the language, also use their knowledge of the rules for using language, that is, their communicative competence, as we discussed in Section 2.2. These communicative rules determine, for example, how you should formulate a polite request, and how you can decode the 'deeper', indirect meaning and the communicative intent of the speaker from the literal meaning of the utterance in question. In English, for example, it is usual for speakers to add the word *please* to the question in (21), which then makes it clear that this is not a simple question but a request. See Section 4.2.

2.4.5 *From Speech Recognition to Interpretation*

Language comprehension, as we have demonstrated in this section, consists of at least four different sub-processes: sound recognition, word recognition,

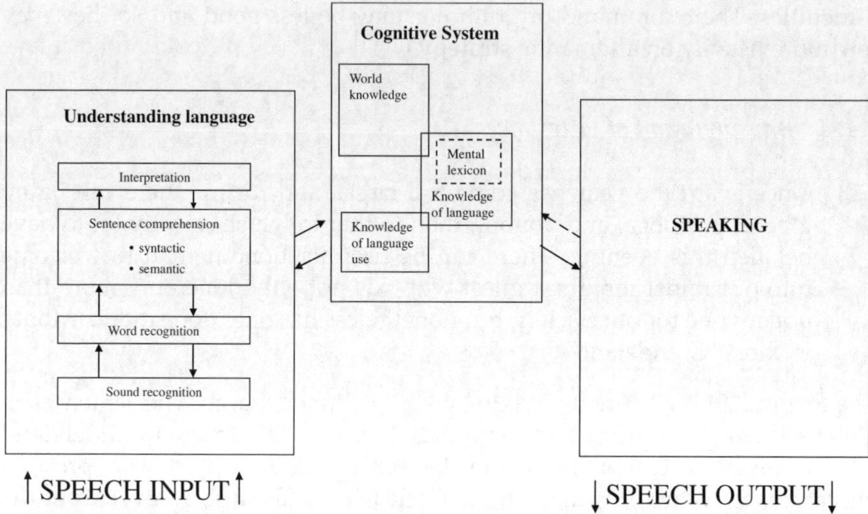

Figure 2.5 The four sub-processes for language comprehension and their relation to the cognitive system.

sentence comprehension and interpretation. This enables us to fill in the left box in Figure 2.1 (see Figure 2.5). The four sub-processes do not work in isolation but interact and influence each other. That is, we do not only proceed from smaller units to larger ones, in bottom-up processing, but we also use information from larger units, including the context and our knowledge of the world, in top-down processing. The interplay of these two forms of processing will – if all goes well – lead to a proper understanding of the sentences we hear or read.

The role of the context can be so strong that world knowledge can be suspended and 'normal' sentences are processed as being semantically strange. In a story about a Mr Peanut, the peanut figure becomes animate. A sentence such as *He falls in love*, referring to the peanut, is then perfectly acceptable. When the participants in an experiment listened to this story and were subsequently presented with the sentence 'the peanut is salty', the ERP measurements showed a semantic deviation similar to the one registered for sentence (9b) discussed in Section 2.3.

2.5 Language Production

(22) . . .and then I go with wa-. . .eh with water. . .no with. . .yes with water yes. . .to make and then eh. . .

In example (22) an aphasic patient is trying to say that he starts the day by washing himself. Due to the brain damage they have suffered, aphasic patients can have extreme difficulties in speaking. But healthy language users also regularly produce speech errors. This suggests that there are all kinds of complex processes going on in our heads, long before an intended utterance is actually produced. A closer look at these processes will reveal how easy it is for things to go wrong – it is almost a miracle that things go as well as they do.

We can distinguish three stages in the speech process: thinking out and planning the utterance, formulating the utterance, and finally the actual pronunciation of the utterance. The formulation stage can be subdivided in two further sub-processes: grammatical encoding, and phonological encoding. These four processes will be discussed in more detail in the following sections.

2.5.1 *What Do You Want to Say?*

In general a speaker will have to think of a 'message' before saying anything. So, what exactly will it be? What information is to be conveyed? Or what should be requested? Should the request be made in a diplomatic manner, or is it better to be blunt?

When thinking out and planning an utterance, that is **conceptualising** the message, the speaker will have to take a number of decisions about the content. For example, a speaker who begins a lecture with sentence (23) is working on the assumption that the listeners know who Chomsky is. Otherwise this speaker would have had to start with sentence (24).

(23) Chomsky argued that...
(24) In the late fifties there was an American linguist, Chomsky, who argued that...

So, speakers must make an assessment of the level of knowledge of their conversation partner(s) and of the information they want to share. They must also decide in which order to present the information. Speakers often keep to the chronological order of events: first event A, and then B and then C. What happened first is mentioned first. Listeners appear to follow this principle, too, when they are interpreting the utterances they hear. Examples (25) and (26) may report roughly the same facts, but the cause and effect will be interpreted differently.

(25) She got interested in dance and failed her university exams.
(26) She failed her university exams and got interested in dance.

It is not completely clear what other principles may guide language users when they plan an utterance. One thing is clear – in a conversation they will usually try to link up with what has just been said. As a consequence, a new utterance will often begin with a reference to something that was said in a previous utterance.

The planning process is difficult to study in natural situations. It is rather hard to determine whether a speech error originated at the planning stage of an utterance. It is true that speakers in such cases say something different than they originally intended, but how can we be aware of this, especially if the speaker does not notice and does not correct the utterance?

Freudian slips of the tongue, named after the famous psychoanalyst, are thought to be the result of repressed thoughts and emotions that interfere with the planning of the utterance. The example in (27) is taken from a student who asked for the postponement of an exam but lied about the reason.

(27) Last night my grandmother *lied* (instead of *died*).

This student appears to have been so preoccupied with lying that the verb *lie* was activated. The word form *lied* was therefore activated before the target form *died*. This speech error or slip of the tongue was probably helped further by the sound similarity between the two words.

As well as speech errors, pauses and hesitations also reveal how planning takes place. While speaking, we not only pause for breath, but also for planning purposes, and sometimes to find the right word. From the study of hesitations we know that they often occur within sentences, just before a new part of a sentence or when there is a difficult choice of words. These are the locations within the utterance where the continuation is not self-evident. This suggests that speakers, while speaking, have to take a moment to plan what else they are going to say.

When the speaker knows what the message will be and has completed the planning stage, the utterance does not yet have a linguistic shape; it is still a **preverbal message**. Below, we will discuss the way in which such a preverbal message is given a verbal form and becomes a spoken sentence.

2.5.2 *Formulation: Grammatical Encoding*

(28) I take my sugar with coffee.

In utterance (28) something has gone wrong with the formulation. The language user undoubtedly knew what he or she wanted to say, but the **grammatical encoding** of the preverbal message is not as intended. What happens at this second stage of the speaking process?

Under the heading of 'grammatical encoding' we are actually talking about processes at the word and sentence level. The construction of an utterance is guided by concepts in the preverbal message, and these concepts activate the associated words in our mental lexicon.

Suppose a speaker wants to say that Sven is giving his girlfriend a book on art. The preverbal message will be something like: GIVE [SVEN, HIS GIRLFRIEND, BOOK ON ART]. The next step is that the speaker will have to activate the right words. The concept GIVE will activate the entry *give* in the mental lexicon, a verb that nearly always involves someone who gives something to somebody else. When *give* is selected from the mental lexicon, it brings along its combinatorial properties, that is that it has to be used in a sentence with (preferably) an open slot for the giver, one for the given object, and one for the receiver (see Section 7.5 for the precise linguistic terms). These slots have to be filled by the speaker on the basis of who is the giver, what is given and who it is given to. The candidates for those open slots are words that have been activated by other concepts from the preverbal message. In the process of grammatical encoding verbs play a central role since the choice of verb largely determines the rest of the sentence structure.

As was just outlined, the first step in grammatical encoding is to activate the right words. Each word brings along its own meanings and syntactic properties. By combining these, the speaker is able to construct and formulate the structure of the utterance. At this stage, the focus is on word selection. The composition of the word form (sound shape) and morphological structure will have to wait until a later stage of the speaking process.

During the grammatical encoding process it is easy to make mistakes that can lead to speech errors. For example, words can end up in the wrong slot in the verb structure, and as a result the intended *I take my coffee with sugar* became the sentence as actually uttered in (28).

A different kind of error occurs when a mistake is made in the selection of words. In this case, the speaker is heading in the right direction as far as meaning is concerned, but comes up with *fork* where *spoon* was needed, for example. Here, the two words share so many semantic and grammatical properties that the unintended rival gets activated sooner or more strongly than the right word.

In fragment (29) an aphasic patient is trying to describe the picture of a boy flying a kite in Figure 2.6.

(29) There's a boy flying a kite. There's a k...k...kite up in a tree. One of the guys a...after it. The girl she's waving to the m...man...flying the kite. There's a *boy* dog on the f...lawn. There's a duck in /earn/. He's a...there's a *lane lean* er driveray going up to the house. It is has a /Is/...has it has a stroke uh...it has a no urn lkr\sl...it has the...smoke...on the chimney. It has a...E...J. Smith from the mailbox. It's got lots of...rolling acres. There's...there's a pond in the front lawn...*ice pond*...er...water pond.

The words in italics show that this patient has great difficulty in selecting the right words. He pronounces some words incorrectly and some are

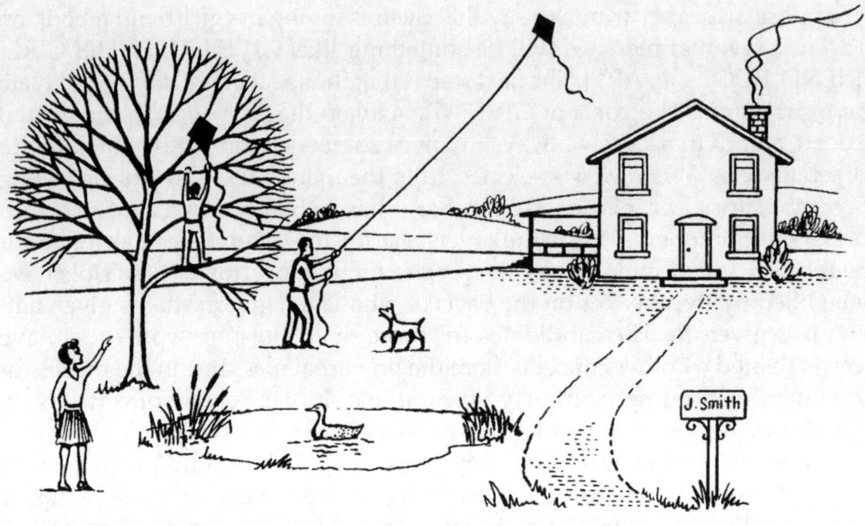

Figure 2.6 Elicitation picture from the Minnesota Test for Differential Diagnosis of Aphasia. Illustration taken from Card Materials for the Minnesota Test for Differential Diagnosis of Aphasia (Pack One) by Hildred Schuell and Lawrence Benson, University of Minnesota Press © 1965 University of Minnesota.

uninterpretable (indicated between slashes). In very serious cases of aphasia, patients may no longer be capable of selecting the right content words at all, even though the sentence structure may still be reasonably intact. This is the case in particular when Wernicke's area has been damaged (see Section 2.3), which can result in totally incomprehensible gibberish. The intended words have not disappeared from the patient's lexicon, though; it is just that they are no longer easy to access. But under different conditions the patient may well be able to produce them.

2.5.3 *Formulation: Phonological Encoding*

(30) Could you pass me the buit frowl, ah... fruit bowl, please.

In (30) we have another **slip of the tongue**. The speaker has chosen the right words for his intended utterance, but arriving at the last words, things go wrong in the word form. The first sound of the second syllable *-bowl*, the consonant *b*, has changed places with the first consonants *fr* of the first syllable *fruit-*. From speech errors like these we can infer how speakers proceed with the **phonological encoding** of their words. Words are probably built up syllable by syllable. Syllables in turn are built from speech sounds, some of which form a sound cluster that stick together, such as *fr-* in *fruit* (see Chapter 16 for the structure of syllables). In (30) we had a case where two consonants were interchanged, but in the next sentence (31) the speaker has chosen the wrong word although it is related in sound structure to what he intended.

(31) There were 53 subscriptions. . .eh. . .submissions.

Mispronunciations as in (30) can also occur in normal signers of sign languages, in which case they are often called **slips of the hand** instead of slips of the tongue. A signer who means to sign HOTEL in German Sign Language may end up making the wrong movement, and as a result erroneously produce the sign meaning 'fashion' (32). Errors such as these indicate that signs are also composed from separate building blocks, such as the shape of the hand, the location of the sign and the movement. In this respect, signs are entirely comparable to words.

(32)

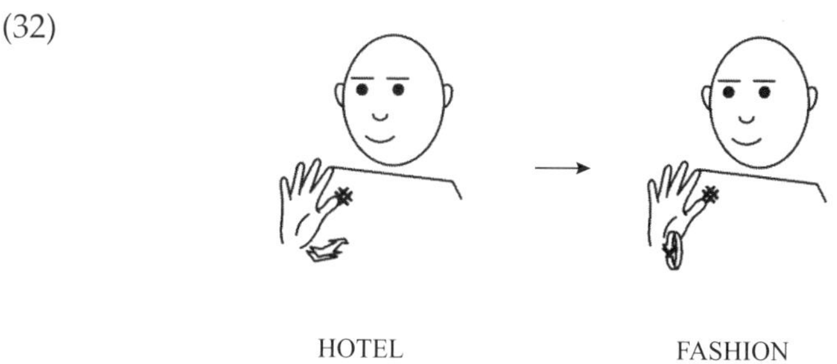

HOTEL FASHION

As we can see, parts of words and signs can go wrong during phonological encoding, but it can also happen that a word form cannot be activated at all, even though we know which word we want to use. Most of us have, at some point or another, been in a situation where a word is, so to speak, on the tip of our tongue, but we just cannot find it. We very often know something about the word we are looking for, like the number of syllables it has, or the location of the main stress, and often also its initial and/or final sound(s). And we immediately recognise the word when someone else says it. Very often, though, the speaker remains stuck on a similar-sounding word form, and cannot go beyond saying 'It is something like tatascope'. Here the word node, at the meaning level, has been activated in the mental lexicon, but the connection with the form of the word remains incomplete. The word form becomes available only in bits and pieces, showing quite clearly that activating the right word form is not an all-or-nothing-process. The word form is clearly not one single unit. Note, by the way, that searching for words in the mental lexicon is often more problematic in a second or foreign language than in your mother tongue. Many people who have learned English as a foreign language will know a word like *relief*, meaning 'ease' or 'alleviation' in the context of pain, but when asked to produce the word on the basis of these meanings will find it difficult to do so.

Aphasic patients can have great difficulties with phonological encoding. Such patients, particularly when they are aware of their problem, often do not manage to produce fluent speech, as they are continuously searching for the intended word forms. In example (22) above, the patient could not find the word *wash*, although he knew that it began with *wa-*, indicating too the use of the cohort.

The context can sometimes help in finding the right word form. An introductory sentence like *The submarine uses its. . .*, for example, can help to prompt the word *periscope* where the speaker at first was stuck with *ta-ta-scope*. It may also help when attention is not focused on the search itself. Thus, an aphasic patient, when asked, was unable to produce the name of his little daughter and became quite desperate (33).

(33) Oh my poor Jacqueline, now I don't even know your name anymore!

In phonological encoding all kinds of different speech errors can occur, but interestingly, nearly all of them follow the rules of the language in question. That is to say that the wrong word is usually another existing word or at least a 'possible' word. An example would be when someone mispronounces the name of the store Marks & Spencer as Sparks & Mencer. An error such as Mpencer & Sarks would be very unlikely since the group of consonants *mp* does not occur at the beginning of a word in English.

2.5.4 *Articulation*

The phonological encoding of words and their grammatical properties leads to the elaboration of a **phonetic plan.** This plan contains all the information needed to actually produce the utterance. This phonetic plan is usually realised unconsciously and without error. Even if an error has taken place at the phonological level, as *buit frowl* in (30), the articulation will be correct. When all words have been given their phonological form, the phonetic plan is ready. During the pronunciation or **articulation** phase, the 'abstract' word forms that have been activated in the brain are turned into speech movements. This transformation requires a good coordination of nerves and muscles. As we observed in Section 2.1, uttering a speech sound involves the combined activity of about a hundred muscles, both large and small, in order to get the right timing needed for the proper pronunciation. In one second of speech, humans can produce some fifteen different speech sounds. Fluent speech thus clearly requires the articulatory organs to be highly coordinated (see also Chapter 14).

It is impossible for speakers to stop and think which muscles they need to use every time they have to produce a new speech sound – that would take far too much time. A plausible idea is that language users have a little standard program for each individual sound wired into their brain that triggers the appropriate muscle activity. This is an attractive idea, but on closer inspection it does not hold water. If computers are programmed to produce speech in this way, they sound extremely unnatural. It turns out that the pronunciation of a particular speech sound is always dependent on the sounds preceding and following it: co-articulation as we called it in Section 4.2.1. To check this, just compare the position of the mouth for the *t* in *tick* and in *tock*. They are slightly different. It is therefore better to take the syllable as the unit of articulation, rather than the individual speech sound.

Furthermore, people produce speech under very different conditions, for example smoking a cigarette or chewing on sweets or gum. Speakers are obviously able to adapt their speech to these varying situations, something that fixed standard programs for individual sounds could never do.

2.5.5 *Speaking: From Intention to Articulation*

We began by distinguishing four steps or sub-processes: thinking and planning or conceptualising the utterance; grammatical encoding, phonological encoding (which together form the formulation stage); and finally the actual pronunciation or articulation of the utterance. A schematic representation is given in Figure 2.7, specifically filling in the right-hand block that was still empty in Figure 2.5.

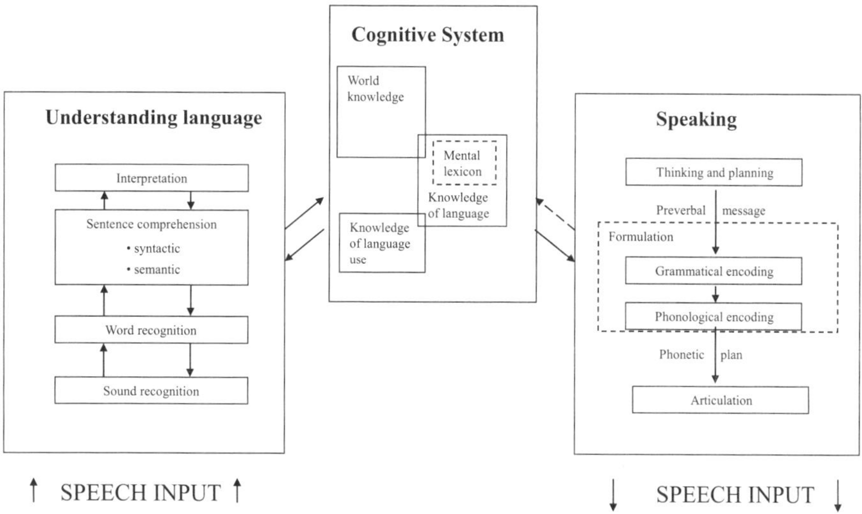

Figure 2.7 The four sub-processes of speaking in the whole system of language use.

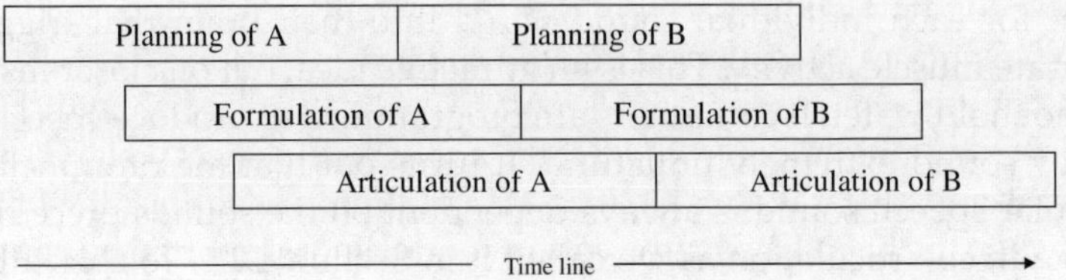

Figure 2.8 The incremental process of language production.

While taking these four steps, speakers can do more than one thing at a time. It is not the case that an utterance A is first exhaustively planned, then completely formulated, and only after that finally pronounced, before the speaker starts on utterance B. If this really were the case there would be gaps between successive utterances. But in actual fact, this does not happen. When hesitations do occur, it is not really so much *between* utterances, but rather *during* them. When people are busy producing an utterance, they are evidently already planning the next. A number of cognitive processes clearly run in **parallel**. When only part of an utterance has been planned, the speaker already begins with the formulation, while the remaining content of the sentence is still being developed. This view of speaking as an **incremental process** is represented schematically in Figure 2.8. While the planning of utterance A is not yet complete, the formulation phase has already started. And while A is still being pronounced, B is already being planned, etc. Figure 2.8 shows how complicated, but also how intriguing, the process of language production really is.

SUMMARY

In order to be able to communicate with others, a language user needs various kinds of cognitive abilities: **linguistic competence**, **communicative competence**, and **knowledge of the world**. These kinds of knowledge form part of the **cognitive system** that humans have at their disposal. An important part of linguistic competence is the **mental lexicon**. When a word from this lexicon is used, it is **activated**. This activation spreads to other words that are somehow connected to the one that has been activated; this is called **activation spreading** or **spreading activation**.

In speaking and understanding a language, that is, in **performance**, other cognitive abilities play a role, such as memory and attention. As a consequence, language use is rarely perfect. In most language users, linguistic competence is localised in certain areas in the left hemisphere of the brain. The language use of humans whose brain damage has caused language disorders **(aphasia)**, provides insight into the functions of these brain areas, and so do neuro-imaging techniques used also on healthy subjects.

In the comprehension of spoken language we can distinguish four processes: (1) speech recognition, when the hearer analyses the speech signal which is **continuous** and also – as a result of **co-articulation** – **variable**; (2) word recognition – when the hearer, using the **cohort model** and supported by **context** and **priming**, tries to identify as quickly as possible the various words; (3) sentence parsing – when the hearer, on the basis of **syntactic** and **semantic strategies**, tries to group words together in order to arrive at the correct meaning of the sentence; and (4) interpretation – when the hearer tries to establish not only the content of the message but also the communicative intention of the speaker. In the comprehension of spoken language we work from both ends: on the one hand, in **bottom-up processing**, we use smaller units (speech sounds, syllables, words) as a basis for the interpretation of the whole sentence; on the other, in **top-down processing**, we use our knowledge of the world and the context in order to properly recognise and interpret those smaller units.

Speaking starts with the thinking out and planning (**conceptualising**) of the **preverbal message** that the speaker wants to utter. This message then needs to be verbalised in language. To this end, suitable word meanings are accessed from the mental lexicon and fitted into the syntactic structure that links up with the verb (**grammatical encoding**). Next, the corresponding word forms are activated (**phonological encoding**). This results in a **phonetic plan** that contains all the information necessary for **articulation**. The fourth and final phase of the speaking process consists in the pronunciation of the sounds that form part of the utterance. The complexity of the speaking process can result in **slips of the tongue**, or in **slips of the hand** in signing, and these often help to reveal what is going on in the various phases of the process.

Because speaking involves complex processes, which need to result in fluent speech, the speaker will carry out many of these processes in **parallel**. As soon as part of the utterance has been planned or formulated, it will be put through to the next phase in the speaking process. Little by little, the utterance 'grows' in size and shape at all levels. The process is therefore **incremental**.

Assignments

1. When introduced to people of higher status, many people will say something like 'How do you do?' When meeting a good friend they are more likely to say 'How's things?' Is this part of their 'linguistic competence', or of their 'communicative competence'?
2. Can the words *poplar*, *partition*, *meal*, and *dog* be included in the network in Figure 2.2?

3. Carry out the following experiment with someone who has not read this book. Point to something white (e.g. a piece of paper) and ask what colour it is. Do the same with something else that is white, and if you can, do it a third time with yet another white object. Then ask: *What does a cow drink?* Chances are the answer will be *milk*. Why does this happen?
4. Why is it that we can usually interpret an utterance like *Whassup?* or *Howyadoing?* without too much difficulty?
5. Take the following two sentences:
   (a) In the zoo we saw a new-born zebra.
   (b) He was talking enthusiastically about the new-born zebra.
   Why will *zebra* be recognised more easily in (a) than in (b)?
6. Explain why one can be easily fooled by the sentence:
   The girl said it liked meat.
7. Compare the following two English sentences:
   (a) The guest expected to be late arrived.
   (b) The guest arrived later than expected.
   Which of these two (a or b) will be more difficult to understand? Why?
8. Give an explanation of the following slip of the tongue: *Britannia waives the rules*. What can you conclude from this slip about the language production process?
9. Try and find someone you can bring into the tip-of-the-tongue state, for example by giving a description of a well-known but rarely used object, such as 'What is the name of that thingy with a gradient which you use at sea to establish where you are by measuring the angle of the sunlight?' (*sextant*), or 'What do you call the thing you use to tap the speed when you are playing music?' (*metronome*). Now find out and note down what this person knows about the form of the word that is on the tip of his or her tongue.
10. When someone prematurely gives away the clue or the point of a joke, in which particular phase of the speaking process is this person making an error? Explain your answer.

Test Yourself

1. Which three kinds of knowledge must language users have at their disposal in order to be able to communicate adequately?
2. What is the difference between linguistic competence and performance?
3. Explain why a hearer usually does not have great difficulty in understanding spoken language, despite the fact that the speech signal is variable and continuous?

4. How does the so-called 'priming effect' operate?
5. What is the difference between semantic and syntactic strategies in understanding sentences?
6. Which components or phases can be distinguished in the speaking process?
7. What are 'slips-of-the-hand'? What can we learn from studying them?
8. Explain why speaking can be considered an 'incremental' process?

ACKNOWLEDGMENTS AND FURTHER READING

Good introductions to psycholinguistics are Aitchison (1976) and Carroll (1999) and a recent basic book on the relationship between language and cognition is Byrd and Mintz (2010). More extensive information can be found in Traxler and Gernsbacher (2006) and Gaskell (2007). Levelt (1989) gives a detailed description of the speaking process. A good non-scientific introduction to the study of aphasia is by Parr, Byng and Gilpin (1998); a more scientific overview is to be found in Sarno (1998). A thorough overview of language and speech disorders is by Damico, Müller and Ball (2010). The psycholinguistics of sign languages is discussed in Baker *et al.* (in preparation). Further examples of ambiguous headlines can be found at http://www.fun-with-words.com/ambiguous_headlines.html.

Brown and Hagoort (1999) and Ahlsén (2006) provide an excellent introduction to the neurological basis of language. For an evolutionary perspective we refer to Deacon (1998). A detailed discussion of language for thought from a philosophical point of view can be found in Aydede (2004).

The quote from Monty Python is from *Monty Python's Flying Circus Vol. II* 1989: 229. The fMRI pictures in Figure 2.4 are taken from MacSweeney *et al.* (2002). The examples from aphasic patients are taken in translation from Prins (1987) and in the original English from Shewan (1988). The elicitation picture in Figure 2.6 is from the Minnesota Test for Differential Diagnosis of Aphasia (Schuell 1972). The ERP experiments were carried out by Atchley *et al.* (2006), Nieuwland and van Berkum (2008), and Pylkkänen and Marantz (2003). An example of a priming experiment is taken from Simpson and Burgess (1985). The German Sign Language example is taken from Leuninger *et al.* (2004).

chapter 3

Language Acquisition

3.1 Introduction

Is it difficult to learn a language? If you ask a group of ordinary English speakers about their language learning experiences, you will get all different kinds of reactions:

'German? Oh no! Those awful cases.'
'French is a beautiful language but really quite difficult.'
'I wouldn't get anywhere with Chinese or Japanese.'

The answers do not usually make any reference to the speakers' first language, English. Apparently, everybody accepts that learning your mother tongue is not really difficult at all. But English can be a difficult language to learn for people who have not learned it as a child. For many learners English is difficult since it is so different from their first language.

In example (1) below, Grégoire, a little French boy of three, is in conversation with an adult, Christian. Anyone who has only had a few years of French at school will see with surprise, and perhaps some envy, how much Grégoire has learned in those three years and how well he can express himself (1).

Linguistics, First Edition. Edited by Anne E. Baker and Kees Hengeveld.

(1) Grégoire: Tu vas pas me laisser tout seul?
'You are not going to leave me all alone?'
Christian: Mais non, Grégoire, je vais rester avec toi et puis après il y a Adrien qui va venir.
'Of course not, Grégoire, I will stay with you, and then Adrien will come.'
Grégoire: Parce que si tu me laisses tout seul, je vais avoir peur des monstres, moi. Tu vas partir quand?
'Because if you leave me all alone, I'll be afraid of the monsters. When are you going?'
Christian: Tout à l'heure, quand Adrien sera arrivé.
'In a while, when Adrian gets here.'
Grégoire: Tu vas aller où? Dans ta maison à toi? Où elle est ta maison à toi?
'Where are you going? To your own house? Where is your house?'
Christian: A Paris, Rue Mouffetard.
'In Paris, on the Rue Mouffetard.'

The same kind of feelings will be shared by someone learning English as a second language when they read how Liam, who is also three, can express himself in English:

(2) 'Dionne poured hot tea on her leg. She got a big blister and had to go to hospital in an ambulance.'

Why is it so much more difficult for adults to learn another language than for children to learn their first language? Are there perhaps circumstances that make language learning easier or harder? Do all children learn their first language with equal ease? How do they learn language anyway? They make mistakes too. Liam at the same age as he told the story in (2) formed the plural of *nest* as *nesses*, and made the past form of *go* as *goed*. How do children learn to stop making these mistakes? These are the questions that will be discussed in this chapter.

First we will look at first language acquisition, and then at second language acquisition. In the next section, 3.2, we will consider a range of theories that aim to explain why children manage to acquire their first language relatively quickly and easily. Then, in Section 3.3, we will discuss what happens in language learning during the first four or five years of a child's life.

In the second half of this chapter we will consider the acquisition of a language other than the first language or mother tongue. We will refer to this as 'second language acquisition'; and the second language will also often be referred to as the 'target language'. First, in Section 3.4, we will review the factors that play a role in second language acquisition, such as age, motivation and the impact of the first language. Then, in Section 3.5, we will discuss the actual process of second language acquisition. In what order do people learn the various parts of the second language? Does the order of acquisition differ from one learner to the next? And are these processes similar to or very different from those involved in first language acquisition? Finally, there is the issue of bilingual development, when children grow up in a situation where they acquire two different languages at more or less the same time. This phenomenon will be discussed in the closing section, 3.6 (and also in Chapter 20).

3.2 How Do Children Acquire Language?

A mother is sitting with her son Nick who is one year and eight months old – in the following examples children's ages are given in years and months in the following way: 1;8 means '1 year and 8 months old'. Here Nick and his mother are playing in the park with some toys and a friend, Gilbert, is taking their picture.

(3) Mother: who's taking the picture?
Nick: ma... (Nick points to a man)
Mother: Yes, he's a man, isn't he?
Nick: gibe
Mother: Gilbert. Well done. That's right. Got a camera.
Nick: kama
Mother: Yes, a camera. He's taking our picture.

Nick is taking his first steps on the road to mastery of his mother tongue, and his mother is helping him. She names certain objects for him (*camera*). Nick repeats what she says, and in confirmation she says *camera* again. This is really a little language lesson – the mother is asking questions and trying to elicit answers from Nick and she gives him feedback on what he says by repeating what he says but in the correct form. Nick's pronunciation of Gilbert as *gibe* she repeats correctly and rewards him with a *well done* for attempting the difficult name.

From example (3) we may infer that language acquisition is first and foremost a matter of naming, repeating and extending vocabulary. And in fact, these are the principles we encounter quite regularly in early language acquisition. In order to find their way into a language, children have to know the names of things, persons and objects; they have to practice the sounds and sound combinations that build up words; and they have to learn how to combine those things, persons and objects with each other through language. Here the people in the child's environment, in particular parents and carers, provide the necessary models.

For a very long time it was thought that learning in general, and language learning in particular, was a matter of **imitation**. Frequent repetition of language forms would in the end, or so it was thought, lead children to adopt these themselves. When children manage to do this, they deserve to be complimented, for example through confirmation of what they have just said. Nick's mother has clearly followed this principle. In cases where the child's imitation is not right, it will be necessary to correct it, in order to try to prevent the same mistake recurring.

But is this view the right one? To answer this question let us look at examples of language from Chris and Alex. In (4), Chris (2;11) is looking at photos with his dad.

(4) Chris: This me swimming.
Father: Yes.
Chris: I swimmed lots.

In example (5), Alex (3;5) and her mother are going for a walk.

(5) Mother: Let's go up there to where the horses are.
Alex: I want to but my foots don't.

The forms *swimmed* in (4) and *foots* in (5) are unusual. Where did Chris and Alex learn these forms? It is unlikely they have ever heard them in their environment, certainly not from their adult 'models'. But these forms are probably not random structures produced by accident. These and similar forms can be found in the language of many other children learning English. This kind of 'error' shows that language acquisition is more than just a matter of mindless imitation of what other people are saying. There is a system behind these errors. In (5) Alex probably produced *foots* from *foot* on the model of *books* from *book*. Similarly, in (4) *swimmed* may well have been modelled by Chris on the verb *trim – trimmed*. The 'errors' of these two children reveal them as being really rather clever, since they are trying to learn a grammatical rule (see Section 12.5 for further discussion of these rules). Instead of passively imitating what they hear other people say, they are actively working at their own language acquisition. Their 'thinking' about language forms is, however, largely unconscious, just as adults have unconscious knowledge about language as we discussed earlier in Chapter 1.

According to the American linguist Noam Chomsky the language acquisition process we observe here is only possible if a child is born with some fundamental knowledge about language. Chomsky postulates that children have an **innate language faculty** containing the general principles to which any language in the world has to conform. In the course of the acquisition process, the very wide range of (theoretically) possible language rules is reduced, since children at every step have to select from the general principles precisely those rules that apply to their own mother tongue.

From a very early age children succeed in making these complicated choices. Language acquisition is very quick and many types of errors are never made. This must imply, according to Chomsky, that we have such an innate language faculty. Otherwise, we would never be able, in a short period of time and on the basis of a very limited language input, to acquire such a complex system as human language. The innate language faculty helps children to develop hypotheses about the rules of their mother tongue. By trying out these rules in actual speech, they are testing those hypotheses, and if necessary, they will be corrected. According to this view, children do not really make errors, and forms like *swimmed* and *foots* are an integral part of the process of language acquisition. This does not mean, though, that adults should ignore such forms. On the contrary, by correcting, repeating or extending what a child said, adults provide a model that children can use to test and correct their hypotheses, although the form of adult speech to children is sometimes not adult-like. Alex's mother would do well to react with something like *Never mind. Your feet will make it I'm sure.*

The view that language acquisition is mostly a matter of imitation is at odds with the assumption of an innate language faculty. The notion of imitation focuses not on the language-learning child, but on its linguistic environment, as a mirror that it should imitate. The child is then reduced to a kind of parrot that just copies what is said. But in Chomsky's view, precisely the opposite is the case. His focus is on the child, and in particular on the child's innate language faculty. This faculty makes it possible for the child to discover the system in the non-systematic language input. The role of the language environment is in this view far less important.

There is, however, a third view of language acquisition that takes a position in between the two theories. This third view assumes the presence of an innate language faculty, but considers the **language environment** of the child to be equally crucial. In particular the language input offered to the child and the interaction between the child and the environment are important. If the innate language faculty is the motor of the language acquisition process, then the language environment is the petrol that keeps the motor going. The **interaction** between the child and parents/carers and other adults plays a significant part. In example (2) we saw how the mother first introduces the man, Gilbert, to the boy by asking a question about who is taking their picture. She then names the camera and later goes on to say something about it. In this way, mother and child both come to focus on the same conversation topic.

Another important aspect of interaction is that of taking turns. Even before a child utters its first word, it has already experienced the principles of how people talk to each other. During its first year, the child experiments with all kinds of sounds and combinations of sounds. Adults usually react with enthusiasm, and as a result it sometimes looks as if the child is engaged in an extensive conversation. In this period, a child will learn that there is no point in talking all at once, since you cannot then understand each other so

Figure 3.1 Mother and child. Image by Saska Leefsma.

well. Communication works best when people take turns. When one person is talking, the other needs to listen, and vice versa. Later on, children will learn how to manipulate this basic rule, how and when to interrupt each other, how to take over someone else's turn, and how to keep their turn for as long as possible (see Section 4.4).

Adults are also usually quite good at matching the **language input** to the level of the child's language, as are brothers and sisters too. Nick's mother in (2) is a good example. Her sentences are short, at times not more than one word. The longest sentence she utters contains five words. If necessary she leaves out words, as in *got a camera.* Language spoken to children is usually marked by many repetitions, a slower speed of speaking, a higher tone, a sometimes exaggerated emphasis on particular words, as in *got a CAMERA*, and use of special words (see Figure 3.1). There are cultural differences in the language that is offered to children but the input still seems to share many features.

3.3 The Order of First Language Acquisition

A child starts to acquire language at least as soon as it is born. There is evidence that babies start to perceive intonation patterns already in the womb since their cries in the first days of life reflect the different intonation patterns of their surrounding language. For example, French newborns tend to cry with a rising melody contour, whereas German newborns seem to prefer a falling melody contour in their crying. From the moment of birth a baby will often first cry and then be comforted. This is the beginning of interactional communication between the child and the world around it.

The child's language acquisition can be subdivided into a number of stages linked to important linguistic milestones. One such milestone is the moment, often around its first birthday, when the child uses its first word. The period prior to this point is known as the **pre-linguistic stage**. During this first year children are not yet using 'real' language, but they are definitely very busy learning the basic rules of communication and experimenting with sounds and sound combinations. They already understand a lot of what is being said to them.

In the first few weeks babies mostly cry but very quickly they can make their first real sounds. These often resemble vowels and at first they are produced more or less by chance. Later on, these sounds begin to be made on purpose and they become more varied. The children are discovering what they can do with their speech apparatus through constant experimentation. Around eight months, they will produce sequences of constantly repeated syllables such as *babababa* or *gagaga*, known as **babbling**. Although these babbles are beginning to sound like real language, having intonational patterns and such, they are not yet real words. They do not have a constant reference to the same objects every time they are produced. Only when a sound sequence is produced consistently in association with an object or event do we really speak of a word, for example when daddy is always referred to with *baba*, or when a child says *eat* every time it wants something to eat. The same stage is found in children learning a sign language – they babble with their hands.

After the first word new words are quickly learned. Later children begin to combine words, first two at a time, and gradually expanded into utterances of more than two words. This period lasts on average from one to two and a half years of age, and is known firstly as the **one-word** and later as the **two-word stage**. In (6) a young American child, Adam (2;9), is at breakfast with his mother.

(6) Mother: Is it an egg?
    Adam: Yes.
    Egg eat.

At this stage, sentences produced by children contain only the most necessary words. Words that do not have a clear immediate meaning, like articles, prepositions and auxiliaries, are usually omitted. If we reconstruct that Adam wanted to say *I am eating the egg*, then we see that there are **omissions** in Adam's speech like the copula (*is*), and pronouns (*I*). He probably also omits sounds in words like *start* that become *tart*. There are also **substitutions**, especially at the sound level. Children say *hed* instead of *red*, *sis* instead of *this*. Many children in this stage also use words with a wider meaning than in adult language. A child may call all quadrupeds *cat*, and say *uncle* to all men other than her daddy. These are cases of **overextension**.

In due course all kinds of different words will appear in the child's language. For this reason the period between two and a half years old and five is often called the **differentiation stage**. Compared to Adam's speech the language use of Grégoire as we saw in (1) is already, at age three, much more complex. During this stage, children begin to use longer sentences and different word categories. In addition they are also learning the conjugation of verbs and the declination of other words (plurals, adjectival inflection). This is not to say that they will immediately use the correct form. In (4) we saw how Chris formed the past tense of *swim* as *swimmed*. German children often say *fliegte* for *flog*, the past tense of *fliegen* 'to fly'. In both cases the rule for past tense formation of the regular weak verbs is extended to the strong verb *swim* in English and *fliegen* 'fly' in German. This is known as **overgeneralisation**. The difference between overgeneralisation and overextension is that in overextension the meaning of a word is stretched, so that for example a 'helicopter' is also referred to as *airplane*, whereas in overgeneralisation a grammatical rule is being applied where it normally should not be. There are many more areas where overgeneralisation is found, but the specific areas encountered depend on the structure of the language. In (7) we give some more examples where bold marks the incorrect form.

(7) English: the *-er* ending that indicates a comparison between two things is overgeneralised to irregular forms, e.g. *good**er*** instead of *better*.
Dutch: the definite article *de* is overgeneralised to neuter nouns, e.g. ***de*** huis *'the house'* instead of *het huis*.
Chinese: the classifier form used to mark many nouns, *ge*, is overgeneralised to other nouns, e.g. *zhè-**gè** shīzi* instead of *zhè-tóu shīzi* 'this lion'.
French: the masculine form of the adjective is overgeneralised to feminine nouns e.g. *la vache* **blanc** instead of *la vache blanche* 'the white cow'.
Polish: the masculine singular ending to indicate possession, *-a*, is used with other nouns, e.g. *cukier**a*** instead of *cukieru* 'of the sugar'.

As a general rule, such forms will not have been heard from others, but are constructed by the children themselves as a natural part of the language acquisition process. For this reason, such 'mistakes' are also known as **developmental errors**.

Around their fifth birthday, children know the basics of their first language. In some areas things may need to be polished up a bit, for example with certain sound combinations and certain irregular formations. But otherwise vocabulary will continue to grow naturally. The period after the age of five is sometimes known as the **completion stage**. This period has no clear end point, for we will always continue to learn new words, whatever our age. In this sense, the language acquisition process never ends. The following fragment

(8) was recorded when Romy (9 years) was explaining to her father what she had been making in the holidays when her father was away:

(8) Romy: Well, I was ma. I've been making a mar. I've been making a market. And I made it out of matchsticks and em matchboxes. And at the bottom of the matchboxes I, I put, I put matches for for the legs. And then I put four matches at the top. And I put a roof on top – em out of paper. And then I made little things to put on it.
Father: Ah I see. So what colours did you use for what?
Romy: Well for the apples I used green. And for the bananas I used yellow. No, for the apples I used red, and for the pears I used green. And I – that's all I could really make – those kinds of fruits. But I made about two of each kind. And I used brown for my bread rolls, and just put them into a kind of rectangle.

In this conversation Romy has the task of explaining a process to her father who has not seen the end result. She uses long, complex sentences which she strings together into a story using *and* and *and then.* She tries to explain what the market looked like by describing the different parts according to their relationship with one another. She uses prepositions well, which is typical for the completion phase, although they are frequently omitted in the differentiation phase. She uses complex vocabulary such as *rectangle* but tends to overuse the verb *put.* Romy's acquisition is not yet completed. Her fluency in providing information will improve so that there will be fewer false starts and hesitations; her vocabulary will expand and her ability to vary sentence structure will increase.

The ages given for the various acquisition stages are not strict. Infants who have not spoken their first word by their first birthday are not abnormal in the least, and parents do not need to worry. Some children do not utter their first word, usually *mummy* or *papa,* until they are one and half years old, some may take even more time. Children can be very different from one another in speed of acquisition, but they do all go through the same broad sequence of acquisition phases, whichever language they are learning, signed or spoken. If their language faculty is intact, and if there is sufficient stimulation from their environment, the result will be that by the age of five most children will have become excellent at language learning. Note that we are talking here about *speaking* proficiency, and not about written language skills.

There can be circumstances, however, when language does not develop according to the timetable set out above. In such cases, there may be a clear delay or an abnormal pattern in the development of the child's speech and language. If these problems occur in the first five years of the child's life, this is known as a **speech and language developmental disorder**. Speech disorders are mostly to do with the articulation of sounds. This can have a purely physical basis, for example when children are born with a cleft palate (schisis), which makes sound production difficult. There may also be neurological causes, for example when control over the facial muscles is impaired due to a damaged central nervous system.

Language development disorders, on the other hand, affect the acquisition of linguistic structures. These disorders may range from problems in understanding language as the result of having a very limited vocabulary to the production of ungrammatical sentences or providing inadequate linguistic reactions. Just as with speech disorders, there may be various different causes for such problems. Children with a medium to severe hearing loss will often hear no more than half of what is said to them. This will inevitably lead to problems with understanding and producing spoken language. Another cause of language difficulties may be a cognitive disorder, as in the case of children with Down's syndrome, who often function at a quite low level of intelligence. General neurological disorders or a problematic socio-emotional development can also cause language disorders. There are, however, children with language problems where there is no clear cause. These language disorders are known as 'specific language impairment' because they are above all to do with language and not the result of some other disorder. Children with specific language impairment often have difficulties with the grammatical structure of utterances and this is also visible in neuroimaging studies, as discussed in Chapter 2. Such disorders affect about 8% of children under four years.

3.4 Factors that Influence the Acquisition of a Second Language

So far we have been discussing the children's acquisition of their first language, their mother tongue. But that does not mean that language learning stops once that mother tongue is acquired. Many people speak more than one language. According to some estimates, half the world's population is multilingual in the sense that they use two or more languages every day. Millions of people also learn one or more languages at school. A distinction often made here is that between learning a second language and learning a foreign language. **Foreign language learning** usually takes place in schools where the **target language** is not the medium of communication – so, for example, when an American child learns German at school or a French adult takes a course in English with the British Council in Paris. In **second language acquisition**, the target language is learned in the community where this language is spoken – for example, when a Spanish computer consultant has to learn Mandarin Chinese in Beijing, or when an English girl goes to Florence to learn Italian. In the discussion here we will not be too concerned with this distinction. In fact, we will use the term 'second language acquisition' to refer to both categories. So, in what follows, the term 'second language' will include 'foreign', 'third', 'fourth', etc. language.

Most people experience learning a language other than their mother tongue as harder and more demanding than learning their first language. That is, if they can remember at all how they learned their first language, since this will mostly have been, literally and metaphorically, child's play. In contrast, for most people learning a second language when they are older it is a long, hard slog. And still, despite years of dedicated study, they may still not get close to the proficiency of a native speaker. But first – before we explore in more detail the differences between first and second language acquisition and the factors that influence second language learning – let us take a look at what Peter has to say, in (9) below. Peter is German and for the past 12 months has been living in London with his English girlfriend. Here he is in conversation with an English friend, Clive.

(9) Clive: When else do you get to speak English then?
Peter: By my lessons naturally. And with people by my work.
Clive: With your girlfriend?
Peter: Yes. She is very easy with me. The people by my work are more, more difficulty.
Clive: Why?
Peter: They want that I always – er – English speaking. It makes tired. But c'est la vie.

As we can see, Peter can express himself reasonably well in English. He is capable of getting his message across, although he speaks with pauses and hesitations and grammatical errors. In Peter's case, the acquisition of English as a second language is influenced by both positive and negative factors. The first of these is his **first language**, German. Peter will probably have fewer problems than fellow students whose mother tongue is a language further away from English such as Chinese or Turkish. He can benefit from the many similarities between English and German, although German is probably not helping him in his choice of prepositions. Still, not all errors are due to the learner's mother tongue. Peter's use of *more difficulty* is not based on German. Peter here has confused two expressions: *are more difficult* and *cause me more difficulty*. Equally, the word order error in *they want that I always English speaking* may be based on the pattern of German (*sie wollen, dass ich immer Englisch rede*, literally translated as 'they want that I always English speak'). But it could be that Peter has just not yet learned to use the verb *want* with the construction *want to do something*. Such an error is also a developmental error for a second language learner, as we saw for first language learners in the previous section. In the next section we will further discuss the role of the first language in second language acquisition.

The next factor that plays a role in second language acquisition is **age**. At 28 Peter already has experience of life and learning. This and his knowledge of the world will come in handy when learning English. At the same time, however, he is past the **critical period** for language learning. The notion of 'critical period' presupposes that a child will have acquired its mother tongue very early on. There have been cases of children not exposed to even a first language due to neglect. Genie is an example of such a child – she was discovered locked away at the age of nine and could not produce any recognisable words. Trying to teach such children their first language at such a late age has proven to be difficult and suggests that there is a critical period for language learning. After that point it will be impossible, or at least very much harder, to learn a language. It is not totally clear to what extent such a critical period plays a role in second language acquisition. At any rate, children are usually more successful at learning a second language than adults. Adults may have the advantage of a more developed intellect, and they may therefore go faster in the beginning, but in due course the children will catch up and eventually overtake them. If you learn a second language at an early age, you usually do not have an accent, whereas people that start later nearly always retain a distinct accent in their speech. For this reason, the period between ten and twelve is often seen as the optimal age for learning a second language. This is the age when children are still young enough to benefit from their language acquisition abilities and at the same time old enough to deploy their well-developed general intelligence.

Peter speaks English during his lessons, but also with his girlfriend, his friend Clive, and colleagues from work. His opportunity to speak English is not restricted to his time in the English course. Outside it he also has **contact with the target language**. This is the third factor that plays a role in second language acquisition. The time and opportunity you have for using the target language will strongly influence the speed of second language acquisition. As a general rule we can say that the more extensive the input and interaction in the second language, the faster and more effectively the language will be learned.

The fourth important factor that affects the speed and success of second language acquisition is your **motivation.** People may have many different reasons for learning a second language: to improve their job prospects, to extend their social network, to make friends or find romance, to pursue a programme of studies, to migrate, or because they are stuck in a foreign country without the possibility of going home, etc. In Peter's case it was the relationship with his girlfriend, his job and the prospect of a long-term stay in the United Kingdom – all good reasons for him to be motivated to learn English. But his colleagues are making things difficult for him and this could affect his motivation. For other people there could be many other factors leading to lack of motivation, such as being refused refugee status, traumatic experiences when fleeing your home country, culture shock or experiencing discrimination in the host country.

Motivation is closely linked to a fifth factor, your **attitude** to the target language and that language community. Motivation and attitude are not purely individual. Very often they also involve socio-cultural factors. If you are treated positively and find it easy to make friends, you are much more likely to have a positive attitude towards the second language and its speakers than if you feel unwelcome or discriminated against.

Language aptitude is the sixth factor. It can contribute to some degree to the success of learning a second language. It is not easy to define what language aptitude is exactly, but it is an undisputed fact that some people are better, quicker and more successful at learning a second language than others. On the basis of (9) it is impossible to say anything about Peter's language aptitude. But the fact that he uses the French idiomatic phrase *c'est la vie* suggests he is open to foreign phrases.

Finally, the seventh factor in second language acquisition is the role of **teaching and learning**. In contrast to first language acquisition, which is a largely free, natural and unguided process, second language acquisition often takes place in a school situation that is far more structured and directive. Coming from Germany, Peter will be used to a western education system and its conventions, so he will probably adapt fairly easily to the structure of the English course he is taking in London. For him, the combination of structured lessons in school and the personal interaction with colleagues and friends should be quite effective. In a structured learning situation often considerable use is made of written texts. Lack of transparency in the spelling rules in a language can be a hindrance. English is difficult in this respect since there are many different sound/letter correspondences. The letter *a* for example is pronounced in many different ways, as in the words *bath, maker, any, aspirin, local*, etc. Written material may also be in a different script to that of the learner's first language. Having to learn the Devanagari script, for example, in order to learn Hindi is an extra challenge.

3.5 The Order of Second Language Acquisition

Cheo from Colombia has been in the United States for just four months. He is five years old and learning English at a kindergarten in a natural setting.

(10) Adult: what's he eating?
Cheo: uh?
Adult: what's that?
Cheo: una cos con leche
'something with milk'
Adult: what?
Cheo: cosa comer
'something to eat'
Adult: it's an apple
Cheo: Apple?
Adult: um
Cheo: no

Cheo is already showing that he understands English quite well, but he is producing very little in English, mostly imitations. Many second language learners, adults or children, will do the same or restrict their language production to a range of almost formulaic short sentences like *Everything OK? Where toilet? How much cost?* For the rest they will remain silent, and – just like first language learners – spend most of their time and effort on listening to the sounds and words of English, and on trying to understand what is being said. The conversation was difficult for Cheo, so he often resorted to Spanish.

In their first short sentences, those starting out on the process of second language learning often use a fixed order, with the verb either always at the beginning (11) or at the end (12) of the sentence.

(11) *Talk* to bakerman
(12) Boss workers *ask*

Sentences such as the one in (11) are typical for Moroccan learners, those in (12) for Turkish learners. The different word orders show a clear influence from their respective first languages – in Turkish the verb is usually placed at the end of the sentence, whereas in Moroccan Arabic it usually comes at the beginning. The examples above can be seen as **transitional structures** on the way to the next phase in the second language acquisition process. The transitional structures in (11) and (12) can be explained by the structure of the first language. In other cases they may be due to developmental errors that also occur in first language acquisition, or there may be several different explanations for a particular incorrect structure, as we saw in the case of Peter's *are more difficulty* in (9).

In the next phase the sentences become longer and the learners begin to experiment with word order. Moon's explanation to her employer as to why she is leaving in (13) contains a number of features of this second stage. Moon is a 25-year-old Vietnamese, whose first language is Vietnamese. She has been learning English for three years.

(13) Now have new job. Must start next week. Sorry, no have anyone for clean. No come Friday.

Though longer than Cheo's sentences, Moon's are still far from complete, and as such resemble those of children learning their first language. Moon leaves out all sorts of words (*I, you, a, on*) and she forms the negative sentence by placing *no* in front of the verb.

Later on in the acquisition process, the missing elements will make their appearance, though not always correctly, as we can see in (14). This is a written text from Inge, a Dutch learner of French who has spent six years learning the language in a school situation. She was asked to make a choice of a holiday destination in a letter to a friend. The words marked in bold indicate her errors.

(14) Pour *moi,* *Maison* *Lory* *Bretagne* *est* ***un*** *autre* *option,*
For me Maison Lory Bretagne is an other option,
avec *son* *petit-dejeuner* *et* ***son*** *aventures* *culinaires.*
with its breakfast and its adventures culinary.
Mais *je* *crois* *que* *la* *proximité* *d'* *un* *village* *avec*
But I think that the proximity of a village with
des ***petite*** ***shops*** *et* *un* *boulanger* *est* *indispensable.*
some small shops and a baker is indispensable.
'For me Maison Lory Bretagne is another option with its breakfast and its culinary adventures. But I think that the nearness to a village with some little shops and a baker is indispensable.'

Inge's French is already a lot more complete and complex than Moon's English, but she is still struggling with gender and number agreement. For example it should be ***une*** *autre option* and ***ses*** *aventures culinaires.* She uses the English word *shop* instead of the French *magasin.* Still, she is not very far from the last stage of the acquisition process when the use of language is as complex as that of native speakers, with only occasional clues that she is a non-native speaker, for example when infrequent and irregular forms are used wrongly, when some sounds and words are not pronounced correctly, or when a word or expression is used in a way that is slightly different from the way native speakers would use it.

The examples given above represent different levels in the process of learning a second language. The technical term for this is **interlanguage** or **interlanguage stages**. As the terms suggest, language learners are moving towards a steadily increasing proficiency in the second language, beginning at level zero and going all the way to complete mastery. The process of second language acquisition can now be described as a sequence of different interlanguages. The transitional structures mentioned above are part of the interlanguage; they belong to a particular stage in the acquisition process. A series of such transitional structures constitutes a developmental sequence. As an example, we present in (15) the steps in the acquisition of negation in the interlanguage of adult, native Spanish-speaking second language learners of English who have acquired their English mostly outside the school system.

(15) Stage 1: The element *no* is placed before the verb, as in 'I no can see'.
Stage 2: The form *don't* is used, but as an alternative for *no*. Other combinations of *to do* and *not* do not yet occur. Examples: *He don't like it* and *He don't can explain.*
Stage 3: The combination of an auxiliary verb and a negation element is used, initially mostly with the auxiliaries *is* and *can*, as in *It isn't dangerous* and *He can't see.*

Stage 4: The form *don't* is no longer an alternative for *no*, and other combinations of *to do* and *not* now appear in the interlanguage, as in *It doesn't matter* and *I didn't even know.*

It is not the case that these different stages and transitional structures appear neatly one after another in the learner's interlanguage. For example, *don't* often appears very soon after *no*, and both forms are then used interchangeably. That is, the different stages run over into each other. Also, second language learners do not by any means all end up at the same final level. It may well be that an individual learner never reaches stage 4 and will go on producing sentences like *He don't can do it*.

Only a few second language learners manage to come close to the level of proficiency of a native speaker. Many people, even learners who have been living in the second language community for many years, stay below this level. When the second language acquisition process stops before it has reached this final level, we use the technical term **fossilisation**. Thus some people are referred to, rather impolitely, as 'fossilised second language learners'. Such fossilisation is more likely as the second language learner ages. The marked difference in second language proficiency between adult migrants and their children is a case in point. Fossilisation may occur at different levels of interlanguage, even at a rather high level of proficiency. A Spanish native speaker with a very good command of English may therefore still use the present tense to refer to a future event, as in *I see her this evening* instead of *I will see her this evening*. Ahmed in (16) first learned German from his Turkish parents and they were first-generation learners of German. At thirty years of age, although fluent, he still makes some errors.

(16) Ahmed: *Meine Muttter, sie fragt immer zu mir: was willst du essen*?
'My mother, she asks always to me: what want you eat?'

Ahmed overgeneralises the structure of the verb *sagen* to the verb *fragen* and says *zu mir* instead of *mich*. This will probably never change. The structure is fossilised. To take another example, Chinese learners are reported to still have problems with English pronunciation, articles, tense and agreement after many years of learning the language. The examples in (17) are taken from a Mandarin speaker who had started to learn English as a young adult and had been living in the United States for ten years.

(17) a. We all same size, you know? (instead of *We are all the same size, you know?*)
b. This kind of appear four time in Bible. (instead of *This kind of appeared four times in the Bible.*).

As well as the different levels of proficiency they reach, we also find differences between second language learners in their speed of acquisition. In the previous section we discussed the various factors that play a role here, such as age, contact with the target language, motivation and language aptitude. But in general learners all learn the various elements of the target language in roughly the same order. Many second language learners of English will, for example, first acquire the simple past, and only later the complex forms of the past tense. That is, there is a certain **order of acquisition**. Again, it is not the case that first structure A is acquired completely and only then structure B. Learners of English do not wait until they have mastered the simple past in order to learn the perfect tense. But it is the case that they achieve a reasonable command of the simple past sooner than they do the perfect. This order of acquisition of *different elements* in the target language is therefore completely different from the order of transitional structures in the acquisition of *one single element*, such as the developmental sequence in the acquisition of negation in English by Spanish speakers that we discussed above.

There are in fact striking similarities between second language learners with different first languages in their transitional structures and the order of acquisition of different elements. There may be some variation between learners in the fine detail, due to differences in the first language, as we saw in the position of the verb in examples (11) and (12). But for the process as a whole the similarities clearly outweigh the differences. Moreover, the order in which a second language is acquired is more or less the same as that for the first language. This has led to the hypothesis that there is a natural, universal order of language acquisition. The examples also demonstrate that the strategies used by language learners – regardless of whether it is in first or in second language learning – are broadly the same, especially with respect to deleting or substituting elements and making overgeneralisations and overextensions.

Overgeneralisation, as we saw in Section 3.3, is when a rule is applied where it should not be. Second language learners who are acquiring the past tense in English may produce *-ed* forms where they do not really exist, as in *he stealed my pen* instead of *stole*. Overextension occurs less with older second language learners than with children learning their first language. Overextension is especially likely when the target language makes a distinction where the first language does not. English learners of French, for example, often overextend the form *vous*, which is the polite form of you and the plural form in all situations, and fail to use the informal form *tu*. Learners of Spanish often overextend the use of *preguntar*, which means 'to request information' where they should use *pedir*, meaning 'to request a favour'. Another example of overextension is the use of general words where a native speaker would be more precise. This is usually due to lack of vocabulary, so for example second language learners of English often use *say* where a native speaker would use *tell*, *relate*, *debate*, etc.

We have discussed the idea of a universal order of acquisition and similarity of transitional structures between learners with very different first languages. There is another, older theory, which holds that the role played by the first language is crucial. From the perspective of this theory the first language is something of a hindrance when learning a second language. The more similarities there are, the better and faster the acquisition process should be; conversely, the fewer the similarities, the slower and more difficult. In the first case we speak of **positive transfer**. The two languages are similar, as for example English and French, which both place the verb next to the subject in subordinate clauses. In (18) and (19) we can see how an English speaker could transfer his first language structure to French. The structural similarity between the two languages will benefit the leaning process, or so it is thought.

(18) I know that he *likes* carrots.
(19) Je sais qu'il *aime* les carrottes.

In contrast, when two languages are very different, we have **negative transfer**. In (20) we see that, unlike French and English, German does not place the finite verb *mag* next to the subject *er* in this construction.

(20) Ich weiss, dass er gelbe Rüben mag.
I know that he carrots likes.

It is not appropriate in this case for German learners of English and French to transfer their first language structures. As a consequence of this word order difference they will probably have more difficulty in learning English than their French fellow students. However, in practice, such predictions are not always correct. Where negative transfer is predicted, it does not always occur. Conversely, where two languages are very similar and positive transfer is expected, errors are made in constructions that are actually the same in the two languages. We have to conclude that the influence of the mother tongue on the process of second language acquisition is less than initially supposed. Still, we have to make allowances for some influence from the first language, especially when the similarities or differences between the two languages are really large. Germans will have an easier time learning Dutch and English than when they try to learn Japanese or Swahili. Similarly, English people will find Spanish far easier to learn than, say, Chinese, Urdu or Indonesian. The influence of the first language is most noticeable in pronunciation, especially when the second language is learned after puberty. However high the proficiency in the second language, there will often still be a recognisable accent that can be traced to a different mother tongue. For example, many French people who speak fluent English may still say *ze* instead of *the*.

3.6 Bilingual Development

The more multicultural societies become, and the more international migration increases, the greater the number of children who grow up bilingual. These are, very often, children from mixed marriages where each parent speaks a different language. When a father and a mother both communicate with their child in their own language, the child will acquire these two languages at the same time. This parallel acquisition is called **simultaneous bilingualism**.

In general, children are quite capable of learning two languages at once, especially when parents and teachers are consistent in their use of language with the child. Parents are usually advised not to switch from one language to the other, but always use their own language with the child. When the mother uses one language and the father the other, this is known as the 'one-person-one-language-strategy'. In this situation the child usually picks up the one language as easily as the other. Quite often, however, the language input the child receives is not exactly the same in the two languages, for example because one of the parents is away during the day, or because the language of one of the parents happens to be the dominant everyday language of the community in which the child is growing up. Nick from example (3) is growing up in the Netherlands learning Dutch from his mother and English from his father. He receives far more input in Dutch than in English but nevertheless both languages are developing well. His vocabulary at age two years was the same in both languages. At that age he was also already showing an awareness of having two languages since he could give the equivalent Dutch word if asked 'And how does mummy say that?' If the language input to a child is heavily weighted in favour of one language, however, then this can result in different levels of proficiency in the two languages.

In other situations we also find bilingualism but it is **sequential**. Cheo, who we discussed in Section 3.5, was learning English at five years of age and was a sequential bilingual. Vicki has Greek-speaking parents and moved to London at three. She attended an English-speaking play group during the day. She became more fluent in English in some domains – for example, in language related to games and songs and other things to do with the play-group environment – whereas everything to do with her home, family and direct living environment she learned in Greek. This kind of division can lead to an imbalance in the child's language development. In general the later the bilingualism starts, the more difficult it is for the child to learn both languages equally well. This is again a possible reflection of the critical period. Many of the factors influencing second language acquisition as discussed in Section 3.4 can also have an influence on the learning of the two languages in child bilinguals.

Interference between the two languages can also occur in bilingualism, as in second language acquisition, but it is often difficult to work out if errors are a result of interference or a developmental error. Jo, for example, at age four had not yet acquired the English negative form *don't*, as is common in young children learning English. She persisted in making errors such as the one in (21).

(21) I want not eat that.
'I don't want to eat that.'

But once you know that Jo is bilingual and her other language is German, then you might put this error down to interference, since the German equivalent in (22) is very close to her structure in (21).

German
(22) Ich will das nicht essen.
I want that not eat.

Disentangling the source of such errors in bilingual children is quite problematic.

Bilingual children also often mix their two languages. This may be due to not knowing the equivalent word in the other language but it can also be a reflection of the high level of bilingualism in the child's environment. The switch from one language to another can also be done for a specific reason. Isabella, aged three, is growing up bilingual in Spanish and English. In (23) she wants to be comforted by her mother whose first language is Spanish. In the conversation with her mother Isabella switches to Spanish to accomplish this.

Spanish
(23) Mother: Now, which is your favourite colour Isabella?
Isabella: Mmmmm. Pink.
Mother: Pink, Wow!
Isabella: Mi duele a barriga.
'I have a stomachache.'
Mother: ¿Y por qué? tienes hambre?
'Why? Are you hungry?'
Isabella: Sí.
'Yes.'
Mother: Tienes hambre, vamos a hacer la comida mejor,
'You are hungry, let's make our meal better.'
Isabella: ¿Tu duele la barriga?
'Do you have stomachache?'
Mother: Sí, un poquito, porque yo tambien tengo hambre.
'Yes a little bit, because I'm hungry too.'
Isabella: A mí también.
'Me too.'

Children who grow up bilingual may also show a fossilised acquisition in one language at some point in time, especially if that language is not the majority language or if the exposure to that language becomes less over time or restricted in use. A bilingual speaker who had learned Spanish as a first language later became bilingual in English and lived in the United States. In his re-telling of the fairy story Little Red Riding Hood he makes a number of errors in his first language (indicated in bold face) (24), even though he had continuously used both languages.

(24) La niña está **camina** y ve **una** perro que quiere comer la niña
The girl is walk and sees a dog that wants eat the girl
pero el hombre con **la** **ax** mata el perro
but the man with the axe kills the dog
'The girl was walking and saw a dog that wants to eat the girl but the man with the axe kills the dog.'

In this example we see wrong uses of verb forms (*camina* instead of *caminando*), wrong use of gender forms (*una perro* instead of *un perro*) and interference from English in lexical choice (*la ax* instead of *la hacha*).

Further features of adult bilingualism, including the mixing of the two languages, will be explored in Section 20.5 and Section 20.6.

Summary

Children are capable of learning their mother tongue in a relatively short period of time. The general assumption today is that they enter the world with an **innate language faculty**, and that **imitation** plays only a limited role in the process of language acquisition. A key factor for unhindered language learning is the **linguistic environment**. This encompasses the **language input** offered to the child from birth, and the **interaction** of the child with its environment. Children go through several phases in their language development: a **pre-linguistic stage** (0–1 year), a **one-word and two-word stage** (1–2;6), a **differentiation stage** (2.6–5), and a **completion phase** (from 5 years old). During these years nearly all children go through the same processes of **babbling**, **omission** and **substitution** of sounds and words, making **overextensions** in meaning and **overgeneralisations** in grammatical rules. Language forms that are constructed by a language learner on the basis of overgeneralisation are known as **developmental errors**. If in the first five years a child's speech and language development shows clear signs of being delayed or deviant, this is known as a **speech and language developmental disorder**.

In addition to learning their first language, people are capable of learning other languages: a **second language** (which is spoken in the learner's linguistic environment) or a **foreign language** (which is not used in the language community of the learner). Sometimes the two are put together under the term **second language acquisition**; the language to be acquired is known as the **target language**. Speed and success in second language acquisition depend on factors such as **first language**, starting **age**, degree of **contact** with the target language, **motivation** and **attitude**, degree of **aptitude**, and the kind of **teaching** you are exposed to. There appears to be a **critical period** in learning a second language.

There are clear similarities between the processes involved in first and second language acquisition. Just as children go through several stages in first language acquisition, so we can distinguish **transitional structures** in the language of second language learners. These are part of what is known as **interlanguage** or **interlanguage stages**, a series of intermediate stages going from the first contact with the second language up to complete mastery. In older second language learners we often find **fossilisation**. Second language learners with different first languages but the same target language usually exhibit the same **order of acquisition**. There are also, however, a number of clear differences between first and second language learners. In second language acquisition there is no babbling, and also there may be interference from the first language. This is known as **transfer**, which can be either **positive** or **negative**, that is stimulating or inhibiting.

Many young children grow up in a **bilingual situation**. They can learn both languages at the same time and be **simultaneously bilingual** or learn the second language somewhat later and be **sequentially bilingual**. In principle this does not have to have negative consequences for the child's level of achievement or mastery of either of the languages concerned.

Assignments

1. A child of two can say things like *Mummy cook dinner* (= Mummy is cooking the dinner). What does this tell us about the role of imitation in the process of language acquisition? How can you explain the occurrence of these forms?
2. Consider the following interaction between a mother (M) and her child (C). What can you deduce from this conversation about the role of interaction in early mother tongue acquisition?
   M: Where is your cup? Pick up your cup. Cup is on the table.
   C: Cup. . .Cup table.
   M: Yes, pick up your cup.
3. Determine whether the following sentences are typical for the one-word stage, the two-word stage, the differentiation stage or the completion stage:
   (a) Mama take sock. (Mummy has to pick up the sock.)
   (b) John give me it yesterday. (John gave it to me yesterday.)
   (c) mimi (windmill)

   (d) Not do that.
   (e) Cos you gotta do that, that's why.
4. In the following sentences identify cases of (1) omission, (2) overextension or (3) overgeneralisation.
   (a) They big gentlemans. (They are big gentlemen.)
   (b) He want you see it. (He wants you to see it.)
   (c) Nobody gived it me. (Nobody gave it to me.)
   (d) That's a mouth. (*pointing to a crescent moon*)
5. The verb *jaghmel* in Maltese has many possible translations in English: make, form (part of), spend (time), do (something), hold (an event), pluck up (courage), get (something done), give (a headache). What can you predict about the kind of errors Maltese students may make when writing an essay in English?
6. The following sentences were produced by a non-native speaker of English, who did not learn English in school:
   (a) Work not
   (b) I not work
   (c) I don't work

   What is the linguistic term for the structures in (a) and (b)? Are they just plain wrong, or is it possible to take a different view?

Test Yourself

1. Why can language acquisition in young children not be explained solely on the basis of imitation?
2. Which specific claims are involved in the hypothesis that humans have an innate language faculty?
3. List and identify five different features of the parental language input that children are exposed to.
4. What is the difference between a babble and a word?
5. Which of the following statements is correct:
   (a) Developmental errors only occur in children.
   (b) Developmental errors only occur in second language learners.
   (c) Developmental errors occur both in first and second language learners.
6. When do we speak of a language developmental disorder?
7. Name five factors that can influence the process of second language acquisition.
8. What is meant by the term 'interlanguage'? Is this a language somewhere in between the first language of a second language learner and the target language?

9. What do we mean when we speak of positive transfer in second language acquisition?
10. In bilingual education, what is meant by the 'one-person-one-language-strategy'?

Acknowledgments and Further Reading

The standard work on children's language, and which gives information about the acquisition of many different first languages, is Slobin (1985, 1992). Good introductions to first language acquisition are the books by Clark (2003), Berko Gleason (1997) and Fletcher and MacWhinney (1995). The study of early infants' crying is by Mampe *et al.* (2009). A theoretical account is given in Tomasello (2003). Acquisition of sign languages is discussed in more detail in Baker *et al.* (in preparation). A discussion of cultural differences in input to children can be found in Simmons and Johnston (2007). Introductions to second language acquisition are Ellis (1994), Gass and Selinker (1994), De Bot, Lowie and Verspoor (2005), Larsen-Freeman and Long (1991) and Mitchell and Myles (1998). A discussion of the critical period hypothesis is provided by Birdsong (1999). A detailed study of the child Genie is in Curtiss (1977). A book more directed at the theories is VanPatten and Williams (2006). Many of the examples of children's language are taken from the CHILDES database available online. The example from Romy is from Freeborn *et al.* (1993), Cheo from Lakshamanan (1994) and Isabella from Arias and Lakshamanan (2005). The example from Inge is taken from Kuiken and Vedder (2008). ERP research with children is reported in Atchley (2006). The examples from a Chinese learner of English are taken from Lardiere (2008) and from the Spanish bilingual from Montrul (2009). The picture of a mother and her child in Figure 3.1 is by Saskia Leefsma.

Language and Interaction

Humans use language to communicate with each other. In this second part of the book we will focus on verbal interaction, the largest unit of analysis in linguistics. This falls within the area of **pragmatics**. Chapter 4 is entitled *Discourse*. This will deal with conversations and longer stretches of text produced by language users. Among other things we will discuss the characteristic features of discourse, focusing in particular on cases such as conversations where language users collaborate to ensure coherence.

Language users often do not say directly or literally what they mean. Language utterances may acquire a certain communicative meaning in interaction, where they function as speech acts. This will be the subject of Chapter 5, *Speech Acts*.

chapter 4

Discourse

4.1 INTRODUCTION

Compare the conversations in (1) and (2).

(1) a. Fred: A laugh a day keeps the doctor away.
    b. Leo: He doesn't know anything about it.
    c. Fred: My bicycle is at the mender's but. . .
    d. Leo: Have you seen Charles lately?

(2) a. Anita: When could you mend my bike?
    b. Liz: Sorry, that's difficult just now.
    c. Anita: Oh, that's a shame.

In (1) the conversation is not really a conversation. Each of the four utterances (1a – d) is comprehensible in its own right, but in combination it is difficult to make sense of the conversation. There is no apparent link in meaning between the utterances. In (2) there are such links and in such cases we can talk of the utterances as forming a **text** or **discourse**. Here we use 'discourse' as the general term, since 'text' is often taken to refer more narrowly to monologues or to a piece of written language produced by one single language user. In this chapter we will consider various characteristic properties of discourse and illustrate these using conversations like those in (1) and (2).

Linguistics, First Edition. Edited by Anne E. Baker and Kees Hengeveld.

In (1b) Leo uses the word *he*, but it is not clear what element in the context he is referring to. It could be *doctor* in (1a), but that is unlikely since in the expression *A laugh a day keeps the doctor away* no particular individual doctor is intended. The only possibility is that Leo is pointing to someone that Fred can also see. In (2) Liz uses the word *that* but this clearly refers back to *mend my bike*. Here we see a typical feature of discourse, that is that speakers usually make it possible for their listeners to interpret their utterances on the basis of the context. This feature will be further explored in Section 4.2. Sentence meaning is constructed using the context, but the communicative intention of the utterance is often also left implicit. So, to ensure effective communication, speaker and listener need to cooperate. For example, a listener will assume that what a speaker says is relevant in the context of their conversation. Fred and Leo are clearly ignoring this in (1). There is no connection whatsoever between Leo's remark in (1b) and Fred's reply in (1c). The basic principles for cooperation between speakers and listeners will be discussed in Section 4.3. In Section 4.4 we will then consider the overall organisation of a conversation in successive turns. For example, in (1c) Fred is trying to complete his turn, but Leo does not let him. In successful conversations, people usually employ a range of subtle strategies to ensure better turn-taking than we find in (1). A good example is Anita's answer in (2c), where she uses the word *that* to refer back to the mending of the bike being difficult mentioned in Liz's reply in (2b). In so doing, Anita creates coherence between the two utterances.

The various discourse properties to be discussed in this chapter all help turn a series of utterances into a coherent discourse.

4.2 Interpretation and Inference

How do we know who is meant by the word *she* in the following two answers to the question *Who broke the window?*

(3) *She* broke the window.
(4) The girl next door confessed *she* broke the window.

In order to come up with a good interpretation of *she*, different strategies have to be used. When interpreting *she* in (3), the listener will have to look in the context for a female person, taking cues from the speaker's pointing and looking behaviour. In this case, what is important is the non-verbal context, as it was in trying to make sense of Leo's reply in (1b). But for an interpretation of *she* in (4), the listener first has to look at the sentence as a whole. From the construction of this sentence it is clear that *she* must be interpreted as *the girl next door*. In this case, it is the verbal context that provides the key to the interpretation, in particular the use of the verb *confess* that requires that the person confessing is responsible in some way for what is being confessed. Thus, in both cases the listeners who are interpreting utterances are using information from the context. The notion 'context' can be used in a broad way, referring to the non-verbal context as in (3) and in a more narrow way referring to the verbal context as in (4).

The communicative intention of the speaker is another aspect of discourse that becomes clear in the context. Let us look at the following short dialogue (5):

(5) Anne: Would you like to go to the cinema with me tonight?
Carlos: My bookshelves just collapsed.

The meaning of the sentences in (5) is clear enough. But the question is – what is Carlos trying to tell Anne? How should she interpret his reply? Is it just a statement to let her know that his bookshelves have collapsed? Let us assume that Carlos' reply is meant as a real answer to Anne's question. Carlos probably expects Anne to understand that he urgently needs to do something about his collapsed bookshelves, thus making it impossible for him to go with her to the cinema. He is not saying this directly though, but makes it clear in an indirect way. Such an indirect message, which the listener, with the help of the context, has to try and extract by inferring from an utterance what it may mean, is known as a **conversational implicature**.

As we see here, in addition to establishing the meaning of a certain language form, there is a further interpretation problem, namely working out the communicative intention of the speaker. This type of problem occurs when speakers do not make their intention explicit. When a speaker uses conversational implicature, contextual information is always important. Young children often make errors in interpreting the communicative intentions of their conversation partners. They may not yet be adept at handling contextual information, or they may not yet have sufficient knowledge of the world. This is illustrated in the conversation with John, aged four (6).

(6) Adult: So, did you go on holiday?
John: Yes.
Adult: Where did you go?
John: France.

John answers the questions with very short replies; he does not yet understand that the adult's questions are intended as a prompt for him to continue talking about his holiday. This is typical for four-year-olds.

When constructing an interpretation, a listener not only uses the information that is present in words, but also uses information from the context, both broad and narrow. So, speakers do not have to formulate everything explicitly. If they did, utterances would grow into totally unwieldy units like (7) – this is the totally explicit version of the conversation in (2).

(7) a. Anita: When could you mend my bike?
b. Liz: Sorry, mending your bike is difficult just now.
c. Anita: Oh, the fact that mending my bike is difficult is a shame.

Listeners, in turn, enrich the utterances they hear by inferring what is meant on the basis of contextual information. And since speakers know that listeners do this, they can leave a lot unsaid. Speakers and listeners cooperate in their speaking and understanding in conversation. In Section 4.3 we will take a closer look at this process of cooperation.

4.3 Cooperation

What is the matter with the following conversation (8)? What coherence, if any, does it have?

(8) Julie: Could I please borrow your bike tomorrow?
Eric: That woman next door is something, you know.
Julie: I need it to go to Hampstead tomorrow.
Eric: She painted her nails a different colour three times this week.
Julie: I am going to see my nephew for his birthday.
Eric: You'd better watch out, if you see her on the stairs.

Julie and Eric are not talking to each other; they are apparently ignoring what the other one is saying. What coherence there is exists only between their own utterances, but these do not link up with the utterances of the other. There is no cooperation between the two, and as a consequence there is no coherence in the conversation. The effect is that there is no communication, just two monologues. If people want to communicate with each other, they have to cooperate. They take turns in conversation as listener and speaker, contributing to the same topic, and in this way build up the conversation. This fine-tuning between speakers and listeners is known as the **cooperation principle**. The short conversation in (9) can illustrate this principle.

(9) Frank: Could I borrow some money off you, please?
Ronald: My wallet's in the kitchen.

Does this mean that Ronald is going to lend Frank some money? Ronald does not reply to Frank's question with a simple yes or no. So Frank will have to work out how exactly Ronald's answer relates to his question. Since Ronald is telling him where his wallet is, Frank may infer that Ronald's answer is meant to be positive. If Frank did not intend to lend him the money, there would be no need for Frank to know where the wallet – and the money – is. This is again an example of conversational implicature as we saw in (5). Speakers and listeners try to match their speaking and comprehension activities when they want to communicate with each other. The cooperation principle is a sort of tacit agreement between conversation partners that they will work together in communication. Speakers take into account what has been said, and how the conversation is developing, when they formulate their next utterance. They assume that the person they are speaking to is following the same principle. For listeners the cooperation principle offers guidance for their interpretation of the utterances that make up the conversation. Listeners assume also that speakers are formulating their utterances in accordance with this principle. The cooperation principle is based on a number of basic assumptions or **maxims**. Here we will discuss the three most important of these maxims.

The conversation in (9) was an example of conversational implicature. The affirmative intent of Ronald's answer cannot be found in the meaning of the words he used. Frank can only infer that he meant yes if he assumes that Ronald's answer relates to his question. This is an example of the **maxim of relevance**: the assumption that the contribution of the last speaker will be relevant to the further development of the conversation. When, as in (8), speakers do not pay enough attention to this maxim, it becomes very difficult to communicate.

The conversation in (10) illustrates the second assumption.

(10) Mrs Smith: I really have to post these letters and need some stamps. Would you know where I can find a post office around here?
Passer-by: Yes, right around the corner here, on your left there's one.

Suppose the passer-by knows that the post office is closed and there are no stamp machines. Then his answer does not really provide what Mrs Smith, in view of her question, is entitled to conclude – that she will be able to get stamps there. A listener should be able to rely on a speaker providing him or her with sufficient information, not more, not less. This is the **maxim of quantity**. If a speaker does not stick to the maxim, the listener will draw the wrong conclusion. This can result in very awkward situations. Mrs Smith in (10) should be able to assume that the passer-by has given her the right amount of information.

Our next conversation (11) takes place between a lecturer and a student who has completely forgotten to do the necessary reading for the class.

(11) Lecturer: What did you think of the article for today?
Student: I found it very difficult.

The lecturer will assume on the basis of the answer that the student did in fact read the article and if the student does not answer questions about it well, she will not be surprised since the student said he had found it difficult. But in fact the student has violated a basic principle of communication, namely that he should offer information that is correct to the best of his knowledge, and not deliberately provide information that is not correct. In other words speakers should not lie. This is the **maxim of quality**.

The cooperation principle forms a basic condition for linguistic communication. If speakers and listeners operate from too strongly diverging presuppositions, communication will become impossible. To ensure good communication, speakers and listeners normally keep to the maxims we have discussed. We will summarise them once more for clarity:

- relevance: the contribution is relevant for the development of the conversation;
- quantity: speakers provide as much information as is necessary in the communicative situation, not more, not less;
- quality: speakers provide information that is correct to the best of their knowledge, and do not deliberately give information that is not true.

The maxims are formulated here from the point of view of the speaker and function as instructions. Listeners make assumptions about the speaker's behaviour on the basis of the maxims.

The maxims of quality, quantity and relevance require use of language that is clear and informative. There are other types of language use where some degree of obscurity and ambiguity is expected. Poetry, riddles, or the wordplay of stand-up comedians are obvious examples. In the language of politics or advertising, too, the first priority is not always to be informative, clear and unambiguous, as we see in (12) and (13).

(12) Greece: the real experience.
(13) We shall ensure that the health service will meet the needs of the people.

An advertisement for holidaying in Greece (12) does not make explicit what the experience will be nor that it will necessarily be good. The political claim to meet the needs of the people is also less than clear in (13). In everyday situations, too, language users may well be deliberately vague, ambiguous or mendacious. How the maxims are strictly applied is determined by the expectations speakers and listeners have of each other. For successful communication it is necessary that conversation partners follow the same basic principles. The principles themselves may be applied differently in different contexts.

4.4 Conversations

In a conversation the participants take turns speaking and listening. Let us look at a conversation taken from a modern novel where two friends, Ray and Ruth, are talking about a drawing Ray has done (14).

(14) Ruth: You hung it up. I think it's really good.
Ray: You and me and nobody else. My mum thinks it's good.
Ruth: She's intense, Ray. No wonder you are such a freak-a-delic.

The representation in (14) of this conversation between Ray and Ruth is actually idealised. In an 'ideal' dialogue, first one speaker talks, then it is the other's turn, etc. There are no repetitions or hesitations.

But are conversations really like that? We saw examples in Chapter 2 that showed clearly that real conversations do not always follow this 'ideal' script. Turn-taking can be a little chaotic. Sometimes turns remain unfinished; people may interrupt each other, or talk at the same time. And there may be pauses and gaps. Example (15) contains a conversation fragment as it actually happened. Dots (. . .) represent longer pauses; italics indicate when the participants were speaking at the same time. James and Vic work as janitors in a New York store and a window has been broken.

(15) James: Alright. Because, it's insured anyway, when I call the office, they'll send a man up eh to put that glass in.
Vic: *Well,*
James: *But* this person *that did it,*
Vic: *If I see the person,*
James: -is got to be. . .hh taken care of. You know what *I mean,*
Vic: *Well James,* if I see the person
James: Yeh right. e(hh) !e(hh)!

In this example we see a considerable amount of simultaneous talk and unfinished sentences. A hiatus can occur in the middle of a turn. In (15) we can find an example of this, when James in his third turn clearly needed time to plan his utterance (see Section 2.5). He staked out his claim to the next turn by filling it in with little words such as *eh*. Vic tries to take his turn but is not successful since his utterances remain incomplete.

There are considerable differences between languages as to the amount of simultaneous talk that is allowed. In some languages, such as American English or Dutch, overlaps are quite common but usually quite short. They often occur when a speaker is already rounding off their turn and the next speaker comes in early. Other languages, such as Spanish or Hebrew, allow even more simultaneous talk. Some languages, on the other hand, permit quite long silences between turns. Swedish is an example. There is of course also considerable variation within a language between speakers and between situations (see Section 18.5)

Speakers know (unconsciously) how a turn is structured in their own language. They know when a turn is finished and someone else can take over. They know the rules of **turn-taking**. A turn may be handed to the next speaker by asking a question like *Don't you think?* or *Isn't it, Thomas?* or by asking a more elaborate question such as *Who wrote that novel again?*. Some languages have special forms to indicate that speakers consider their turn to be finished. In Mandarin Chinese, for example, the word *le* at the end of a sentence is used to explicitly hand your turn to your conversation partner (16).

Mandarin Chinese

(16) (student to a fellow student, waiting in a queue to pay his college fees):

xuéfèi	tài	guí	*le*!
College fee	too	high	*end of turn*

'The college fees are too expensive.'

By adding *le* Chinese speakers indicate that they have finished saying what they wanted to say, so the listener knows that now it is their turn to speak. In many languages a question particle like *nicht?* in German can be used, or a tag question like the English *isn't it?*.

A conversation turn can also be handed over through body language, for example by looking at the next possible speaker, head movements or by making a gesture in their direction. Such non-verbal signs are not absolutely necessary for turn-taking, since in telephone conversations turn-taking also runs quite smoothly. Nevertheless, in that situation speakers also produce a great deal of non-verbal behaviour, such as smiling and eyebrow movements, even though the other person cannot see them (see Figure 4.1a and Figure 4.1b).

If speakers want to keep their turn, they must ensure that their conversational partners do not get the impression that they are (almost) finished. They can do this by immediately starting a new utterance after finishing the previous one, even if they do not yet quite know what to say and how to formulate it. Speakers can also use filler words as we saw in (15) and illustrated again in (17).

(17) I think I'm going to book such a last-minute journey, *and eh*. . .

Here the speaker makes sure there is no gap, especially not at a sentence boundary. He uses the words *and eh* to signal that he has not yet finished. It is important to do this at a sentence boundary, since this is precisely the point at which someone else is likely to try to take over. Turn-taking provides a frame for a conversation. In our next dialogue (18) coherence in the conversation is the result of turn-taking.

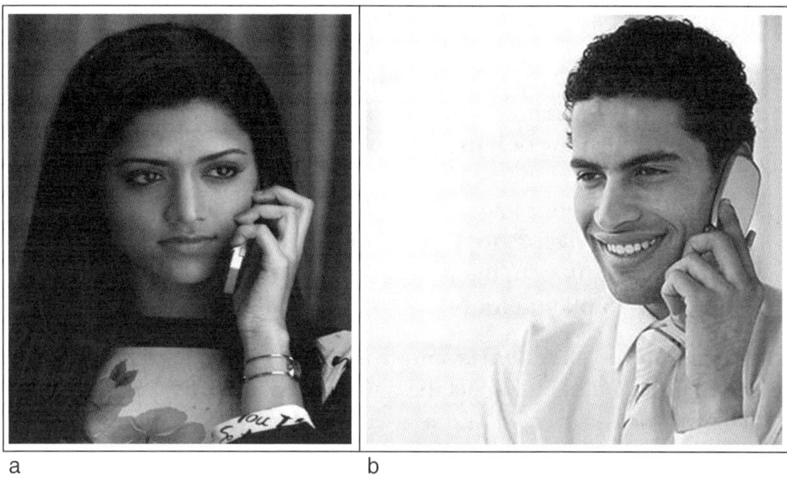

a b

Figure 4.1 Non-verbal behaviour in a telephone conversation (a and b): Montrul, S. 'Research methods in L2 acquisition and bilingualism' 6th EMLAR (Experimental Methods in Language Acquisition Research), Utrecht, The Netherlands, February 3–5, 2010.

(18) A: Are you going on holiday?
B: Yes, in two weeks' time.
A: Where are you going?
B: I'm thinking of Spain.

This short dialogue consists of two question-and-answer-pairs. In each pair, the first part, the question, elicits the second part, the answer. Such a question-and-answer-pair is an example of an **adjacency pair**. An adjacency pair consists of two utterances, produced by different speakers, in a fixed order. Other examples are a greeting and counter-greeting, a request or an offer and its acceptance or refusal.

In some cases, the form of a successive pair is more or less fixed, or allows only limited variation, for example in the case of greeting and counter-greeting in English (19).

(19) Mrs Barrett: Good afternoon, Mr Jones.
Mr Jones: Good afternoon, Mrs Barrett.

Some pairs in greetings require fixed formulas but these are different according to the role of the speakers. In Turkish, for example, the person taking leave says *allahısmaladık* but the person staying replies with *güle güle*. In most adjacency pairs, however, there is much more freedom, as in the case of question and answer. A question can be put into words in many different ways, and the same holds true for answers. In the adjacency pair 'question-and-answer' as in (18) an answer must come in some form but there is freedom in the formulation. This is different from the fixed combination of two specific utterances as in (19).

In the adjacency pair offer and acceptance/refusal there are two options for the second part of the pair. From the point of view of the speaker one of these is the preferred option. A speaker who makes a request or an offer, is usually aiming for acceptance rather than refusal. In this light, it is useful to look at the two possible reactions of B in (20).

(20) A: Shall I carry your bag?
B: (a) Oh yes, please do. How kind.
(b) No, thank you, there's no need, it's not very heavy.
But thank you for offering.

B's acceptance of the offer in (a) is simple and straightforward. In (b), however, where the offer is declined, B feels the need to explain why, and to account for his choice of the less-expected and less-valued reaction.

Some languages use certain politeness adjacency pairs for offering and receiving something, for example at the dinner table. In German this pair is *Bitte* (literally 'please') followed by the reply *Danke schön* 'thank you'. In French the first part is *s'il vous plait* 'please' followed by *merci* 'thank you'. English does not have such a pair, nor do many other languages like Afrikaans or Hindi. Words such as *please* are often restricted in such languages to requests as in Grace's utterance in (21). Second language learners of languages that do have such an adjacency pair for offering/receiving often use the word *please* wrongly in their conversation, as Günther's response in (21b). This response is pragmatically incorrect in English and this is indicated by the question mark in front of it. Grace may well think that Günther is requesting something himself. He should have replied as in (21b').

(21) a. Grace: Please may I have the butter?
b. Günther: ? Please (passing the butter)
b'. Günther: Here you are.

Although adjacency pairs often consist of two turns, they can also contain more than two. In French the offering-receiving sequence can also be followed by the person making the offer saying *je vous en prie* (literally 'I beg you'), or in German *nichts zu danken* (literally 'nothing to thank'). In example (22) we see another example of three turns in close adjacency. What is the function of the third turn of the teacher?

(22) Teacher: Tell me, Mary, what is the Pythagoras' theorem?
Student: A square plus eh plus B square is C square.
Teacher: Right, yes, exactly. That is Pythagoras' theorem.
And what can you use it for, Mary?

First the teacher asks a question, then the student answers the question. Then the teacher evaluates the answer. This is an example of the so-called three-step, commonly used in education and well known from conversations between parents and children when they are reading a book together or doing a jigsaw puzzle. After the three-step the teacher asks another question and a new three-step begins.

Jokes often consist of three steps, in the form of a strict question-and-answer routine as in example (23).

(23) A: What is the difference between a crazy rabbit and a counterfeit coin?
B: I don't know.
A: One is bad money, and the other is a mad bunny.

It would be quite inappropriate for B to attempt to answer A's initial question since it would spoil the joke. This joke involves a play on words that is called a pun. These joke routines are very popular amongst children when they are about eight years old. But they are very difficult for children who have severe speech difficulties due to physical problems and have to use a speech computer that produces their speech when they indicate what they want to say. Researchers in Scotland have invented a computer program called STANDUP that generates jokes like this so that such children can join in the joking conversations. The formulation of the jokes adheres to strict rules so that the computer program is able to generate them.

Should the second part of an adjacency pair always follow immediately after the first part? Let us take a look at the next conversation in (24).

(24) A: Would you like something to drink?
B: What have you got?
A: Well, eh, wine, beer. . .some fruit juice, I think.
B: I'll have a beer, please.

Before B can answer A's opening question, he first needs some additional information. In order to get this, he asks A a counter-question. Only after this has been answered is B in a position to answer A's original question. In this case, the middle pair of 'question-and-answer' has been embedded into the opening pair. Such embeddings can go on for quite a while, as we can see in the next example and indicated by the indented pairs (25).

(25) A: Have you seen Carmen around?
    B: Carmen? Which Carmen?
        A: You mean you don't know her?
            B: Should I?
            A: Well, eh, no, I just thought you knew her.
        B: No, I don't think so.
    A: She was here last year on an exchange.
B: Oh, that Carmen! Why didn't you say? Yes, I saw her yesterday.

Of course, not all conversations are as highly structured as the examples we have just discussed. Often the second part of an adjacency pair will get lost, certainly in complex embeddings like (25), when with each turn the conversation may well take a completely different direction.

Conversations do not begin, or end, just like that. Not everybody knows the secret of how to start a conversation with an attractive stranger. But in most situations speakers do know how to open a conversation, and also how to bring it to a close. There is often a certain pattern to **conversation openings** and **conversation endings**. In (26) and (27) we have examples of conversation openings.

(26) Did you see last night's match?
(27) You know what happened to me today?

The listener will use the context to interpret these as openings rather than as a strict yes/no question and, as we saw in (6), children have to learn to make this interpretation.

To bring a conversation to a close often takes more than one turn, as we can see in the following fragment of the end of a telephone conversation.

(28) A: Why don't we all go and have dinner all together?
B: Brilliant! In the Riverside Restaurant?
A: Yes.
B: Good.
A: Shall we have a drink first, say at six at the pub on the corner?
B: OK.
A: Is that all right?
B: Yes fine, thanks very much.
A: You're welcome.
B: So, I'll see you there.
A: Yes, around six.
B: Good.
A: Good, see you.
B: Cheers.

When A closes the conversation, B also has to say something to bring it to a close. But this can trigger a new reaction from A, etc. Sometimes language users can play this out ironically, by continuing to say *bye* to each other, as in a famous film scene with Laurel and Hardy.

Some languages have special words or expressions to signal that one of the speakers wants to end the conversation. In Spanish, for example, a speaker may use the expression *pues, nada* (literally: 'so, nothing') to indicate that he wants to close the conversation. If learners of Spanish as a second language have not learnt this, and continue the conversation, they may end up in an increasingly uncomfortable situation. A comparable element can be found in

Koryak, a language spoken in the Kamchatka peninsula in north-east Siberia. In this language a narrator will indicate that his story is finished by saying the word *acco'ct*. In English, the narrator of a fairy story can say *The end*, and someone delivering a lecture will often round off by saying *Thank you.*

4.5 Coherence Through Linguistic Form

A discourse consists of a series of utterances. These can be either oral or written, and they can come from one person (monologic discourse) or from more than one (dialogic discourse). However, not every series of utterances constitutes a discourse, as we saw in the strange exchanges in (1) and (8) where there was no link in the content of the utterances. In (29) there is a link in the content but the sentences do not fuse together well.

(29) Wash two aubergines. Slice the aubergines. Put the aubergine slices on an oven tray.

For a text, it is necessary to have **coherence** between the constituting utterances. That is, they should be related to both the verbal and the non-verbal context in which they appear. They should also be related in content, and each individual utterance should make a contribution to the building up of the text's subject. In (29) there is some coherence in terms of content but not in the way the sentences are formulated. Compare example (29) with (30).

(30) First wash two aubergines. Then slice them and put the slices on an oven tray.

It will be immediately clear that in (30) there is more coherence than in (29) in terms of the linguistic forms used. Possibly, if (29) were spoken, the speaker would use gestures to denote the passing from one action to the next. This would create more coherence but non-verbally. The extra coherence in (30) is of a special kind, since it is created by the use of specific language forms. In (30) it is the use of time adverbs that gives continuity to the actions *first* and *then*. The use of the pronoun *them* in the second sentence also creates coherence since it refers back to the sentence element *two aubergines* that was mentioned earlier (see Section 7.9 for more details over pronouns). *Two aubergines* is the antecedent of *them*. This is an example of **anaphoric reference** since the pronoun refers back to another linguistic element (see Section 10.4). This type of reference enhances (30) as a text, since it establishes a link between a pronoun and its antecedent, which both refer to the same person or object. Cases like this, where coherence is achieved with linguistic means, are known as instances of **cohesion**. Cohesion is a narrower notion than coherence, since coherence also includes non-linguistic means.

Children have to learn how to use cohesive means such as pronouns. In (31), Janet, aged five, is telling a story of a boy looking for his lost frog. She does use time adverbs like *then* but she does not use pronouns.

(31) Janet: The boy climbed the tree. The boy called the frog. And the boy fell down. Then the bees chased the dog.

If Janet had used pronouns, this text would have had far more cohesion. Pronouns have little specific meaning in themselves. As a result, the way in which they come back to their antecedent is not very emphatic. Repetition of a full noun like **the boy** in (31) is a far more emphatic way of referring back to him. Pronouns usually indicate that the element being referred to is already known to the reader or listener. The referent is mentioned again to be able to add information about it. Pronouns are pegs on which to hang the content development in the text.

Children of five know how to use pronouns in conversations but may still not be able to use them in a story. Or if they do – as Dominic aged eight does in (32) in telling the same story about the boy, his dog and the lost frog – something may not be quite right.

(32) The boy and the dog fell in the water. He was cross.

It is not quite clear which character *he* refers to, the boy or the dog. This is an example of the problem that can occur with anaphoric use of pronouns: for our interpretation we will need to be able to recover the intended antecedent. Recovery of the antecedent is easier when the pronoun is marked for number (for example, singular or plural) and gender (for example, masculine, feminine or neuter). When pronoun and antecedent agree with each other in number and gender, these shared features help the reader to find the antecedent, as we can see in (33).

(33) Mary was walking beside her brother. Suddenly *he* slipped, so *he* slid down the bank into the water.

Since the pronouns here are overtly marked as masculine, the reference is clear: *he* refers back to the masculine antecedent *her brother*. There can be no doubt that it is Mary who stayed completely dry, and that her brother fell into the water.

However, the features of number and gender do not always solve the problem. Take for example the fragment in (34). Can we say what *he* in the third sentence in this text refers to?

(34) In Paris the talks were proceeding well when the British foreign affairs minister suddenly became impatient. The junior minister was summoned to the meeting. He refused to explain what the matter was.

In (34) the intention is for the last *he* to refer back to *foreign affairs minister*. But when the reader comes to this *he*, its intended antecedent is not so easily 'within reach'. The reader will tend to first link this *he* to the nearest person in the preceding context that fits the bill in terms of number and gender, and that is *the junior minister*. The phrase *the foreign affairs minister* is not so accessible because of the intervening words. It is more difficult to make the link with *he* in the last sentence of (34). As a result the reader will consider the interpretation that it was the junior minister who refused to explain. This interpretation is unlikely on the basis of what we know about junior ministers but it is not impossible. It is likely to be rejected on the basis of world knowledge as we saw in Section 2.2 and Section 2.4.3.

In (35) we see a different mechanism for organising cohesion.

(35) a. Ingrid needn't have worried about the wine. There was enough Ø.
b. I just love roses but I only want red Ø in my garden, not blue Ø.

Here, cohesion is the result of a concise sentence construction, in which elements (*wine* and *roses*, respectively) have been omitted. Such omissions, represented by Ø in (35), are possible only if the omitted element can be reconstructed from the immediate context, and thus be understood by the reader/listener. The omission has the effect of forcing the reader/listener to establish the link with the relevant language element that has been mentioned before. The omitted element must be the same in form and meaning as the one mentioned before. In (34a) *There was enough* can only mean 'There was enough wine' and not 'There was enough booze' or something like that. In this way – through **ellipsis** – a cohesive relation is established between two different sentences. This is similar to the anaphoric reference we discussed earlier. In an elliptic construction a language element that has been mentioned before is highlighted or activated by choosing a sentence pattern that forces the reader/listener to think of this referent. Not all languages allow ellipsis in every context; there can be quite strict restrictions (see Section 8.6 for further discussion).

Ellipsis and anaphoric reference are similar in that both devices reactivate a text element that was mentioned before. In (34) we saw that the use of anaphoric reference led to ambiguity in the closing sentence. Using ellipsis there would lead to an ungrammatical sentence in English, as we see in (36a). Note that the asterisk here indicates that a sentence is ungrammatical, as we indicated in Chapter 1.

(36) a. *refused to explain what the matter was
b. The foreign affairs minister refused to explain what the matter was.

The solution should have been to repeat the full noun as in (36b). Repetition is a more emphatic option than ellipsis or anaphoric reference, since it consists of reintroducing in its full form an element that has been mentioned before.

Sometimes such a repetition can be disruptive, as in Janet's story in (31). The way out, in a case like this, would be to choose an alternative description or a **paraphrase**. The writers of brochures often use this technique, so for example *Paris* can later be referred to as *the French capital* or as *the City of Lights*, etc. Another example of paraphrase can be seen in (37).

(37) But, for director Steven Spielberg, it was merely another step along a familiar path. 'I wasn't trying to make this movie bigger or better,' *the iconic filmmaker* states, relaxed and unruffled just weeks before the film makes its global début at the Cannes Film Festival.

Steven Spielberg is first mentioned by name, and then again as *the iconic filmmaker*. This re-phrasing is less heavy than a fully-fledged, literal repetition, and helps to establish cohesion almost without the reader noticing.

The various cohesion phenomena discussed above, such as anaphoric reference, ellipsis, repetition and paraphrase, are all to do with the way in which we refer to people or objects involved in the events being described. However, cohesion can also be achieved by establishing a direct link between the events themselves. Consider the following examples in (38).

(38) a. Dawlish arrived home. He opened the door carefully, and turned on the small lamp. He hid his gun in the small desk drawer. Then he checked his phone for messages.
b. After coming home and carefully opening the door, Dawlish turned on the small lamp before hiding his gun and checking his phone for messages.

In (38a) each of the various verb forms used – *arrived, opened, turned on, hid* and *checked* – serves to situate each of the narrated events in the past. This makes each event stand on its own and does not foreground the relation in time between these events. In (38b) we have the opposite effect. Only one event, *Dawlish turned on the small lamp*, is firmly situated in the past by the verb form *turned on*; all other events are presented relative to this one, as either preceding or following it (see Section 10.5 on tense). This arrangement emphasises the cohesion between the events. The style in (38a) can, however, be deliberately used to build up tension, since with each action, the unexpected may occur.

By using these linguistic means for cohesion together with content that is well linked we can create maximum coherence in a text. Experimental research has shown that the more coherence there is the easier texts are to read.

Summary

A **text** or **discourse** comes about when utterances are linked to each other. In interpreting those utterances the listener operates on the premise that there are such links. The context in which utterances appear is used to uncover their meaning. In addition to meaning the listener also has to understand what the communicative intention of the speaker is. If the communicative intention is not contained in the meaning of the utterance, the listener will need to determine its **conversational implicature**.

Establishing the conversational implicature of an utterance works only if speakers and listeners apply the **cooperation principle**. That is, in conversation, the speaking and listening activities of the participants should be in keeping with certain **maxims**, specifically that the information contributed to the conversation meets the requirements of **relevance**, **quality** and **quantity**.

In conversation, participants build up coherence by **taking turns**. These turns may be organised in **adjacency pairs**. The structure of the conversation as a whole is marked by characteristic **openers** and **closers**.

When utterances in a text are interlinked, this is known as **coherence**. When linguistic means are used to create coherence, the text also has **cohesion**. To this end one may use **anaphoric reference**, **ellipsis** as well as lexical means such as **repetition** and **paraphrase**. The choice of sentence structure may also contribute to the cohesion of a text.

Assignments

1. Consider the following mini-dialogue, in which Lia associates a particular conversational implicature with Mike's question. Which conversational implicature is this? And in return, which conversational implicature could Mike associate with Lia's answer?

   Mike: Shall I go to the parents' evening by myself?
   Lia: There you go again. As if I don't want to go.

2. On the assumption of relevance a reaction should link up with the preceding utterance of your conversation partner. Now consider the following dialogue and adopt the position of the hearer/listener. What could B be trying to signal with his reaction to A's question? And what could A in return be trying to say with her reaction to B's reaction?
   A: Have you heard about Mary and Tom?
   B: I have been working hard all day.
   A: Are you too superior to listen to gossip?
3. In the following joke one of the assumptions of the cooperation principle is violated. Which one?
   A farmer meets another farmer and says: 'Hi John, my donkey has got a terrible gut infection. Didn't yours have that too a while ago? What did you give him to cure it?' 'Paint thinner,' says John. A week later they meet

again. The first farmer is angry. 'I gave my donkey paint thinner, like you said, and now he is dead.' 'Mine too,' says John.

4. Which of the following pairs is not an adjacency pair? Explain your answer.
   (a) question-answer;
   (b) greeting-counter greeting
   (c) question-counter question
   (d) statement-denial;
   (e) request-rejection.
5. What are the successive pairs in the following little dialogue?
   A: Have you got a pen on you?
   B: (looks in shirt pocket) Blue or red?
   A: Blue
   B: (gives A the blue pen) There you go.
6. Engage someone in conversation, then try and hang on to your turn for as long as possible. How long can you keep this up? What means do you use? How does your conversation partner react? Describe what happened.
7. What is wrong with the following text fragment?

   Peter is going to move house and his brother is coming over to help him. He is not looking forward to it.

8. Which two cohesive means are used in the following sentence to create coherence?

   I bought a cabriolet, a red one, and am planning to drive to Turkey in it.

9. Example (8) of this chapter presents a text fragment which lacks coherence. Texts without coherence are characteristic of people with schizophrenia. They have no access to one of the types of knowledge identified in Chapter 2, and used by humans in their production and understanding of language. Which type of knowledge is this?

Test Yourself

1. What is a conversational implicature?
2. Name and define three maxims that form the basis of the cooperation principle.
3. Identify two ways in which speakers can transfer their turn to someone else.
4. Give an example of an adjacency pair.
5. What is the difference between coherence and cohesion?
6. What is ellipsis?

Acknowledgments and Further Reading

A good overview of pragmatics is to be found in Levinson (1983) and in a more recent book by Huang (2006). A study of coherence and reading can be found in McNamara and Kintsch (1996). The classical study of cohesion in English is by Halliday and Hasan (1976). Cross-cultural communication is a big topic and is discussed in Gudykunst and Mody's handbook (2002).

The example from Mandarin on turn-taking is from Li and Thompson (1981). The dialogue about the broken window was taken from Schegloff (2000) in an adapted form of transcription. The information on the pun-generating software STANDUP is taken from Waller *et al.* (2009). The Laurel and Hardy film is *Perfect Day* (1929). Information about Koryak is to be found in Bogoras (1917). The dialogue from a modern novel was adapted from *The Lovely Bones* by A. Sebold (2002). The photographs of a phone conversation were reproduced with permission from Montrul (2009).

chapter 5

Speech Acts

5.1 Introduction

In the last chapter we discussed a range of phenomena that occur when language is used in interaction. These all form part of pragmatics as introduced in Chapter 1. This chapter also deals with pragmatics, but in contrast to Chapter 4, where we focussed on discourse, we will now consider the pragmatic aspects of individual utterances.

The following example (1) illustrates the three different perspectives to be explored in this chapter.

(1) Go play in the park!

Sentence (1) has a specific content, but in addition its form indicates what the communicative intention of the speaker is. The speaker aims to have the utterance interpreted as an order. In this respect, the utterance represents an act on the part of the speaker. In Section 5.2 we will explore utterances as acts.

The various parts of sentence (1) do not all have the same information value. If you use (1) to address children that are playing in the street, the word *play* will have no news value. The really new information is the speaker's wish that the playing take place in a different location, expressed in the phrase *in the park*. To mark this, this constituent will receive extra emphasis in the intonation

Linguistics, First Edition. Edited by Anne E. Baker and Kees Hengeveld.

pattern of the sentence. In Section 5.3 we will further discuss the way in which utterances convey information.

If sentence (1) is produced by a mother to children playing in the street, they are likely to listen to her. But if a secretary finds her boss playing a computer game in the lunch break on her computer, she is not likely to express her wish to reclaim the computer in the form of (1). A particular utterance may be more suitable in one context than in another. This topic – that is, how an utterance can be used to express a social relationship between speaker and hearer – will be discussed in the last section, 5.4.

5.2 An Utterance is an Act

Suppose John told Birgit:

(2) I'll bring you the book tomorrow.

Then, when Birgit sees John the next day, it turns out he does not have the book with him. She gets cross and tells him off. Is she being unreasonable?

When John uttered (2), he had a certain communicative intent. His utterance is more than just a statement to Birgit that he is going to do something for her the next day. By uttering (2) he has made a commitment to Birgit. He has made her a promise: that he would bring the book for her the next day. And Birgit is entitled to complain when he fails to deliver. Speakers utter sentences in order to achieve something in their contact with other human beings. Their use of sentences is a form of social action. They may use them to make a promise, to question somebody, to make a bet, to greet or thank somebody, etc. For this reason, utterances are known as **speech acts**. The promise made by producing (2) is a case in point.

Utterances thus have two different aspects. On the one hand they have a purely linguistic aspect: their sounds, words, structure, and the meaning of the sentence as a whole. To a very large extent, these can be described without regard to how an utterance is used in a particular situation. On the other hand, utterances also have a functional aspect, namely the speech act that they can perform. These two different aspects of utterances are known respectively as **locution** (its form) and **illocution** (its function as a speech act). Instead of (2) John could have said (3).

(3) I promise I will bring you the book tomorrow.

The verb *promise* means 'to undertake an obligation to do something for someone'. By using this verb in (3), the illocution is explicit and therefore more clearly expressed than in (2). The difference between (2) and (3) is that the speech act character of (3) is expressed in so many words within the sentence, and in (2) this is not the case. Verbs like *promise*, which express the illocution of an utterance, are **performative verbs**. Other examples in English are: *inform*, *warn*, *ask*, *protest*, *advise* and *summon*. Utterances such as (3) are known as **direct speech acts**: they contain a performative verb in the present tense, they have a first person subject and, if necessary, a second person representing the addressee. Utterances like (2), on the other hand, do not contain a performative verb. So when Birgit constructs an interpretation of the sentence, she will have to deduce what its illocution is, in the same way as she would look for its conversational implicature (see Section 4.2). This second type of speech act is known as an **indirect speech act**.

Children have to learn how to interpret such indirect speech acts. In (4), George, aged five, is told by his mother one Friday night about a possible trip.

(4) We may go to the beach tomorrow.

Then on the Saturday morning, when they do not go to the beach because it is raining, George gets very angry. He complains to his mother (5).

(5) But you promised.

However, his mother had not promised. The word *may* in (4) makes it clear that her speech act is not a promise, but a statement about a possible future event. George still has to learn the difference. If she had said *We'll go to the beach tomorrow*, then George would have had a point, since the indirect speech act could well have been a promise.

Given what we have said about speech acts so far, which speech act is expressed in the first part of (6)? And is this a direct or an indirect speech act?

(6) I hereby name this ship the *Pathfinder*. God bless all who sail in her.

This utterance is clearly a direct speech act with the verb *name*. It is usually accompanied with the smashing of champagne against the hull of the ship (see Figure 5.1). Compared to (3) the speech act is more emphatically expressed here, as the word *hereby* makes explicit 'by pronouncing this utterance'. In everyday language this would be exaggerated, but ritual and ceremonial situations as in the launching of a ship often require the use of formulaic expressions, and then it is certainly appropriate.

Most speech acts are indirect, that is they do not contain a performative verb. Here the form of the sentence may help in interpreting the illocution of the utterance. For example, English has declarative, interrogative and imperative sentence forms. But this is not to say that these three sentence types are always only used to make statements, ask questions or issue orders respectively. The relationship between sentence form and speech act is not absolutely fixed, as we can see in the following examples (7), (8) and (9).

(7) Is the plumber coming?
(8) Could you open the window?
(9) Patrick, would you mind putting your clothes away before you go to school?

Figure 5.1 Launch of the *Pathfinder*, 1941. NOAA Photo Library, NOAA Central Library; Association of Commissioned Officers.

All three examples have the form of an interrogative sentence. But is the speech act expressed in all three cases really that of asking a question? In (7) the speaker will indeed expect a positive or negative answer. The speaker does not know whether the plumber is coming, and would like to know. But is this also the case in (8)? Is the speaker here also expecting a yes/no answer? That is highly unlikely. A speaker who produces (8) is not interested in a positive or negative answer; rather, the addressee is expected to be able to open the window, and (8) is addressed to that person in order to bring about the opening of the window. The speaker hopes that the addressee will come to the same conclusion and will interpret the utterance of (8) as an (indirect) request. In other words, the speech act of (8) is not a question, but a request. In (9), Patrick's father is not interested in his son's state of mind, but is putting into words, indirectly, what he expects of him. Thus, (9) functions as an order.

As we can see, there is no fixed correspondence between the grammatical form of (7), (8) or (9) and their function as a speech act. There is no one-to-one relation between locution and illocution in interrogative sentences. Does this hold true more widely, for all language forms and speech acts? Take for example the declarative sentence (10), and try to decide what the speech act is.

(10) I feel that a white line between paragraphs would look more attractive.

It is not too difficult to think of a context in which (10) would be a *request* to put a white line between the paragraphs, or a situation in which (10) is a piece of *advice*, or indeed a situation where it is just a *statement* of the speaker's feelings. Out of context, the sentence is ambiguous as to its speech act function. In general this does not cause undue problems for language users. Usually they manage very quickly to come to an appropriate interpretation, using their knowledge of the situation and context to deduce the speaker's intention as expressed in the speech act (see Section 4.3).

One locution may be linked with a number of different illocutions, as in (10). Conversely, different locutions may be used to express one single illocution. Which speech act is being performed in (11), (12) and (13)?

(11) Make me another coffee.
(12) I wouldn't mind another coffee.
(13) Could you give me another coffee, please?

Sentence (11) has the imperative form, sentence (12) is declarative in form, and sentence (13) is an interrogative. But each of these three sentences is making a request for some more coffee. One and the same illocution can be formulated using all three sentence types. Speakers may consciously exploit this ambiguity, as we can see in the conversation in (14).

(14) Ellen: The rubbish bin is still in the kitchen.
Dick: Can't you put it out this time? I did it last week.
Ellen: I didn't ask you. All I ever said was it's still in the kitchen.

Ellen's first utterance could be a statement expressing an observation; it could equally be an indirect request. This is how Dick interprets it – and he promptly refuses. Then Ellen replies denying the correctness of Dick's interpretation of her utterance as a request; she claims she intended it as a statement. She may of course have deliberately phrased the utterance in this ambiguous way, so as to be covered if Dick refused her request.

There are quite a few languages that have more sentence types than the three we discussed for English. The more sentence types there are in a particular language, the more specific the function of each type becomes. The number of possible interpretations for each type then also decreases. In Tauya, for example, a language of New Guinea, there is a separate sentence form for pronouncing a prohibition, which makes use of a so-called prohibitive verb form. In (15) the prohibitive marking and the singular marking are inseparable, which is indicated in the gloss by the use of the full stop.

Tauya
(15) Yate-?atene.
go-*prohibitive.singular*
'Don't go!'

A South American Indian Language, Tucano, uses a sentence type for encouragement called a hortative alongside an imperative, as we can see by contrasting (16a) and (16b).

Tucano

(16) a. apê-ya!
play-*imperative.2nd person plural*
'Play!'

b. apê-râ
play-*hortative.1st person plural*
'Let's go play!'

Mandarin Chinese, finally, has a special 'admonitive' construction that is used for issuing a warning (17).

Mandarin Chinese

(17) Xiăoxin ou.
careful *admonitive*
'Be careful!'

In all three languages the particular form of the sentence, the locution, expresses clearly and directly the speech act function, the illocution, of its utterance. But even in languages that have a more restricted number of sentence types, it is not possible to use each sentence type for each type of illocution. In most of the examples we have discussed it was quite clear which speech act was intended. We can clearly explain why (7) is a question, (8) a request, and (9) an order. In (7) the speaker does not know whether the plumber will come, and he or she would like to know. In (8) this is different. Here, it is highly likely that the speaker already knows that the addressee is able to open the window, and so the question form of (8) is then interpreted as an indirect request. This sounds more polite in English than the order in (18).

(18) Close the window!

In (9), too, Patrick's father does not expect an answer in the form of *yes* or *no*. He is indicating in an indirect way what he expects of Patrick, that is that he will clear up his clothes before going to school. But if Patrick is indeed of the rebellious type, he might choose to interpret the locution as directly matching the illocution, that is as a question, and say *yes*, thus provoking his father.

The interpretation of a particular utterance as a certain speech act depends on the context. In (7) the speaker assumes that the addressee has the information necessary to answer his question. With the request in (8) the speaker assumes that the addressee is capable and willing to accept it. With the order in (9) Patrick's father assumes that the content of the order and the social relation to his son will justify his issuing it. He also expects that his son will recognise this and will find the order reasonable. But suppose Patrick is a rebellious teenager. Would (9) then still be the appropriate form for an order?

In order to function well in a given context and situation as a question, request or order, an utterance must satisfy certain conditions and these are specific for each of these of speech act types. If these conditions are not met, the speech act will not be successful. For instance, if (9) was uttered by Patrick's younger sister, the speech act (of issuing a polite, indirect order) would not be successful, since she does not have the social position to be able to give him an order. These conditions are known as **felicity conditions**.

Imagine a top criminal talking to one of the men in his gang, as in example (19).

(19) I promise I will break your neck.

Is (19) a promise? The phrase *I promise* definitely expresses a commitment to do something. This creation of an obligation is one aspect of what it means to make a promise. The speaker undertakes an obligation to do something to the addressee, that is, to break his neck. But in strong contrast to a normal promise as in (3), where the speaker commits himself to doing something positive for the addressee, in (19) the speaker commits himself to doing something negative. These different felicity conditions make the illocution of (3) a promise, but of (19) a threat, despite the use of the performative verb *promise*. The verb *threaten* cannot in fact be used as a performative verb in English: **I threaten I will break your neck*.

When interpreting an utterance or locution as having a specific illocution, it is important to establish what felicity conditions are involved. The context of the utterance is critical here. The relationship between the speaker and the addressee is also important, and the situation in which the utterance is produced. Imagine the utterance from (8) *could you open a window?* produced when looking at a skyscraper from another building or when sharing a room on holiday (see Figures 5.2a and 5.2b).

The interpretation as a request is evident when the speaker enters a room and poses the question to the person already there (see Figure 5.2b). When looking at an office skyscraper (see Figure 5.2a), however, that interpretation is

a b

Figure 5.2 a. View of skyscrapers. b. Window in room.

a lot less evident; it might just as well be a yes/no question about the physical possibility of opening windows in such a building.

Languages differ, as we have seen, in the directness of the link between locution and illocution. These differences mean that it can be difficult for second language learners to interpret the illocution correctly. This can be of critical importance in business or political situations. We will return to this point in Section 5.4.

5.3 Information Structure

With every sentence they produce, speakers and writers aim to provide their listeners and readers with information. This is particularly true in the context of answering a question. In (20) to (22) B is answering the questions of A. How do we know what the *new* information is in B's answers?

(20) A: When will we know what Anita's going to do?
B: We'll know next week.
(21) A: What's the matter with your little sister?
B: She was bitten by a dog.
(22) A: What are you writing?
B: I've got to finish my thesis.

In (20) the words *next week* contain the new information for A. The rest of B's sentence merely repeats elements already contained in the question. Since these elements do not offer any new information, they could also be left out. The phrase *next week* would also be an adequate answer. In (21) the most important information is *bitten by a dog*. In (22) B's noun phrase *my thesis* has the highest informative value. The informative part of the sentence is called the **focus**. It is the main point of the utterance.

In the answers in (20) to (22), the elements forming the focus are placed towards the end of the sentence. This is no coincidence, for there is a connection between sentence structure and informative value. This is known as the **information structure** of a sentence. One of the factors that can be used to mark information structure is word order. In a considerable number of languages, including English, an element with a higher information value is placed after an element with a lower information value. That is, in these languages, the information value of sentence elements increases from beginning to end in a sentence. The final position in such languages is then the main focus position. In such languages the first sentence element has the lowest information value. The first element in the sentence is usually known to the listener/reader. In B's answer in (20) there is nothing new in *we*, which only repeats an element already mentioned in A's question. As such it offers a good starting point, and the rest of the sentence will then provide further information about this *we*. In a sense, *we* offers the addressee an anchor for the interpretation of the rest of the sentence, and this is only possible if this initial element is sufficiently known to the addressee. The sentence element that presents known information is the **topic** of the sentence. In (20) the topic is *we*; in (21) it is *she*, which refers back to *your little sister*; and in (22) the topic is *I*, which refers to the addressee B, and at the same time refers back to *you* in A's question.

Some languages use markers to express information structure. In the African language Gungbe of the Kwa family, the focussed element occurs first and is marked as the focus with the particle *wɛ̀*. In (23) we see the focus marked both in the question and again in the reply marking *bicycle* as the new information.
Gungbe

(23)	a.	Étɛ́	wɛ̀	Kòfí	xɔ̀ ?	b.	Kɛ̀kɛ	wɛ̀	Kòfí	xɔ̀.
		what	did	Kòfi	buy		bicycle	did	Kòfí	buy
		'What did Kòfi buy?'					'Kòfi bought a bicycle.'			

Just as Gungbe uses *wɛ̀* to mark focus, Japanese uses *wa* or *wo* to mark topic (see example 9 in Chapter 1 and example 32a below). Some sign languages mark topics using eyebrow movement and head tilt.

In many languages focus can also be indicated by stressing the phrase in focus, that is by giving the phrase more emphasis (see Section 16.4 for more detailed information on stress). In English and other languages that use final position usually to indicate focus, a focus constituent can even be placed at the beginning of the sentence if it is stressed, as in (24). By shifting the main stress (indicated by capital letters) in the sentence, an element not in final position can be marked as carrying the highest information value.

(24) A: When will we know what Anita's going to do?
B: NEXT WEEK we'll know.

This contrast with the normal stress pattern in the sentence has a clear effect: the element *next week* gets special emphasis. Stress works in spoken language, but in written texts writers often have to rely on word order.

In order to create the correct information structure in terms of word order, the appropriate grammatical structure has to be chosen. Let us consider the sentences in (25).

(25) a. Ahmad gave the book to Caroline.
b. Ahmad gave Caroline the book.
c. To Caroline Ahmad gave the book, and to Irene the magazine.

Sentence (25a) has neutral word order in English – that is the sentence begins with the person giving, then what is given, and last the person to whom the object is given. If no other element gets special stress, the element *to Caroline* would normally be interpreted as the constituent in focus. This would be a typical answer to the question *Who did Ahmad give the book to?* In (25b) *the book* is the constituent in focus. This has been achieved by changing the order of the elements *Caroline* and *the book*. This would be a typical answer to the question *What did Ahmad give Caroline?* In (25c) *To Caroline* has been moved into topic position and in the following part *to Irene* is also in topic position. The elements *the book* and *the magazine* are in focus positions. This order is not so common in English but would be quite appropriate as an answer to the question *What did Ahmad give to Caroline and Irene?* These different information structures are the result of moving sentence elements into different positions. But not every element can be simply moved to last position in English.

So how could *Ahmad* become the focus element using word order? If word order is going to be used, then this will require a rather more drastic change of the construction of (25a), as for example in (26).

(26) The book was given to Caroline by Ahmad.

In (26) the construction of (25a) has been replaced by what is called a passive structure. In passive sentences the object or person (here *the book)* that is the target of the verb (here *give*) is made the subject of the sentence, and the person doing the action (here *Ahmad*) is put last, with the preposition *by*. This operation brings along a change in word order such that *Ahmad* is in last position, that is the focus position for English. Another option would be to replace the verb *give* in (25) with its opposite, *receive* or *get*, as in (27).

(27) Caroline got the book from Ahmad.

At the beginning of a story all the information is new. How do narrators get around this problem in languages that place their focus at the end of the sentence? Let us compare (28a) and (28b).

(28) a. A king once had seven daughters.
b. Once upon a time there was a king who had seven daughters.

In (28b) a construction is used with *there was* in the beginning followed by an indefinite noun (*a king*) as the grammatical subject. This is the traditional fairytale opening in English. At the beginning of the story the referent of *a king* will be completely unknown. This has two implications. First of all, since it is unknown, this sentence element is not a suitable topic and cannot function as anchor for the interpretation of the information in the rest of the sentence. Secondly, for the same reason, *a king* is a good focus element, since it is unknown and has high information value. On both counts, (28a) is not very good. In (28b), on the other hand, the construction with *there was* forces *a king* into focus position. Once the king has been introduced, he can be used as the topic of the following clause. There *who* refers back anaphorically to *king*, and serves as anchor for the introduction of further new information, that is *the seven daughters* that are then in focus position in that clause. This sort of construction, called the 'presentative', also occurs in everyday narratives, which very often begin with *Well, there was a man on the bus, and he* .... Here again, the referent of *a man* is unknown.

Which sentence element is the focus in the sentences in (29)?

(29) a. The Mickey Mouse cartoon got the most votes.
b. It was the Mickey Mouse cartoon that got the most votes.
c. The one that got the most votes was the Mickey Mouse cartoon.

In (29a) *the most votes* is in focus; in (29b) and (29c) the focus is on *the Mickey Mouse cartoon*. In (29b) and (29c), it is as if the construction from (29a) is split in two; this is why these are called 'cleft sentences'. In the special focus construction (29b), *the Mickey Mouse cartoon*, the subject of (28a), is placed in focus position, with the rest of the sentence following on as a relative clause *that got the most votes*. In (28c) the subject of (28a) is again placed in focus position, but this time with the clause *the one that got the most votes* in topic position.

French uses a cleft construction as in (29b) very frequently, far more frequently than English, to place a noun in focus position. An example is given in (30).

French

(30) Ce sont des soldats qui marchent là-bas.
it are *indefinite* soldiers who march there-down
'There are soldiers marching down there.'

In (30) the phrase *des soldats* 'the soldiers' is in focus position.

Children have to learn to manage information structure and it can take some time for them to do this. However, sentence (31) was produced by a three-year-old French girl, Anne.

French

(31) C(e) est Maminou (qu)i me l' a donné là.
it is Maminou who me it has given there
'It was Maminou who gave me that one there.'

French children are much quicker to learn these constructions than English children because they are so frequent. Learning to manage information structure is of course also important in a second language but it can take some time to master.

Summarising, the information structure of a sentence should match the context in which it is used. Languages use different devices to mark topic and focus – we have discussed word order, marking and stress. The form of utterances needs to be appropriate to the information structure. In the next section, we will again consider the appropriateness of utterances, but from a different perspective.

5.4 Pragmatic Appropriateness

Native speakers of English usually get quite a shock when they learn a second language like French and suddenly realise that they have to decide on their relationship with the addressee when choosing the second person pronoun. In English there is only *you* but in French you have to choose between *tu* and *vous*, in Italian between *tu*, *voi* and *Lei*, in German between *du*, *ihr* and *Sie*, in Hindi between *tum* and *ap*. These different forms of address in these languages cannot be used interchangeably in every situation. It depends on the social relationship between the speaker and addressee: how well they know each other, the difference in social status and age, and the formality of the occasion. In Hindi the *tum* form is used amongst friends but can also be used to a socially inferior person by someone higher on the social ladder. In German and French secondary schools both teachers and students are likely to use *Sie* and *vous* respectively, but at primary school both teachers and pupils are likely to use the familiar forms *du* (singular) or *ihr* (plural) and *tu* (singular) or *vous* (plural). Even if two people know each other well, they usually use the familiar form, but in a formal situation, such as in court or at an official meeting, they will switch to the formal form.

When a relationship develops such that the more informal form can be used, the switch is often made quite explicit. There are even verbs derived from the personal pronouns to use in this situation. So a German speaker might say something like *Wollen wir uns dutzen*? 'Shall we use the familiar form?', the verb *dutzen* being derived from *du*. In French, *tutoyer*, 'to use the informal form', is derived from *tu*. The conditions governing the use of these forms are not so much to do with the content of the utterances as with the circumstances under which they are produced. These kinds of usage conditions constitute the **social meaning** of a language form.

Other languages have a system of forms of address that are even more complicated. In Japanese, for example, an element like *-san* or *-kun* (called a honorific) has to be added on to the name of the addressee. A man named *Yamamoto Jiroo* (where *Yamamoto* is his family name) has to be addressed as *Yamamoto-san* by someone who does not know him. Once they have become more closely acquainted, he may be addressed as *Jiroo-san*. But the really intimate form of address is *Jiroo-kun*. This 'intimate' suffix *-kun* may not, however, be used for women. The choice of suffix depends on the difference in age and status between speaker and addressee, and on their sex. There are far more forms that have social meaning. The form of the verb in Japanese is also dependent on the social relation between speaker and addressee. In forming a request, for example, the speaker has to take into consideration the age difference, the status difference, the closeness of the relationship and the imposition of the request. In (32) both sentence forms are requesting the loan of a pen, but (32a) is appropriate for a student addressing a professor and (32b) is appropriate for a student making the request to a fellow student.

(32) a. pen-wo kashite kudasai mas-en-ka?
pen-*topic* lend *honorific.humble* *auxiliary-negation-question.formal*
'Would you be so kind as to lend me your pen please?'
b. pen aru?
pen exist?
'Got a pen?'

If an extremely polite form is used with someone of the same status, they are likely to think that the speaker is being ironic.

Knowledge of the **pragmatic appropriateness** of specific language forms is part of communicative competence. In a particular context of use, language utterances must not only satisfy the maxims of quantity, quality and relevance that follow from the cooperation principle (Section 4.3), they must also fit into the social circumstances of that context. The key factors here are the social relation between language users and the social function of the occasion where language is being used. **Style** is regarded as the fourth maxim of the cooperation principle.

The social meaning of language forms is not directly related to the main content or message speakers are trying to present. Social meaning derives from the social factors in the context of usage. These differences in style can be divided into two categories, **formal** and **informal style** (see also Section 18.6). As we have seen, in French *tu* is a more informal language form, whereas *vous* belongs to a more formal style. Such stylistic differences between language forms are part of their social meaning.

Such stylistic differences can be seen easily in the choice of words from the lexicon. For example, the words *man* and *gentleman* have the same referential meaning, that is 'male person', but they differ in their stylistic value. If a salesman wanted to refer to an incident involving a customer in the shop, then he would be likely to use the more formal word *gentleman*, as in (33a), especially if the person involved could also hear the conversation. The utterance in (33b), using the more neutral *man*, is more likely if the salesman is reporting to his boss out of earshot of the customer.

(33) a. This gentleman would like to make a complaint.
b. A man wanted to make a complaint.

The difference between formal and informal use of language is of course not absolute. There are many gradations of formality. Talking about the day later in the pub to his friends, the salesman who was the speaker in (33) might well use the even more informal terms *geezer*, *bloke* or *guy* (34). Taken together, these words constitute a stylistic continuum.

(34) This geezer/bloke/guy wanted to complain.

Language users are well aware that in a more formal situation a different use of language is required than in a more informal situation. When a lecturer teaching a class is bothered by the noise being made by some carpenters, she might say (35a) but when during her preparations for her lecture at home she is constantly interrupted by her little son's drumming, she may well produce the request to stop in quite a different form (35b).

(35) a. Could you please do what you have to do a little later, after I have finished?
b. Billy, cut it out, will you, NOW!

Language users do not always do what is appropriate in the situation. They may deliberately use a language form or expression that is not expected. When speakers produce utterances that are different from what we would normally expect, they create a special effect. In Japanese, for example, if more formal formulations are used than the situation requires, then this is often interpreted as irony, as mentioned above.

The notion of pragmatic appropriateness also plays an important role in foreign language learning. How, for example, do you address a waiter in France? Even for someone with an impressive vocabulary in French, a good command of its grammar and a perfect accent, questions such as these may yield unexpected problems. As we saw in Section 4.4, example 21, second language learners may wrongly transfer structures from their own language, assuming that they are pragmatically appropriate in the second language. Children also have to learn these rules but they are often surprisingly quick to pick them up. Fay (2;6) is growing up bilingual in Dutch and English. Her English grandmother wants her to speak English and so when Fay answers her in Dutch, she makes the same request again, but in English (36).

(36) Grandmother: What would you like to drink, Fay?
Fay: Ik wil water.
'I want water.'
Grandmother: How do you say that in English?
Fay: Can I have some water, please?

Fay's second try is not only in English but also contains all the politeness forms necessary in English. She has learned that these are important and can produce this request absolutely appropriately even at this young age. Alex, at age 4, can even reflect on such politeness forms (37), and the fact that they have to be produced frequently in some situations like mealtimes.

(37) at the start of dinner...
Alex: If I say please and thank you now twenty times, is that enough for all dinner-time?

The control of pragmatic appropriateness can go wrong. People who suffer from some neurological conditions can lose their command of pragmatic appropriateness. For example, people with Tourette syndrome (a neuropsychiatric disorder involving physical tics named after a nineteenth-century French neurologist, Gilles de la Tourette) frequently use swear words and other taboo expressions where there is no occasion for them to be used. They use inappropriate language forms, and often do so to an extreme degree.

Despite all the attention we have been paying to styles of language use that are contextually bound, we should not forget that all these variants share a common core of language forms, the set of grammatical and other features that are present in every style. This common core in the sentences in (38) is clear. The pragmatically neutral style is exemplified in (38a) and contrasts with a more formal style in (38b) or informal style in (38c).

(38) a. That girl has a difficult job.
b. That young lady is in onerous employment.
c. That chick really has to graft.

If a situation does not explicitly call for either a formal or informal style of language, the neutral style of (38a) will be used.

SUMMARY

In language use, utterances function as **speech acts**. In each utterance we can distinguish between **locution** (form) and **illocution** (communicative intent). Utterances constitute **direct speech acts** when they contain a **performative verb**. When the nature of the speech act needs to be deduced from the context, it is an **indirect speech act**. Depending on the situation and the form of the utterance, there are different **felicity conditions** for speech acts.

Language utterances usually present both known information (**topic**) and new information (**focus**). The **information structure** plays a role in the construction of utterances. Languages can use word order, stress and marking of the topic or focus to indicate this structure.

When language forms are subject to conditions that specify the social circumstances under which they can be used, these conditions constitute the **social meaning** of those language forms. When language utterances need to fit in with a particular context of use, this is known as **pragmatic appropriateness**. As a result there will be **stylistic differences**, in particular between **formal** and **informal** language elements.

ASSIGNMENTS

1. Which of the following verbs are performative verbs: *trust*, *ask*, *use*, *conclude*?
2. Each of the following sentences violates a felicity condition of the speech act *promise*. Explain for each of these sentences which condition has been violated.
   (a) I promise you that the sun will rise tomorrow.
   (b) I promise you that I won't kill you tomorrow.
   (c) I promise you that I will help you move house tomorrow, but I might go to the beach.
3. Which speech acts are involved on the bumper sticker in the picture? Which felicity condition is violated?

> Be nice to America
> Or we'll bring democracy to
> your country

4. In the following examples the sentence stress falls on the word in capital letters. Read these sentences out loud and find out what is problematic about the information structure of the sentences:
   (a) Last year, the company BOOKED a net profit of one billion euros.
   (b) Because of the falling oil prices, many gas consumers need to PAY less.
   (c) The minister MADE the proposed new law public.
5. In this chapter we have discussed, among other things, felicity conditions and pragmatic appropriateness. Each of the following example sentences violates either a felicity condition or is pragmatically inappropriate. Explain the violation in each of these sentences.
   (a) Doctor to patient: Open your mouth now!
   (b) Doctor to patient: Herewith I order you to open your mouth.
   (c) Judge to accused: You must answer all my questions by keeping silent.
   (d) Judge to accused: You are lying through your teeth.
6. Describe as precisely as possible the rules for addressing people in your own language in different social situations, ranging from very informal to very formal. Now compare these rules to the rules for addressing people in another language you know.

Test Yourself

1. What is a performative verb?
2. What is the difference between the locution and the illocution of an utterance?
3. Give an example of a direct speech act.
4. What is a felicity condition?
5. Name three means of indicating the information structure of a sentence.
6. What is the social meaning of a language form?

Acknowledgments and Further Reading

Speech act theory was first set out by Austin (1962) and Searle (1969) and discussed further in Levinson (1983), Saeed (1997), Schiffrin (1994), and Thomas (1995). Information structure is discussed in detail in Brown and Yule (1983). The use of pauses and stress in information structure is discussed in van Donzel (1999). The example from Tauya is taken from MacDonald (1990), the Tucano example from Ramirez (1997), the one from Mandarin Chinese from Li and Thompson (1981), and the one from Gungbe from Aboh (2004). The Japanese example was found on the internet.

Sentences and Their Meaning

In Part II we discussed the largest unit of linguistic analysis, the text. The next unit to be focused on in this part of the book is the sentence. When people talk to each other, they use sentences that have a certain structure and meaning. When studying the structure of sentences it is important to identify groups of words that belong together, as well as to name the different categories of words. This will be the subject of the Chapter 6, *Constituents and Word Classes*.

Chapter 7, *Simple Sentences*, will then go into more detail about sentence structure and the role of constituents within it. Languages may differ quite significantly in this respect, and this variation will be discussed in this chapter.

Speakers are not restricted to the use of simple sentences such as 'Liz is going to the market.' They can combine such simple sentences and string them together into a more complex whole such as 'Liz is going to the market, because they're selling ripe mangoes.' Chapter 8 will discuss such types of *Complex Sentences*.

An important feature of sentence structure is that word order is usually rather fixed, although, again, there are interesting differences between languages here. This will be the subject of Chapter 9, *Constituent Order*. Chapters 6 through 9 cover the domain of what is known as syntax.

The last chapter in this part of the book is also concerned with sentences. But instead of looking at their formal properties and syntax, it will be concerned with their meaning. The crucial point about language use is that a certain form is used to express a certain meaning. Chapter 10, *Sentence Meaning*, will take us into the field of semantics.

chapter 6

Constituents and Word Classes

6.1 Introduction

As we discussed in Section 2.4.3, the example in (1) can conjure up two different situations.

(1) The Prime Minister has decided on the high-speed train.

In the first situation the high-speed train is the thing the Prime Minister decides on buying or travelling in, while in the second situation he takes a decision while being on the train. In the first case the word *on* combines with the verb *decided* to form *decided on*, while in the second case it combines with *the high-speed train*, to form *on the high-speed train*. It all depends on how we analyse the sentence into units. Sentence units such as these are called **constituents**. Constituents are thus the meaningful parts that make up a sentence. We will discuss their properties in this chapter.

The second subject we will discuss in this chapter is that of **word classes**. The clause in (1) consists of nine different words. In the written language these are separated by spaces. These nine words serve different functions in the clause, not all of them equally important, as we can see when we turn (1) into a newspaper heading (2).

(2) Prime Minister decides on high-speed train.

Linguistics, First Edition. Edited by Anne E. Baker and Kees Hengeveld.

Example (2) consists of words with a clear, concrete meaning, such as *decides* and *train*, which are indispensable for understanding the content of the clause. Words with an abstract meaning such as *the* and *has* have been omitted, but, interestingly, this does not make the clause harder to understand. Still, words like *the* and *has* serve an important structural function in the sentence, as we will see in the course of this chapter.

In the first part of this chapter we will discuss constituents, and in the second part word classes. What exactly are constituents? How can we recognise them? These questions are discussed in Section 6.2. In Section 6.3 we distinguish between two types of constituents, clauses and phrases, and then go on to consider different types of phrases in Section 6.4. Next, we will discuss the internal organisation of phrases that consist of more than one word, such as *the angry woman*. Here, the word *angry* can be omitted, but not the word *woman* – so some words are more important than others, and in Section 6.5 we will see which words fit into which category. In Section 6.6 we will look into the different ways in which the structure of clauses can be represented in terms of the phrases they contain. Then in Section 6.7 we look further at the relationship between phrases and words. Finally, we will draw an important distinction between two different kinds of word classes: content words, discussed in Section 6.8, and function words, discussed in Section 6.9.

6.2 CONSTITUENTS

Suppose you had to split up the following sentence into exactly three coherent and meaningful parts, what would those parts be?

(3) The student bought a computer yesterday afternoon.

It is not very likely that your answer would contain the parts *computer yesterday* or *student bought a* or just *the*. Probably you have divided (3) into the three parts in (4) (here and in further examples we will represent the relevant boundaries between constituents with square brackets).

(4) [The student] [bought a computer] [yesterday afternoon].

The reason we divide the sentence this way is because a sentence is not just a random collection of individual words. On the contrary, within a sentence words are organised into groups that belong together semantically and therefore behave as coherent units. We call these groups constituents.

Example (3) consists of three such constituents. This can be demonstrated in a number of ways. First of all, a group of words that make up a constituent can be replaced by simpler expressions, as for example in (5).

(5) [He] [did so] [then].

Here we have the following replacements (6).

(6) the student – he
bought a computer – did so
yesterday afternoon – then

Another way in which the three groups of words in (3) can be replaced by another element is when they are replaced by means of a question word, as in (7) to (9).

(7) Who bought a computer yesterday afternoon? – the student.
(8) What did the student do yesterday afternoon? – buy a computer.
(9) When did the student buy a computer? – yesterday afternoon.

In (10) we have the replacements.

(10) the student – who?
bought a computer – what?
yesterday afternoon – when?

Using these replacement tests we can establish that (3) consists of three constituents. Note that these tests also show that a constituent may consist of just one word, such as *he* in (5) and *who* in (7).

A second type of test for 'constituenthood' is the movement test, which is illustrated in example (11). Here we see that one of the constituents of (3), *yesterday afternoon*, can be moved to the front.

(11) [Yesterday afternoon] [the student] [bought a computer].

If a language allows movement, then a constituent can occur at different positions in the sentence and be placed somewhere as one single unit. This shows us that *yesterday afternoon* in (3) and (11) is a constituent.

Not all constituents can be moved around. For instance, in sentences (3) and (11) the constituents *the student* and *bought a computer* have to occur in that order. In English this order cannot be inverted as in sentence (12).

(12) *[Bought a computer] [the student] [yesterday afternoon].

The fact that this sentence is ungrammatical in English is indicated by the asterisk preceding it.

There is one type of constituent in (3) that is actually internally complex: the constituent *bought a computer* itself contains a further constituent, *a computer*. That *a computer* is a constituent can again be demonstrated by replacement and movement tests. Consider the alternatives to (3) in (13) to (15).

(13) The student bought *it* yesterday afternoon.
(14) *What* did the student buy yesterday afternoon?
(15) *A computer* the student bought yesterday afternoon.

Note that (15) is possible but only in a contrastive context, for instance when the expectation is that the student bought a bicycle rather than a computer. All three tests show us that *a computer* is a constituent too, yet it is one that is contained in another constituent, *bought a computer.* A more accurate representation of the constituent structure of (3) is therefore the one in (16).

(16) [The student] [bought [a computer]] [yesterday afternoon].

This bracketing shows that the constituent *bought a computer* contains itself another constituent *a computer*. Another way of saying this is that sentence (3) actually answers four different questions: (17) to (20).

(17) *Who* bought a computer yesterday afternoon? – The student.
(18) *What* did the student do yesterday afternoon? – Buy a computer.
(19) *What* did the student buy yesterday afternoon? – A computer.
(20) *When* did the student buy a computer? – Yesterday afternoon.

To sum up, both the replacement tests and the movement test demonstrate that the real building blocks of sentences are not words but constituents, which may themselves contain other constituents. Constituents may consist of several words, but they may also consist of just one word.

6.3 Sentences, Clauses and Phrases

The constituents we have looked at in Section 6.2 are all relatively simple. But constituents can actually be far more complex. Consider the examples in (21) and (22).

(21) He knows the answer.
(22) He knows that the earth is round.

If we apply a simple constituent test to (21) and (22) we get the results in (23) and (24).

(23) What does he know? – the answer.
(24) What does he know? – that the earth is round.

This shows us a very simple but also very important thing: the sentence part *that the earth is round* in (22) is just as much a constituent as the sentence part *the answer* is in (21). So if they are both constituents, what is the difference between the two? For now it will be sufficient to say that the constituent *that the earth is round* in (22) is not only a constituent of a sentence, but is pretty much like a sentence itself. In fact, in this case we just have to drop the word *that* to end up with a complete English sentence. In order to avoid confusion in the use of the term 'sentence', we will from now on use the term **sentence** only for complete independent sentences, such as *He knows the answer* in (21) and *He knows that*

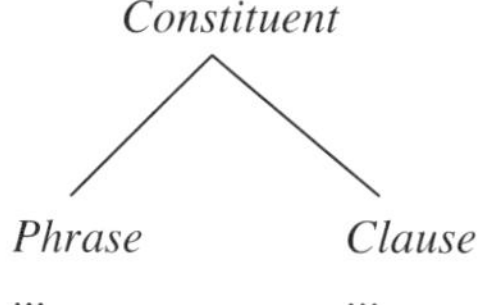

Figure 6.1 Types of constituent (simplified version).

the earth is round in (22). The two 'subsentences' that make up sentence (22) we will call **clauses**. In (24) the clauses are as in (25).

(25) Clause 1 = He knows Clause 2
Clause 2 = that the earth is round

Clause 1 in (25) is called a main clause, Clause 2 an embedded clause. Sentence (22) may now be divided into clauses as shown in (26).

(26) [He knows [that the earth is round]].

We will discuss complex sentences such as (26) in detail in Chapter 8.

Now let us return to the other type of constituent, the type that is not a clause in itself like *the answer* in (21). This type of constituent is called a **phrase**. It is characterised by the fact that its central element is a word, in this case *answer*. We do not need to explain what is meant by central element here, but we return to that in Section 6.5. For the time being it is sufficient to say that all constituents that are not clauses are phrases. Phrases come in different types, and we will discuss these now.

Summarising, sentences are built up out of constituents. These constituents may be clauses (to be discussed in Chapter 8) or phrases (to be discussed in the next section). This subdivision is shown in Figure 6.1, and will be discussed and expanded further in Section 6.4 to Section 6.9.

6.4 Phrase Types

A clause, whether main or embedded, normally consists of a number of phrases. But not all phrases make the same sort of contribution to the structure of the clause. As a first approximation, they can be divided into several different classes on the basis of this contribution. To demonstrate this we will take another look at the example from Section 6.2 (27).

(27) [The student] [bought [a computer]] [yesterday afternoon].

First of all, *bought a computer* has a function that is quite different from *the student*. The phrase *the student* refers to a person: it identifies an entity in the external world. The phrase *bought a computer*, on the other hand, predicates an action of that person. That is the action is said to be true of *the student* and is applicable to *the student*. Phrases such as *the student* and *a computer* are primarily used to refer to entities (objects, individuals, but also more abstract entities such as properties and events). In contrast, phrases such as *bought a computer* are primarily used to predicate a relation between or a property of entities. A phrase that is primarily used to refer is called a **noun phrase** (NP). It has a **referential function**. A phrase that is primarily used to predicate is called a **verb phrase** (VP). It has a **predicative function**.

In addition, there is in (27) a fourth phrase, *yesterday afternoon*. This phrase does not refer to an entity and neither does it predicate a relation or property, and so falls outside the distinction we have just made. It is an example of a third kind of phrase, those which are primarily used to attribute properties or features to something else. In this case the phrase *yesterday afternoon* attributes a property to the event *the student bought a computer* that is described in (27). The property attributed here is the time that the event happened.

Phrases with such an **attributive function** do not only occur within clauses but also within other phrases, as we can see in (28) and (29).

(28) [The [[very] nosy] man] kept looking at her.
(29) The woman [laughed [[extremely] loudly].

In (28) *the very nosy man* is one constituent; it can be replaced by the single word *he*. Here we have a noun phrase containing the phrase *very nosy*; this constituent has an attributive function, since it specifies a property of *man*. In (29) the attributive phrase *extremely loudly* is contained within the verb phrase *laughed extremely loudly*. So attribution may occur at various places within the clause.

When a phrase with attributive function is primarily used to specify a property of a noun, it is known as an **adjective phrase** (AdjP). For instance, the adjectival phrase *very nosy* specifies a property of *man*. When a phrase with attributive function is primarily used to specify properties of something that is not a noun it is known as an **adverbial phrase** (AdvP). For instance, the adverbial phrase *extremely loudly* attributes a property to the verb *laughed* in (29), and the adverbial phrase *yesterday afternoon* attributes a property to the whole of *the student bought a computer* in (27).

A last type of phrase is one that has a **relational function**. Examples of this type of constituent are given in (30) and (31).

(30) I met him [in [the garden]].
(31) the man [in [the garden]]

The word *in* in (30) and (31) specifies a locational relation between the *event of my meeting him* and *the garden* in (30) and between *the man* and *the garden* in

(31). In both cases the word *in* introduces an NP (*the garden*). A phrase with a relational function such as *in the garden* in (30) and (31) is called an **adpositional phrase** (AdpP). Adpositional phrases may be subdivided into prepositional and postpositional phrases, depending on whether the adposition precedes (32) or follows (33) the NP.

(32) *into* the house

Turkish
(33) yol *üzere*
road on
'on the road'

Note that, just as VPs may contain further NPs, AdpPs contain a further obligatory NP. Thus, just as the VP *bought a computer* in (3) contains the NP *a computer*, the AdpP *in the garden* in (30) and (31) contains the NP *the garden*. This is shown by means of brackets in (34) and (35).

(34) [bought [a computer]]
(35) [in [the garden]]

We can now return to the ambiguous sentence in (1) at the beginning of this chapter and pinpoint where the ambiguity lies, namely in the type of constituents involved, as shown in (36).

(36) a. [The Prime Minister] [has decided on [the high-speed train]].
b. [The Prime Minister] [has decided] [on [the high-speed train]].

In (36a) the clause contains an NP and a VP, the latter containing a second NP. In (35b), on the other hand, there is one NP, one VP, and an AdpP, the latter containing a second NP.

Table 6.1 summarises the various types of phrases we have distinguished so far.

And we can now expand Figure 6.1 into Figure 6.2.

Table 6.1 Types of phrases

Primary function	Type of constituent	Abbreviation
Referential	Noun phrase	NP
Predicative	Verb phrase	VP
Attributive, within NP	Adjective phrase	AdjP
Attributive, outside NP	Adverbial phrase	AdvP
Relational	Adpositional phrase	AdpP

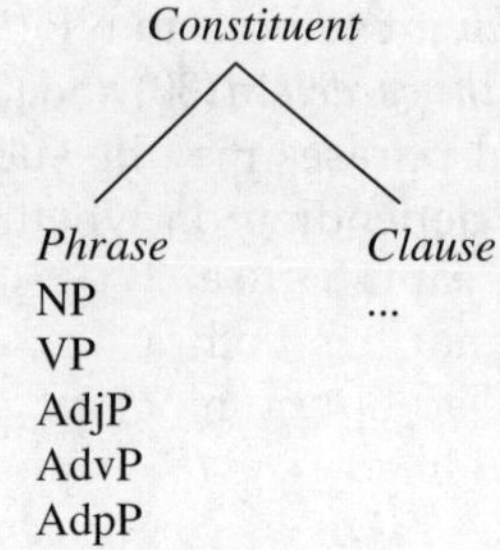

Figure 6.2 Types of constituent (expanded version).

6.5 Heads and Modifiers

Not every element within a phrase is necessarily always present, as we can see in examples (37) to (41). The (b) variant in each case leaves out a different element than the (c) variant. The asterisk (*), as explained above, indicates that an example is not correct, that is, not grammatical.

(37) *Noun phrase*
a. She ate [a nice sandwich].
b. She ate [a sandwich].
c. *She ate [a nice].

(38) *Verb phrase*
a. He [laughed excessively].
b. He [laughed].
c. *He [excessively].

(39) *Adjective phrase*
a. The [extremely nosy] man laughed.
b. The [nosy] man laughed.
c. *The [extremely] man laughed.

(40) *Adverbial phrase*
a. He ate [rather grossly].
b. He ate [grossly].
c. *He ate [rather].

(41) *Adpositional phrase*
a. It lives [ten feet below [sea level]].
b. It lives [below [sea level]].
c. *It lives [ten feet [sea level]].

What conclusion can we draw from these examples? In some cases an element can be left out, in other cases this is not possible. That is, within a phrase we can distinguish between an obligatory nucleus and the possible or optional additions to it. The obligatory nucleus is the **head**, the optional additions are the **modifiers**. This distinction applies to all types of phrases. The (a) examples above all contain a phrase that has both a head and a modifier, in the (b) examples the phrase has a head but no modifier, and in the (c) examples the phrase has a modifier but no head. The (c) examples are all ungrammatical, that is, the modifiers *nice*, *excessively*, *very*, *rather*, and *ten feet* cannot occur on their own in these cases.

With this test we can clearly distinguish heads from modifiers in the examples above. But we will need to be careful when applying this test, for in some cases the head of, for example, a noun phrase can be left out, as long as it is clear from the context what sort of entity is involved. In English, when you leave out the head of a NP, it is often replaced by the substitute head *one*, as in B's answer to A' s question in (42a).

(42) A: Would you like the red or the blue pen?
B: (a) I'd prefer [the blue one].
(b) I'd prefer [the blue Ø].

In other languages, Spanish being an example, an answer of type (42b) is the only option.

Spanish
(43) Prefiero el azul.
I prefer the blue.
'I prefer the blue one.'

El azul in (43) is then still a NP, with the head noun understood from the context.

Interestingly English does not allow the (42b) option if the indefinite article is used. It is not possible to say **I'd prefer a blue Ø.* Second language learners of English often make this mistake, especially if their first language is one like Spanish, where this construction is possible.

6.6 Constituent Structure

We saw in Section 6.3 that clauses consist of constituents, and in Section 6.4 we looked in greater detail at different types of phrases acting as constituents. The examples in Section 6.4 and Section 6.5 have shown that not only do clauses consist of constituents, but that constituents themselves can be complex too. Consider the following example (44) and its constituent structure.

(44) The very rude man laughed excessively.

The application of a replacement test shows us that there are just two constituents here (45).

(45) a Who laughed excessively? The very rude man.
b What did the very rude man do? Laugh excessively.

At the level of the clause we can therefore distinguish between two constituents: the NP *the impolite man* and the VP *laughed excessively*. Each of these phrases contains a head – *man* and *laughed* respectively – and modifiers: the AdjP *very rude* as part of the NP *the very rude man* and the AdvP *excessively* as part of the VP *laughed excessively*. Within the AdjP *very rude* we again distinguish a head *rude* and a further AdvP *very* as a modifier. The exact analysis would be as in (46) (ignoring, for the time being, the status of the article *the*). The successive steps of analysis are shown using indentation.

(46) Clause: The very rude man laughed excessively.
    NP: the very rude man
        Head: man
        AdjP: very rude
            Head: rude
            AdvP: very
                Head: very
    VP: laughed excessively
        Head: laughed
        AdvP: excessively
            Head: excessively

The same kind of information can also be represented in the form of a tree, as shown in Figure 6.3.

Note that in, for instance, the AdjP *very rude*, the head is *rude* and the modifier is *very*. This modifier in turn is a phrase in its own right – an AdvP consisting of just one word. This single word, *very*, is then the head of its phrase.

There are various usages and conventions for describing the constituent structure of an example like (44). In (46) we used the indentation method. An alternative way of representing the hierarchical structure of (44) is the tree diagram in Figure 6.3. Yet another possibility is the bracket method in (47), which was already used in simplified form in Section 6.2. Here the brackets are used to mark the boundaries of the constituents; the type of constituent involved is marked by subscripted abbreviations; heads are marked with H; and the C at the end of (47) stands for 'Clause'.

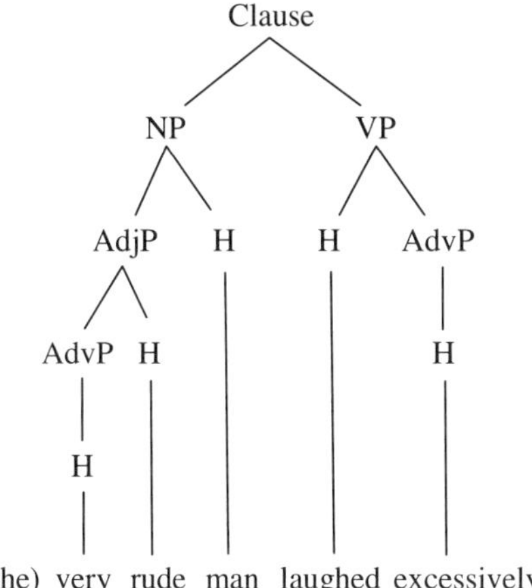

Figure 6.3 Tree diagram of (44).

(47) [[(the) [[very$_{H}$]$_{AdvP}$ rude$_{H}$]$_{AdjP}$ man$_{H}$]$_{NP}$ [laughed$_{H}$ [excessively$_{H}$]$_{AdvP}$]$_{VP}$]$_{C}$

The analysis in (47) is visually less transparent than the one in (46), but it takes up less space. It takes a little time to get used to, but then it clearly states, for example, that *laughed excessively* is a VP with *laughed* as its head. For a quick check count the left and right brackets: for the clause as a whole the number of left brackets should always equal the number of right brackets.

Let us go through the same steps again with the more complicated example in (48).

(48) The unbelievably tall woman rode remarkably slowly on the totally new bicycle.

With the help of a replacement test we can identify the phrases that this clause is made up of (49).

(49) a. Who rode remarkably slowly on the totally new bicycle?
The unbelievably tall woman.
b. What did the unbelievably tall woman do?
Cycle remarkably slowly.
c. On what did the unbelievably tall woman cycle remarkably slowly?
On the totally new bicycle.

At the level of the clause we can thus distinguish three constituents:

- the NP *the unbelievably tall woman;*
- the VP *rode remarkably slowly;*
- the AdpP *on the totally new bicycle.*

Each of these phrases contains a head: *woman*, *rode*, and *on* respectively, plus further phrases as obligatory constituents or as modifiers:

- the NP *the totally new bicycle* as part of the AdpP *on the totally new bicycle;*
- the AdjP *unbelievably tall* as part of the NP *the unbelievably tall woman;*
- the AdvP *remarkably slowly* as part of the VP *rode remarkably slowly.*

Within these phrases we again distinguish a head (*bicycle*, *tall*, and *slowly* respectively, and other phrases as modifiers:

- the AdjP *totally new* as part of the NP *the totally new bicycle;*
- the AdvP *unbelievably* as part of the AdjP *unbelievably tall;*
- the AdvP *remarkably* as part of the AdvP *remarkably slowly.*

And so we may continue the analysis until we have reached the last head. The exact analysis is as in (50) using the indentation method (leaving open, again, the status of the article *the*).

(50) Clause: The unbelievably tall woman rode remarkably slowly on the totally new bicycle.
- NP: the unbelievably tall woman
  - Head: woman
  - AdjP: unbelievably tall
    - Head: tall
    - AdvP: unbelievably
      - Head: unbelievably
- VP: rode remarkably slowly
  - Head: rode
  - AdvP: remarkably slowly
    - Head: slowly
    - AdvP: remarkably
      - Head: remarkably
- AdpP: on the totally new bicycle
  - Head: on
  - NP: the totally new bicycle
    - Head: bicycle
    - AdjP: totally new
      - Head: new
    - AdvP: totally
      - Head: totally

Figure 6.4 presents the same information in the form of a tree.

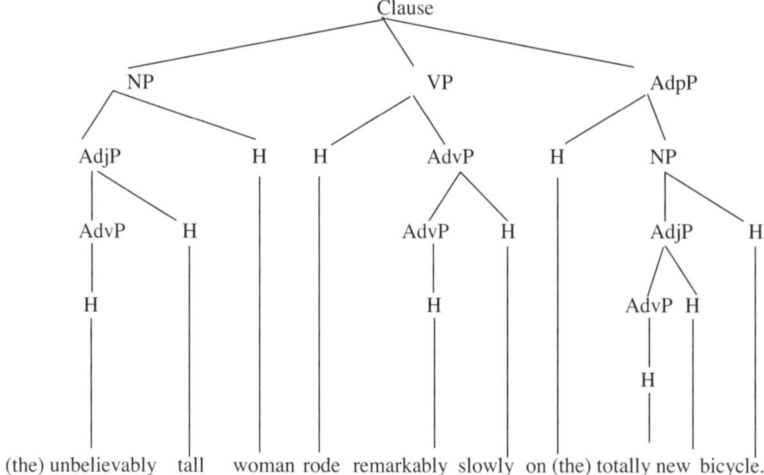

Figure 6.4 Tree diagram of (48).

And finally, the same information is given once more using the bracket method in (51).

(51) [[(the) [[unbelievably$_{H}$]$_{AdvP}$ tall$_{H}$]$_{AdjP}$ woman$_{H}$]$_{NP}$
[rode$_{H}$ [[remarkably$_{H}$]$_{AdvP}$ slowly$_{H}$]$_{AdvP}$]$_{VP}$
[on$_{H}$ [(the) [[totally$_{H}$]$_{AdvP}$ new$_{H}$]$_{AdjP}$ bicycle$_{H}$]$_{NP}$]$_{AdpP}$]$_{C}$

With some practice this type of analysis gets easier and easier.

6.7 Phrases Versus Words

In our analysis of (44) and (48) above we have moved from the overall, abstract constituent structure of the clause down to the level of individual words. First we divided the clause into phrases. Then we identified within each phrase its head, and set it apart from the remaining material. This remaining material was then again divided into one or more phrases, for which we identified the heads, etc. We continued our analysis until we only had heads left. These heads are the individual lexical words that constitute the clause.

This leaves us with one category of unanalysed words. In our analysis of (48) we have not yet said anything about the article *the*. This word is clearly part of the NP *the unbelievably tall woman*. The word *the* cannot be the head of this constituent, but neither does it have a modifying function within it. To clarify the status of this little word, we will have to make use of the distinction between content words and function words, first mentioned in Section 2.3 and to be discussed more in depth in Chapter 11. Words that are heads of phrases are all content words, that is words with a more or less concrete meaning.

Words that are not heads of constituents, at any level of analysis whatsoever, are function words, that is words with an abstract meaning and which have a structuring function in the construction of clauses. They are, as it were, the mortar between the bricks of the content words.

Thus, from the perspective of syntax (within which phrases are important units of analysis), it makes sense to divide words into content and function words. In the next two sections we will discuss these two, first content words and then function words.

6.8 Word Classes: Content Words

In the preceding discussion we have identified five types of phrases: NPs, VPs, AdjPs, AdvPs, and AdpPs. In English, the heads of these five phrase types belong to different **word classes**. The head of an NP is a **noun**, the head of a VP a **verb**, the head of an AdjP an **adjective**, the head of an AdvP an **adverb**, and the head of an AdpP an **adposition** (a preposition or a postposition, see Section 6.4). By way of illustration consider example (52).

(52) The new students answered the questions intelligently in class.

It is not too difficult to establish to what word categories the seven **content words** belong here. *Students*, *questions*, and *class* are nouns, *answered* is a verb, *new* is an adjective, *intelligently* is an adverb, and *in* is an adposition.

These word categories serve as the heads of their respective phrases, as we can see in the representation in (53).

(53) Clause: The new students answered the questions intelligently in class.
- NP: The new students
  - Head: students (**noun**)
  - AdjP: new
    - Head: new (**adjective**)
- VP: answered the questions intelligently
  - Head: answered (**verb**)
  - NP: the questions
    - Head: questions (**noun**)
  - AdvP: intelligently
    - Head: intelligently (**adverb**)
- AdpP: in class
  - Head: in (**adposition**)
  - NP: class
    - Head: class (**noun**)

The key principle here is that, in general, it is impossible for these five word categories to serve as the head of a different type of constituent. For instance, adjectives can modify nouns, adverbs cannot; adverbs can modify verbs, adjectives cannot, as illustrated in (54).

(54) *The newly students answered the questions intelligent in class.

Another way of stating this principle is to say that word categories are syntactic classes of words that are specially geared to serving as the head of a particular type of phrase.

Though this is to a large extent the case in English, it is not true for all languages. Not every language distinguishes a separate word category for each separate type of phrase head, as we can see in Samoan, a Polynesian language. From a syntactic point of view, any content word in this language can be used as the head of any type of phrase. The examples in (55) and (56) illustrate this flexibility of Samoan content words.

Samoan

(55) (a) Ua malosi le *la.*
aspect strong the sun
'The sun is hot.'
(b) Ua *la* le aso.
aspect sun the day
'It is a sunny day.' [Literally: 'The day sun-s.']

(56) (a) E *alu* le pasi i Apia.
generic aspect go the bus to Apia
'The bus goes to Apia.'
(b) o le pasi *alu* i Apia
presentative the bus go to Apia
'the going of the bus to Apia.'

The word *la* 'sun' is used in (55a) as the head of a NP, and in (55b) as the head of a VP. Similarly, in (56a) *alu* 'go' is used as the head of a VP, and in (56b) as the head of an AdjP. So, in addition to languages like English, which have specialised word classes serving as the head of different types of phrase, we also have languages like Samoan, where the function of head of various different types of phrase can be implemented by one single word category.

We conclude this section with a few remarks about what are traditionally called pronouns. Taken literally, a 'pronoun' stands for a noun, or rather for an NP. In the following example the word *him*, a personal pronoun, replaces a NP as in (57).

(57) *Caroline's husband* has left the city. I saw *him* take a train at the railway station.

Another example is given in (58), in which *who*, an interrogative pronoun, replaces a NP:

(58) *Who* is that? That is *Caroline's husband*.

The term 'pronoun' is sometimes also used for words that can replace other types of constituent, as in (59) and (60).

(59) *Which* car is John's? The *red* one.
(60) *How* does Gloria write? She writes *well*.

But the term 'pro-noun' is used incorrectly here. In (59) the question word replaces an AdjP and is therefore a 'pro-adjective', in (60) it replaces an AdvP and is therefore a 'pro-adverb'. In other languages we furthermore find question words that can systematically replace VPs. For instance, Dyirbal, an Australian Aboriginal language, has the verb *wiyami* meaning 'do what?' Dyirbal thus has a class of 'pro-verbs'.

6.9 Word Classes: Function Words

In Section 6.7 we made a distinction between content words and function words. Content words have a concrete meaning and they serve as the head of a phrase. Function words, in contrast, have grammatical meaning and structure the clause.

Some function words were originally content words and behave in the same way as content words as regards their form. This is for instance the case of *has* in (61).

(61) Carla *has* stolen a car.
(62) Carla *has* a car.

In (62) *has*, as a separate and individual word, has a concrete meaning (*possesses, owns*). *Has* is a content word in this example. In (61), however, *has* does not have a concrete meaning and only serves as a grammatical function word that marks the temporal localisation of the event that is being reported. But in terms of its form *has* in (61) behaves exactly like the lexical verb *has* in (62). Verbs like *have* in (62) are therefore called auxiliary verbs. Other auxiliary verbs in English are *be, must*, and *will*.

Example (63) gives an example from Spanish of a function word that behaves as if it were a content word.

Spanish

(63)	*este*	hombre	y	*esas*	mujeres
	this.*masculine.singular*	man	and	that.*feminine.plural*	women

'this man and those women'

Like other function words, *este* and *esas* in (63) do not contribute to the concrete meaning of the sentence. In telegraphic speech (see Section 2.3) we can leave out these two words without damage to the clause's content. Yet at the same time, *this* and *that* behave in many respects as if they were adjectives, as can be demonstrated with example (64).

Spanish

(64)	el	hombre	viejo	y	las	mujeres	viejas
	the	man	old.*masculine.singular*	and	the	women	old.*feminine.plural*

'the old man and the old women'

Just like the adjectives in (64), the words *este* and *esas* in (63) change their form depending on whether a noun is of the masculine or feminine gender and on whether it is in the singular or the plural. Thus the function words in (63) behave in certain ways like the content words in (64). They are called demonstratives.

Pure function words, those that have no corresponding content word class, have an invariable form and cannot be modified. They are usually called **particles**. The role of particles is to give a further specification of individual constituents. Take example (65) from Modern Greek.

Modern Greek

(65)	Tha	ime	edo	meta	ti	deftera.
	future	I.am	here	after	*the*	monday

'I will be here from Monday on.'

The definite article *ti* ('the') in (65) specifies the noun phrase *ti deftera* 'Monday' and characterises this as known to the listener. The time reference *tha* specifies the clause as a whole and places the event that is described in this clause in the future. Each of these two particles thus specifies a particular syntactic constituent. In (66) to (68) we see some more examples from Mandarin Chinese.

Mandarin Chinese

(66)	Nǐ	kāxīn	ma?
	you	happy	*question*

'Are you happy?'

(67)	Xiǎoxīn	ou.
	careful	*warning*

'Be careful, OK?'

(68)	Wǒmen	zǒu	ba.
	we	go	*encouragement*

'Let's go!'

As we showed in Section 5.2, languages use various means to indicate how a sentence should be interpreted as a speech act, that is, with what intention the speaker utters the sentence. Mandarin Chinese uses sentence final particles with this function. Thus the particle *ma* in (66) indicates that the sentence should be interpreted as a question, the particle *ou* in (67) that the sentence should be interpreted as a friendly warning, and the particle *ba* in (68) that the sentence should be interpreted as an encouragement.

SUMMARY

Independent **sentences** are made up of **constituents**. When these are sentence-like themselves they are called **clauses**, when they are based on a lexical head they are called **phrases**. Depending on their primarily **referential**, **predicative**, **attributive** or **relational** function we can distinguish between **noun phrases**, **verb phrases**, **adjective phrases**, **adverbial phrases** and **adpositional phrases**. Within each type of phrase we can further distinguish between obligatory **heads** and optional **modifiers**. Phrases may contain further phrases. Words that can serve as heads of phrases are **content words**, which can be subdivided into **word classes** (**noun**, **adjective**, **verb**, **adverb** and **adposition**), depending on the type of phrase of which they can be the head. In addition to content words there are **function words** that have a structuring function in the clause. These may borrow their form from other word classes, as in the case of auxiliary verbs; if they do not, they are called **particles**.

ASSIGNMENTS

1. In order to establish the psychological reality of syntactic rules and elements, researchers have carried out so-called 'click'-experiments. In one of these, people were presented with the following sentences and heard a click at the *-sign:
   (i) Your hope of marrying An*na was surely impractical
   (ii) In her hope of marrying An*na was surely impractical
   Why would the subjects in this experiment hear the click in (i) and (ii) in a different place than it really occurred?
   In which direction are they likely to have moved the 'click' in (i) and in (ii), and why?
2. Divide the following sentences into their main constituents and indicate whether these are NPs, VPs, AdjPs, AdvPs or AdpPs:
   (i) The young nurse seduced the rich patient with very sweet talk.
   (ii) On a beautiful day the old couple took a bus to the beach.
   (iii) Every four years a very important art exhibition is held in Kassel.

3. Determine what are the heads and the modifiers of the following constituents:
   (a) tough luck
   (b) a golden heart
   (c) remarkably simple
   (d) simply remarkable
4. In this chapter we have demonstrated three different ways of representing the complete constituent structure of sentences. Choose one of these to give a representation of the following sentence:
   (i) The badly prepared minister gave a thoroughly rude answer to the opposition.
5. Give a representation of the constituent structure of the following sentence, using one of the methods that you did not choose in the previous assignment:
   (i) Yesterday I met a very young professor in Linguistics.
6. Aphasia patients with brain damage in the Broca area (see Section 2.3) speak in a way that is illustrated in the fragment below, where incomprehensible words are represented as XXX. What strikes you as typical of the language of this patient, in particular in the domain of word classes?

Test leader	*Patient*
What do you usually do in the daytime?	Yes. . .yes. . .yes. . .yes. . .uu. . .be, a bit, knitting,. . .XXX
Some knitting?	Yes. . .be. . .kni. . .kni. . .knitting
Yes.	Yes. . .yes
Knitting. What are you making?	XXX [Moves a finger up and down and laughs]
Oh yes	No. . .no. . .no
With a needle, yes?	Yeesss
Yes. . .	Yes. . .XXXwer. . .yes
What else do you do?	Reading. . .writing
Writing?	Yes
Yes	Writing. . .yes. . .yes. . .yes
Writing letters	Writing letters

7. For each and every word in the sentence below, indicate its word class:
   (i) I am very much in love with the son of my neighbour.
8. Check where in the sentences below we have prepositions, postpositions, and particles:
   (i) He will probably not show up at the party.
   (ii) Well, in my opinion she should be at school more often.
   (iii) He took the shoes from under the table.
   (iv) If he doesn't show up I'll never talk to him again.

Test Yourself

1. Which tests can one use to establish how many constituents there are in a clause?
2. What type of constituent has a primarily referential function?
3. What is the crucial difference between adjectival and adverbial phrases?
4. Explain which element is the head and which is the modifier in the following example: *A beautiful book*.
5. What is the difference between content words and function words?
6. How does one define a noun?
7. Name two types of adpositions.
8. Which types of phrases can be replaced by pronouns?

Acknowledgments and Further Reading

There are many good introductions to syntax and constituent structure. Some recent ones include Fabb (2005) and Moravcsik (2006). The books written about the problems of word classes and word class systems could fill several libraries. A good general introduction is Evans (2000). The Samoan examples are from Mosel and Hovdhaugen (1992), the Dyirbal example is from Dixon (1972), the Greek example from Joseph and Philippaki-Warburton (1987), the Turkish from Lewis (1967), and the Mandarin Chinese from Li and Thompson (1981).

chapter 7

Simple Sentences

7.1 Introduction

In Chapter 6 we discussed how sentences can be divided into constituents and we saw how these constituents can be either clauses or phrases. On the basis of their semantic and syntactic properties five types of phrases could be distinguished: nominal, verbal, adjectival, adverbial, and adpositional phrases. This was in turn the basis for establishing word categories such as nouns, verbs, adpositions and so on. Within words a distinction was made between content words and function words. In Chapter 6 we were thus particularly concerned with the **categories** of constituents and words.

In this chapter, in contrast, we will discuss the **functions** that phrases serve in the construction of sentences. The point here is that phrases belong to a category on the one hand, but on the other hand serve a function in the clause. This point is of great importance in understanding many syntactic phenomena. To illustrate the distinction, let us consider the examples in (1).

(1) a. the least experienced burglar of the lot
    b. the police
    c. by the police
    d. was caught

Linguistics, First Edition. Edited by Anne E. Baker and Kees Hengeveld.

All examples in (1) are phrases. To identify the category of such phrases, all we need to do is to examine their structure. Thus, in (1a) and (1b) we see we have noun phrases, in (1c) an adpositional phrase, and in (1d) a verb phrase. But when it comes to identifying the function of phrases, we cannot take the phrases just on their own. On the basis of (1a) and (1b) alone we can say nothing about the functions that these two noun phrases may have in a sentence. Take an example like (2).

(2) *The least experienced burglar of the lot* was caught *by the police.*

It is only when we know its syntactic context that we can say that the noun phrase *the least experienced burglar of the lot* is the subject of the sentence. This same noun phrase may, however, also be used in a different syntactic context, as in (3).

(3) *The police* caught *the least experienced burglar of the lot.*

In this case, the first element in the sentence is not *the least experienced burglar of the lot*, but *the police*. In fact the distribution of syntactic roles in (2) is different from that in (3). At the same time, however, the meanings of (2) and (3) are not so very different. In both cases it is the police who are doing the catching, and the burglar who is being caught. In other words, the distribution of the roles of the participants in (2) and (3) is the same.

In Section 7.2 we will discuss in more detail the different functions that phrases may serve in a sentence. Then in Section 7.3 we will demonstrate that some phrases require the presence of one or more other phrases. Semantic roles will be discussed in Section 7.4, grammatical roles in Section 7.5, and how these are marked in Section 7.6. Finally, in Section 7.7, Section 7.8 and Section 7.9 we will discuss three situations in which it is possible to leave out a phrase or where it is necessary to express it in a specific way.

7.2 Functions of Phrases Within the Sentence

In sentences (4) to (7) the italicised parts belong to different phrase categories, but they all serve the same function.

(4) John *laughed.*
(5) Ian's mum is *seriously ill.*
(6) Mary is *my best friend.*
(7) The dog is *in the garden.*

The function that all these phrases have in these sentences is that of **predicate**. A predicate expresses a relation between the referents of other constituents in the clause or it specifies a property of the referent of another constituent. In (4) *laughed* says something about *John*; in (5) *seriously ill* says something about

Ian's mum; in (6) *my best friend* says something about *Mary*; and in (7) *in the garden* says something about *the dog*. As explained in Section 6.4, the function of predicate is typically expressed by verb phrases, as in (4). But other types of phrase are equally possible. In (5) the predicate is an adjective phrase, in (6) it is a noun phrase, and in (7) an adpositional phrase. In languages like English, nominal, adjectival, and adpositional phrases have to be accompanied by the auxiliary verb *to be* when they are used as predicates, thus forming a verb phrase. In many other languages this is not the case. In Russian, for example, such an auxiliary verb can be left out under certain conditions, as we can see in example (8).

Russian
(8) Jego anglijskoe proiznošenie otličnoe.
his English pronunciation excellent
'His pronunciation of English is excellent.'

This also holds for Tamil, spoken in India and Sri Lanka (9), the variety of Arabic spoken in Cairo (10), and British Sign Language (11).

Tamil
(9) Avaru oru daktar.
he one doctor
'He is a doctor.'

Cairene Arabic
(10) Hijja mudarris-a.
she teacher-*feminine.singular*
'She is a teacher.'

British Sign Language
(11) There is a toilet.

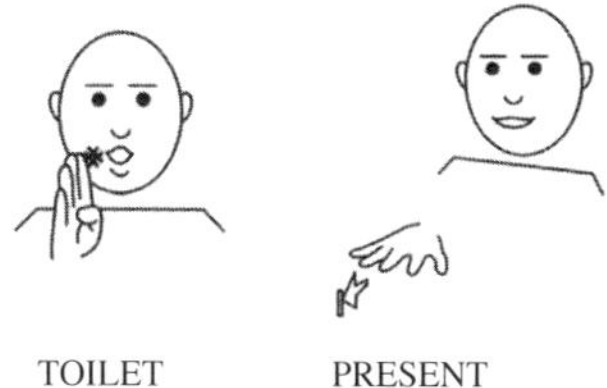

From such examples we can see that, although verb phrases typically act as predicates, other types of phrases can have the predicative function as well.

In addition to the function of predicate, phrases may have two other functions at the level of the sentence: argument and adjunct. It is important to distinguish these two functions and example (12) illustrates the difference.

(12) Yesterday Sylvie walked along the beach.

Here, the verb *walked* functions as the predicate of the clause. The event described by *walked* requires at least one participant, that is the one who did the walking. For a correct use of this predicate, the clause therefore needs to contain at least one other constituent, the noun phrase that describes the one who did the walking. In (12) this is *Sylvie*. A variant of (12) such as (13) that does not contain this phrase is ungrammatical.

(13) *Yesterday walked along the beach.

Phrases that are obligatorily associated with a predicate are known as **arguments**. In (12) therefore, *Sylvie* is an argument of *walked*. Note that the linguistic term 'argument' as used here is different in meaning to the term 'argument' in everyday English.

Returning to (12) we can see that it also contains phrases like *yesterday* and *along the beach*, that are rather more loosely associated with the predicate. These phrases can in fact be left out without any problem, as we can see in the following variant of (12), which is grammatical.

(14) Sylvie walked.

Constituents that are not required by a predicate are known as **adjuncts**. The constituents *yesterday* and *along the beach* in (12) are therefore adjuncts.

We saw earlier that there is no one-to-one-relation between the function of predicate and the type of constituent which serves that function. In the same way the functions of argument and adjunct can be expressed by a range of different types of constituent. In (12), for example, we have an adverbial phrase (*yesterday*) and an adpositional phrase (*along the beach*) serving as adjuncts. Arguments are very often expressed by noun phrases such as *Sylvie* in (12), but we also find other types of constituents serving this function, such as the adverbial phrase *rather badly* in (15), or the adpositional constituent *in Paris* in (16).

(15) Richard behaved rather badly.
(16) Richard lives in Paris.

The verb *behave* as it is used in (15) requires two arguments, representing the person who does the behaving and the way in which he or she behaves. The latter is expressed in (15) by the adverbial phrase *rather badly*. The verb *live* likewise requires two arguments in (16), representing the person who lives somewhere and the place where he or she lives. The latter is expressed in (16) by the adpositional phrase *in Paris*.

7.3 Valency

The key point that emerges from the preceding section is that the predicate has a central role in determining the various functions within the sentence as a whole. For the formation of a grammatical sentence, it is necessary for a predicate to co-occur with a specific number of arguments. Take for example the verb *buy* in the sentences in (17). How many arguments does it require?

(17) a. Charles bought the newspaper.
b. *Charles bought
c. *Bought the newspaper

On the basis of (17) we can say that *buy* requires two arguments, one to describe the buyer, the other to describe what is bought. The number of arguments that necessarily accompanies a predicate is its **valency**. A predicate that requires just one argument is known as a **one-place predicate**; if it requires two arguments it is a **two-place predicate**; and with three arguments it is a **three-place predicate**. One-place predicates are also known as **intransitive**, and two- and three-place predicates as **transitive** and **ditransitive** respectively. The examples in (18) to (24) contain predicates with different valencies. The grammatical version is shown in (a) and the ungrammatical variants in (b) and (c), showing that the various arguments are indeed obligatory.

(18) a. Gianni walked. [one-place predicate: *walk*]
b. *Walked

(19) a. Hadil is a carpenter. [one-place predicate: *(be) a carpenter*]
b. *Is a carpenter

(20) a. Anne is outside. [one-place predicate: *(be) outside*]
b. *Is outside

(21) a. The queen cut the ribbon. [two-place predicate: *cut*]
b. *Cut the ribbon
c. *The queen cut

(22) a. Mary is fond of chocolate. [two-place predicate: *(be) fond of*]
b. *Is fond of chocolate
c. *Mary is fond

(23) a. Lisa is from China. [two-place predicate: *(be) from*]
b. *Is from China
c. *Lisa is from

(24) a. Mabel put the book on the shelf [three-place predicate: *put*]
b. *Put the book on the shelf
c. *Mabel put the book
d. *Mabel put on the shelf

The valency of a predicate determines the number of arguments that must accompany it. We must immediately add here that in certain contexts an argument may be left out, for example in the case of the three-place predicate *give*. In example (25) all three arguments have been realised.

(25) Sophie gave Sarah the paint box.

But in a context where two people are queuing to give Sarah a birthday present, that is in a very clear context, it is possible for Tom to ask Sophie the question in (26).

(26) What are you giving then?

In this case the three-place predicate *give* has not, all of a sudden, turned into a two-place verb. Rather, the third argument, Sarah, is understood. In the non-linguistic context this is clear enough, and so it is not necessary to make the argument explicit.

When we want to determine the number of arguments of a particular predicate, we have to be able to do it leaving all sorts of special contexts aside. A handy way of doing this is to replace the arguments by indefinite words such as *somebody*, *something* and *somewhere*, as in the examples (27) to (31).

(27) Walk - *somebody* (1) walked.
(28) Carpenter - *somebody* (1) (is a) carpenter.
(29) Cut - *somebody* (1) cut *something* (2).
(30) Love - *somebody* (1) loves *something* (2).
(31) Put - *somebody* (1) put *something* (2) on *something* (3).

So far we have restricted ourselves to predicates with one, two or three arguments. Predicates with more than three arguments are rare but not impossible, as with the English **four-place predicate** *exchange* (32).

(32) Exchange - *somebody* (1) exchanged *something* (2) with *somebody* (3) for *something* (4).

Now ask yourself how many arguments are required by the predicates in (33) and (34).

(33) a. snow
b. (be) nice weather

(34) a. (be) six o'clock
b. (be) night

As you will have noticed, these predicates do not require any argument at all: they are **zero-place predicates**. These predicates describe events which do not require the presence of one or more participants. The weather and time expressions in (33) and (34) belong to this category. It is impossible to specify an argument for these predicates as we can see in (35) and (36).

(35) a. snow: **somebody*/**something* is snowing.
b. (be) nice weather: **somebody*/**something* is nice weather.

(36) a. (be) six o'clock: **somebody*/**something* is six o'clock.
b. (be) night: **somebody*/**something* is night.

There are languages that do not allow zero-place predicates to be used. Such languages, among them English, French or Danish, require a dummy word instead, as a kind of pseudo-argument, as in such constructions as (37), (38) and (39).

(37) *It* is raining.

French
(38) *Il* pleut.
it rains
'It is raining.'

Danish
(39) *Det* fryser ti grader.
it freezes ten degrees
'It is ten below zero.'

It is easy to demonstrate that words like *it* (36), *il* (37) and *det* (38) are indeed pseudo-arguments. They cannot be replaced by words with a more specific meaning, not even by general words such as *somebody* or *something*, as we saw in (34) and (35).

In many other languages such as Latin (40), Indonesian (41) or Basque (42) zero-place predicates are realised without such dummy words or pseudo-arguments.

Latin
(40) Pluit.
rains
'It is raining.'

Indonesian
(41) Hujan.
rains
'It is raining.'

Basque
(42) Izotza egin du.
ice done has
'It has been freezing.'

As we showed in example (26) it is possible to leave an argument unexpressed when it is understood from the context. The following Spanish example (43) illustrates this again.

Spanish
(43) Lleg-ó.
arrive-*past.third singular*
'He arrived.'

Here the verb *llegar* 'arrive' does require an argument, the person arriving, but Spanish allows this argument to remain unexpressed when it can be retrieved from the context.

Quite clearly then, verbs differ in the number of arguments they require and languages vary considerably as to whether and how they have to realise such arguments.

7.4 SEMANTIC ROLES

Noun phrases describe entities, as we explained in Section 6.4. But when we consider noun phrases in their function of argument or adjunct, we find they describe entities that play different roles in the event described in the sentence. These roles are known under the technical term of **semantic roles**. The following example (44), describing the game of Cluedo, can demonstrate what we mean by this.

(44) Colonel Mustard killed Miss Scarlet in the kitchen with a gun.

In (44) there are four participants: *Colonel Mustard*, *Miss Scarlet*, *the kitchen* and *a gun*. Note that just like 'argument', the term 'participant' here has a different meaning from that of the same word in everyday language, which only refers to persons who are taking part in something. The first two participants are obligatory; the verb *kill* is a two-place predicate that requires two arguments: the person killing, and the living thing that is killed. The last two participants in (44) may be left out; if they are, we still have a grammatical clause. In the event that is described here, *Colonel Mustard* was the person carrying out the action, *Miss Scarlet* the one undergoing it, *the kitchen* the place where the action was carried out, and *a gun* the instrument with which the action was carried out. The technical terms for these four roles are:

- **Agent**: the entity that takes the initiative for an event, the acting person;
- **Patient**: the entity undergoing the action;
- **Location**: the place where an event occurs or an entity is located;
- **Instrument**: the entity used to carry out the action.

Example (45) also contains an agent and a patient, but this time they are accompanied by a **recipient**, that is the entity that receives something, and (46) contains a **source**, that is the entity something originates from.

(45) *The millionaire* (agent) donated *his fortune* (patient) to *Médecins sans Frontières* (recipient).

(46) *The student* (agent) took *a book* (patient) from *the shelf* (source).

7.5 Grammatical Roles

Consider now the distribution of roles in (47).

(47) a. Hannibal Lecter murdered two detectives.
b. Two detectives were murdered by Hannibal Lecter.

The semantic roles in (47a) and (47b) are exactly the same. In both cases *Hannibal Lecter* is the agent, and the *two detectives* the patient. The two clauses describe the same event, with the same distribution of roles amongst the participants. The differences in form between (47a) and (47b) do not point to a difference in meaning between these two clauses, but to a difference in formulation (see Section 2.5.2). Example (47a) presents the event from the perspective of the agent, and example (47b) from the perspective of the patient. To describe this more precisely, we say that, as well as having a semantic role, a constituent also has a **grammatical role**. The constituent that determines the perspective of a sentence has the grammatical role of **subject**. We call this a grammatical role because to a very large extent the subject determines the construction of the clause. The different structure of (47a) and (47b) is a case in point: (47a) is an **active** clause, (47b) a **passive** clause. An active clause is a clause with a transitive predicate where the agent is the subject. A passive clause also has a transitive predicate but here the patient is the subject. In English, the verb in active clauses has a specific form called 'active', whereas in passive clauses the passive auxiliary *to be* has to be added.

The examples above serve to illustrate a number of properties of subjects. In many languages the subject occupies a special position. For example, the constituents *Hannibal Lecter*, agent and subject in (47a), and *the two detectives*, patient and subject in (47b), both occupy the initial position in the sentence.

In many languages the form of the verb depends on the subject too. Thus, in (47b), the form *were* is determined by the plural subject *two detectives*, other forms of the verb *to be* are not possible, as we see in (48).

(48) *Two detectives was murdered by Hannibal Lecter.

Another characteristic property of the subject is that often its semantic role is not explicitly marked. In (47a), in which the agent is the subject, there is no specific marking. On the other hand, in English the agent role of *Hannibal Lecter*, where it is not the subject, is marked in (47b) using the preposition *by*. Again, this is obligatory, as (49) shows.

(49) a. *By Hannibal Lecter murdered two detectives.
b. *Two detectives were murdered Hannibal Lecter.

Now consider the two examples in (50). What are the semantic roles of the phrases here, and which one is the subject?

(50) a. The father gave a Mercedes to his daughter.
b. The father gave his daughter a Mercedes.

Again we see that, despite differences of form, the semantic roles expressed are the same. Both in (50a) and (50b) *the father* is the agent, *a Mercedes* is the patient and *his daughter* the recipient. In both clauses *the father* is also the subject. So here, the differences in form are not related to the semantic roles nor to the grammatical role of subject.

The grammatical similarity between (50a) and (50b) becomes clearer when we compare the patient *a Mercedes* in (50a) and the recipient *his daughter* in (50b). Both occupy the same position in the clause, immediately to the right of the verb, and both occur without a preposition. Despite their different semantic roles, the grammatical behaviour of these two constituents is exactly the same, and this is a reflection of the fact that they serve the same grammatical role, that of **object**. In (50a) the patient *a Mercedes* is the object, and in (50b) the recipient *his daughter* is the object. Again, as with the active-passive distinction in (50a-b), this involves a difference in the perspective from which the event is being presented. This time, however, it is not the subject perspective, but the so-called secondary perspective, that of the object.

In terms of their semantic and grammatical roles we can now describe the similarities and differences between (50a) and (50b) as in (51).

(51)					
	a.	The father	gave	a Mercedes	to his daughter.
		agent-subject		patient-object	recipient
	b.	The father	gave	his daughter	a Mercedes.
		agent-subject		recipient-object	patient

Note that in many approaches to grammar the term 'direct object' is used for what we here call 'object' and where we use the term 'recipient' the term 'indirect object' is often used. This traditional terminology, however, obscures the distinction between semantic and grammatical roles that we are emphasising here.

7.6 The Marking of Semantic and Grammatical Roles

Languages use different means to express semantic and grammatical roles. Consider first the English example (52).

(52) Charlie was hit with a hockey stick by Susan.

Example (52) has three participants that are involved in the event that is described by the predicate *hit*: an agent (Susan), a patient (Charlie) and an instrument (a hockey stick). As we can see here, English can use prepositions to express semantic roles. That *Susan* is the agent is indicated by the preposition *by* in (52) and that the *hockey stick* is the instrument is clear from the use of *with*. English does not need a preposition to indicate the patient. Grammatical roles are instead marked through the absence of a preposition, as shown in (53).

(53) Susan hit Charlie with a hockey stick.

In (53) Susan is still the agent of the action of hitting, yet this is no longer marked by the preposition *by*, as Susan is the subject of the sentence here.

In Finnish – as we can see in (54) – semantic roles are expressed in a quite different way.

Finnish

(54)	Annan	kirja-n	tei-lle.
	I.will.give	book-*accusative*	you-*dative*
	'I will give you the book.'		

In this example the different roles of the participants in the event are not indicated, as in English, by separate words such as prepositions, but by changing the form of the head of the noun phrase. Such special forms of noun phrases are known as **cases**. Finnish is a language rich in case. In (54) the so-called accusative case is used to indicate the patient, and the dative case marks the recipient.

Marathi, a language from India, uses the instrumental case to mark instruments (55).

Marathi

(55)	Mī	sābṇā-ne	hāt	dhutle.
	I	soap-*instrumental*	hands	washed
	'I washed my hands with soap.'			

Languages vary in whether they use case forms or adpositions to express semantic roles and, if they do use them, there is also considerable variation in that use.

7.7 Reduction of Valency

Having seen the various functions and roles that constituents can serve within a clause, we now return to the distinction between transitive and intransitive predicates we first introduced in Section 7.3. The transitive/intransitive distinction is not expressed in the same way in all languages. We begin with some clauses from English in (56) to (58).

(56) The waiter is opening the windows.
(57) The windows are being opened (by the waiter).
(58) The windows are opening.

Example (57) is the passive variant of (56). But what about (58)? Is that a passive clause too? In (56) we can infer from the singular form of the verb that the agent-argument *the waiter* is the subject of this active clause. In (57) the subject is *the windows*, and so the verb has a plural form. In passive clauses the constituent with the semantic role of patient always has the grammatical role of subject. In (58), however, we find a construction that is not passive, but still has the patient argument *the windows* as its subject, again reflected in the plural form of the verb.

There are a number of parallels in the structure of (57) and (58). Both have the patient-argument to the left of the verb, which in English is the subject position. In both the verb is plural and agrees with the plural subject. There are also, however, at least two important differences. Example (57) is definitely a passive clause, since it has the passive auxiliary, whereas (58) does not. The second important difference is that the agent can be expressed in (57), while this is impossible in (58), as (59) demonstrates.

(59) *The windows are opening by the waiter.

The various similarities and differences between (57) and (58) are all related to the fact that in (57) we have the transitive verb *open*, a two-place predicate which takes an agent and a patient as its arguments. In (58), on the other hand, we have the intransitive verb *open*, which only takes a patient-argument. Passivisation can only take place when the subject role is assigned to the patient-argument of a transitive predicate. *Open* in (56) and (57) is such a transitive predicate, *open* in (58) and (59) is intransitive.

In English this difference is not expressed in the form of the constituents that are involved. In many other languages, however, this is quite common. Examples (60) and (61) show how Swahili makes this distinction. The addition of the bracketed part in (61) results in an ungrammatical sentence.

Swahili

(60) Juma a-li-fungu-a mlango.
Juma he-*past*-open-*indicative* door
'Juma opened the door.'

(61) Mlango u-li-fungu-k-a (*na Juma)
door it-*past*-open-*intransitive-indicative* (*by Juma)
'The door opened.'

The base form of the verb *fungu* 'to open' is transitive, as we can see in (60). In (61) we see that the intransitive variant of this verb is formed by adding the element -*k* 'intransitive'. This suffix reduces the valency of the predicate *fungu* from two arguments to one: the agent-argument can no longer be expressed in (61). This phenomenon – the lowering of the number of arguments that is required by a verb – is known as **valency-reduction.** This process is clearly visible in Swahili, but is just as relevant to the analysis of English.

While in Swahili reduction of valency is marked by a change in form of the verb, in other languages it may be expressed through separate words, as for example in the Spanish examples (62) and (63).

Spanish

(62) Juan rompió el vaso.
John broke the glass
'John broke the glass.'

(63) El vaso se rompió (*por Juan).
the glass *intransitive* broke (*by John)
'The glass broke.'

In (63) the little word *se* indicates that the valency of the transitive verb *romper* ('break') has been reduced. The resulting verb *romper-se* (literally 'break itself') cannot take an agent-argument, as (63) demonstrates: the addition of *por Juan* results in an ungrammatical clause. We can summarise the situation in Spanish as follows: if a transitive verb (*romper*) changes into an intransitive verb (*romper-se*) through reduction of valency, the derived intransitive verb describes a situation in which only one participant is involved. In (63) this is *el vaso*. The original verb, the transitive *romper*, was a two-place predicate describing a situation involving two participants, an agent (*Juan*) and a patient (*el vaso*).

7.8 Reflexive Constructions

Languages like Spanish make use of a word such as *se* (as in *romper-se* 'break itself') for the reduction of valency. A comparable form in German is *sich*, illustrated in (64).

German

(64) Das Kind wäscht sich.
The child washes itself
'The child is washing itself.'

How many participants are involved in this German example? The verb *waschen* is a two-place predicate (*somebody* washes *something*), which takes an agent (*das Kind*) and a patient (*sich*). But in (64) there is only one participant, the child, which both carries out and undergoes the action of washing. That is, the two arguments, *das Kind* and *sich*, refer to the same entity. In a sense, therefore, (64) is expressing the sentence in (65), assuming that the two children are identical.

(65) Das Kind wäscht das Kind.
The child washes the child
'The child is washing the child.'

Put differently, we can say that in this case the agent and the patient have the same referent. They are **co-referential**. Instead of repeating the noun phrase *das Kind*, German uses the **reflexive pronoun** *sich*. Example (64) is a **reflexive construction**.

Notice that in this German reflexive construction we do not have reduction of valency, since *waschen* in (64) is and remains a two-place predicate. So there is a clear difference between valency reduction and reflexivisation. Yet in many languages reflexive constructions and constructions realising valency reduction closely resemble each other. Thus, in (63), Spanish expresses the valency reduction of *romper* with the word *se* and this is also the reflexive pronoun, as shown in (66).

Spanish

(66) Juan se lava.
John himself washes
'John is washing himself.'

In (66) *se* is a reflexive pronoun, which – just as in the German example (64) – expresses the co-reference between agent and patient. But in (63) *se* is an expression of the reduction of valency; it does not express any (co-)reference, but is part of the derived intransitive verb *romper-se* ('break').

Reflexive constructions and constructions with valency reduction are thus very similar. The key point is that in both cases we have a construction that has one referent less than is usual in the transitive construction. In reflexive constructions, such as (64) and (66), the one referent has a double role: it occurs as an argument twice and with two different semantic roles. The verb still is a two-place predicate. In constructions with valency reduction, on the other hand, the one referent has only a single role. One of the two arguments, together with its semantic role, has disappeared – the meanings have fused and the verb has changed into a one-place intransitive predicate.

7.9 Pronominalisation

As we saw in Section 7.8, example (64), *Das Kind wäscht sich* really stands for *Das Kind wäscht das Kind* (65). An alternative way of saying this is that the second *Kind* in (65) has been replaced by *sich* in (64). The use of *sich* here is a case of **pronominalisation**. Let us now look at examples (67) and (68). How can we explain the differences between them?

(67) Eve sent the letter to herself.
(68) Eve sent the letter to her.

In (67) *Eve* is both agent and recipient. There is co-reference here between these two arguments, and the form *herself* is used to express this. In (68), on the other hand, Eve is the agent but another female person is the recipient. So we do not have co-reference and therefore do not need a reflexive pronoun; the regular personal pronoun *her* will suffice. Pronouns such as *her* in (68) can be used when an entity in the speech situation is sufficiently known to the hearer, as we discussed already in Section 4.5 and will deal with in more detail in Section 10.4. In (69) we find the same situation. Here, the two pronouns in the second clause refer back to two entities that have been mentioned in the preceding clause. Rather than repeat *Charlie* and *the book*, the pronouns *he* and *it* are used respectively.

(69) Charlie got a book. *He* read *it* the next day.

In this context everyone will interpret *he* as 'Charlie' and *it* as 'the book'.

In a number of languages pronouns can be left out when they are the subject. As we showed earlier in Section 7.3, Indonesian is such a language, and so is Latin. Try to determine for the Latin example in (70) which arguments the verb *habere* 'have' has, and how these arguments are expressed.

Latin
(70) Libr-um habe-o.
book-*accusative* have-*1.singular.present*
'I have a/the book.'

The verb *habere* has two arguments (*somebody* has *something*). Yet in (70) only one argument, the object *librum*, is expressed as a separate noun phrase. The subject – the first person singular who carries out the action *habere* – can only be identified on the basis of the verb ending *-o*; there is no pronoun here to refer to the 'I'. This is in contrast to languages such as English where the subject always has to be expressed separately. The phenomenon of leaving out the subject is known as **pro-drop**: the pronoun is 'dropped'.

The various sections of this chapter have demonstrated that, if we want to understand a range of syntactic phenomena, it is important to carefully distinguish between the various functions which constituents can serve. In this chapter we concentrated on syntactic phenomena within clauses. In the next chapter we will take a closer look at relations between clauses.

SUMMARY

Phrases not only belong to a particular type or **category**, but they also serve particular **functions** within a sentence. Within a sentence we distinguish between the functions of **predicate**, **argument** and **adjunct**. The way in which phrases serving the first two of these functions can be combined with each other is determined by the **valency** of the predicate. Predicates may be accompanied by one, two, three, four or zero arguments and are then called **one-place**, **two-place**, **three-place**, **four-place** or **zero-place predicates** respectively. A one-place predicate is also known as **intransitive**, while predicates with two and three arguments are known as **transitive** and **ditransitive** respectively. Arguments and adjuncts can be further characterised by their **semantic** and **grammatical roles**. Amongst the semantic roles we find **agent**, **patient**, **instrument**, **location**, **recipient**, and **source**, while **subject** and **object** are grammatical roles. The bound expression forms of semantic and grammatical roles are called **cases**. The need to distinguish between these different kinds of roles is highlighted by the existence of **active** and **passive** sentence pairs, which can be seen as the outcome of the assignment of the grammatical role of subject to constituents with different semantic roles. Related to passive sentences are constructions involving **valency reduction**. Formally, these are often related to **reflexive constructions**. In the latter type of construction two arguments have the same referent: they are **co-referential**, and one of the arguments is expressed by a **reflexive pronoun**. In reflexive constructions we therefore encounter **pronominalisation**, a concept that is also necessary for a proper understanding of the process of **pro-drop**.

ASSIGNMENTS

1. For each of the italicised parts of the following sentences, indicate whether it is a predicate, an argument, or an adjunct, and why this is so:
   (a) *The doctor* is not at home.
   (b) *As a doctor*, I have to warn you not to smoke.
   (c) The chairman is *a doctor*.

2. Determine for each of the following words how many arguments it takes:
   (a) put
   (b) brother
   (c) go
   (d) ill
3. Identify the semantic roles of the participants in the following sentences. Then do the same for their grammatical roles:
   (a) The chimpanzee opened the coconut with his teeth.
   (b) The stowaway was thrown overboard by the captain.
   (c) The rings were handed to the bridegroom by his best man.
4. Consider the following Indonesian sentences:

   (a) John mem-buka pintu itu.
   John *active*-open door that
   'John opened that door.'
   (b) Pintu itu di-buka (oleh John).
   Door that *passive*-open (by John)
   'That door was opened by John.'
   (c) Pintu itu ter-buka.
   Door that *intransitive*-open
   'That door is open.'

   Can you give a systematic comparison and description of the similarities and differences in valency and subject between these sentences?
5. Reduction of valency is only one way in which a verb can be derived from another verb. How would you describe the derivation of the causative verb in Hungarian, in sentences (b), from the non-causative verbs in (a)?

   (a) Mari kimos-t-a a ruhak-at.
   Marie.*nominative* wash-*past tense-3.sing* the clothes-*accusative*
   'Marie washed the clothes.'
   (b) Peter Mari-val kimos-at-t-a a ruhak-at
   Peter.*nom* Marie-*instrument* wash-*causative-past-3.sing* the clothes-*accusative*
   'Peter made Marie wash the clothes.'

6. In which of the following sentences do we have co-reference?
   (a) Peter excused himself.
   (b) I am going to do it just like you.
   (c) She told him clearly.
   (d) The only one he has to thank for this luck is himself.
   (e) In itself, it won't do any harm if you tell him the truth.

Test Yourself

1. What is the difference between the type of a phrase and its function?
2. Which three important functions must be distinguished at the level of the sentence?
3. Give two examples of zero-place predicates.
4. How can semantic roles be expressed in form?
5. What is the difference between semantic and grammatical roles?
6. What is a reflexive construction?
7. What are the characteristics of a pro-drop language? Is English a pro-drop language?

Acknowledgments and Further Reading

The importance of functions in the analysis of clauses has been emphasised in particular in the framework of Functional Grammar (Dik 1997) and of Role and Reference Grammar (Van Valin and LaPolla 1997). The role of semantic functions in grammar was described in Fillmore (1968). The Russian example was provided by Igor Nedjalkov. The Tamil examples are taken from Asher (1982), the Cairene Arabic from Olmsted and Gamal-Eldin (1982), the Swahili from Ashton (1944), and the Marathi from Pandharipande (1997).

chapter 8

Complex Sentences

8.1 Introduction

In Section 6.3 we briefly discussed the distinction between simple and complex sentences using examples (1) and (2).

(1) He knows [the answer].
(2) He knows [that the earth is round].

In (1) the two arguments of the verb *know* are realised as noun phrases, *he* and *the answer*. In (2) one argument is realised as a noun phrase, *he*, but the other one is not a phrase, but a sentence-like construction. We called such sentence-like constructions clauses. They combine with a main clause to form a sentence as in (2). In Chapters 6 and 7 we focused on sentences with phrases as constituents, as in (1), but in this chapter we will concentrate on sentences with clauses as constituents. We will look in more detail at clauses of the type as in (2), called embedded clauses, in Section 8.2, and at the forms they can take in Section 8.3. In some cases main and embedded clauses interact with each other, when, for example, they have the same subject. The consequences this can have will be discussed in Section 8.4. Finally we will discuss a different

Linguistics, First Edition. Edited by Anne E. Baker and Kees Hengeveld.

type of clause, in which the clause is not an argument of the main clause but is more independent, as in (3).

(3) Fatima is a hairdresser and her sister is a carpenter.

The clauses of sentences like (3) are called coordinated clauses and will be discussed in Section 8.5. The forms they can take will be studied in Section 8.6.

8.2 The Functions of Embedded Clauses

In Chapter 7 we looked at the functions of phrases in the construction of sentences. Embedded clauses may have the same functions as phrases. In order to illustrate this, take a look at (4) and decide what the predicate is.

(4) Eve believes Charles stole this bicycle.

The predicate of (4) is *believes*. This predicate requires two arguments (*somebody* believes *something*). The 'believer' in this case is Eve, and what she believes is not *Charles*, or *this bicycle*, but the whole of the rest of the clause, that is *Charles stole this bicycle*. This is also evident when we apply the substitution test as in (5).

(5) Eve believes it.

In other words, one of the arguments of the predicate *believe* is not expressed by a noun phrase, but by a clause, which in turn has a complex structure itself. Example (4) thus demonstrates that clauses (Cl) can contain other clauses as their constituents. To see this most clearly we need a detailed analysis of the constituent structure of (4).

(6) Cl: Eve believes Charles stole this bicycle.
- VP: believes
  - Head: believes
- NP: Eve
  - Head: Eve
- Cl: Charles stole this bicycle
  - VP: stole this bicycle
    - Head: stole
    - NP: this bicycle
      - Head: bicycle
  - NP: Charles
    - Head: Charles

As can be seen clearly in (6), the clause *Eve believes Charles stole this bicycle* contains another clause, *Charles stole this bicycle*. A clause that is contained within another clause is known as an **embedded clause**. A clause that is not embedded is known as a **main clause**.

An embedded clause is often introduced by a conjunction. A conjunction is a grammatical word. In Sections 6.6 and 6.7, when analysing simple sentences, we ignored grammatical words such as articles, and we will do the same here. We will thus leave conjunctions unanalysed when establishing the constituent structure of a sentence. An example of such an analysis is given in (7).

(7)	Cl:	Sheila walked to the shop because she needed sugar.				
		NP:	Sheila			
			Head:	Sheila		
		VP:	walked			
			Head:	walked		
		AdpP:	to the shop			
			Head:	to		
			NP:	the shop		
				Head:	shop	
		Cl:	because she needed sugar			
			VP:	needed sugar		
				Head:	needed	
				NP:	sugar	
					Head:	sugar
			NP:	she		
				Head:	she	

So there are clauses that may serve as constituents within other clauses, often with the intervention of a conjunction. The convention we shall follow in the remainder of this chapter is to put such embedded clauses within square brackets, as we did in earlier chapters with other types of constituent.

The question now is: What functions can such constituents serve in the clause as a whole? Try to work out the functions of the embedded clauses in examples (8) to (11).

(8) Fatima thought [that the bus wasn't running].
(9) Fatima stayed at home [because the bus wasn't running].
(10) Fatima's reason for staying at home was [that the bus wasn't running].
(11) The bus [that wasn't running] was an oldtimer.

The predicate in (8) is *think*. This is a two-place-predicate (*somebody* thinks *something*). The person doing the thinking is *Fatima*; what she thinks is *that the bus wasn't running*. This embedded clause therefore has the function of an argument. An embedded clause with this function is known as a **complement clause**. In (8) it is an object-argument.

In (9) *stayed* is the predicate. This is a two-place predicate (*somebody* stays *somewhere*). The person who stayed is *Fatima*, and the place where she stayed

Table 8.1 Various types of embedded clauses and their functions

Function	**Name**
Argument	Complement clause
Adjunct	Adverbial clause
Predicate	Predicate clause
Modifier (within an NP)	Relative clause

is *at home*. The embedded clause *because the bus wasn't running* is not required by the predicate, so it is an adjunct. An embedded clause with this function is known as an **adverbial clause**.

The predicate in (10) is the embedded clause *that the bus wasn't running*, introduced by the copula *was*. (See Section 7.2, where we encountered sentences of the type *Mary is my best friend*.) This predicate takes only one argument (*something* equals *that the bus wasn't running*), in this case *Fatima's reason for staying at home*. An embedded clause that functions as a predicate is known as a **predicate clause**.

Finally, in (11), the predicate is *an oldtimer* plus the copula *was*. This is a one-place predicate (*something* is *an oldtimer*). The thing that is an oldtimer is *the bus that wasn't running*. The embedded clause *that wasn't running* (with the relative pronoun *that* substituting for *the bus*) therefore does not have a function at clause level. It occurs as part of the noun phrase *the bus that wasn't running*. Within this noun phrase the embedded clause has the function of modifier, since it gives a further specification of the head, *bus*. That is, the embedded clause has the same function as an adjective here. An embedded clause that serves the function of modifier of a nominal head is known as a **relative clause**.

In Table 8.1 we have listed the various types of embedded clauses and their functions.

We now have identified a number of clause types, just as we identified a number of phrase types in Chapter 6. We are therefore in a position to complete Figure 6.2 from that earlier chapter and expand it into Figure 8.1.

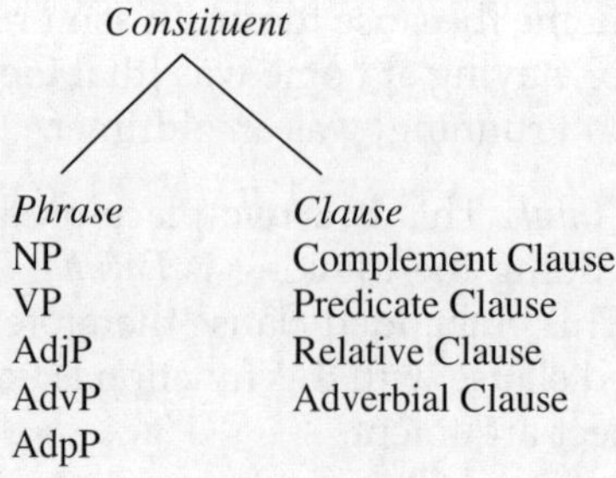

Figure 8.1 Types of constituent (final version).

8.3 The Forms of Embedded Clauses

In the previous section we looked at the different types of embedded clauses but we did not consider their form. This can in fact vary a great deal. Consider examples (12) and (13).

(12) She hopes [that he reads this book].
(13) She hopes [to read this book].

The predicate *hope* is a two-place predicate (*somebody* hopes *something*). What is hoped for in (12) is *that he reads this book*, and in (13) *to read this book*; so in both cases we have a complement clause. In (12) the complement clause looks like a main clause since there is a clear subject *he* and a verb *reads* and so on. However, the embedded clause in (13), *to read this book*, looks different; its infinitive *to read* can never by itself serve as a main clause predicate. However, we can still conclude that (13) contains an embedded clause since the construction *to read a book* has a predicate, namely the two-place *read* (*somebody* reads *something*). Of the two possible arguments of this predicate only one, however, is expressed within the embedded clause, that is the patient-argument *the book*. The other argument, the agent, is not mentioned in the embedded clause but can be derived from the information in the main clause. It is the subject of the main clause, *she*, which is also the (non-expressed) subject of the embedded clause.

The same reasoning applies to examples (14) and (15).

(14) [The books [that Jim reads]] are difficult to digest.
(15) [The books [to be read by Jim]] are difficult to digest.

The clauses between brackets in (14) and (15) serve the same function. They both function as modifiers within the noun phrase that has *book* as its head. Both embedded clauses are relative clauses. They are both clauses, because both have a predicate, the two-place *read*. The agent-argument *John* is expressed explicitly within the relative clause. The patient-argument *the book* is the head of the noun phrase of which the relative clause forms a part. The difference between the two constructions is again that the predicate of the embedded clause in (14) could be used in a main clause as well, while this is not the case with the infinitive in the embedded clause in (15).

In sum, a constituent is an embedded clause when it contains a predicate of its own. The exact form of an embedded clause can be different, as we saw in (14) and (15). The most important distinction is that (14) is a finite embedded clause and (15) a non-finite embedded clause. A **finite** embedded clause contains a verb form which can also be used in a main clause. In many languages such a verb form is marked for tense and person. The examples (12), *She hopes [that he reads this book]*, and (14), *The books [that Jim reads] are difficult to digest*, both contain finite embedded clauses. **Non-finite** embedded clauses contain verb forms that cannot occur as main clause predicates. Such verb forms are normally not marked for tense and person, or if they are, only to a limited extent. There are several different types of non-finite embedded clauses: infinitival constructions, nominalisations and participial constructions.

Infinitival constructions are non-finite embedded clauses that contain a verb form, the infinitive, that is not marked for tense or person. Example (16) is from Spanish.

Spanish

(16)	Quier-o	[le-er	este	libro].
	want-*first.person.present*	read-*infinitive*	this	book

'I want [to read this book].'

In many languages where infinitives like *leer* 'read' occur as in (16) it is not possible to express the subject. The non-expressed subject of the infinitival construction must then be identical to an argument in the main clause. In other words, the non-expressed subject of the infinitival construction and the relevant argument of the main clause must be co-referential, to use a term that we introduced in Section 7.8. Thus, (16) is an alternative way of expressing the more explicit but ungrammatical (17).

(17)	*Quiero	[que	(yo)	lea	este	libro].
	want-*first.person.present*	that	I	read-*first.person.present*	this	book

'I want [that I read this book].'

The co-reference in (16) is between the two subjects. In many languages this is a necessary condition on infinitival constructions such as (16). In those languages infinitival constructions are not possible when the unexpressed subject of the infinitive is different from the subject of the main clause. This is not the case in English, where the object *him* of the main clause can be the subject of the infinitive, as in (18).

(18) I want him [to read the book].

But in Dutch, for instance, such a construction is not possible, as illustrated in (19). It would be necessary to use a finite embedded clause instead, as in (20).

Dutch

(19)	*Ik	wil	[hij/hem	dit	boek	te	lezen].
	I	want	he/him	this	book	to	read
	'I want him to read this book.'						

(20)	Ik	wil	[dat	hij	dit	boek	leest].
	I	want	that	he	this	book	reads
	'I want that he reads this book.'						

Nominalisations are non-finite embedded clauses that closely resemble infinitival constructions. The difference is that in nominalisations the verb behaves in some respects like a noun, as we can see in (21) and (22).

(21) [The bishop's sudden killing of the fox] took everybody by surprise.
(22) [That the bishop suddenly killed that fox] took everybody by surprise.

In contrast to the finite embedded clause in (22), the nominalisation in (21) shares a number of properties with noun phrases. The verb form *killing* is accompanied by the article *the*, and by the adjective *sudden* instead of the adverb *suddenly*. Furthermore, the agent is expressed by means of the genitive marker *'s*, and the patient by the preposition *of*, both again typical of noun phrases, as in (23) and (24).

(23) my best friend's brother
(24) the brother of my best friend

Non-finite constructions that can by themselves be used attributively (i.e. that can replace finite relative clauses and adverbial clauses) are called **participle constructions**. They can be either adjectival or adverbial in character. Example (25) from Swedish illustrates the adjectival option.

Swedish

(25)	Det	[hem-bak-ade]	brödet	är	bäst.
	the	[home-baked-*adjectival participle*]	bread	is	best
	'Home-baked bread is best.'				

Here the participle *hembakade* modifies the head noun *brödet*, so this is an adjectival participle construction that directly modifies the noun.

Constructions with an adverbial participle may occur directly – that is without the use of a conjunction or preposition (see Section 6.9) – as an adjunct. This is illustrated in (26) from Russian.

Russian

(26)	[Vernu-všis'	domoj],	Xèvgun	načal	novuju	žizn'.
	return-*adverbial participle*	home	Khevgun	began	new	life
	'Having returned home, Khevgun began a new life.'					

These examples from Swedish and Russian contain participles that are used exclusively either as adjectival or adverbial constructions. In other languages, such as for example Italian, we find participles that can be used both as an adverb (27) and as an adjective (28).

Italian

(27) [Arriva-ta a casa Maria], ho saputo la notizia.
[arrive-*participle* at home Maria], I have known the news
'When Maria came home, I learned the news.'

(28) La raggaza [arriva-ta un momento fa] è Maria.
the girl [arrive-*participle* a moment ago] is Maria
'The girl who just arrived is Maria.'

In (27) *arrivata Maria a casa* is an adverbial participle construction; *-ta*, the suffix at the end of *arriva*, indicates that this is the participle; the construction as a whole qualifies the following main clause. In (28) *arrivata un momento fa* is again a participle construction, but this time, since it modifies the nominal head *ragazza*, it is an adjectival participle construction.

8.4 Interaction between Main Clause and Embedded Clause

As we have seen, an embedded clause can be quite different in form from a main clause. Our examples so far have concentrated on the form of the verb in the embedded clause. But the way the arguments of a verb are expressed may also be quite different in an embedded clause. In the next section we will discuss three processes that are involved here.

8.4.1 *Equi-Deletion*

Under certain conditions some arguments of an embedded predicate do not have to be realised. What are the rules that govern this phenomenon? When exactly can we leave an argument of an embedded predicate unexpressed? In an attempt to find out, we will first consider the infinitival constructions (29 and 30) and nominalisations (31 and 32).

Infinitival construction

(29) Jane forgot [to finish the assignment].

(30) The English teacher forced Jonathan [to finish the assignment].

Nominalisation

(31) She made a significant contribution [to maintaining the prohibition of alcohol].

(32) The police praised her [for maintaining the prohibition of alcohol].

In the complement clauses (29 to 32) a non-finite verb form is used in the embedded clause and the clause shares an argument with the main clause. This phenomenon – where an argument in the embedded clause is not realised when it is co-referent with an argument in the main clause – is known as **equi-deletion**. In (29) and (31) the subject of the embedded clause is identical with the subject of the main clause; in (29) *Jane* and in (31) *she*. In (30) and (32) the subject of the embedded clause is identical to the object of the main clause, in (30) *Jonathan*, in (32) *her*.

Participle constructions behave in a similar way, as we can see in examples (33) and (34).

Participle constructions
(33) [Cycling through Oxford] I happened to see Madelon.
(34) I saw Madelon [cycling through Oxford].

The embedded clauses in (33) and (34) are adjectival constructions. In (33) only one interpretation is possible: the subject of the participle construction is identical to the subject *I* in the main clause. Example (34), however, allows two possible interpretations; it is an ambiguous clause. The most likely interpretation is where the main clause object *Madelon* is the subject of *cycling*, but it is possible to interpret (34) with the main clause subject *I* as the subject of *cycling*.

In all these cases there has to be co-reference between an argument in the main clause and one in the embedded clause. It is only under this condition, and then only in an embedded construction which is non-finite, that equi-deletion is allowed in English. Other languages may have very different rules for cases like these. For instance, the languages of the Balkan such as Greek or Bulgarian hardly ever use non-finite verb forms and do not have a rule of equi-deletion.

8.4.2 Raising

Consider examples (35) and (36), in particular their subjects, and try to determine in what way they are different.

(35) It appears that John is ill.
(36) John appears to be ill.

The content expressed in these two clauses is more or less the same. The difference between (35) and (36) lies in which constituent is the subject of the main clause. In (35) the subject of *appears* is the embedded clause *that John is ill*. This clausal subject is introduced by the dummy-word *it*. Such dummy words we discussed in connection with zero-place predicates in Section 7.3 as in *it is snowing*. In (36), on the other hand, the subject of *appears* is *John*. This can be easily checked by making both sentences plural as in (37) and (38). The verb form only changes in (38).

(37) It appears that John and Franklin are ill.
(38) John and Franklin appear to be ill.

Nevertheless, from a semantic point of view, *John* in (36) is an argument of the embedded clause *John to be ill*. When an argument of an embedded clause behaves as if it is an argument of the main clause, this is known as **raising**.

After raising, the subject of the embedded clause in (37), *John and Franklin*, behaves as the subject of the main clause in (38). But in examples (39) and (40) this is not the case. What is the matter here, and how do the grammatical roles change in these cases of raising?

(39) Bill believes that Sheila is ill.
(40) Bill believes Sheila to be ill.

In (39) the noun phrase *Sheila* is the subject of the complement clause *that Sheila is ill*. In (40), after raising, this same constituent functions as the object of the main clause predicate *believes*. In (40) the only indication for this is the position of *Sheila*. But when we replace *Sheila* by a personal pronoun, the effect of raising is also visible in the form of the pronoun.

(41) Bill believes that *she* is ill.
(42) Bill believes *her* to be ill.

In (41) the pronoun *she* is in the nominative case used for subjects; in (42) the pronoun *her* is in the accusative case used for objects.

8.4.3 Sequence of Tenses

Equi-deletion and raising are cases of interaction between the main clause and the embedded clause. The interaction affects the way in which arguments are expressed. Let us consider a different kind of interaction. Imagine Aziza has to report what Michael, the little boy in the picture (Figure 8.2), says to his friends (43).

The likely result is either (44) or (45). They both contain (43) as an embedded clause, in this case Michael's words. But in (44) the form of the verb in the embedded clause is *is* just as in Michael's original words and in (45) it is *was*.

(43) The boat is aground.
(44) Michael says that [the boat is aground].
(45) Michael said that [the boat was aground].

In (44) the present tense is used both in the main clause and in the embedded clause; in (45) it is the past tense in both clauses. This phenomenon – that is when the tense form in the embedded clause adapts itself to the tense form of

Figure 8.2 Michael with a boat gone aground. Montrul, S. 'Research methods in L2 acquisition and bilingualism' 6th EMLAR (Experimental Methods in Language Acquisition Research), Utrecht, The Netherlands, February 3–5, 2010.

the main clause – is known as **sequence of tenses**. As we already indicated, the tense form of the embedded clause in (45) no longer corresponds to the tense form of the original clause that is being reported. Note that this is not obligatory in English. Example (45) could have the present tense in the embedded clause as well, for instance if the boat is still likely to be aground at the moment Aziza reports what Michael had said, as in (46).

(46) Michael said that [the boat is aground].

Other languages apply similar rules. Consider some examples from Spanish (47 to 49).

Spanish

(47)	María	va	a	venir.		
	María	goes	to	come		
	'María is going to come.'					
(48)	Carlos	dice	que	[María va	a	venir].
	Carlos	says	that	María goes	to	come
	'Carlos says that María is going to come.'					
(49)	Carlos	dijo	que	[María iba	a	venir].
	Juan	said	that	Carlos went	to	come
	'Carlos said that María was going to come.'					

The sentence in (47) contains Carlos' exact words. In (48), with present tense in the main clause, the original tense form of (47) is retained in the complement clause, whereas in (49) the past tense of the main clause triggers the use of the past tense in the complement clause.

Speakers of English and Spanish learn this sequence of tenses as part of the grammar of their language. But for second language learners this aspect of English or Spanish grammar can be problematic if your first language does not have sequence of tenses (see Section 3.5 on negative transfer in language learning). One such language is Russian, as we can see in (50) and (51).

Russian

(50)	Ja	pridu	četyrnadcatogo	maja.
	I	will.come	fourteenth	May

'I will arrive on the fourteenth of May.'

(51)	Kolja skazal,	čto	[on	pridět	četyrnadcatgo	maja].
	Kolja said	that	he	will.come	fourteenth	May

'Kolja said that he would arrive on the fourteenth of May.'

Example (50) has been embedded into the main clause of (51), which has a verb in the past tense (*skazal*, 'said'). The embedded verb, however, retains its future tense (*pridět*, 'will come'), as we can see in the literal, word-by-word, rendition. It is as if this verb remains loyal to its original form whatever happens. This is so even if the future tense used in (51) would be completely at odds with the real time that is being referred to. If, for example, (51) had been uttered on May 15th, that is the day after Kolja's arrival, it would still have the same form, including the future tense, because this corresponds to what Kolja actually said in (50).

8.5 Coordinated Clauses

So far in this chapter on complex sentences we have been discussing embedded clauses. There are, however, other ways in which clauses can be combined, as we can see in (52) and (53).

(52) Fatima is a hairdresser and her sister is a carpenter.
(53) Peter is poor but Mabel is rich.

As we saw earlier, an embedded clause functions as a constituent of another clause, the main clause. Both in (52) and (53) we do have two clauses, but neither of these is a constituent of the other. In this case such clauses are called **coordinated clauses**, that together form a sentence. The two clauses that could occur separately in (54) and (55) combine to form (52) and the main clauses in (56) and (57) form (53).

(54) Fatima is a hairdresser.
(55) Her sister is a carpenter.
(56) Peter is poor.
(57) Mabel is rich.

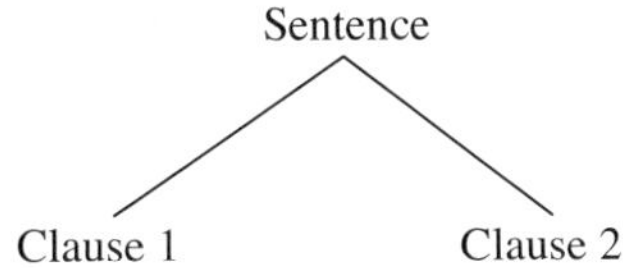

Figure 8.3 The constituent structure of coordinated clauses.

Thus we can say that the constituent structure of (52) and (53) is as in Figure 8.3.

Coordination can occur between clauses, but also between phrases, as we can see in the following examples.

(58) *Fatima and her sister* went home.
(59) A *fast and expensive* car.
(60) He has been *muttering and moaning* all day.
(61) She came in *quickly and silently*.
(62) They arrived *by car and with their dog*.

In example (58) two noun phrases have been coordinated, in (59) two adjectival phrases, in (60) two verb phrases, in (61) two adverbial phrases, and in (62) two adpositional phrases.

Coordinated clauses and coordinated phrases are often connected by a conjunction such as *and* or *but*. These are known as **coordinators**. Their presence is not always required. In (63) and (64) we have coordination without a coordinator.

(63) A fast, expensive car.
(64) Fatima is a hairdresser, her sister a carpenter.

These examples appear to show that we can take two clauses or phrases and just put them next to each other like that. But is this really the case? In the next section we will take a closer look at this question.

8.6 The form of Coordinated Clauses

When clauses are coordinated, we are looking at a combination of two or more main clauses. As a consequence of the coordination these main clauses may take a form that is different from the form they would take in isolation. It is possible that equi-deletion takes place, as example (65) illustrates.

(65) Charlie has a bike, but never rides it.

In (65) the clause that follows the coordinator *but* is incomplete, or at least it would be incomplete, and ungrammatical, if used in isolation, as we can see in (67).

(66) Charlie has a bike
(67) *Never rides it.

The second part, if it stands alone as a main clause, should have the form as in (68).

(68) Charlie never rides it.

When we coordinate this clause with (66) we get (69).

(69) Charlie has a bike, but Charlie never rides it.

These two coordinated clauses have the same subject, *Charlie*, and in this case the second subject is normally left out, resulting in (65).

Other parts of coordinated clauses may also be left out, as we can see in (70).

(70) Fatima bought a car and Charlie a bike.

Again we have a coordinated clause, where the second part cannot occur on its own in isolation, as shown in (71) and (72).

(71) Fatima bought a car.
(72) *Charlie a bike.

This second part, on its own, would have to be (73).

(73) Charlie bought a bike.

When (71) and (73) are coordinated, the result is (74).

(74) Fatima bought a car, and Charlie bought a bike.

Here the two coordinated clauses have the same predicate, *bought*, and in this case the second predicate may be left out, resulting in (70). The deletion or leaving out of identical predicates in a coordinated construction is known as **gapping**.

SUMMARY

A clause can take on the role of a constituent within a sentence. Such a clause is then an **embedded clause** within a **main clause**. According to their function, such embedded clauses can be subdivided into **complement clauses** (arguments), **adverbial clauses** (adjuncts), **relative clauses** (modifiers) and **predicate clauses** (predicates). According to their form, they can be subdivided into **finite** and **non-finite** clauses. The latter category can be further subdivided into **infinitival constructions**, **nominalisations** and **participial constructions**. The interaction between main clauses and embedded clauses can give rise to such phenomena as **equi-deletion, raising and sequence of tenses**. Clauses can also be **coordinated**, rather than embedded, and are then often linked by a coordinator. The interaction between coordinated clauses can result in **gapping**.

Assignments

1. Give an analysis of the constituent structure of the following sentences:
   (a) I think that Agnes hit the man who is walking there.
   (b) If it's raining, she won't come.
   (c) That this famous actor tried to woo her with the most flattering words left her stone-cold.
2. What is the function of the embedded sentences in the following examples:
   (a) Mustafa went out [to do the shopping].
   (b) My neighbour [who has been retired for many years] has bought a house in Spain.
   (c) Paula thinks [her brother is ill].
   (d) John forgot [to do the dishes].
   (e) Charles went home [to do the dishes].
3. Name the form of the embedded sentences in the following examples:
   (a) I want [to stay at home].
   (b) I know [that you would rather stay at home].
   (c) I hate it [when Charlotte always wants to stay at home].
   (d) [Walking along the coast] I saw various ships at sea.
   (e) [Her constant yelling] bothers me.
4. Does English have participles, and if so, are these adjectival, adverbial or both? Make sure you support your answers with examples.
5. Do the following sentences contain a form of coordination? If not, what kind of embedding do they illustrate?
   (a) She looked as if she had seen a ghost.
   (b) The minister first visited Baghdad, and then Teheran.
   (c) He did not agree with her, but did not dare to say so.
   (d) When preparing a salad dressing, most people will use oil and vinegar.
6. Do the following sentences have (a) equi-deletion, (b) gapping, (c) both, or (d) none? Give evidence for your answer.
   (a) Charles believed Peter to be ill.
   (b) Frank ate a herring, John a healthy snack. Nicola did both.

7. The following example is from Amele, a language spoken in Papua New Guinea. Is this an example of sequence of tenses?

   Uqa uqadec jobon na hugen ec maten.
   he tomorrow village to come.*first.person.future* that he.said
   'He told me that he would come to the village tomorrow.'

TEST YOURSELF

1. What is recursion?
2. What is the difference between embedding and coordination?
3. Which types of embedded clauses can be distinguished on the basis of function?
4. Which types of embedded clauses can be distinguished on the basis of form?
5. What are the characteristic properties of infinitival constructions?
6. What is raising?
7. Give an example of gapping.

ACKNOWLEDGMENTS AND FURTHER READING

Excellent introductions to the various topics in this chapter can be found in Shopen (ed.) (2007), which contains chapters on complement clauses (Noonan 2007), adverbial clauses (Thompson, Longacre and Hwang 2007), relative clauses (Andrews 2007) and coordination (Haspelmath 2007). The Russian examples are from Haspelmath (1995) and from Comrie (1985), the Amele example from Roberts (1987). The picture of a boy with a boat in Figure 8.2 is from Montrul (2009).

chapter 9

Constituent Order

9.1 Introduction

In Chapter 6 we saw that the constituents that make up a clause do not just occur in random order. But is that order always completely fixed? Look at the sentences (1), (2) and (3). What constituents are involved in these sentences, and what are their semantic and grammatical roles?

(1) He ate the pizza yesterday.
(2) Yesterday he ate the pizza.
(3) The pizza he ate yesterday (, the salad today).

It does not take long to establish that each of the sentences (1) to (3) has the same constituent structure and the same distribution of semantic and grammatical roles, as follows:

NP/Subject:	he	
VP:	ate the pizza	
	V:	ate
	NP/Object:	the pizza
AdvP:	yesterday	

Linguistics, First Edition. Edited by Anne E. Baker and Kees Hengeveld.

So (1), (2) and (3) are similar in these respects, but not in the order of their constituents. As we will show later in this chapter, in this case the different orders have to do with the information structure of the clause, as discussed in Section 5.3.

Constituent order, the subject of this chapter, is often referred to as 'word order'. As the previous examples show, the latter term is not entirely appropriate, as it is constituents that are assigned a position in the linear order of the clause. In Section 9.2 we will demonstrate that the constituent structure of a clause determines the amount of variation possible in constituent ordering. In Section 9.3 we will discuss the basic constituent order within clauses, as it can be identified for individual languages. In Sections 9.4 to 9.7 we will survey the four key factors that play a role in determining the basic constituent order patterns of languages, that is clause type (Section 9.4), the difference between main and embedded clauses (Section 9.5), the complexity of constituents (Section 9.6), and the information status of constituents (Section 9.7). In Section 9.8 we move from the clause level down to the level of the constituent, which in general allows less variation. The various ordering properties of languages show interesting correlations, which are discussed in Section 9.9. The chapter will close with a discussion of constituents that can be split into two parts (Section 9.10).

9.2 Constituent Order and Levels of Analysis

As we saw in Chapter 6, clauses are not random collections of words. They have an internal, hierarchical structure. This is important to keep in mind when studying constituent order, as examples (4) to (9) make clear.

(4) The unbelievably intelligent boy read very fast.
(5) *Read very fast the unbelievably intelligent boy.
(6) *The boy unbelievably intelligent read very fast.
(7) *The unbelievably intelligent boy very fast read.
(8) *The intelligent unbelievably boy read very fast.
(9) *The unbelievably intelligent boy read fast very.

If we want to understand why sentences (5) to (9) are ungrammatical, we need to know the constituent structure of (4) first. It is given in (10).

(10) Sentence: The unbelievably intelligent boy read very fast.
    NP: The unbelievably intelligent boy
        Head: boy
        AdjP: unbelievably intelligent
            Head: intelligent
            AdvP: unbelievably
                Head: unbelievably

VP: read very fast
    Head: read
    AdvP: very fast
        Head: fast
        AdvP: very
            Head: very

Sentence (5) is ungrammatical because it violates a constituent order rule at the sentence level. The sentence contains a VP (*read very fast*) and an NP (*the unbelievably intelligent boy*), but in English **declarative clauses** (clauses formed to express assertions), a VP does not normally occupy initial position.

Sentence (6) is ungrammatical because it breaks a constituent order rule that applies within the NP. The NP contains a nominal head (*boy*) and an AdjP (*unbelievably intelligent*). In English (with some exceptions) an AdjP precedes the head it modifies.

Sentence (7) is ungrammatical because it does not respect a constituent order rule within the VP. The VP contains a verbal head (*read*) and an AdvP (*very fast*). In English the AdvP usually follows the head it modifies.

Sentence (8) is ungrammatical because it does not conform to a constituent order rule within the AdjP. The AdjP contains an adjectival head (*intelligent*) and an AdvP (*unbelievably*). In English the AdvP must precede the adjectival head it modifies.

Finally, sentence (9) is ungrammatical because it breaks a constituent order rule within the AdvP. The AdvP contains an adverbial head (*fast*) and another AdvP (*very*). In English an AdvP, such as *very* in (9), always precedes the adverbial head it modifies.

As we see in the examples (5) to (9), constituent order rules operate at the level of the sentence and within the different phrase types. We will now first consider a number of constituent order phenomena at the sentence level.

9.3 Constituent Order at the Sentence Level

As examples (1) to (3) demonstrated, even within one single language there can be a great deal of variation in the constituent order within clauses. Yet, in almost every language there is also one 'normal' constituent order pattern, the so-called **basic constituent order** of the language in question. When determining this basic order, we look at the order that occurs in (i) declarative clauses that are (ii) main clauses, with (iii) two nominal (not pro-nominal) arguments, which have (iv) equal information status, that is they are presented with the same degree of emphasis. These four conditions will be discussed in more detail later, when we will see that variation in each of these four aspects may result in different patterns of constituent order.

Amongst the languages of the world we can distinguish three different, frequently occurring basic constituent order patterns. The following sentences – (11) from Fijian, (12) from English and (13) from Turkish – represent these three basic patterns. What can we say about the crucial differences between these patterns? The first thing to notice here is the position of the predicate.

Fijian

(11)	Sa	yalana	o	Viliame	a	ona	ti'i	ni	qele.
	aspect	demarcate	*article*	William	*article*	his	piece	of	land

'William demarcates his piece of land.'

English

(12) Sophie is reading the newspaper.

Turkish

(13)	Ressam	bize	resimlerini	gösterdi.
	artist	us	his.paintings	showed

'The artist showed us his paintings.'

The key difference between the constituent order patterns of these three languages is that in Fijian the predicate is positioned at the beginning of the clause; in English we find the predicate in the middle, and in Turkish at the end. In another respect, however, the three languages are very similar, for in their basic constituent order patterns the subject always precedes the object. In (11) *Viliame* 'William' comes before *a ona ti'i nu qele* 'his piece of land'; in (12) *Sophie* precedes *the newspaper*; and in (13) the subject *ressam* 'the artist' is positioned to the left of the object *resimlerini* 'his paintings'. This gives us the following basic patterns:

Fijian:	Predicate	Subject	Object
English:	Subject	Predicate	Object
Turkish:	Subject	Object	Predicate

Logically speaking there are three other possible orders, where the object precedes the subject. Examples can be found of languages that have these basic constituent orders, though they are very rare.

Malagasy (Madagascar):	Predicate	Object	Subject
Hixkaryana (Brazil):	Object	Predicate	Subject
Warao (Venezuela):	Object	Subject	Predicate

Often the abbreviation 'V' (for verb) is used rather than 'P' (for predicate), so that Fijian is then described as a VSO language, Hixkaryana as an OVS language, etc.

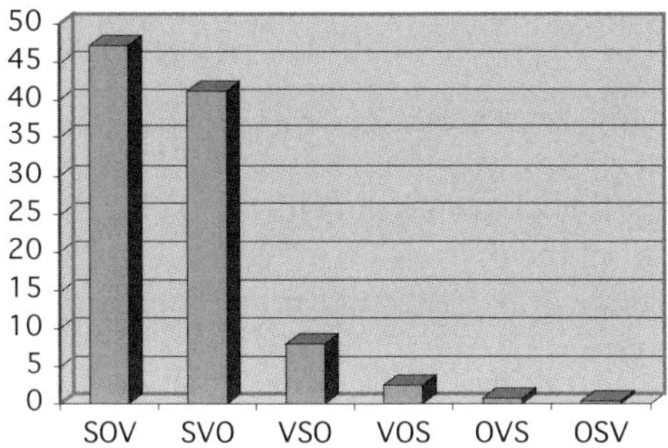

Figure 9.1 Approximate distribution of Basic Constituent Orders.

Figure 9.1 shows the approximate quantitative distribution of the six basic constituent orders using these abbreviations.

There are also languages that belong to a mixed type, when clauses exhibit two different basic constituent order patterns. German and Dutch are examples of this, partly following the English model (12), and partly the Turkish pattern in (13) (see Section 9.5).

Most languages, however, have one basic, neutral constituent order in their clauses, although they possibly allow some other orders. The four key factors that play a role in these alternative orders were mentioned at the beginning of this section. We will now take a closer look at each of these four factors.

9.4 Clause Type

When establishing the basic constituent order of a language, our starting point is, as we saw in Section 9.3, the declarative clause. But **interrogative clauses** (clauses formed to express questions) and **imperative clauses** (clauses formed to express commands) may well have a different constituent order. So, let's consider what impact clause type has on constituent order in Spanish by comparing (14), (15) and (16).

Spanish

(14)	Pilar	escribió	una	carta.
	Pilar	wrote	a	letter
	'Pilar wrote a letter.'			
(15)	¿Escribió	Pilar	una	carta?
	wrote	Pilar	a	letter
	'Did Pilar write a letter?'			
(16)	¡Escribe	una	carta!	
	write	a	letter	
	'Write a letter!'			

Spanish has as its basic constituent order the following pattern:

Declarative clauses: Subject – Predicate – Object (14)

If we look at interrogative clauses as in (15), we see a difference in order from (14). We will here restrict the discussion to 'yes/no' questions, that is questions where the expected answer is either *yes* or *no*. The pattern we find in (15) can be specified as follows:

Interrogative clauses: Predicate – Subject – Object (15)

In imperative clauses like (16) the Subject is not expressed, so there is nothing we can say about its position. The constituent order is as follows:

Imperative clauses: Predicate – Object (16)

Summarising across these clause types, we find the following:

Declarative clauses:	Subject	Predicate	Object	(14)
Interrogative clauses:	Predicate	Subject	Object	(15)
Imperative clauses:	Predicate	Object		(16)

As we see, there are both differences and similarities in constituent order between these different clause types: both interrogative clauses and imperative clauses start with the verb; both declarative and interrogative clauses have the subject before the object. Yet at the same time, we note that in all three types the relative order of Predicate and object remains the same, in the sense that the verb always precedes the object within the clause.

9.5 Embedded Clauses

In determining the basic constituent order pattern of a language the main clause is the basis, as we mentioned earlier. But in some languages the constituent order in embedded clauses is different. This rather exceptional situation is found, for example, in German, as we can see in examples (17) to (19).

(17) Alex und Jasmina lasen die Zeitung.
Alex and Yasmina read.*past* the newspaper
'Alex and Yasmina read the newspaper.'

(18) *Ich sah, dass Alex und Jasmina lasen die Zeitung.
I saw that Alex and Yasmina read.*past* the newspaper
'I saw that Alex and Yasmina were reading the newspaper.'

(19) Ich sah, dass Alex und Jasmina die Zeitung lasen.
I saw that Alex and Yasmina the newspaper read.*past*
'I saw that Alex and Yasmina were reading the newspaper.'

The key difference with English is that the main predicate is placed at the end of the embedded clause. The constituent order pattern of German clauses is as follows:

Main clause: Subject – Predicate – Object
Embedded clause: Subject – Object – Predicate

9.6 COMPLEXITY

The main clause used to determine a language's basic constituent order must also contain two nominal arguments, as we mentioned in Section 9.3. When other arguments are involved, the orders we find may be quite different, as we can see in examples (20) to (22).

French
(20) Jean a donné le livre à son frere.
John has given the book to his brother
'John gave the book to his brother.'

(21) Jean l' a donné à son frere.
John it has given to his brother
'John gave it to his brother.'

(22) Jean a dit à son frère qu' il est malade.
John has said to his brother that he is ill
'John told his brother that he is ill.'

Sentences (20) to (22) are based on three-place predicates (see also Section 7.3). In (20) all three arguments of *donner* are realised as noun phrases (*Jean*, *le livre*, *son frère*). The subject (*Jean*) precedes the verb (*a donné*), which is followed first by the object (*le livre*) and then by the third argument, the recipient, which is neither subject nor object (*son frère*).

In (21) the object *le livre* has been replaced by an unstressed pronoun, a clitic (see Section 11.2). In contrast to (20), where the full nominal object follows the verb, this clitic object, *l'*, immediately precedes the verb.

In (22), finally, the object of the verb *dire* is an embedded clause (see Section 8.2). In contrast to (20), where the object, a noun phrase, immediately follows the verb, here this object-clause (*qu'il est malade*) does not follow the verb but is placed at the end of the main clause, after the recipient (*son frère*).

Comparing these three different constituent order patterns results in the following patterns:

Subject – *Object* – Predicate – Other argument (object = pronoun) (21)
Subject – Predicate – *Object* – Other argument (object = noun) (20)
Subject – Predicate – Other argument – *object* (object = clause) (22)

In each of these three patterns the object moves a place to the right. This has to do with the internal complexity of the object in question: a simple clitic pronoun, a full noun phrase, or a clause. As the **complexity** of the object increases, it is positioned farther to the right in the main clause. A possible explanation for this is that the more complex a constituent may be, the easier it is to produce and interpret when it is farther towards the end of the clause.

9.7 The Information Status of Constituents

The fourth and final criterion used to determine the basic constituent order pattern of a language has to do with the information status of constituents (see Section 5.3). The **information status** of a constituent depends on whether or not the information contained in that constituent is known or unknown in a given communicative situation. According to the information status of a constituent, its position may be changed as a consequence. Let us consider the Polish example in (23). Since this is a main clause with two arguments it reflects the basic constituent order in this language.

Polish
(23) Moj przyjaciel teraz odrabia swoje zadania_domowe.
my friend now makes his homework
'My friend is now doing his homework.'

As we can see, the basic constituent order of Polish is SVO: the subject precedes the verb, which is followed by the object. In Polish this basic order is not affected by the type of clauses, as we see in (24). Yes/no questions start with a question particle, but are otherwise exactly the same as the declarative main clause in (23). The same goes for embedded clauses, as we can see in (25).

Polish
(24) Czy moj przyjaciel teraz odrabia swoje zadania_domowe?
Question my friend now makes his homework
'Is my friend now doing his homework?'

(25) Wiem, ze moj przyjaciel teraz odrabia swoje zadania_domowe.
I.know that my friend now makes his homework
'I know that my friend is now doing his homework.'

But now consider sentences (26) to (28).

Polish
(26) Moj przyjaciel teraz odrabia swoje zadania_domowe.
my friend now makes his homework
'My friend is now doing his homework.'
(27) Teraz moj przyjaciel odrabia swoje zadania_domowe.
now my friend makes his homework
'Now my friend is doing his homework.'
(28) Swoje zadania_domowe moj przyjaciel odrabia teraz.
his homework my friend now makes
'His homework my friend is now doing.'

In each case there is a different constituent in initial position, although the other constituents retain their original position in the basic constituent order. To explain the different interpretations associated with these different orders would require an extensive discussion, which we cannot go into here. But the key factor that determines whether the order in (26), (27) or (28) is appropriate is what information is already given in the context (see Section 5.3). This given information will end up in initial position. Thus, sentence (26) will be used in a context where 'my friend' is given; sentence (27) in a context where 'now' is already known; and (28) in a context where 'his homework' has been mentioned before, in answer, for example, to a question like 'When is your friend going to do his homework?' These sentences demonstrate how in Polish the initial position of declarative clauses is used for the topic of the sentence (Section 5.3). Depending on the context, the information status of constituents may override the basic constituent order.

9.8 Constituent Order within Constituents

The key point we have established so far is that each language has a basic constituent order, and possibly in addition a range of other constituent order possibilities, depending on clause type, embedding, complexity, and the information status of constituents. All of this takes place at the clause level. At the constituent level, in contrast, variation in constituent order is much less frequent. It is actually rather difficult to find languages that show a degree of variation at this level that is of any significance. Here we shall briefly consider two key constituent types, noun phrases and verb phrases.

9.8.1 *The Noun Phrase*

Within a noun phrase, a variety of elements have to be ordered. Example (29) is a noun phrase containing the following elements: the article *the*, the numeral *two*, the adjective *glitzy*, the nominal head *limousines*, the adpositional phrase *from the hotel*, and the relative clause *that are parked over there*. In theory there would be 720 (= 6 x 5 x 4 x 3 x 2 x 1) possibilities for combining these six different elements, but in actual fact only one way of ordering them is acceptable in English.

(29) the two glitzy limousines from the hotel that are parked over there

So, clearly, there are strong restrictions on order variation within a noun phrase in English. The few cases where there actually is some variation are therefore all the more interesting. Consider the examples in (30) and (31).

(30) the singing girl
(31) the girl that sings

Both (30) and (31) contain a relative clause which acts as a modifier of the head, *girl*. In (30) this is an embedded clause in the form of a participle construction; in (31) it is a finite relative clause (for participle constructions and relative clauses see also Section 8.2 and Section 8.3). The participle construction in (30) precedes the nominal head; the finite relative clause in (31) follows it. This is a further example of the role of complexity in determining constituent order in English. The relative clause is internally more complex and is realised later in the clause.

The Spanish examples in (32) and (33) demonstrate that the information status of elements is a factor not only at the clause level and the order of constituents (see Section 9.7), but also at the level of constituents themselves and within noun phrases in particular.

Spanish
(32) su linda casa
his beautiful house
'his beautiful house'
(33) su casa linda
his house beautiful
'his BEAUTIFUL house'

In (32) the house is known, there is only one house and it belongs to someone; it is this house that is characterised as beautiful (*linda*). Sentence (33), in contrast, can only be used when the person who owns this house has other houses as well, and the house we are talking about is being identified as *linda* in contrast to those other, not so beautiful, houses. The information status of *linda* in these two cases is very different indeed, and this is reflected in the different positions the two adjectives occupy in (32) and (33).

9.8.2 *The Verb Phrase*

Within the verb phrase, too, there is in general only very limited variation in constituent order. Consider example (34).

(34) Gerald *was dancing beautifully.*

In English the auxiliary verb (*was*) has to precede the verbal head (*dancing*), and adverbs which denote the manner (*beautifully*) usually follow this head.

In Dutch, on the other hand, there is, rather exceptionally, some variation possible here, depending on the presence or absence of an auxiliary, as we can see in (35).

Dutch

(35) a. Susan *danste mooi.*
Susan danced beautifully
'Susan danced beautifully.'

b. Susan *heeft mooi gedanst.*
Susan has beautifully danced
'Susan danced beautifully.'

In (35a) the adverb *mooi* follows the predicate *danste*; in (35b) it precedes the predicate *gedanst.*

A further example of variation in Dutch can be found in the order of auxiliary verbs and main verbs in embedded clauses, as in (36b). Here the auxiliary verb *heeft* can either precede or follow the predicate *gedanst.*

Dutch

(36) a. Ik weeet dat Susan *mooi danste.*
I know that Susan beautifully danced
'I know that Susan danced beautifully.'

b. Ik weet dat Susan *mooi gedanst heeft / mooi heeft gedanst.*
I know that Susan beautifully danced has / beautifully has danced
'I know that Susan danced beautifully.'

Example (36a) illustrates that in embedded clauses the manner adverb precedes the finite verb, rather than follows it, as in main clause (35a). When an auxiliary verb has to be expressed, it can either be placed in the final or in the medial position of the verb phrase (36b).

9.9 Correlations

In our discussion so far we have treated a range of related constituent order phenomena as if they were separate and unconnected. But in reality there are clearly correlations between the basic constituent order at clause level and at constituent level, called word order universals. These universals are best described starting from the basic constituent order at clause level. At this level we have two very clear, extreme positions, that is, languages with the predicate either in initial position, or in final position.

Fijian is a good example of the first type of language, as shown in Section 9.3 and illustrated again in (37). We find various relationships between constituent order at clause level and at constituent level in this type of language. In example (38) we can see that in the noun phrase of such a language the adjective phrase follows the nominal head. The same goes for the noun phrase that expresses the possessor, as we can see in (39).

Fijian

(37) Sa moce na gone.
aspect sleep *article* child
'The child is sleeping.'

(38) na vale levu
article house big
'the big house'

(39) na nona vale na turaga
article his house *article* leader
'the house of the leader'

Within the verb phrase of a language of this type the auxiliary or any particle that serves this function usually precedes the predicate, whereas adverbs follow it. Both phenomena are illustrated in (40). A final property of this type of language is that it uses prepositions and not postpositions, as we can see in example (41).

Fijian

(40) Sa tabaki vakavula.
aspect print monthly
'It is printed monthly.'

(41) e na lawa
in *article* net
'in the net'

Turkish, on the other hand, is a language with the predicate in final position (42). In this type of language, the adjective phrase usually precedes the head of a noun phrase (43), and the same goes for the nominal expression of the possessor (44).

Turkish

(42) Ressam bize resimlerini gösterdi.
artist us his.paintings showed
'The artist showed us his paintings.'

(43) büyük ev
big house
'the big house'

(44) çiftçi-nin ev-i
farmer-*genitive* house-*possessive.3.singular*
'the house of the farmer'

Within the verb phrase of a language like Turkish we usually find that auxiliaries and particles that serve the same function follow the predicate (45), whereas manner adverbs will normally precede the predicate (46). In this type of language relations between constituents are usually expressed with postpositions, not prepositions (47).

Turkish

(45) Bir zelzele ol-du.
an earthquake be-*past tense*
'There was an earthquake.'

(46) Iyi çalışır.
good he.works
'He works well.'

(47) bugün-den evvel
today-*ablative* before
'before today'

Table 9.1 shows the correlations for these two types of language.

As can be deduced from Table 9.1, the patterns for Fijian and Turkish are exactly the mirror image of each other, and this is true for many VSO and SOV languages.

Table 9.1 Constituent order correlations

	Fijian	**Turkish**
Clause: Basic Constituent Order	Pred S O	S O Pred
NP: Order of N – AdjP	N – AdjP	AdjP – N
NP: Order of N – Possessor	N – Poss	Poss – N
VP: Order of V – Auxiliary	Aux – V	V – Aux
VP: Order of V – AdvP	V – AdvP	AdvP – V
AdpP: Order of Adp – NP	Adp – NP	NP – Adp

Other languages, where the predicate occupies a middle position in the basic constituent order of the clause, are less consistent than the two extreme examples above, although they are often closer to the VSO type of language, such as Fijian. In English clauses, the predicate is in medial position (48), the possessor follows the nominal head (49); the auxiliary precedes the predicate; and manner adverbs follow the predicate (50). In addition, English has prepositions (51).

(48) Jasmina is reading the newspaper.
(49) the son of my neighbour
(50) She is dancing beautifully.
(51) in the living room

Although there are properties that English shares with Fijian, there are also a number of features it shares with Turkish. For example, the possessor may occur in a position preceding the nominal head of the NP (52); and AdjPs always precede their nominal head (53).

(52) my neighbour's daughter
(53) a big house

The word order universals thus provide a framework for understanding the correlations and interconnections that exist between a range of different constituent order phenomena in different types of languages.

So far we have discussed the position of constituents as if they always form a coherent unit or whole that occupies a single space. In the next section we will see that this is not necessarily so.

9.10 Discontinuous Constituents

As a general rule, constituents form one uninterrupted whole or unit. But consider (54) and (55).

(54) She had the books brought over from the Treasury.
(55) Gwen completely took him in.

Which constituents are not realised as a continuous unit here, but broken up into different parts? In (54) the auxiliary *had* is separated from the predicate *brought over* by the object *the books*. This is in conflict with the general rule that all verbal elements should stay together and, in English, occupy the position between subject and object. Instead, whereas the finite auxiliary is in second position (as it should be), the non-finite predicate is not. What we have here is a **discontinuous verbal cluster**. Something similar is the case in (55), where the phrasal verb *take in* has been split into two parts: the finite element *took* in second position and the particle *in* at the end, with the object *him* in between.

In addition to discontinuous verbal clusters we also find discontinuous NPs (56).

(56) I gave him a book for his birthday which I myself had not yet been able to read.

In this example the relative clause *which I myself had not yet been able to read* belongs to the head *a book*. These two parts of the noun phrase have been split apart by the adverbial phrase *for his birthday*. If *for his birthday* had been placed in final position, the resulting sentence would have been awkward and difficult to process (see Section 2.4.3). The head of the NP is in the normal position for the object, that is to the right of the main verb, whereas the relative clause obeys the general tendency for more complex units to be placed farther to the right, near the end of the clause. The relative clause has in fact been detached from its head. This movement of the relative clause outside the NP is known as **extraposition**.

With this topic we come to the end of our chapters on syntax. Now, as we know, language is much more than just form. Syntactic units also have meaning. This will be the subject of the next chapter.

SUMMARY

Constituent order can be investigated both at the level of the sentence and within constituents. At clause level almost all languages have a certain **basic constituent order**. Deviations from that basic pattern are determined by the clause type (**declarative**, **interrogative** and **imperative**), by the difference between main and embedded clauses, by the **complexity** of constituents and by the **information status** of constituents. At constituent level, deviations from the basic order are not very frequent. Within noun phrases, information status and complexity may play a role in the positioning of adjectives and relative clauses. The correlation between constituent order at clause and at constituent level comes out clearly in constituent order universals. When there is a conflict between constituent order rules at clause level and those at constituent level, this may result in split constituents, as in the case of **discontinuous verb clusters** (for example, with phrasal verbs), and in **extraposition**.

ASSIGNMENTS

1. Here are some sentences from young German children, aged between 1;8 and 2;4. What can we deduce about the acquisition of word order rules in this language?

(1;8) teddy mofa fahren
Teddy moped drive
'Teddy is driving the moped.'
(1;10) meike fenster gucken
Meike window look
'Meike is looking out of the window.'
(2;2) mal sehen, dass fort ist
Just see that away is
'Let's see that it has gone away.'
(2;4) Bubi hat kein hunger
Bubi has no hunger
'Bubi is not hungry.'
(2;3) ich gehe in die schule
I go in the school
'I go to school.'

2. German has properties of languages where the verb occupies the middle position, but also of languages where the verb occupies end position. Which phenomena in the following sentence belong to which type of language?
German
Ich weiss, dass Johann in die Zimmer gelaufen ist.
I know that Johann into the room walked is.
'I know that Johann walked into the room.'
3. The next example is from Samoan. Can you predict on this basis whether Samoan will have prepositions or postpositions?
Samoan
Na pa'u le teine.
past tense fall the girl
'The girl fell.'
4. How can you explain the position of the object in the following sentence:
I found the book for John that he had always wanted to read.

Test Yourself

1. What is the definition of 'basic constituent order'?
2. Which constituent is most important in determining the basic word order pattern of a language?
3. Which factors can cause deviations from the basic word order of a language?
4. How can the information status of a constituent influence word order?

5. What is the most likely position of the adjective relative to its noun in languages where the predicate occupies sentence-initial position?
6. Does the following sentence contain a discontinuous verbal cluster, or do we have extraposition here, or both?

    I let the chickens out yesterday belonging to my neighbours.

Acknowledgments and Further Reading

Thorough discussions of word order phenomena can be found in Hawkins (1983), Tomlin (1986) and Siewierska (1988). The word order universals of Greenberg were first presented in Greenberg (1963). The Fijian examples are from Dixon (1988), the Turkish examples from Lewis (1967) and the Samoan examples from Mosel and Hovdhaugen (1992). The examples from German child language are taken from Mills (1985).

Acknowledgments and Further Reading

chapter 10

Sentence Meaning

10.1 Introduction

In everyday situations we often come across sentences that can be interpreted in more than one way. The newspaper headline in (1) is a good example.

(1) New chairs now too expensive

In the context of an article on higher education, this clause wishes to convey that new professorial positions cost too much. But there is a possible different interpretation: in the context of an article about the refurbishing of the New York Opera House it means that the seating now costs too much. Example (2) also allows two different interpretations.

(2) The opposition demanded arms checks for the police.

The author of (2) meant to say that the political opposition wanted the police to have the right to check suspected criminals for firearms. But an equally valid alternative interpretation is that the police themselves should be checked for firearms.

Both example (1) and example (2) allow two different interpretations, but the ambiguity of (1) is of a different nature to that of (2). Example (1) can have different meanings because the word *chair* has more than one meaning.

Linguistics, First Edition. Edited by Anne E. Baker and Kees Hengeveld.

The ambiguity here is a matter of **lexical meaning**. In (2) this is not the case. Here, the words have the same meaning in each of the two interpretations. The ambiguity lies in the fact that the police can be either the subject or the object of the firearms checks demanded by the opposition. In the one interpretation we mentally fill in the police as the subject of checks (the police check for arms), in the other we fill in police as the object (other people check the police for arms). This ambiguity does not lie in the individual words and their meanings, but instead relates to the way in which the clause is constructed. This ambiguity is a matter of **compositional meaning**, since it arises from the possible constituent structures of the clause in (2). As we saw in Section 2.4.3, this type of ambiguity makes clauses more difficult to understand.

We define **meaning** as the information that is inextricably linked to the forms of language, whether these are words (lexical meaning) or constructions (compositional meaning). The subfield of linguistics that is concerned with the study of meaning is known as **semantics**.

The intricacies of lexical meaning will be discussed in Chapter 11. Here we will focus on the problem of the compositional meaning of clauses, following on from the discussion of the structure of clauses and their constituents in the previous chapters. After a number of general remarks concerning compositional meaning in Section 10.2 we will discuss the meaning of noun phrases in Section 10.3 and Section 10.4, and the meaning of verb phrases in Section 10.5 and Section 10.6.

10.2 Compositionality

In each of the pairs of sentences (3a,b), (4a,b), and (5a,b) the words are the same but they are presented in different orders.

(3) a. The teacher irritated the girl.
 b. The girl irritated the teacher.
(4) a. The man with the hammer destroyed the car.
 b. The man destroyed the car with the hammer.
(5) a. The car was not sold by Caroline.
 b. Not the car was sold by Caroline (, but the motor bike).

In (3b) *the girl* and *the teacher* in (3a) have swapped places. This change corresponds to a complete change in meaning, a change in role between the one who irritates and the one who is irritated. In (4b) the man used the hammer to destroy the car but (4a) just states that the man who destroyed the car had a hammer in his possession. The different positions of *not* in (5a) and (5b) indicate that in these two sentences different things are being negated. In (5a) *not* covers the whole sentence and means 'it is not the case that the car was sold by Caroline'. In (5b) *not* only covers what immediately follows and means 'it was not the car that was sold by Caroline'.

These examples show how the meaning of a sentence is not only determined by the meaning of the individual words it contains but also by the way in which these words have been combined. This principle is known as the principle of compositionality, which, as we showed in Section 1.2, is a defining feature of natural languages. This principle means that the meaning of a clause is not simply the sum of the meaning of the constituent words, but includes the syntactic relations between them. Note that this principle also applies at the level of constituents and compound words, as we can see in (6) and (7).

(6) a. right in front of the palace
    b. in front of the right palace
(7) a. shark hunter
    b. hunter shark

In (6a) the word *right* modifies the adposition *in front* of, but in (6b) the noun *palace*. The compound in (7a) means a person who hunts sharks whereas (7b) refers to a type of shark. Compound words as in (7) will be further discussed in Chapter 13. Here we will focus on sentential constituents.

10.3 Noun Pphrases: Reference

Let us go back to nineteenth-century Britain under the reign of Queen Victoria. The queen goes out for a walk in the park and is recognised by one of her subjects. This person could then make one of the following remarks (8) or (9).

(8) There's *Victoria* in the park.
(9) There's *the queen* in the park.

In this context, *Victoria* and *the queen* refer to the same person. *Victoria* and *the queen* are both noun phrases (NPs). As we saw in Section 6.5, NPs have a noun or pronoun as head. This head can be accompanied by one or more other elements. The key contribution which NPs make to the meaning of a clause is that they **refer** to people and objects. These in turn are the **referents**. Thus, in (8) the NP *Victoria* refers to the person we introduced above; and this person is the referent. The relationship between the NP and the person or object referred to is known as **reference** (see also Section 4.5, Section 7.8, and Section 7.9).

Examples (8) and (9) contain two different NPs that refer to one single referent. But whereas *Victoria* and *the queen* have the same referent, it is not possible to say that they have the same meaning. The two constituents may refer to the same person, but the information they give about this person is different. The NP *the queen* in (9) clearly indicates that we are talking about a reigning sovereign; with the NP *Victoria* in (8) this is not necessarily so. It follows that the reference and the meaning of an NP are not the same. This gives rise to the question of what the relation between meaning and reference is.

As we said in Section 10.1, meaning is the information that is tied up with a particular linguistic unit. Reference, on the other hand, is the link between a linguistic unit and the person or object it refers to. Meaning takes precedence over reference, since we may use various different kinds of semantic information to refer to the same person. The key point here is that it is meaning that makes reference possible. The information contained in the NPs *Victoria* or *the queen* forms the basis to be able to refer to that particular person (see also Section 4.5).

The NP *Victoria* has the proper name *Victoria* as its head. Proper names are nouns used by language users to refer to certain unique people or objects. Such proper names are consciously and often explicitly assigned to the particular person or object they refer to. This is not the case with other words such as *table* or *queen*. Nobody ever decided that a 'table' should be called *table*, or a 'queen' *queen*. The fact that these words refer to what they refer to has its foundation in an age-old convention in the English-speaking community. By contrast, the name *Victoria* used for this person was explicitly chosen, in this case by her father (interestingly after considerable discussion in the royal household), and conferred on June 21, 1819 when she was baptised. The link between a proper name and the person it refers to is therefore not conventional. It can be the result of an explicit act of naming as in *I baptise this child* .... In the case of a nickname there can be an explicit act of naming or it could be that one person starts using the name and others pick it up: *Mrs Brown* in Queen Victoria's case.

The NP *the queen* has the common noun *queen* as its head. Common nouns are nouns such as *baker*, *girl*, *bird*, *home*, *river*, *soap*, *cattle*, *length*, *joy*, and *bank*, and we can use these to refer to people and objects that belong to a certain category. The meaning of these terms defines what kind of person or object is meant. With the term *baker* we refer to people whose profession it is to bake and sell bread and other baked products. The term *queen* refers to female persons whose role it is to rule a country as a sovereign.

In examples (8) and (9) the NPs *Victoria* and *the queen* are used for **specific reference**, that is, when speakers refer to a referent that is known or familiar to them. This is the case in (8) and (9), where the speaker actually sees the referent walking in front of him. Proper names such as *Victoria* or *Mrs Brown* can of course be used for specific reference because they name a specific person or object. But what about common nouns? In contrast to proper names, common nouns do not necessarily refer to specific individual people, objects or concepts. In the particular case of (9), however, the NP does refer specifically since the referent of *the queen* is known to the speaker.

The opposite of specific reference is **non-specific reference**. This is the case when a speaker refers to a referent that is not known, as in example (10).

(10) Actually, does Sweden have a king or *a queen*?

With the NP *a queen* in (10) the speaker does not refer to a specific known referent. We are not concerned here with the identity of the head of state, but rather with the question of whether there is in Sweden somebody who can be described as *queen*. The difference between specific and non-specific can thus be defined as follows:

Specific reference: referent is known to the speaker
Non-specific reference: referent is not known to the speaker

Within each of these two categories we can make further distinctions. We will first discuss these distinctions, and then give examples of the ways in which languages express these distinctions.

Within the category of specific reference we must first distinguish **definite** and **indefinite reference**. The difference can be explained with examples (11a to d).

(11) a. There's the president in the limousine.
b. There's a president in the limousine.
c. There are the presidents in the limousine.
d. There are presidents in the limousine.

In these four examples the speaker refers to specific referents. Within the relevant context, the referent or referents are known to the speaker; in each case the speaker can actually see the referent(s) in front of him. So what is the difference between these examples? Let us start with (11a) and (11b). These differ in the use of the articles *the* and *a*. The use of *the* in (11a) indicates that the addressee, in the eyes of the speaker, should be able to identify the referent of the expression *the president*. The speaker assumes that the addressee has sufficient information to understand which president is meant. This is definite reference. In (11b), in contrast, the use of *a* signals that the speaker does not assume that the addressee knows or can find out which president is meant. The speaker is not presenting the referent of *a president* as identifiable for the addressee. This is indefinite reference.

In (11c) and (11d) we are talking about more than one president, but the same distinctions apply. In (11c), just as in (11a), the article *the* indicates that the reference is definite; the speaker expects the addressee to be able to identify which presidents are being referred to. In (11d), in contrast, there is no article, and in combination with the plural noun, this absence of an article means that the reference is indefinite. The presidents mentioned here are not presented as identifiable for the addressee.

We may thus define the distinction between definite and indefinite reference as follows:

Definite: referent is identifiable for the addressee according to the speaker
Indefinite: referent is not identifiable for the addressee according to speaker

Within the category of non-specific reference we can also make a further subdivision, that between generic and categorial reference. Example (12) illustrates the first type, that of nonspecific-generic reference.

(12) *The Siberian tiger* is almost extinct.

In (12) *The Siberian tiger* does not refer to an individual member of the species *Panthera tigris altaica*, but to the species as a whole, that is, to all possible members of the category 'Siberian tiger'. When, as in (12), reference is made to the species or category as a whole, this is known as **generic reference**. Generic reference is non-specific, since it does not concern a particular person or object, as we can see when we compare (12) with (13).

(13) **A Siberian tiger* is almost extinct.

Extinction is a process that applies to a biological species as a whole, and not to individual members of a species. In (12) the reference of the Siberian tiger is generic; what is referred to is the species; and this is the kind of referent to which the meaning of the predicate *extinct* can be applied. In (13), on the other hand, *a Siberian tiger* refers to a particular specimen of the category; and it is not possible to apply the notion of 'being extinct' to one animal. Example (13) is therefore not acceptable.

The second type of non-specific reference is **categorial reference**, as illustrated in (14).

(14) What is the best way to learn *a foreign language*?

In (14), *a foreign language* does not refer to a particular member of the category 'foreign languages', so we do not have specific reference here. But neither does it refer to the class of foreign languages as a whole, so we do not have generic reference either. What is being referred is a random member of the category, as we can see when we compare (14) to (15).

(15) Yesterday I heard Edith speaking *a foreign language*.

In (15) we have specific reference, even though this is indefinite. Edith was speaking a specific foreign language, but the speaker does not specify which one it was. In (14), on the other hand, the question refers to the learning of a foreign language in general. In this context *a foreign language* does not refer to one specific foreign language, but to any foreign language, that is the category, hence the term categorial reference. In this type of reference one of the category that is not further identified represents the category in question.

Generic reference and categorial reference have in common that no reference is made to a specific individual member of a category. The difference is that in generic reference we refer to the category as a whole, whereas in categorial reference the reference is to a random member of the category. The various kinds of reference we have distinguished so far are set out in Figure 10.1.

<table>
<tr><td rowspan="4">Reference</td><td rowspan="2">Specific
(known to the speaker)</td><td>Definite
(identifiable for the addressee)</td></tr>
<tr><td>Indefinite
(not identifiable for the addressee)</td></tr>
<tr><td rowspan="2">Non-specific
(not known to the speaker)</td><td>Generic
(category as a whole)</td></tr>
<tr><td>Categorial
(random member of category)</td></tr>
</table>

Figure 10.1 Schematic representation of the different types of reference.

One of the ways in which languages give formal expression to the different types of reference is by using articles. The way the English system operates in this respect, at least in the singular, can be illustrated using our previous examples (16) to (19).

(16) *Specific-definite*
There's the president in the limousine.
(17) *Specific-indefinite*
A president is in the limousine.
(18) *Nonspecific-generic*
The Siberian tiger is almost extinct.
(19) *Nonspecific-categorial*
What is the best way to learn *a foreign language?*

The situation in English is rather complex. The definite article *the* can be used for specific-definite (16) as well as for nonspecific-generic reference (18). The indefinite article *a*, on the other hand, can be used both for specific-indefinite (17) and for nonspecific-categorial reference (19). The system can be represented as in Figure 10.2.

In Turkish we find a similar system of semantic distinctions. Where English uses the indefinite article *a*, Turkish will use the indefinite article *bir;* and where English uses the definite article *the*, Turkish will not use an article. In addition, however, Turkish systematically distinguishes between specific and non-specific reference, although this is limited to patient arguments (for the notion of patient, see Section 7.4). Specific patient arguments in Turkish will

<table>
<tr><td>Specific-definite

the</td><td>Specific-indefinite

a</td></tr>
<tr><td>Non-specific-generic

the</td><td>Non-specific-categorial

a</td></tr>
</table>

Figure 10.2 Different types of reference in English.

be marked for this role by what is called the Accusative case; non-specific patient arguments will not be marked for this case. The examples in (20) to (23) illustrate the Turkish reference system.

Turkish

(20) *Specific-definite*

Bu	*gazete-yi*	çıkarmak	zor	bir	iş.
this	newspaper.*accusative*	publish	heavy	*article*	job

'It is hard work publishing this newspaper.'

(21) *Specific-indefinite*

Her	gün	*bir*	*gazete-yi*	okuyorum.
every	day	*article*	newspaper.*accusative*	I.read

'Every day I read a (particular) newspaper.'

(22) *Nonspecific-generic*

Gazete	çıkarmak	zor	bir	iş.
Newspaper	publish	heavy	*article*	job

'It is hard work publishing newspapers.'

(23) *Nonspecific-categorial*

Her	gün	*bir*	*gazete*	okuyorum.
every	day	*article*	newspaper	I.read

'Every day I read a (any) newspaper.'

In examples (21) and (23) *gazete* is accompanied by the indefinite article *bir*, which is comparable to English *a*, as we can see in the translations. In (20) and (22) *gazete* has no article, where English would have used *the* in (20) and no article in (22). An important difference between Turkish and English is, however, that in the specific examples (20) and (21), but not in the non-specific examples (22) and (23), the accusative case is used for the patient, hence *gazete-yi*. In (20) we have this *gazete-yi* because the clause is about the difficulties involved in publishing one particular newspaper, whereas (22) is about newspaper publishing in general. In (21) the accusative *gazete-yi* appears because the speaker is a regular reader of one particular newspaper; in (23), in contrast, the speaker also reads a newspaper every day, but this time it can be any newspaper. The Turkish system is summarised in Figure 10.3.

Specific-definite *accusative* + *Ø*	Specific-indefinite *accusative* + *bir*
Non-specific-generic *Ø*	Non-specific-categorial *bir*

Figure 10.3 Different types of reference in Turkish.

Specific-definite *le*	Specific-indefinite *le*
Non-specific-generic *le*	Non-specific-categorial *se*

Figure 10.4 Different types of reference in Samoan.

A different reference system operates in Samoan. In this language we find a single article, *le*, which is used for specific-definite, specific-indefinite and nonspecific-generic reference; a different article, *se*, is used exclusively for nonspecific-categorial reference, as we can see in examples (24) to (27).

Samoan

(24) *Specific-definite*
Sa nofo *le* *fafine* i *le* *fale*
past sit *article* woman in *article* house
'The woman sat in the house.'

(25) *Specific-indefinite*
Sa iai *le* *ulugalii*
past exist *article* couple
'Once there was a couple.'

(26) *Nonspecific-generic*
E aina *le* *gatta*
general.time be.eaten *article* snake
'Snakes are edible.'

(27) *Nonspecific-categorial*
'Aumai *se* *niu*
Bring *article* coconut
'Bring me a coconut.'

The article *se* only occurs in (27). This is a clear example of non-specific reference, since the speaker is asking for a coconut that is not known to him. At the same time the reference is categorial, for the speaker is not asking for the category or species as a whole but for any member of it. The Samoan system is presented in Figure 10.4.

10.4 Noun Phrases: Deixis and Anaphora

In Section 10.3 we discussed noun phrases with a noun as their head. Here we will consider noun phrases with a pronoun as their head (see also Section 7.4).

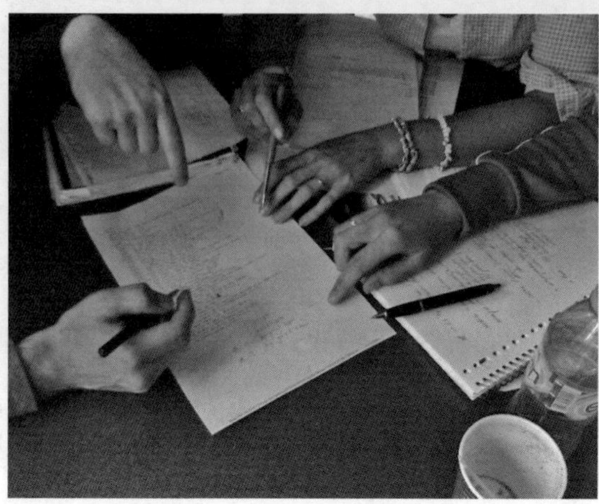

Figure 10.5 Use of deictic terms. Image courtesy of Esther Parriger.

Imagine you are working with some other students on a paper and the conversation in (28) takes place, as illustrated in Figure 10.5:

(28) Toby: Shall *I* rewrite *it* for *you*?
Eva: Yes, *you* will need to send the text to *us*.
Toby: When do you need that version by?

The pronouns (in italics) in these clauses refer in a way that is different from noun phrases that have a noun as their head. Pronouns refer to people or objects with the help of a very limited number of distinctions, such as person and number.

Within the category 'person' the key distinction is that between the speaker (first person), the addressee (second person) and somebody or something that is neither the speaker nor the addressee (third person). In the category 'number' we usually find singular and plural, but in some languages also more specific distinctions such as dual (involving two) or paucal (involving a few). Within the set of non-singular forms sometimes a distinction is made between inclusive and exclusive. In inclusive reference the addressee is included, in exclusive reference it is not. In English that distinction is not made in the form; the pronoun *we* can be used in both ways and it is only clear from the context. Thus *us* in (28) is used exclusively, that is, excluding Toby, the person addressed.

Figure 10.6 contains a survey of the distinctions employed in Tokelau, a Polynesian language.

The distinctions that operate in the Tokelau pronominal system are between first, second, and third person, and between singular, dual, and plural. The first person also has a further distinction between 'inclusive' and 'exclusive'.

	singular	dual	plural
1st person inclusive		*ki taua/ki ta* 'the two of us (me and you)'	*ki tatou* 'we more than two (me, you, and others)'
1st person exclusive	*au* 'I' *kita* 'poor me'	*ki maua/ki ma* 'the two of us, (me and someone else, not you)'	*ki matou* 'we more than two (me and others, not you)'
2nd person	*koe* 'you'	*koulua* 'the two of you'	*koutou* 'you more than two'
3rd person	*ia* 'he, she, it'	*ki laua/ki la* 'they two'	*ki latou* 'they more than two'

Figure 10.6 The pronominal system of Tokelau.

Additionally, within the 'first person exclusive' there is a distinction between 'neutral' and 'emotive': *au* means I, and *kita* 'poor me'.

Semantic categories such as person and number enable the addressee to identify the referents of the pronouns. Returning to the conversation in (28), we can see that *I* refers to the speaker (Toby), and *you* to the rest of the group. The reference here is dependent on the roles of the speaker and the addressee in this utterance. When Eva answers the question, *you* has a different referent from *you* in Toby's utterance. *It* in (28) is more ambiguous than *I* and *you*. The word *it* refers to a single object, not a person. In this case Toby is pointing to the text (see Figure 10.5), and this makes the reference clear. Where words refer to entities that can be identified on the basis of a common frame of reference within the speech situation we use the term **deixis** (from Greek for 'pointing'). The personal pronouns *he, she, they* can also be used deictically, referring to people who are neither the speaker nor the addressee, as in (29).

(29) I don't want to give the money to her (pointing to a girl).

In addition there is a range of other deictic elements, such as the demonstrative pronouns *this*, *that*, and *these*, and adverbs such as *here* and *now*. *Now* refers to the time at which the conversation takes place, and *here* to its location.

In (30) and (31) we have personal pronouns with a different kind of reference.

(30) This boy goes past here every day, but I don't even know who *he* is.
(31) How is Michaela? I haven't seen *her* for a long time.

In (30) *he* does not refer directly to a person present in the speech situation. So the reference here is not deictic. *He* refers back to the noun phrase *a boy*. Similarly, in (32), *her* refers back to *Michaela*. That is to say, the referents of *he* and *her* are retrieved indirectly, namely on the basis of the noun phrases *a boy* and *Michaela* introduced earlier. The pronouns *he* and *her* refer back to

Figure 10.7 Elicitation test picture. Montrul, S. 'Research methods in L2 acquisition and bilingualism' 6th EMLAR (Experimental Methods in Language Acquisition Research), Utrecht, The Netherlands, February 3–5, 2010.

these noun phrases. When a pronominal element does not 'point' directly to a referent present in the speech situation, but refers back to a constituent introduced earlier, known as the antecedent, reference is called **anaphoric** (see also Section 4.5).

Reflexive pronouns, as were described in Section 7.8, can only be anaphoric pronouns. Imagine that you hear the story in (32) together with the picture (Figure 10.7).

(32) Rob is Tom's boss. Rob just came into Tom's office and he looks angry. Rob is pointing a finger at Tom. Tom is very upset about this. Tom is upset that Rob is pointing at himself.

Would you judge the story in (32) to be true about the picture? You probably would not, since Rob is pointing at Tom, not at himself. Reflexive pronouns in English can in fact only refer to noun phrases within the same clause. Therefore *himself* can only refer back to Rob, not to Tom. In other languages such as Chinese or Korean it can refer to both. First and second language learners make many errors in this area of language when learning English.

10.5 Verb Phrases: Tense and Aspect

In contrast to noun phrases, verb phrases refer to something that involves the passage of time. This can be an action, an event, a process, or a state. The general term used here is **situation**, a collection of circumstances that is the case at a certain moment. Consider the examples in (33).

(33) a. Jane is knitting a sweater for Charlie.
b. The children are playing in the garden.
c. Carlos fell down the stairs.
d. Our train arrived at platform 3.
e. A fuel tank exploded behind the flat.
f. Marita knows a lot about computers.
g. Uncle Herbert is living in London.

Each of the situations described in (33a to g) covers a period of time that may be longer or shorter; here, events such as in (33e), that take a minimal amount of time to occur, are the shortest. This is a key difference between VPs and NPs; NPs name people, objects, and ideas without, in principle, referring to any period of time. Nominal expressions such as the *girl, a dog, books, Coleridge, we,* and *this* all name their referent but do not place them in time. This does not hold for all NPs, though, since there are expressions such as *the meeting, the match,* and *the concert* that name events involving a certain passage of time. Time is, however, in general not part of the meaning of NPs. In VPs, on the other hand, the time element necessarily forms part of the meaning.

The global temporal meaning of verb phrases is, in many languages, realised through the grammatical category of **tense**. Tense localises the time of the situation described in a clause. Compare the clauses in (34).

(34) a. Theo is clearing the table.
b. Theo cleared the table.
c. Theo will clear the table.

The verb forms *is clearing, cleared,* and *will clear* indicate where the clearing of the table is located in time in relation to the moment of speaking. We may imagine time as a line on which situations can be ordered from left (past) to right (future), as in Figure 10.8. On this line we can then locate situations with respect to the moment of speaking (S). The moment in time when a situation takes place is usually represented as E (an abbreviation of *event time*). When we do this for the three situations in (34a to c), we get the following result: in (34a) the period of table clearing (E) includes the moment of speaking (S); in (34b) the period of table clearing lies before S; and in (34c) it comes after S.

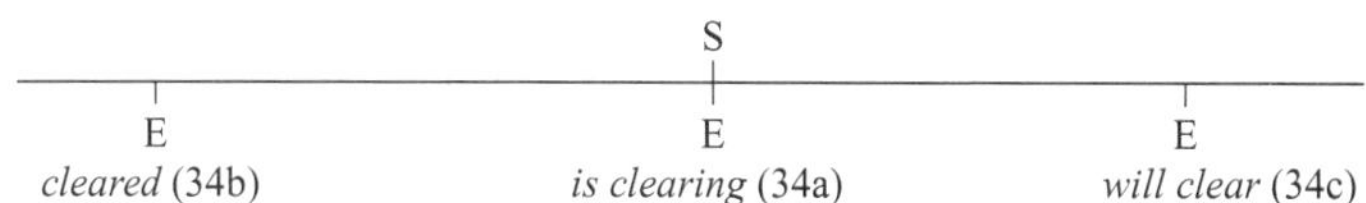

Figure 10.8 Tense in (34) (E = event time, S = moment of speaking).

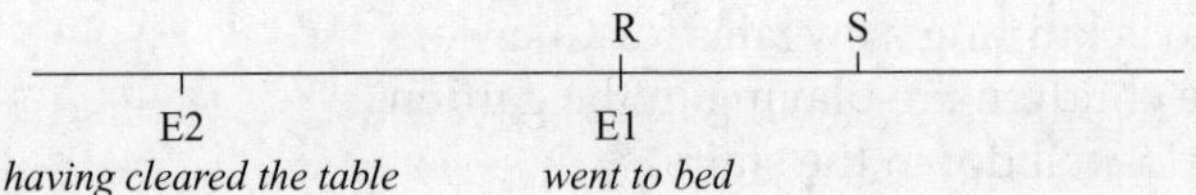

Figure 10.9 Absolute and relative tense in (35) (E = event time, R = point of reference, S = moment of speaking).

The three different meanings distinguished in (34) are expressed through the grammatical category of tense, specifically its three subcategories of **past**, **present**, and **future**.

These three tenses are interpreted here in relation to the speech moment (S). This is known as **absolute tense**. But is tense always absolute? Take example (35). Is the speech moment (S) here also the point of reference?

(35) Theo went to bed after having cleared the table.

In this example, two different situations are located in time: Theo's going to bed, and his clearing of the table. The moment when his going to bed takes place, E1, is located in time relative to the moment of speaking (S). The fact that the past, an absolute tense, is used here makes clear that Theo's going to bed took place before the moment of speaking. But now the moment E1 serves as a point of reference (R) for determining when exactly the table clearing took place, E2. Here the use of the auxiliary *having* plus the participle *cleared* indicates that Theo's table clearing took place before his going to bed. When, as in this case, the point of reference is a moment in time that is different from the moment of speaking (S), we have to do with **relative tense**. Figure 10.9 gives a schematic representation of the difference between absolute and relative tense, as expressed in example (35).

The relative character of the construction with *have* plus *cleared* comes out even more clearly when we place the whole event in the future. Suppose that someone at the table, before it had been cleared, said (36).

(36) Theo will go to bed after having cleared the table.

When does the table clearing take place now? Again, before Theo's going to bed, but now after the moment of speaking, as represented in Figure 10.10.

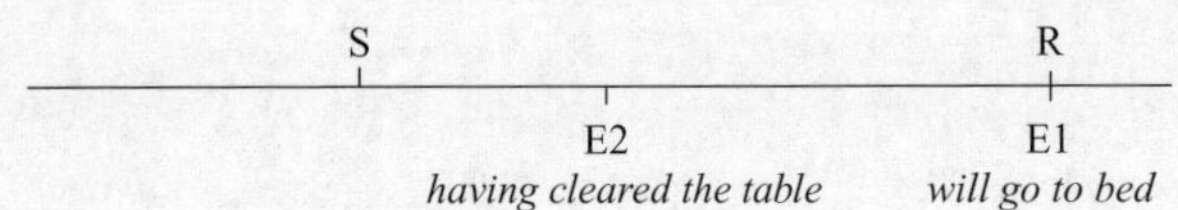

Figure 10.10 Absolute and relative tense in (36) (E = event time, R = point of reference, S = moment of speaking).

Some languages do not use the grammatical category of tense. Instead they use lexical elements such as *tomorrow* or *last year* to refer to points in time and to locate events and situations in time. Such expressions are not considered to be part of the category tense. Only changes in the form of verbs or other grammatical elements such as auxiliaries and particles can be considered expressions of tense.

When languages do use tense, the range of tenses may be rather limited. Quite a few languages only distinguish between the past and everything else that is not part of the past. On the other hand, there are languages such as Amele, a language spoken in Papua New Guinea, which has a very rich set of distinctions. In this language we find no less than three different verb forms that refer to the past: the past on the same day, the past of yesterday, and the past sometime before yesterday. The examples in (37) illustrate these different options.

Amele

(37) a. Ija dana eu fi -g -a
I man that see *-1.singular* *-past(today)*
'I saw that man (today).'

b. Ija dana eu fi -g -an
I man that see *-1.singular* *-past(yesterday)*
'I saw that man (yesterday).'

c. Ija dana eu fi -em
I man that see *-1.singular.past(before yesterday)*
'I saw that man (before yesterday).'

As we see, the time element in the meaning of verb phrases can be expressed in a range of different ways through the category tense. Tense links the situation described in a clause to the timeline, and in this way makes clear where this situation is relative to the moment of speaking or to some other point of reference.

In the two examples in (38) the time element is also expressed, but this time we encounter something new.

(38) a. Yesterday at half past eleven Laura began to wash her car.
b. Yesterday at half past eleven Laura was washing her car.

The time reference is the same in both cases. Both the lexical expression *Yesterday at half past eleven* and the grammatical forms *began* and *was* serve to firmly locate the event that is being described at a moment in time well before the moment of speaking. The difference is that (38a) presents the car washing from its starting point, whereas (38b) presents the same situation while it is in full swing. This difference does not arise from the choice of a particular tense, since this is the same in both cases (*began* and *was*), so both situations are connected to the timeline in exactly the same way. Rather, the difference is one of presentation and perspective. In (38a) the situation is presented from the perspective of its beginning ('Laura is beginning to wash her car'), whereas in (38b) the perspective is that of its going on ('Laura is busy washing her car'). Such differences of presentation and perspective are related to the grammatical category of **aspect**: in (38a) we have ingressive or inchoative aspect, and in (38b) progressive aspect. The aspect category does not link a situation to the timeline, but specifies the temporal perspective from which the speaker is presenting the situation.

In addition to the aspectual distinctions in (38), another, frequent, aspectual distinction is between **perfective** and **imperfective aspect**. In a clause with perfective aspect the situation is presented as a finished and completed whole; in a clause with imperfective aspect the situation is presented as being in progress. The Italian example in (39) illustrates this distinction.

Italian

(39)	Gianni leggeva	quando	entrai.
	Gianni read.*preterit.imperfective*	when	enter.1.*sing.preterit.perfective*
	'Gianni was reading when I came in.'		

The perfective verb form *entrai* ('I came in') describes a finished situation; the event of 'entering' has been completed. The imperfective *leggeva* ('he was reading'), on the other hand, describes a situation as it is going on and developing; this situation was already going on when the speaker came in.

10.6 Verb Phrases: Situation Types

A verb phrase refers to a situation, a collection of circumstances that exists at a given moment and involves a certain passage of time. The kinds of situation referred to by VPs can, however, be extremely varied. There are two key distinctions that result in four **situation types**.

The first distinction concerns situations in which something changes versus situations in which this is not the case. The first type of situation is known as **dynamic**, the second type as **static**. Dynamic situations are illustrated in (40a and b), static situations in (41a and b).

(40) a. Mary sat down on the sofa.
b. Mary grew weak.

(41) a. Mary was sitting on the sofa.
b. Mary was weak.

In the situations in (40), something changes. At first, Mary was not sitting on the sofa, and then she completed the action of sitting down (40a). In (40b) she was first reasonably strong and then that changed. The examples in (41) describe situations where nothing changes: Mary remained sitting in (41a); in (41b) she was already weak and stayed so.

Dynamic situations are different from static situations in that they develop at a certain rate. If we want to determine whether a situation is static or dynamic, a good test is to try and add an adverbial expression such as *slowly*. In a dynamic situation such an expression is acceptable, but not in a static situation. In (42) and (43) we apply this test to examples (40) and (41).

(42) a. Mary sat down slowly on the sofa.
b. Mary slowly grew weak.
(43) a. *Mary was sitting slowly on the sofa.
b. *Mary was slowly weak.

Various languages systematically differentiate in their grammars between dynamic and static VPs. One of these is Abchaz, a language spoken in the Caucasus. In this language we find a special declarative marker that marks a clause as a statement. The form of this marker is dependent on the type of situation involved. If the clause involves a dynamic situation and uses a dynamic verb, the marker is *yt'*; but if it involves a static situation and verb, the marker is *p'*. We can see this in the following examples, where (44) uses the dynamic verb *taa* 'visit', and (45) the static verb *taxe* 'want'.

Abchaz
(44) Dynamic

Də	-s	-táa	-wa	-yt'.
3.sing.male	*-1.sing.*	-visit	*-progressive*	*-declarative*

'He is visiting me.'

(45) *Static*

Yə	-s	-taxé	-w	-p'.
3.sing.irrational	*-1.sing*	-want	*-present*	*-declarative*

'I want it.'

A second important distinction is that between **controlled** situations, that is where one of the participants controls whether the situation can happen, versus situations that are **non-controlled** by one of the participants. Controlled situations are illustrated in (46), situations that are non-controlled in (47).

(46) a. Mary sat down on the sofa
b. Mary was sitting on the sofa.
(47) a. Mary grew weak.
b. Mary was weak.

Mary can decide for herself whether she wants to sit down on the sofa, or whether she wants to stay seated (46), but she cannot control whether she will grow or remain weak (47).

The difference between controlled versus non-controlled situations is that controlled situations can be the subject of an order. If, on the other hand, something is not under the addressee's control, there is not much point in ordering them to do it. This provides us with a handy test for determining whether a sentence describes a controlled situation or not. For a controlled situation it should be possible to turn the sentence into an order, but not for a non-controlled situation. Applying this test to (46) and (47) we see that the test gives the right results: the first pair involves controlled situations (48), and the second pair non-controlled situations (49).

(48) a. Sit down on the sofa!
b. Stay seated on the sofa!
(49) a. *Grow weak!
b. *Be weak!

In some languages the distinction between controlled and non-controlled VPs is expressed in their grammar. A good example of this is the Chickasaw language where we find the distinctions marked as in (50) and (51).

Chickasaw
(50) Sa -ttola.
1.sing.noncontrol -fall
'I fell (over).'

(51) Ittola -li.
fall *-1.sing.control*
'I fell (deliberately).'

Examples (50) and (51) contain the same verb *ittola* ('fall'). In (50) we have a non-controlled situation; the fall is an accident; the person falling has no control over it. But in (51) the fall is intentional, the person falling allowed himself to fall down. In Chickasaw this difference is expressed through a different conjugation of the verb. In (50) the prefix *sa-* indicates that the subject is first person singular and has no control; in (51) the suffix *-li* also marks the subject as first person singular, but this time it signals that the referent of the subject has control.

Together, the two distinctions we have discussed here, dynamic/static and control/non-control, produce four different situation types, as schematically represented in Figure 10.11.

In Figure 10.11 the names of the four situation types are in italics. Examples (40a and b) and (41a and b) are used to illustrate these four situation types, distinguished using the various tests we described above. Dynamic situations have a certain speed, static situations do not. Controlled situations can be the subject of an order, but non-controlled situations cannot. Let us now apply these tests to some other examples (52) to (55).

	dynamic	static
controlled	*action* 'Mary sat down on the sofa.'	*position* 'Mary was sitting on the sofa.'
non-controlled	*process* 'Mary fell ill.'	*state* 'Mary was ill.'

Figure 10.11 Four situation types.

(52) a. Pyotr finished reading the book.
b. Pyotr slowly finished reading the book.
c. Finish reading the book, Pyotr!

An action as in (52a) is a dynamic controlled situation. So an adverbial expression like *slowly* is acceptable (52b); and equally, the clause can be turned into an order (52c).

(53) a. Jessica kept very silent.
b. *Jessica slowly kept very silent.
c. Keep very silent, Jessica!

Preserving a state of being, as illustrated in (53a), is static and controlled. Adding the adverbial *slowly* is therefore not acceptable (53b); but the clause can be changed into an order (53c).

(54) a. Ling turned deadly pale.
b. Ling slowly turned deadly pale.
c. *Turn deadly pale, Ling!

The opposite of a state is a process, as in (54a), which is dynamic but non-controlled. So, we can add *slowly* (54b), but we cannot turn the clause into an order (54c).

(55) a. Ali is bald.
b. *Ali is slowly bald.
c. *Be bald, Ali!

Sentence (55a) is a good example of our fourth and final situation type, a state that is neither dynamic nor controlled. A state does not have any speed, so *slowly* is not acceptable here (55b); and equally, we cannot turn this clause into an order (55c).

The examples we have discussed here demonstrate that the situation type that is being expressed in a VP does determine the syntactic options available for that VP. This underlines, once again, the close relation between syntax and compositional semantics.

Summary

Meaning is information which stands in a fixed relation to the forms of language. Such information may be contained in words (**lexical meaning**), but also in constructions (**compositional meaning**). The subdiscipline of linguistics that is concerned with the study of meaning is known as **semantics**. The way in which words are formed and then combined into constituents and clauses of various types determines the meaning of the construction. This is the principle of compositionality.

Noun phrases are used to **refer** to people or objects. The person or object that is being referred to is the **referent**. The relationship between the noun phrase and the person or object that is being referred to is known as **reference**. Reference is **specific** when it is made to a referent that is known to the speaker. It is **non-specific** when the referent is not known to the speaker. Specific reference is **definite** when the referent can be identified by the hearer; it is **indefinite** when this is not the case. Non-specific reference is **generic** when it is made to a kind in general; it is **categorial** when the reference is to a random member of that kind.

In addition we need to distinguish between **deixis** and **anaphoric reference**. This distinction matters in particular for pronouns. In deixis, the reference is dependent on the speech situation. In anaphoric reference, the reference is dependent on the surrounding text.

Verb phrases describe situations. It is a characteristic feature of situations that they involve (the passing of) time. The temporal meaning of a verb phrase can be further specified within the grammatical category of **tense**, which concerns the localisation of a situation in time, either in the **past**, the **present** or the **future**. We further distinguish between **absolute tense**, that is when the tempus expression needs to be interpreted in relation to the moment of speaking, and **relative tense**, when the tense-expression has to be interpreted relative to a moment in time that has been introduced earlier. Tense as a grammatical category needs to be distinguished from another category, **aspect**, which concerns the temporal perspective from which a situation is being presented. A frequently occurring aspectual distinction is that between **perfective** (finished, completed) aspect and **imperfective** (non-complete) aspect.

Verb phrases can give expression to various different **situation types**. Here, important distinctions are that between situations in which something changes (**dynamic**) and situations where this is not the case (**static**), and between situations which are **controlled** and those that are **non-controlled**.

Assignments

1. Explain the compositionality principle by giving three pairs of examples where the same words, when ordered differently, produce different meanings.

2. Discuss the difference in reference of the noun phrase *a second-hand car* in the following three sentences:
   (a) He drives a second-hand car
   (b) He wants to buy a second-hand car
   (c) A second-hand car is always trouble
3. Determine for each of the pronouns (in italics) below whether they are used deictically or anaphorically.

   Marilyn and Arnie were sitting on a terrace, when an old acquaintance of *theirs* walked past. 'Look, there is Stan,' said Arnie and *he* called out to *him*. 'Hey, long time no see, how are *you* today?' answered the passerby, turning around. '*I* am a daddy now,' said Arnie happily. 'And *you* know who is the mother?' '*She* is, I suppose,' answered Stan, and *he* cast a glance at Marilyn.

4. Indicate whether the verbs (in italics) in the text below express absolute or relative tense, and say as precisely as possible which tense it is.

   Yesterday I *met* Gerard. He *said* he *had* just *been* to the hairdresser's, and he *was* very unhappy with the result. 'I *am* totally embarrassed by this haircut,' he *said*, 'Tomorrow I *am going* back and you bet I *will give* him a piece of my mind, that amateur! But I don't *want* to walk around like this any longer, so believe me, by then I *will have had* my hair cut properly.'

5. Give four examples of sentences to illustrate the four different types of situation: dynamic, static, controlled, non-controlled.

TEST YOURSELF

1. What is meaning?
2. What is the difference between lexical meaning and compositional meaning?
3. 'The meaning of a sentence is more than the sum of the meanings of the words in that sentence.' What is the name of this principle?
4. What is the difference between specific and non-specific reference?
5. What is generic reference?
6. What is the difference between deixis and anaphoric reference?
7. Why are the words *I* and *you* always deictic?
8. What is the difference between tense and aspect?
9. What is the name for a tense that needs to be interpreted relative to a moment in time that is different from the moment of speaking?
10. What is a dynamic situation type?
11. Give an example of a controlled situation type.

Acknowledgments and Further Reading

A good introduction to the various aspects of sentence semantics is Saeed (1997). For reference, deixis and anaphora see Lyons (1977). Universals of situation type and aspect are discussed in Smith (1991) and Dik (1997). Comrie (1976) and (1985) are two succinct monographs about aspects and tense respectively. Bybee, Perkins and Pagliuca (1994) contains an extensive typological survey of tense, aspect and modality. The examples are from the following sources: Turkish – Lewis (1967); Samoan – Mosel and Hovdhaugen (1992); Tokelau – Hovdhaugen *et al.* (1997); Amele – Roberts (1987); Abchaz – Spruit (1986); Chickasaw – Munro and Gordon (1982), cited in Comrie (1989). The picture in Figure 10.5 is by Esther Parigger, the picture in 10.7 is taken from Montrul (2009).

Words and Their Meaning

In the previous chapter we discussed the meaning of sentences. In this part we will take a closer look at words and their meaning. In Chapter 11 we will focus on the vocabulary of a language, also known as its lexicon. Here we will discuss, among other things, the various types of word that can be distinguished, the different kinds of information contained in the lexicon, and the sorts of relations that can occur between words.

Words may consist of various meaningful elements. For instance, we may create new words such as *greenish* in the process of derivation, thereby expanding the lexicon with a word that consists of the two meaningful elements *green-* and *-ish*. Another process is that of inflection, which enables us to fit a word into the grammatical structure of a sentence, as for example when the verb *(to) work* appears as *worked* in the sentence *He hardly worked*. Again the word consists of two meaningful elements, *work-* and *-ed*. These two processes, derivation and inflection, will be the subject of Chapter 12 on word formation.

In the last chapter of this part, Chapter 13, we will discuss the meaning of combinations of words, in compounds such as *underground* and *wheelchair*, and in (idiomatic) expressions such as *all the rage*, used to describe something that is widely popular.

chapter 11

Lexicon

11.1 Introduction

It is not difficult to establish how many words there are in the following sentence:

(1) When the mayor had not shown up by three, the organising committee began to get worried.

Counting the units in (1) that are separated by a space, we arrive at a total of sixteen words. It appears that writing conventions determine what can count as a word here. But what if we find a sentence as in (2)?

(2) Thassit!

Here we write more or less as we speak, and if we keep to the convention that spaces indicate what can count as a word, then it follows that we have only one word here. Not many people will agree with this, though. The form *thassit* is a contraction of the three elements *that*, *is* and *it*, which in other contexts may each be used independently of one another. Conversely, a form like *daisycutter*, a term for a fragmentation bomb, combines two elements, *daisy* and *cutter*, which each have an identifiable and independent meaning on their own, but which taken together form one new word with a single new meaning.

Linguistics, First Edition. Edited by Anne E. Baker and Kees Hengeveld.

So, are there better ways to establish what a word is than by this writing convention? Indeed, there are, and these will be discussed in Section 11.2. Next, in Section 11.3, we will discuss the relationship between the form of a word and its meaning, and we will see that in most cases this relationship is arbitrary. In Section 11.4 we will consider the distinction between content words and function words, since this plays an important role in many different aspects of language. From Section 11.5 onwards we will discuss the inventory of words that make up a language, its lexicon. In Section 11.6 we will take a look at the various kinds of information a lexicon contains. In Section 11.7 we then discuss various types of dictionaries, which in different ways try to capture the lexicon of one or more languages. In Section 11.8 we focus on word meanings and the various kinds of relations that can exist between them. In Section 11.9 we will see how the meaning of a word can be described. Finally, in Section 11.10, we will explore the causes of the similarity of words across languages. Thus, in contrast to the previous chapter, which was devoted to sentence meaning, here we will concentrate above all on words and their meanings.

11.2 What is a Word?

In order to establish whether a certain language element is or is not a **word**, we may use two criteria. These involve (a) sound shape, and (b) syntax.

In English the sound shape of a word requires the presence of at least one vowel, as in *first* and *black*, which contrast with impossible word forms such as *frst* and *blck*. In Czech the sound shape of a word requires the presence of a vowel or of one of the sounds *l* or *r*. In this language you find words such as *prst* 'finger' and *vlk* 'wolf', whereas words such as *pmst* or *vnk* are impossible. Despite the differences between these two languages, in both cases there are clear restrictions on possible word forms that are definable in terms of their sound shape.

Among the syntactic conditions for a word is the requirement that it should be possible to place it in different positions in a clause and that it should freely combine with other words (see also Chapter 6). For example, the expression *that is it* from (2) can be converted into the question *is that it?*, showing that the three elements that compose these clauses can occupy different positions with respect to each other. Similarly, the element *bread* can be combined with the element *the* in *the bread*, or with *sliced* in *sliced bread*. Another syntactic condition on words is that they cannot be interrupted. For instance, if someone wants to say the word *antidisestablishmentarianism* and accidentally says *antidisestablishrentarianism*, the only way to repair this is by starting all over again.

There are, however, difficult cases, where it is not immediately clear whether we can say of a language element that it is a word. An example is the following opening sentence of Virgil's *Aeneid* in (3).

Latin
(3) Arm-a vir-um=que can-o.
weapon-*plural.accusative* man-*acc*=and sing-*1.singular*
'I am singing of the weapons and the man.'

The form =*que* 'and' is closely linked to *vir-um* 'man-*accusative*' and cannot be pronounced separately. Syntactically, however, this =*que* certainly does not belong to *vir-um*, but to the combination of *arm-a* and *vir-um*, since it links these two together. This kind of word, which cannot have a stress of its own, is called a **clitic**. This term comes from the Greek verb for 'to lean' – the clitic element leans, so to speak, on another word that supports it. To show the difference between elements which form part of a word and clitics (which are words by themselves), the symbol '=' is used to indicate the boundary between the word and the clitic in those cases where the standard orthography would write them together.

Another example of clitic elements comes from Spanish in (4).

Spanish
(4) a. Dá=me=lo
give.*imperative*=me=it
'Give it to me.'
b. ¿Me lo das?
me it give.*indicative.present.3.singular*
'Do you give it to me?'

The words *me* 'me' and *lo* 'it' do not carry a stress of their own and cannot be pronounced separately. These clitics follow imperative verb forms, as in (4a), but precede indicative verb forms, as in (4b), where they are also written separately from the verb. The fact that clitics such as these occur in different orders shows that clitics are syntactically independent, but phonologically dependent, units.

11.3 The Relation Between Word Form and Meaning

A word has a form and a meaning. The form of a word is usually arbitrary. There is nothing in the form of the word *horse* that tells us what kind of animal is meant. This animal may be referred to by quite different forms in other languages, even in closely related languages (French *cheval*, Polish *koń*, Dutch *paard*). That the form of most words is arbitrary becomes quite clear when we compare them to the exceptional cases where there is a certain natural relation between form and meaning, such as *cuckoo*, *cock-a-doodle-do*, and *atishoo*. Even these words are different from one language to the next, as we can see from the examples in (5):

(5)

English	*French*	*Polish*	*Dutch*
cuckoo	coucou	ku ku	koekoek
atishoo	atchoum	apsik	hatsjoe
cock-a-doodle-do	cocorico	kukuryku	kukeleku

The arbitrary nature of words goes hand in hand with their conventional character. That is, the form-meaning relationship is based on social convention, a kind of unconscious agreement between users of the same language. If there is no natural reason to prefer one particular word form over another, the members of a particular language community will simply have to keep to the convention that *horse* is used for HORSE and *cow* for COW (remember that we use capitals to represent concepts, Section 2.5.2).

There are, however, languages in which the form of a rather large number of words is not arbitrary, particularly in sign languages, where about a third of the signs used are iconic. In (6) there are pictures of signs from several different sign languages.

(6)

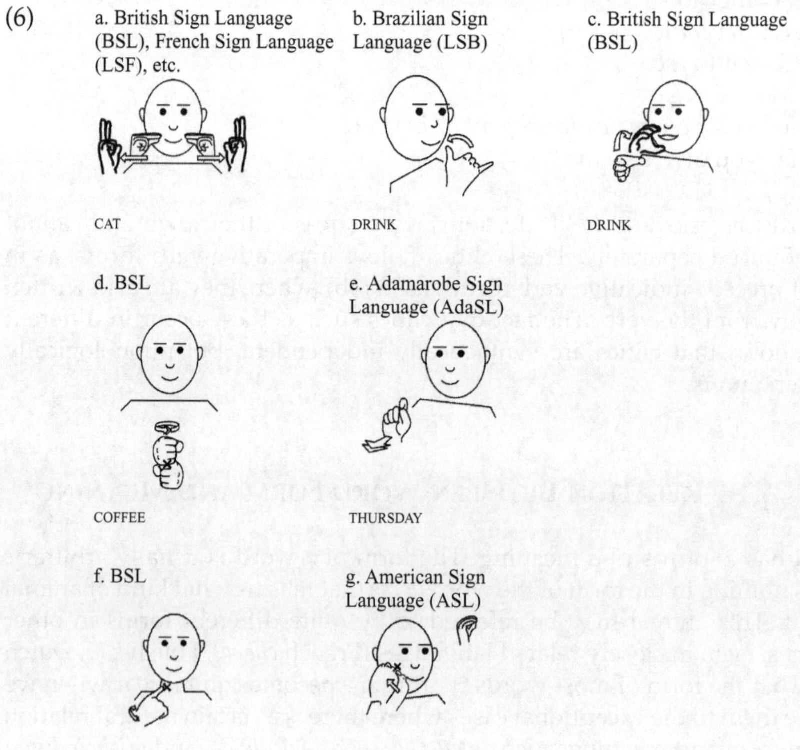

The sign in (6a) is the sign for CAT as it is used in British Sign Language (BSL), French Sign Language, and Sign Language of the Netherlands (NGT) and many other sign languages. This sign is highly iconic, portraying the whiskers of the cat; the meaning can be guessed without much context. However, although in (6b) and (6c) the signs glossed as drink in British Sign Language (BSL) and Brazilian Sign Language (LSB) are both iconic, they are different in form. The BSL sign incorporates the holding of a cup whereas the LSB sign represents the shape of a drinking jug. The BSL sign for coffee (6d) is also iconic but far less so. You have to know that coffee is ground in a mill where the top part turns above the bottom part in order to see the **iconicity**. The same is true for the sign Thursday in (6e) from Adamarobe Sign Language from Ghana. The hand shape and movement represent the use of a small hammering tool. Only if you are familiar with the culture and know that Thursday is market day and that tools are repaired at the market does the iconicity become clear. The signs in (6f) and (6g) are arbitrary, there is no relation between form and meaning here. [Note that the cross in (6f) and (6g) means that there is contact with the body part.]

At first sight the existence of these iconic signs would appear to constitute a crucial difference between spoken languages and sign languages. But the question is what role such an iconic element actually plays in the system of language. Research suggests that over time the iconicity of signs tends to decrease, and sometimes even disappears completely. The ASL sign in (6g), meaning home, is an example of this – the sign used to be a compound consisting of the signs eat (movement at the mouth) and bed (touching of the cheek) but in the course of time the compound has fused and the iconicity that was in the two original signs has disappeared.

Spoken languages also have some iconicity, as we discussed in Section 1.4 in onomatapoeic words. Most spoken languages also have some so-called ideophones. These are words that are used to vividly describe situations by means of a sound that usually accompanies them. For instance, the Australian language Bininj Gun-Wok has ideophones such as *wurr* 'sound of tree falling, crash!', *ngam* 'gulp!', and *lerre* 'rattling of snail-shell collars placed around dogs'.

11.4 Content Words and Function Words

Suppose you had to produce a sentence using the following words: *agreement, decide, environment, ministers, on, sign*. Your sentence could possibly be as in (7).

(7) The ministers have decided to sign an agreement on the environment.

Whatever your solution, the six words that were given above were not enough to make up a complete sentence. More were needed.

Now what is the difference between the original six words and the others that were added to produce (7)? Each of the words *agreement, decide, environment, ministers, on,* and *sign* has a meaning of its own. Together they make up the core of the meaning of the sentence as a whole. In Section 6.8 we identified these words as content words. The other words in (7), *an, have, the,* and *to,* serve a different purpose. They act like the mortar that keeps the bricks, the content words, in place. These words were identified as function words in Section 6.9. In Chapter 6 we saw that content words can be syntactic heads, whereas function words cannot. Here we will consider some further differences between them.

Speakers can use content words to refer to something that exists or obtains in reality or in some fictional world. Function words, on the other hand, primarily serve a function within the grammatical system of the language. In sentence (7), the elements *agreement, decide, environment, ministers, on,* and *sign* determine the core meaning; the other elements add further semantic and pragmatic nuances, establish relations between the lexical elements and connect everything into the grammatical network of the sentence.

What we mean by semantic and pragmatic nuances can be illustrated with examples (8a and 8b).

(8) a. He has *the* book.
  b. He has *a* book.

The definite article *the* in (8a) indicates that a particular book is meant, whereas the indefinite *a* in (8b) signals that we are talking in a more general way, about any book really (see Chapter 10).

Content words belong to word categories that are **open** and extendable. Any speaker of the language is free to add new content words to the vocabulary. This is successful when other language users are also willing to adopt the new item and follow the same convention. The introduction of new grammatical elements, in contrast, is next to impossible. Suppose somebody felt that English needed distinct plural articles like Italian or French. After all, for the definite form there is a single article *the* as in *the shoe, the shoes*, but for the indefinite form there is no article in the plural (*a shoe, shoes*). To systematically express the plural on articles the following system would not be unreasonable, since it makes use of the regular plural ending *-s*:

(9)

	singular	plural
definite	the (book)	*thes (books)
indefinite	a (book)	*as (books)

Despite the transparency of the system, it is extremely unlikely that our speaker would ever succeed in getting other speakers to follow suit and say things as in (10).

(10) *I need to buy *as* shoes.

This is so, because grammatical elements such as articles belong to word classes that are not open but **closed** and non-extendable.

The difference between content words and function words becomes apparent in other contexts. In nonsense poetry we see that function words cannot be replaced, since they form a closed system. Using nonsense content words means that the grammatical structure is recognisable even if the meaning of the nonsense content words is quite unclear. John Lennon's *The Faulty Bagnose* is an example of this, the first stanza of which is given in (11).

(11) Softly, softly, treads the Mungle
Thinner thorn behaviour street.
Whorg canteell whorth bee asbin?
Cam we so all complete,
With all our faulty bagnose?

Newspaper headings and telegrams often only contain content words for the purpose of brevity, as in:

MINISTERS SIGN AGREEMENT ON ENVIRONMENT

Children initially produce sentences containing mostly content words. The first combinations of words in children's language usually consist of lexical elements such as nouns and verbs, as in (12).

(12) a. Drink milk
'I want to drink milk.'
b. Mummy gone?
'Has Mummy gone?'
c. Bear table
'The teddy bear is on the table.'

Such combinations of content words are a characteristic feature of this initial phase of language acquisition, as we discussed and illustrated in Section 3.3. In (13), (14) and (15) there are a few more examples from other languages.

French
(13) Papa couper cheveux.
daddy cut hair
'Daddy has cut his hair.'

German
(14) Max auch male.
Max too draw
'Max wants to draw too.'

Polish
(15) Basia spa-ć.
Basia sleep-*infinitive*
'Basia is sleeping.'

This form of language use is often referred to as telegraphic style, since it is like the efficient language used in telegraphs or telegrams. It is not restricted to small children and first language acquisition. We also encounter it in the speech of adult second language learners, and in some forms of aphasia where the grammatical elements are no longer accessible for the speaker. An example of this type of aphasia was discussed earlier in Section 2.3. We repeat it here as example (16), a conversation between an aphasia patient (A) and an interviewer (I):

(16) A: ...Stratford...upon Avon. And er...beautiful...er...I...nice...walk.
I: Yes...yes where?
A: Where? Er...Stratford upon Avon.
I: You walk all through it?
A: No...cycle or no, er...er...car er...shopping.

The difference between content words and function words also plays a role in borrowing (see Section 20.6). Content words are fairly easy to borrow from other languages, whereas this is far more difficult with function words. Sentence (7), here repeated as (17), can serve as an example.

(17) The ministers have decided to sign an agreement on the environment.

In fact, most of the content words here are not originally English words: *agreement*, *decide*, *environment*, *minister*, and *sign* are in fact all of Romance origin, that is from Latin, French, etc. Most grammatical elements (*an*, *the*, and *to*) belong to the original, Germanic core vocabulary of English (see Section 17.3 for a discussion of the relationships between languages).

As we see from the various examples above, there are a number of significant differences between content words and function words. These differences play an important role in many aspects of language.

11.5 The Lexicon

We will define the lexicon of a language first of all as the set of all its words, both content and function words. This can be interpreted in two different ways. In a practical sense, the lexicon of a language is what a dictionary of that language tries to capture. For example, the *Concise Oxford English Dictionary* (*COED*) offers the following description of the word 'environment' (18).

(18) **environment**
1. physical surroundings and conditions, esp. as affecting people's lives.
2. conditions or circumstances of living.
3. *Ecol.* external conditions affecting the growth of plants and animals.
4. a structure designed to be experienced as a work of art.

As we can see, the dictionary first gives two current and common meanings, and then two more specialist meanings of the word, in ecology and art respectively. The first two meanings have been around for quite a while, whereas the last two appear to be more recent developments, say from the past fifty years. Such changes in views, ideas and interests may have a profound effect on the vocabulary of a language, and this is reflected in dictionaries.

Sometimes dictionaries are seen as authoritative arbiters of what is right and wrong. They are used to that effect in, for instance, scrabble competitions, the USA National Spelling Bee Competition, but also in the courts and in parliament, as if they had the final say about the words of a language. Dr Johnson, who compiled one of the first dictionaries in 1755, for example defined *monsieur* as 'a term of reproach for a frenchman', perhaps because he personally thought that was the case. He also vehemently refused to include words he did not like in his dictionary. It is important to remember that his dictionary, as all other dictionaries, are man-made, and that the properties of the words of a language are not determined by some arbiter but by the way these words are actually used by the members of a speech community. A dictionary is no more – and should be no less – than an attempt to describe as accurately as possible what those properties are. This is not an easy job, not just because it is difficult to define exactly what the meaning or meanings of a word are, but also because both the vocabulary of a language and its meanings are constantly changing. And it is difficult to say at what particular moment in time a certain word or expression ceases to be part of the current vocabulary. Is a word like *demurrage* (with meanings related to the detention of ships) more than a dictionary word? Is it actually used? Sometimes this is hard to ascertain, and in some cases it may take up to a century before a word or expression that is no longer used is removed from the dictionary. In the meantime dictionaries such as the *COED* label the word as 'archaic'.

A further difficulty is that – as time goes by – older words, with their meanings and usages, may come to be considered as discriminatory or insulting from today's point of view. A case in point here is the word *jew* in the *COED*, which in addition to its common meaning 'person of Hebrew descent; person whose religion is Judaism', has a second meaning 'person who drives hard bargains, usurer'. The second meaning arose in medieval times when Jews acted as moneylenders, but is generally perceived as an abusive term. To some people this second meaning is so unacceptable that for them it should not be included in the dictionary at all. A similar issue arose in the United States over the troublesome word *nigger.* In the *Merriam-Webster Collegiate Dictionary* this was described as 'perhaps the most offensive and inflammatory racial slur in English'. To very many people the word is so hateful that they felt insulted by the dictionary simply for including it. Dictionary makers clearly have to tread very carefully through this minefield of social attitudes and sensibilities. But in the end it is their job to come up with an adequate description of even the most offensive of words, their meanings and usage.

To conclude this section we mention one last, but important, feature of the organisation of dictionaries. As we saw above, the word *environment* has four different meanings. These are interrelated, and they are given in the dictionary under one single heading, which is known as a **lemma**. So we can say that *environment* is one lemma with four different, yet related, meanings. But what about a case such as *steer*? This word may mean 'guide, direct' or it may mean 'young male bovine animal'. These two different meanings are clearly unrelated. What we have here instead are two words that happen to have the same outward form. So in the case of *steer*, the dictionary should – as indeed the *COED* does – have two lemmas, each with its own meaning, as indicated in (19).

(19) **steer (1)**
1. guide, direct.
steer (2)
1. a young male bovine animal.

11.6 Kinds of Lexical Information

A monolingual dictionary such as the *COED* contains many different kinds of information about the words of English, as we can see in (20).

(20) **dėmu'rrage** *n.* rate or amount payable to ship owners by charterer for failure to load or discharge ship within time allotted; similar charge on railway trucks or goods; such detention, delay. [f. OF *demo(u)rage* (*demorer*, as DEMUR; see -AGE)]

The first information we are given concerns the form of the word and some aspects of its pronunciation. For example, given the conventions of the *COED*, we know on the basis of the '-sign after the *u* that the main stress falls on the second syllable. Then we are informed about the lexical category of this word: it is a noun (n). We then see that there are two main meanings, one to do with a charge or amount payable for a delay, the other with the delay itself. These meanings are described by a paraphrase in English. From these paraphrases we learn that *demurrage* is used especially in the world of shipping and transport. Finally we are given some etymological information. The information between square brackets is that this word came from (f) Old French (OF) *demourage*, which itself came from the verb *demorer*; and finally we are referred to the entries for *demur* and *-age*.

These various kinds of information offer us many starting points for further inquiry. For example, when checking the link to the entry for *demur* 'to raise scruples or objections', we again come across an etymological reference, this time to French *demeurer* and on to Latin *morari* 'to delay'. The dictionary tells us here that *demur* and *demurrage* share a common root in the past that has to do with the notion DELAY. The link which the dictionary posits here is historical-etymological rather than semantic in character, for in the paraphrase of the meaning of *demurrage* no use is made of *demur*. In fact, as the dictionary tells us, *demur* belongs to the domain of the law, whereas *demurrage* is a term used in the world of shipping. The two words may have started from a common origin, but the meanings they have today, each within their own specialist domain, are quite different.

This example is typical of what we find in general: each and every word of a language has its own often very rich and fascinating history, which can tell us a lot about the cultural and social developments that have taken place in the past. Etymological dictionaries can inform us about all kinds of interesting and unexpected connections between words. Yet at the same time you do not necessarily have to know this history in order to be able to use the word correctly. For the average language user, the different meanings of *demur* and *demurrage* are no longer seen as related today.

There are various other types of information that may be crucial to the correct use of a lexical item that are present in a dictionary entry as in (20). Suppose that somebody needs to translate the sentence *The father did not reckon with his bankruptcy* into French. He takes out his English-French dictionary and produces the sentence **Le pere n'a pas teni compte avec la banqueroute*. A native French speaker will have a number of difficulties with this. First of all, the form *teni* is not correct, since *tenir* is an irregular verb and its past participle is *tenu*, not **teni*. Secondly, the use of the preposition *avec* is wrong, since *tenir compte* always goes with *de*. These mistakes could be avoided if the dictionary contained this information, which is part of the knowledge language users have of the grammatical possibilities of a lexical element. In the case of the French equivalent of the expression *reckon with*, for example, the language user knows that *tenir* has an irregular participle *tenu* and that the use of the preposition *de* is obligatory.

A key question for lexicographers is how much grammar should be included in the dictionary to enable the user to correctly use the words of a language in a sentence. Should they go so far as to add a complete grammar, that is, the complete description of the rule system of the language in question? This may be overdoing it, and linguists and lexicographers are today looking for the optimum rather than the maximum. They are trying to find a good balance between what should be in a grammar and what in a lexicon, exploring in particular what relationships exist between the two.

At a minimum, a complete dictionary contains a description of all those properties of words that cannot be derived using rules. It will need to describe all those properties of the words of a language that speakers have to learn by heart if they are to use those words correctly. If you have never heard the past tense of *drink*, there is no easy rule to derive the form *drank*, and you may end up with the past tense *drinked*, as children do in the differentiation phase of language acquisition (see Section 3.3). That is, *drank* is a non-derivable verb form in English, and should therefore be in the lexicon. The opposite is the case with the verb *laminate*. Even if you have never heard this verb before, you can still predict that its past tense and participle will be *laminated*. These two verb forms can clearly be derived according to general rules; so in this case the lexicon can restrict itself to just one base form or stem for the verb in question, which will then represent all the other forms that can be regularly derived from it. This base form is usually the simplest or least complex form of the word, in this case *laminate*. In general this means that we do not list all derived forms for every verb.

Another aspect of the form of a lexical element is its characteristic sound pattern. Two words may consist of exactly the same sounds, but differ in their stress pattern. Here we will mark the stress in the usual way for linguists, that is, with an accent on the stressed syllable as opposed to after it as it is done in the *COED*. English examples are the words *protést* (verb) versus *prótest* (noun), *permít* (verb) versus *pérmit* (noun). And of course, differences in stress patterns need to be accounted for in the lexicon. This holds more in general, too, since word stress is one of the form properties of lexical items that is often difficult to predict. And it is important to get it right: the word *elephant* pronounced with the main stress on the second or third syllable may still be understandable, but we should know that the main stress ought to go on the first (see Section 16.3).

11.7 Dictionaries

Dictionaries, and the lexical information they contain, come in many shapes and forms. The *COED*, from which we have already drawn a number of examples, is a monolingual dictionary that also offers etymological information. In addition there is a range of other kinds of dictionaries, which we will quickly survey below.

(a) A *bilingual dictionary* offers, for each word in a given language, the nearest equivalent in a different language.

(b) A *frequency dictionary* describes how often certain words occur in a particular type of text. A collection of texts is known as a 'corpus', and the study of such text collections as 'corpus linguistics'. For many languages we now have large computer corpora that aim to be as representative as possible. For English, there is for instance the British National Corpus (BNC), and the International Corpus of English (ICE).

(c) A *thesaurus* presents an ordering of words that is not alphabetical but conceptual. It explains the synonyms or alternative expressions that are available in a broad range of conceptual domains. A thesaurus would group together, for example, the names of all sorts of drinks (*water, tea, coffee, beer, orange juice, vodka*) or the various verbs that describe the preparation of fruit and vegetables (*to peel, to skin, to strip*). Example (21) contains the short list given in *Roget's Thesaurus* of the various words for coffee, itself mentioned in the domain of 'soft drink', which is again part of the domain of 'food: eating and drinking':

(21) coffee, café au lait, café noir, Irish coffee, Turkish coffee, espresso, cappuccino

(d) A *concordance* is a special type of dictionary that indicates for any word in a given text, for example the Bible or Shakespeare's plays, all the places where it occurs plus the context in which it occurs. Such concordances are an invaluable tool for the scholarly study of important texts. In the past, the production of a concordance used to be a veritable labour of love that might take many years to complete. Today, we just scan a text into our computer, which will then help us to search in a variety of ways for words, combinations of words and other text features that are of interest to us.

(e) A *retrograde dictionary* presents the words of a language in alphabetical order, but starting from the end of the word. So a word like *idler*, which normally comes under the letter I, will now feature under R. In (22) we can see how the same word list would appear very differently in a normal dictionary and in a retrograde dictionary.

(22)

Alphabetical	*Retrograde*
attack	public
bake	bake
corpus	take
enjoy	offensive
girl	attack
gym	girl
offensive	gym
public	rotten
rotten	zero
take	corpus
zero	enjoy

Apart from being helpful when looking for rhyming words, retrograde dictionaries are also extremely useful in linguistic inquiry, as they greatly facilitate the search for words with the same endings since, for example, all words that end in *-ake* or *-able* will be listed together.

Figure 11.1 Violão

(f) A *picture dictionary* offers a visual alternative to an ordinary dictionary. It contains pictures of what the words in it represent. The words may be listed alphabetically or according to content. A picture dictionary may come in very handy when travelling in a foreign country or when learning a foreign language. From a picture dictionary it is immediately clear that a Brazilian Portuguese *violão* is a guitar and not a violin (Figure 11.1).

The discipline which is concerned with the production of these various kinds of dictionaries is known as **lexicography**. This is a thriving sub-domain of applied linguistics that caters for the great and growing need for accurate lexical information. Recent developments in information technology have made it possible to produce dictionaries on cd-rom and on-line, which actually are a combination of the various kinds of dictionaries discussed above. Sign Language dictionaries are also available in multimedia format, offering video images that demonstrate the correct way of producing the signs.

11.8 Meaning and Meaning Relations

The most important, but also the most difficult, part of lexical description is the representation of word meanings. This is part of the sub-discipline of semantics. In Chapter 10, a number of aspects of sentence meaning were discussed. Here we will take a look at some properties of word meaning. Let us look at the utterance in (23).

(23) Their game was excellent

Without further context it is not easy to know what the exact meaning of (23) is, since the word *game* can have more than one meaning, as we can see in (24) and (25).

(24) a. A leisure activity such as soccer, as in *Chelsea's game was excellent*.
b. A part of a tennis match, as in *They won the next game forty-love*.
c. Make-believe, as in *They were playing games all the time*.

(25) a. Wild animals hunted for sport, as in *The hunters brought back a lot of game.*
b. The meat obtained from wild animals, as in *The main course was game with baked potatoes.*

There is an important difference between the meanings in (24) and those in (25). They constitute two different lemmas, a notion we introduced in Section 11.5. The various meanings in (24) have something in common, since they all relate to the notion of *play*. So here we have one word, *game*, with various different, but not unrelated, meanings of a single lemma. That is, we have here a case of **polysemy**. In (25) on the other hand, we have a completely different word *game*, with a completely different meaning, and it is only its form which happens to be the same as in (24). For this reason, *game* in (24) and (25) are considered to be **homonyms**, that is they constitute different lemmas that happen to coincide in form.

Polysemy and homonymy can give rise to **ambiguity** in situations where it is not clear which of the various possible meanings is intended. In sentence (23) it is not immediately clear which of the various meanings in (24) and (25) is intended by the speaker. Usually, however, the potential ambiguity of words can be resolved, because words are always used in context, and other words in the linguistic context or the situation will often make it clear enough which particular meaning is intended.

Starting from (26) we will now take a closer look at some other aspects of word meaning. The question here is: What is the relation between the pairs of words in (26a to c)?

(26) a. tea – beverage
b. black – white
c. dress – frock

In (26a) tea is a kind of beverage; in (26b) we have two terms that denote opposites and in (26c) we have two different words for the same female garment. Each of these word pairs exhibits a different type of **semantic relation**: **hyponymy**, **antonymy** and **synonymy** (discussed in that order).

Hyponymy refers to semantic subordination and involves hierarchic relations within the lexicon. We say that A is a hyponym of B, if A is a kind of B. *Tea* is a kind of *beverage*, just as a *chair* is a kind of *furniture*, and a *car* a kind of *vehicle*. Between verbs, too, we find relations of hyponymy: *cycling* is a kind of *driving*, *driving* is a kind of *moving about*, and this in turn is a kind of *moving* in general.

Antonymy refers to semantic opposition: *black* is an antonym of *white*, just as *night* is an antonym of *day*. Many words occur in such antonymic pairs, with each member carrying a meaning that is in some respect the opposite of the other member's meaning, as in (27).

(27) man – woman
large – small
buy – sell

Synonymy, the third semantic relation in example (26), has to do with identity of meaning: A and B are synonyms if they have exactly the same meaning, although it is doubtful whether complete synonymy really exists in natural human language. Consider again the words *dress* and *frock*. These are synonyms, since they both refer to the same object. But if the words were really completely one hundred per cent synonymous, they should always be interchangeable, in any and all contexts. But this is by no means the case, as we can see in (28).

(28) a. She bought this way-out dress.
b. ?She bought this way-out frock.

Frock is a more old-fashioned term and does not combine felicitously with a modern adjective like *way-out*, as in (28b). This adjective can be combined with the neutral term *dress*, as shown in (28a). That is, the two words are only partially synonymous: they do refer to the same female garment, but the effect of using the one word instead of the other can be quite different.

That words like *dress* and *frock* are only synonymous to a certain extent has to do with the fact that words not only have a **denotation** (that is, what they refer to), but also a **connotation**. The connotation of a word involves its emotional and stylistic value as well as its social meaning (see Section 5.4). Even if words have the same denotation, they almost never have the same connotation. Choosing words with the right connotation is a necessary prerequisite if we want to produce an utterance that is pragmatically appropriate. The ability to do this is part of the knowledge speakers have of how to make use of the language in question.

Semantic relations play an important role in processes of language comprehension and language production. People who suffer from certain types of aphasia frequently use the wrong words, as we showed in Section 2.5.2. Often, however, these words are semantically related to the word that was intended, as, for example, when they say *house* instead of *palace*, or *travel* instead of *suitcase*. The same kinds of error may, of course, also be made by language users not suffering from aphasia, when they say something like '*Would you like another cup of coffee...eh, tea I mean?*' Such errors and mistakes can tell us something about the way in which words are stored in our brain. Similar problems may occur when children with developmental language impairment are learning words and choose a general term like *man* over the more specific and contextually appropriate *driver*. This problem may also vex second-language learners, particularly at the stage when they know the word *good* but not yet its alternatives such as *excellent*, *brilliant*, *perfect*, and *fantastic*.

11.9 Semantic Description

In describing the meaning of a word the traditional dictionary gives a paraphrase, using other words from the same language. This gives a descriptive list such as the one in (29).

(29) a: surgeon: doctor who performs operations
b: doctor: person whose profession it is to cure ill people
c: person: a human entity
d: entity: something that exists

Word (29a) is paraphrased using among other words also word (29b); then word (29b) is described using (29c), etc. The semantic relations between these words form a network through the lexicon as a whole.

This type of verbal description can create various different problems. First of all, in practice they are often circular, as when *doctor* is described as 'physician', and *physician* as 'doctor', or when *house* is described as 'dwelling' and *dwelling* as 'house'. Secondly, when descriptions are not circular, as in (29), we may soon end up with words that cannot be described any further with the use of other words. This is the case in particular with general words such as *thing*, *object*, *entity*, etc., which can often only be described in terms of one another. Thirdly, in many cases it is difficult to capture the meaning of a word exhaustively in other words. Most people know what a rose is, but a description such as (30) may cause them problems. It is not easy to give an adequate description of the meaning of a word using paraphrase.

(30) 'The fragrant flower of plants of the genus *Rosa*, from the family of *rosacea*, cultivated in many different varieties, but also occurring in the wild. . . .'

A different way to approach semantic description is to analyze the meaning of a word and split it into little parts, the so-called **semantic features**. In (31) (a part of) the meaning of a number of words is described in terms of such features.

(31)

	Kind	*Gender*	*Age*
man	human	male	adult
woman	human	female	adult
boy	human	male	juvenile
girl	human	female	juvenile
cow	cattle	female	adult
calf	cattle	both	juvenile
steer	cattle	male	adult
chick	fowl	both	juvenile

These semantic features represent values across three dimensions: Kind (human, cattle, fowl), Gender (male, female, or both), and Age (adult, juvenile).

Using these kinds of features we can now explain why sentence (32) is not possible.

(32) *The calf promised to post the letter tomorrow.

The verb *promise* requires a subject with the semantic feature 'human'. The word *calf* does not have that feature. In a fairytale or in more general fictional contexts, (32) might be acceptable, if the feature 'human' is temporarily – say, for the duration of the tale – assigned to *calf*. Similarly, in a dream a chicken may well promise to lay an egg by tomorrow.

11.10 Words Across Languages

Words denoting the same concept, given in capitals, may be strikingly similar across languages, as the groups of examples in (33) and (34) show.

(33)	CAVALIER	CAR(RIAGE)	CROSS
English	cavalier	car	cross
German	kavalier	karre	kreuz
Spanish	caballero	carro	cruz

(34)	TOOTH	TWO	MOTHER
Avestan	dantan	duva	mātar
Latin	dent	duo	mater
Old Irish	dēt	dó	máθir

Yet the reasons for the similarity within these two groups of words are quite different.

The words for the concepts CAVALIER, CAR and CROSS in (33) as used in English, German, and Spanish are very similar in their sound pattern; they are in fact all of Celtic origin. The Celts expanded their territory from the middle of Europe into various directions from 1000 BC onwards, and part of the vocabulary that they brought with them was later taken over by the Germanic and Romance speaking population. The incorporation of these words into the English, German and Spanish lexicon was thus a result of language contact. It is not a coincidence that these words denote concepts that were very prominently present in Celtic culture. This phenomenon of borrowing between languages and language contact will be further discussed in Section 20.6.

The words in (34) are very similar in their sound patterns too, but in this case the reason for the similarity is that these languages as ancient languages are close to a common ancestor, Proto-Indo-European. In the course of time they all evolved differently, while retaining part of the original vocabulary. The Indo-European language family resulting from the many successive changes in varieties of Proto-Indo-European nowadays occupies a large area ranging from the Atlantic Ocean up to Bangladesh. This topic of relationships between languages will be explored in Section 17.3.

In order to be able to distinguish between the two situations illustrated in (33) and (34), linguists make use of basic word lists that capture the concepts that are thought to be relevant to all or a great majority of the cultures of the world. The reasoning behind this is that for a concept that is present in all cultures of the world, languages spoken in these cultures will have a native word. There is then no immediate need to borrow a word with a similar meaning from another language. This can be illustrated by comparing the words for the concepts TWO and OAK in four Romance languages (35).

(35)

	TWO	OAK
French	deux	chêne
Italian	due	quercia
Portuguese	dois	carvalho
Spanish	dos	roble

It is evident from even a superficial comparison of these two columns that the words for TWO are very similar, while those for OAK are not. For instance, all four words for TWO begin with a *d*, and all four consist of one syllable, while the words for OAK vary on both of these points. Detailed further study of the sound patterns of the words would reveal more similarities and differences. Since TWO is considered a basic concept that will occur across a majority of cultures, while OAK is not, the conclusion is warranted that the similarity of forms for TWO is not the result of contact, but points at a common ancestor.

Of course, such a conclusion could never be based on the comparison of the forms for just one single concept such as TWO. There are many lists of concepts around that help us to arrive at more solid conclusions. The most famous of these is the **Swadesh list**, named after the linguist Morris Swadesh who designed it. The short version of this list is given in the Table 11.1.

In Section 17.3, as mentioned above, we will return to the issue of genetic reconstruction, for which the sound correspondences between words for the same concept across languages are crucial.

Summary

Although everybody seems to know what a **word** is, it turns out to be very difficult to give a satisfactory definition of this concept. The two groups of criteria that are most important for such a definition are the sound shape and the syntactic behaviour of a word. Words that cannot occur by themselves but need other words to lean on are called **clitics**. In most cases there is no direct relation between the form of a word and its meaning. When there is such a direct link, as for instance in the signs in sign language, this is called **iconicity**. A further distinction is based on the function and meaning of words. Content words can be distinguished from function words. The number of content words

Table 11.1 The short version of the Swadesh list

1 I	21 LOUSE	41 EYE	61 TO SLEEP	81 CLOUD
2 YOU	22 TREE	42 FINGERNAIL	62 TO DIE	82 SMOKE
3 WE	23 SEED	43 NOSE	63 TO KILL	83 ASHES
4 THIS	24 LEAF	44 MOUTH	64 TO SWIM	84 TO BURN
5 THAT	25 ROOT	45 TOOTH	65 TO FLY	85 ROAD
6 WHO	26 BARK	46 TONGUE	66 TO WALK	86 MOUNTAIN
7 WHAT	27 SKIN	47 FOOT	67 TO COME	87 RED
8 NOT	28 MEAT	48 KNEE	68 TO LIE	88 GREEN
9 ALL	29 BLOOD	49 HAND	69 TO SIT	89 YELLOW
10 MANY	30 BONE	50 BELLY	70 TO STAND	90 WHITE
11 ONE	31 FAT	51 NECK	71 TO GIVE	91 BLACK
12 TWO	32 FIRE	52 BREAST	72 TO SAY	92 NIGHT
13 BIG	33 EGG	53 HEART	73 SUN	93 WARM
14 LONG	34 HORN	54 LIVER	74 MOON	94 COLD
15 SMALL	35 TAIL	55 TO DRINK	75 STAR	95 FULL
16 WOMAN	36 FEATHER	56 TO EAT	76 WATER	96 NEW
17 MAN	37 FISH	57 TO BITE	77 RAIN	97 GOOD
18 HUMAN BEING	38 HAIR	58 TO SEE	78 STONE	98 ROUND
19 BIRD	39 HEAD	59 TO HEAR	79 SAND	99 DRY
20 DOG	40 EAR	60 TO KNOW	80 EARTH	100 NAME

in a language can easily be expanded; these words belong to the **open word classes**. This is not the case with function words, which belong to the **closed word classes**.

Words are described in a dictionary or **lexicon**. Words that can be found in a dictionary and have a different meaning are called **lemmas**. There are different kinds of dictionaries, depending on the way in which they have been composed. In addition to monolingual and bi- or multilingual dictionaries we also have frequency dictionaries, thesauruses, retrograde dictionaries and picture (illustrated) dictionaries. **Lexicography** is the discipline that is concerned with the composition and production of the various kinds of dictionaries just mentioned.

Between words and their meanings, many different kinds of relations are possible. If a word has more than one meaning, we have to do with **polysemy**. If words that have different meanings share the same form, we have **homonymy**. Both polysemic and homonymic words can give rise to **ambiguity**. Other kinds of **semantic relations** are **hyponymy**, **antonymy** and **synonymy** (and the associated notions of **denotation** and **connotation**).

Under each lemma in a dictionary we find different kinds of information, such as a paraphrase of the meaning. Another way to represent semantic relations within the lexicon is to distinguish the various **semantic features** within the meaning of a word.

Correspondences between words across languages may point at a common ancestor or at the influence of language contact. In order to distinguish between the two, linguists use lists denoting basic and culturally independent concepts such as the **Swadesh list** to detect family relationships between languages.

ASSIGNMENTS

1. What are the lexical words in the following sentences:
   (a) The driver forgot for the umpteenth time to stop at the bus stop.
   (b) Carton milk containers are worse for the environment than bottles.
2. What are the function words in:
   (a) John asked whether the problems did not occur in the new software.
   (b) The two birds were flying high in the sky.
3. In the following sentences the most important stresses have been underlined:
   (a) The ministers have signed the agreement on the environment.
   (b) The ministers have signed the agreement on the environment.
   Which of these stress patterns is natural, which isn't, and why?
4. Do we have one or more lemmas in the examples (a) and (b) given below?
   (a) limbo — place of seclusion
   limbo — dance, originally from Latin America, where one wriggles under an ever lower tape with body bent backwards
   (b) window — an opening in the wall or roof of a building or vehicle, fitted with glass in a frame to admit light or air and allow people to see out
   window — a transparent panel on an envelope to show an address
   window — a framed area on a computer screen for viewing information
5. What information would the lexicon have to contain to enable the correct use of the following words?
   (a) buy
   (b) people
   (c) police
6. Which of the following semantic relations – hyponymy, synonymy or antonymy – applies to the pairs of words below? We advise you to consult a dictionary when answering this question.
   (a) stove – cooker
   (b) heavy – light
   (c) transparent – opaque
   (d) newspaper – journal

7. What connotations do the following words have for you?
   (a) charwoman – maid – cleaning lady
   (b) police officer – cop – bobby – flatfoot
8. The famous quote from the comedian Groucho Marx *Time flies like an arrow; fruit flies like a banana* involves some cases of homonymy. Identify these and explain how this play on words works.

Test Yourself

1. Which criteria are most important for determining what a word is?
2. What is meant when we say that the form of a word is arbitrary and conventional?
3. What is the difference between content words and function words?
4. Words may belong either to a closed or to an open class. What does this mean?
5. Is a lemma the same as the meaning of a word?
6. Identify and describe five different kinds of dictionaries.
7. Which discipline is concerned with the writing of dictionaries?
8. When can we say a word is polysemous? When is it a homonym?
9. What is the difference between the denotation and the connotation of a word?
10. What is the purpose of the Swadesh list?

Acknowledgments and Further Reading

The arbitrary and conventional character of the word is – according to de Saussure (1916) – a basic property of natural language. A classical treatment of lexicography is Cruse (1986). Many aspects of word meaning and semantic relations are discussed in detail in another classic, Lyons (1977). Lexical entries were taken from the 1982 edition of the *Concise Oxford English Dictionary* and the 1987 edition of *Roget's Thesaurus of English Words & Phrases*. The examples from Bininj Gun-Wok are taken from Evans (2003). The example from Polish child language is taken from Smoczyńska (1985).

chapter 12

Word Formation

12.1 Introduction

It is not difficult to establish that the words in (1) have something to do with one another:

(1) learned, learn, learnable, learnt, learning, learner, learns

What these words have in common is that they are all related to *learn*. We can say, therefore, that the word *learn* is the core element of all these words. Put differently, the words in (1) can all be dissected into smaller parts, of which *learn* is one in every case.

In this chapter we will discuss how words such as those in (1) are formed. In Section 12.2 we first explain the notion of word formation in more detail. In Section 12.3 we will take a closer look at the functions of word formation. On the one hand, it may facilitate the expansion of our vocabulary (as in *learnable, learning, learner*); on the other, it can help to fit words into the grammatical structure of the constituents and clauses that they are part of (as with *learns, learned, learnt*). The first of these cases is known as derivation, the second as inflection. Both will be discussed in more detail in the two subsequent sections: derivation in Section 12.4, inflection in Section 12.5.

Linguistics, First Edition. Edited by Anne E. Baker and Kees Hengeveld.

New words may be formed by adding one or more elements to an existing word, as for example in *un-learn-able*. Section 12.6 will discuss these and other such word formation processes. The relation between the structure of words and their meaning will be the subject of Section 12.7. Although many kinds of word formation process occur equally in derivation and inflection, there are also a number of differences between the two, as will be discussed in Section 12.8. Apart from this, languages may be significantly different from each other in the word formation processes they apply in their grammar. There is a range, from languages with short and simple words to languages where a sentence may consist of a single long and very complex word. In Section 12.9 we will discuss these and other such differences between languages.

12.2 The Internal Composition of Words

In example (1) we saw that the words of a language can sometimes be split up into smaller parts. The word *learnable* can be divided into *learn* + *able*; and *learned* into *learn* + *ed*. Example (2) shows that as well as the pair *learn-learnable*, there are many other such pairs.

(2)	(a)		(b)	
		know		knowable
		sing		singable
		accept		acceptable
		love		loveable
		adore		adorable

The series in (2b) demonstrates that the element *-able* can be combined with many more words than just *learn*. All words in (2b) consist of more than one part. That is, they are **internally complex**. The words in (2a), on the other hand, just like *learn*, cannot be further analysed into such constituent elements. They are **internally simple**. Now consider the examples in (3).

(3) unknowable
unsingable
unacceptable
unloveable
unadorable

This series clearly shows that words can consist of more than two parts. In other words, they can be multiply complex.

The order in which the various parts are added is not random. The element *-able* has to be added to the basic form *know, sing*, etc., first. Then the element *un-* can be added to the form *knowable, singable*, etc. If you were to do it the other way round, you would first create the form **unknow*, **unsing*, etc., which are non-existent forms. In order to indicate the order in which elements must be attached, bracketed structures are used, not unlike the ones used in syntactic analysis (see Section 6.5), as illustrated in the series in (4).

(4) a. [know-]
b. [[know-] able]
c. [un- [[know-] able]]

Thus, words can consist of various different parts. The smallest identifiable components of a word that carry meaning are known as **morphemes**. In the word *knowable*, the element *know* is a morpheme, and so is *-able*. The sub-discipline of linguistics which is concerned with the properties of complex words, in particular the way in which words are formed or built, is known as **morphology** or the study of word formation.

In examples (2) and (3) we can compare words and series of words with each other, and from this comparison we can draw conclusions as to the form of these words. In the field of morphology such word comparisons constitute an important research instrument. Consider the set of examples from Turkish in (5). What are the morphemes in these examples, and what do they mean?

Turkish
(5) a. Gelmişim.
'I have come.'
b. Geleceğim.
'I will come.'
c. Gelmişin.
'You have come.'
d. Geleceğin.
'You will come.'

It is not difficult to recognise 5 different elements in these words: *gel*, *miş*, *im*, *eceğ*, and *in*. Taken together, the set of examples makes clear that *gel* means 'come', *miş* is a past tense, *eceğ* is a future tense, *im* is first person, and *in* second person. As we will see in Section 12.9, not all languages have a morphology that is as transparent as in Turkish.

12.3 The Functions of Word Formation

When the first computers were invented, they generated a need for people who could write computer programs. As yet, there was no name for this new job, and this was a problem. For example, when recruiting people, it was a bit awkward to advertise this with 'Our dynamic company is looking for someone who programs'. So a word was coined, *programmer*, on the analogy of word pairs such as in (6).

(6) [paint-] [[paint-]er]
[ship-] [[ship(p)-]er]
[write-] [[writ(e)-]er]

This is an example of one of the functions of word formation, that is to expand the existing vocabulary of a language. When the need arises, speakers of a language can make a new word by deriving it from one that already exists.

Adult language users may know up to as many as 40,000 words in one language. They apparently need this enormous vocabulary in order to be able to function properly, and normally they are quite capable of remembering and using all these words. But the collection of internally simple words is, in most languages, considerably smaller. This is where word formation performs an essential role, since words often consist of (re-)combinations of smaller parts. This means, first of all, that the many different sound combinations that are possible in a language are used more efficiently. It also means that it is much easier to remember the words of a language: words that are similar in meaning often also share some feature of form. Thus, from the basic forms *bake* and *brew*, various related words can be formed:

(7) [[bake-](e)r] [[brew-]er] 'person professionally engaged in baking/brewing'
[[bak(e)-]ing] [[brew-]ing] 'activity of baking/brewing'
[[bake-](e)ry] [[brew-]ery] 'place where baking/brewing is carried out'

In this way, six different words can be created from two existing basic forms.

The examples given so far all illustrate a certain type of vocabulary expansion. In all cases we start from an existing word to which something is added that is not itself a word. Put differently, a lexical word is connected with a non-lexical element to form a new word, such as *knowable*, *walker*, or *bakery*. This type of vocabulary extension is known as **derivation**.

There is another way of expanding the vocabulary, however. This is illustrated by the examples in (8).

(8) hay stack
water bed
sun deck

In what way are these different from the derivation examples in (8)? The answer is that they do not consist of a lexical element plus a non-lexical element, but of two lexical elements. Words that are built by combining two (or more) lexical elements or content words are known as compounds. These will be discussed in more detail in Chapter 13.

Apart from serving the purpose of vocabulary expansion, morphology has another important function. Consider the example in (9).

(9) *Yesterday the two opera lover see a new production in Covent Garden.

When we come to the word *opera lover* in (9) we may, at first sight, think that this is a typing error. But the use of *see* is definitely wrong too. Why? The words *opera lover* and *see* are used here in conflict with the grammar of standard English. After the numeral *two* the plural form of the noun is required, hence *opera lovers* and not *opera lover*. Furthermore, with a time adverb like *yesterday*, we must use the past tense of the verb, hence *saw* and not *see*. These two mistakes illustrate the second main function of morphology, which is to fit existing words into the grammatical structure of the sentence they are part of. This part of morphology is known as **inflection**. In the next two sections we will discuss the processes of derivation and inflection in more detail.

12.4 Derivation

In English we have the word *low*, from which we can derive another adjective *lowish*, an adverb *lowly*, and a noun *lowness* but not an adjective **unlow*. From the word *smooth* we can similarly derive *smoothish*, *smoothly*, and *smoothness*. But unlike *low*, we can now form *unsmooth* as well. Also, *smooth* can be used both as an adjective and as a verb, but this is not possible with *low*. If we need a verb here, we will have to add the morpheme *-er* to form the word *lower*. These examples show that derivation is subject to certain restrictions. In this section we will explore the different factors behind these restrictions, and discuss first morphological and lexical restrictions, then phonological conditions, and finally restrictions involving word categories.

In (10) we have a few examples of morphological restrictions on the derivation of adjectives ending in *-ish*. This ending forms an adjective that expresses an approximate quality. In (10a) the result is acceptable, in (10b) it is not.

(10) a. green – greenish
blue – blueish
sheep – sheepish
b. sea green – *sea greenish
indigo blue – *indigo blueish
highland sheep – *highland sheepish

How can we explain that the new formations under (10b) are not grammatical? The restriction we are faced with here has to do with the base word. In (10a) this is an internally simple word, but the base words in (10b) are internally complex. The restriction here is that adjectives in *-ish* can only be derived from internally simple words.

The restrictions illustrated in (11) involve lexical restrictions, here on the derivation of nouns ending in *-er* from verbs. In (11a) the result is acceptable, in (11b) it is not.

(11) a. play – player
dance – dancer
b. steal – *stealer
judge – *judger

Here the restriction has to do with the fact that, although **stealer* and **judger* have been derived according to the same rule as the forms in (11a), there is already an internally simple word in English vocabulary with precisely this meaning, that is *thief* and *judge*. So **stealer* and **judger* are not needed, even though they are well-formed and entirely possible words of English. This is also the reason for the ungrammaticality of **unlow*, mentioned in the introduction to this section: we already have the word *high* in our vocabulary, the existence of which will disfavour the new formation **unlow*.

What is going on here in the derivation process can be described as follows. A speaker may want to use a noun that represents the person who is carrying out a certain action. If that action is checking tickets, speakers will search in their mental lexicon to see if there is already a word there that has this meaning. If this is not the case, they may go ahead and produce the new word *ticket checker*, following the pattern of (11a). If, on the other hand, the action in question is stealing, they are most likely to come across the existing word *thief* in their mental lexicon, and so have no need to proceed any further.

The blocking does not need to be absolute. In English the derived verb *to redden* – see also example (13) – can be used in the sense of the basic verb *blush*, as shown in the examples in (12), found in an internet search:

(12) a. She saw that he blushed, and she wanted to know why.
b. He reddened a little, wondering whether she had some inkling of his secret.

But though both the derived and the basic verb can be used, a simple count based on a similar internet search reveals that the combination *he/she blushed* occurs roughly 423,000 times, while *he/she reddened* only occurs approximately 23,000 times, that is, the basic word is used 18 times more often than the derived verb in this combination. Interestingly, *reddened* is used more often with *he* and *blushed* more with *she*.

As we see, language users do consult their mental lexicon before they go ahead and form new words. So what if someone wants to describe the situation in which their money has been stolen and they do not know the word *thief*? This might well be the case in young children or second language learners of English. They may resolve the problem by forming the word *stealer*, and this will do until they learn that the proper word to use in that context is *thief*.

There is ample evidence from first and second language acquisition data that cases like this do indeed occur.

The examples in (13) demonstrate how phonological restrictions can affect derivation:

(13) a. black – blacken
b. white – whiten
c. red – redden
d. green – *greenen
e. purple – *purplen
f. blue – *blueen

The English suffix *-en* can be added to an adjective 'X' to create the meaning 'to make X', as in *redden* 'to make red'. But this suffix can only be added to verbs ending in certain consonants, such as *k* in (13a), *t* in (13b), and *d* in (13c), whereas it cannot be used with certain other consonants, such as *n* in (13d), *l* in (13e), or with vowels such as *ue* in (13f).

Finally, there are restrictions on derivation that have to do with the word category to which a lexical item belongs. In (14) there are some examples in which a lexical element is combined with a non-lexical item to form a new word. In the left-hand column of (14) we have the base words, in the right-hand column the new formations. What can we say about the word category of the base words versus the derivations here?

(14) a. duke – dukedom
b. pleasant – unpleasant
c. read – reread

The word *duke* in (14a) is a noun, and so is *dukedom*; *pleasant* and *unpleasant* in (14b) are both adjectives; and *read* in (14c) is a verb just like *reread.* Derivation here has left the word category unchanged. But this is not always the case, as we can see in (15).

(15) a. bake – bakery
b. stone – stony
c. hard – harden
d. quick – quickly

In (15) we see that the word category of the base word may indeed be changed in the derivation process. In (15a) the base word is a verb and the derived word a noun; in (15b) a noun is changed into an adjective; in (15c) an adjective is transformed into a verb; and in (15d) an adverb is derived from an adjective.

In order to keep track of the word-class changing effects of derivation, or the lack thereof, we may expand the earlier bracketed representations of the internal structure of words with word-class labels, just as we used syntactic category labels in the analysis of constituents and clauses in Section 6.6. The examples given in (14) and (15) can then be represented as in (16) and (17).

(16) a. $[[\text{duke-}]_{N}\ \text{dom}]_{N}$
b. $[\text{un-}\ [\text{pleasant}]_{Adj}]_{Adj}$
c. $[\text{re-}\ [\text{read}]_{V}]_{V}$
(17) a. $[[\text{bake-}]_{V}\ \text{ry}]_{N}$
b. $[[\text{ston(e)-}]_{N}\ \text{y}]_{Adj}$
c. $[[\text{hard-}]_{Adj}\ \text{en}]_{V}$
d. $[[\text{beautiful-}]_{Adj}\ \text{ly}]_{Adv}$

The analysis of a multiply complex word such as *unpredictability* would look as in (18).

(1) $[[\text{un-}[[\text{predict}]_{V}\text{-able}]_{A}]_{A}\text{-ity}]_{N}$

Here the base form is the verb *predict*, from which the adjective *predictable* is derived. The negative counterpart of this adjective, *unpredictable*, itself an adjective, is derived next. Finally, this adjective is turned into the noun *unpredictability*.

The words in examples in (16), (17) and (18) involve nouns, verbs, adjectives and adverbs, which are all classes of content words (see also Section 11.4). The remaining classes of lexical words may show up in derivational processes too, as (19) demonstrates.

(19) a. inning $[[\text{in-}]_{Prep}\ \text{(n)ing}]_{N}$
b. iffy $[[\text{if-}]_{Conj}\ \text{(f)y}]_{Adj}$

Despite the richness displayed in these examples, there are also restrictions on derivational processes in English that have to do with word classes. Though we have given some examples in (19), it is actually very difficult to find cases in which prepositions and conjunctions serve as the basis for or the result of derivation. Furthermore, function words do not participate in derivational processes, so that we do not find words like **the-hood* on the basis of the definite article, or **a-ness* on the basis of the indefinite article.

We conclude that, while languages in general have many ways to derive new words from existing words, there are also significant and systematic restrictions on derivation. These have to do with word categories or with morphological, lexical and phonological factors that operate in the language in question. In the Section 12.5 we will move from derivation to a discussion of the properties of another sub-domain of word formation, that is, inflection.

12.5 INFLECTION

In contrast to derivation, inflection does not contribute to the expansion of our vocabulary. The function of inflection is to fit words into the grammatical structure of the sentence they are part of, as we explained when discussing example (9). Here we will first consider the examples in (20).

(20)	a. work	b. swim	c. must	d. reread
	works	swims	must	rereads
	working	swimming	–	rereading
	worked	swam	must	reread
	worked	swum	must	reread

The four columns in (20) contain different forms of four verbs. In each column, these are not new words, but different forms of the same word. They are formed on the basis of the **stem**, given in the first line, plus further additions (if any). A stem may be basic, as in (20a to c), or derived, as in (20d), where *reread* is a stem derived from *read*. The list of forms that a particular stem, such as *work* in (20a), can take is known as a **paradigm** (a Greek/Latin term meaning 'example' or 'model'). The paradigm of *work* is a very common one in English. Many verbs are inflected according to this pattern, such as *reread* in (20d). Other verbs follow the irregular paradigms of *swim* in (20b) or *must* in (20c).

Take, for example, the verbs *fell*, as in *the woodcutter felled twenty trees*, and *sell*. From the very similar forms of these words we could never tell that they are in fact inflected according to the two different paradigms listed in (21).

(21)	a. fell	b. sell
	fells	sells
	felling	selling
	felled	sold
	felled	sold

Adult speakers of English will have learnt which paradigm applies to which particular verb, and they will certainly not use forms like **fold* as the past tense of *fell* or **selled* as the past tense of *sell*. It is reasonable to assume that the various forms of a verb, regular or irregular, are linked to a particular paradigm, and in that way are stored in our mental lexicon.

Within the domain of inflection we can make a further distinction between **contextual** and **inherent inflection**. In contextual inflection the form of words is strictly determined by their grammatical context, and the inflection does not contribute independently to the meaning of the sentence in which the words appear. An example of this is given in (22). How can we explain the difference in form between the verbs of (22a) and (22b)?

(22) a. Julia plays football.
b. Julia and Stan both play football.

In (22a) the verb takes the form that agrees with a singular subject *Julia*; in (22b) the verb form agrees with a plural subject, *Julia and Stan*. In both cases we find agreement between the verb and the subject. The choice of *plays* or *play* depends on the singular or plural character of the subject. In other words, the grammatical context determines what form the verb should take. For this reason, verbal inflection for agreement is known as contextual inflection.

In many languages, nouns and adjectives also need to be inflected so as to make them fit into the grammatical structure of the sentence. A clear example of contextual inflection in nouns is inflection for case in German, where the verb *geben* 'to give' imposes three different case forms, the nominative for the giver, the dative for the recipient of the object given, and the accusative for the object given, as we can see in example (23).

German

(23)	Die	Frau	gab	dem	Mann	ein-en	Apfel.
	the.*nominative*	woman	gave	the.*dative*	man	an-*accusative*	apple

'The woman gave the man an apple.'

Contextual inflection of the adjective can be found in Italian, where adjectives accompanying a feminine noun must end in an *-a*, while those accompanying a masculine noun must end in an *-o*, as in (24).

Italian

(24)							
	a.	la	tavola	rossa	il	palazzo	rosso
		the	table	red	the	palace	red
		'the red table'			'the red palace'		
	b.	la	strada	sporca	il	giardino	sporco
		the	road	dirty	the	garden	dirty
		'the dirty road'			'the dirty garden'		

Here again, it is the grammatical context that determines the choice of one ending or the other.

In all other cases, when inflection is not contextual, it is inherent. In example (25), the choice of *girl* versus *girls* does not depend on the grammatical context, but on what the speaker wants to say. If he wants to talk about one girl he will use (25a), but if he wants to say something about more than one girl he will use (25b).

(25) a. The girl was playing in the street.
b. The girls were playing in the street.

The choice between *was* and *were* in (25a and b), on the other hand, is not free. Here the speaker has no option but to do as the grammatical context requires. So, *was/were* is a case of contextual inflection, determined by the number of the subject. But the plural ending *-s* in *girls* is an example of inherent inflection.

12.6 Morphological Forms

Compare the examples in (26) to (29) from Turkish, Jacaltec (a Mayan language from the Guatemalan highlands), Bontoc (a language from the Philippines) and Tamazight (a variety of Berber in Morocco). The parts in italics are lexical elements which constitute the stem of the word, whereas the parts in bold are the non-lexical elements. Note in particular the position of the bold, non-lexical elements as opposed to the italicised stem.

Turkish
(26) *su*-**da**
water-*locative*
'in/on the water'

Jacaltec
(27) **w**-*atut*
1.singular-house
'my house'

Bontoc
(28) *k*-**um**-*ilad*
kilad 'red'; um *'inchoative'*
'he is getting red'

Tamazight
(29) **t**-*ussen*-**t**
ussen 'fox'; t-/-t *'feminine'*
'female fox'

These examples have in common that there are certain non-lexical elements that are somehow attached to the lexical stem of the word. Such attached grammatical elements are known as **affixes**, and the process of attaching them is known as **affixation**. Note that these are different from clitics discussed in Section 11.2. Clitics are words that lean phonologically on other words, while affixes are part of a word. Depending on where exactly they are attached, we can distinguish at least the following four categories of affixes:

1. If they are attached to the end of a word, affixes are known as **suffixes**. The Turkish example in (26) is a case in point. An example in English would be *nerv-ous*.
2. Affixes that are attached to the beginning of a word, as in the Jacaltec example (27), are known as **prefixes**. In English a good example is *be-devil*.
3. In the Bontoc example (28) we find **infixes**, that is, affixes that take up a position inside the stem of the word. Infixes are common in the many languages of Indonesia and the Philippines. The infix -um- in Bontoc adds the meaning of the process of becoming (30).

Bontoc
(30) a. kilad > *k*-**um**-*ilad*
'red' 'he is getting red'
b. fusul > *f*-**um**-*usul*
'enemy' 'he is becoming an enemy'

4. The fourth and final type of affix is, again, not very frequent in the languages of the world, although it does regularly occur. This category consists of affixes that are attached simultaneously to the beginning and the end of a word, as if getting a grip on the stem they hold in between. These affixes are known as **circumfixes**. As we can see in (29), they occur in languages such as Tamazight, where feminine words have a *t-* before and a *-t* after the stem. It is a coincidence that the Tamazight feminine circumfix consists of identical parts, which are both *t*. This is not necessarily always the case, as we can see in the following examples of past participles from German and Dutch that begin with *ge-* and end with *-t* in (31) and (32).

German
(31) *ge*-**kauf**-*t*
kauf 'buy'; ge-/-t *'past participle'*
'bought'

Dutch
(32) *ge*-**kook**-*t*
kook 'cook'; ge-/-t *'past participle'*
'cooked'

An important point about affixes in general is that they may play a role both in derivation and in inflection.

In addition to affixation we find **reduplication**, the process whereby a word is repeated, as in *hush-hush*, or *tut-tut*. In languages like English this process is rather peripheral, and it is mostly used for expressive purposes. In other languages reduplication may have a much more central role. In Indonesian, for example, reduplication is used to form the plural (33).

Indonesian

(33) buku > buku-buku ('books')
anak > anak-anak ('children')

The German sign language DGS similarly uses reduplication to form the plural, that is the sign for book is made twice, with a repetition of the movement, indicated by the doubling of the heads of the arrow.

DGS

(34)

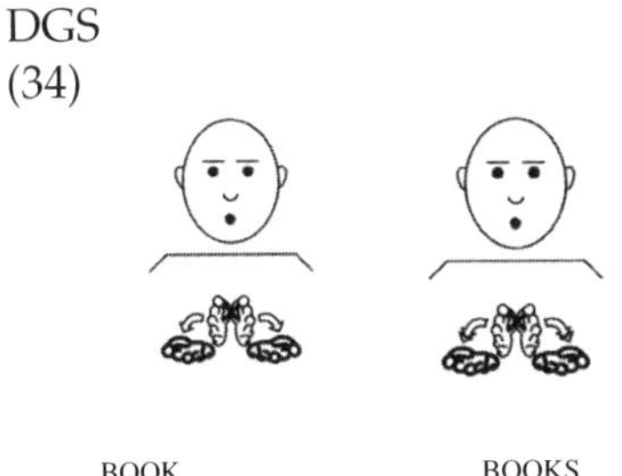

BOOK BOOKS

In Ewe, a West African language, a particular type of infinitive is formed by reduplication (35):

Ewe

(35) a. subo > subosubo
'serve' > 'serving'
b. yi > yiyi
'go' > 'going'

The examples in (33) to (35) are instances of complete or full reduplication. Partial reduplication is also possible, as we can see in Ilocano, another language of the Philippines (36):

Ilocano

(36) a. talon > tal-talon
'field' > 'fields'
b. biag > bi-biag
'life' > 'lives'
c. ulo > ul-ulo
'head' > 'heads'

The morphological processes we have seen so far – affixation and reduplication – all involved some sort of formal difference. However, we also encounter morphological processes without such formal marking, that is, when there is no observable prefix or suffix present. Consider examples (37) from English and (38) from Sranan, the most widely spoken creole language of Surinam:

(37) a. Did you buy (V) this shampoo?
Yes, it was an excellent buy (N).
b. Did you walk (V) all the way home?
Yes, and it was a wonderful walk (N).

Sranan

(38) a. Wan dei Margie ben siki wan bun hebi (A) siki.
One day Margie was sick one very heavy sick
'Once Margie was really very sick.'
b. I no mu hebi (V) a wagi moro.
You not must load the cart more
'You must not load more onto the cart.'
c. A libi kon hebi (N).
The life become burden
'Life becomes a burden.'

The verb *buy* and the noun *buy* can have exactly the same form in English, as we can see in (37). In Sranan (38) the word *hebi* (borrowed from English *heavy*) can be used as an adjective/adverb, as a noun, and as a verb. It is a multifunctional word. In both cases the different uses are not accompanied by a change in form. Such category changes without morphological marking are known as **conversion**.

We conclude this section with a quick look at yet another type of word formation. Consider the series in (39).

(39) a.	b.
be	work
am	work
is	work-s
are	work
were	work-ed
been	work-ed

In example (39b) we have one stem, *work-*, which constitutes the core of the whole paradigm and all its members. In (39a) we also have a paradigm, but this time it is a list of rather disparate and very different elements. That is, for the verb *to be*, in contrast to *work*, we cannot identify one single stem that is common to all members of the paradigm. This phenomenon is known as **suppletion**.

12.7 The Structure of Words and Their Meanings

The examples we have considered so far are words that consist of many different parts and also have a complex meaning. The question is: is the meaning of such words determined completely by their form and structure? In general this appears to be the case. Take example (40) from Yup'ik, an Inuit language.

Yup'ik
(40) a. yuk-pak-cuar
person-big-small
'a small big person, a small giant' (i.e. someone who is small for a giant)
b. yuk-cuar-pak
person-small-big
'a big small person, a big dwarf' (i.e. someone who is big for a dwarf)

The first element in Yup'ik words is the stem, which is followed by elements that give a further specification. In (40a) the stem *yuk* 'person' is followed by *pak* 'big', and together these two elements produce the new meaning 'giant'. Adding on the element *cuar* 'small' gives rise to the meaning 'small giant'. In example (40b) we find a different ordering of the two suffixes *pak* and *cuar*. Now the combination of *yuk* and *cuar* produces the meaning 'dwarf'; then, by adding *pak*, we get the meaning 'big dwarf'. So, the order of suffixes is a decisive factor in determining the meaning of the word as a whole.

Example (41) is from Quechua, a language from South America.

Quechua
(41) Uqya-naya-chi-wa-nqa-n.
drink-*desiderative-causative-1.singular-past-3*
'It made me feel like drinking.'

Starting from the beginning we can build up our interpretation by going step by step through the contribution of the various elements we come across, as shown in (42).

Quechua
(42) *uqya-* drink
uqya-naya- feel like drinking
uqya-naya-chi- to make someone feel like drinking
uqya-naya-chi-wa- to make me feel like drinking, etc.

This pattern of regular interconnection between the structure and the meaning of a word follows from the central principle of compositionality that we introduced at the beginning of this book in Section 1.2, and which was discussed further in Section 10.1.

12.8 Differences between Derivation and Inflection

As we have seen, many morphological forms can be used both in derivation and in inflection. So we may think that these two processes are formally equivalent. Yet, as we will discuss below, there are a number of differences between the two.

The first difference has to do with **productivity**, that is how widely and freely a certain morphological process can be applied. It is a common assumption that inflectional processes are more productive than the process of derivation. By way of illustration we will now consider the contrast between past tense formation in the verbal system and the formation of language names. First we consider the past tense forms of some English verbs in (43).

(43) a. dig – dug
buy – bought
make – made
b. saw – sawed
tag – tagged
wash – washed
c. surf – surfed
email – emailed
skype – skyped

Although, as we can see in (43a), there are irregular and non-productive past tense forms in a range of verbs, the large majority of verbs is regular and forms its past tense in *-ed*, as we see in (43b). Crucially, all new verbs, like the ones in (43c), always take this regular ending in *-ed*. When we now take a look at the way names for nationalities and ethnic groups are formed, the picture is quite different (44).

(44) (a) -ian: Arabian, Russian, Frisian, Brazilian, Australian, Peruvian, Latvian
(b) -Ø: Arab, Greek, French, Dutch, Chechen, Basque, Yoruba, Zulu, Welsh
(c) -ish: Spanish, Turkish, Danish, Finnish, Flemish, Irish, Polish, Yiddish
(d) -ese: Chinese, Balinese, Javanese, Sinhalese, Nepalese, Faroese
(e) -i: Iraqi, Somali, Beluchi, Uzbeki, Apache, Ashanti, Pakistani
(f) -an: German, Samoan, Moroccan, South African, Kosovan
(g) -ic: Arabic, Amharic

What we see here is an enormous diversity of morphological endings. We can identify seven different types of formation, and we can group the various forms that exist into different categories, but we cannot predict which paradigm will apply in each particular case. Why *Somali* and not *Somalian*? Why *Arab, Arabic* or *Arabian* but not *Arabese*? And why *Welsh* instead of *Walesi*? Many examples in (44) look rather more like the accidental results of history than as formations that follow a particular rule or pattern.

The difference between (43) and (44) points to a real and significant difference between inflection and the expansion of our vocabulary through derivation and compounds. While inflection is a regular and productive process, vocabulary extension often is not. The difference is, again, not an absolute one, since in the domain of inflection we also have to account for many irregularities. How can we explain, for example, irregular plural formations such as *sheep*, *feet*, *geese*, *children*, *teeth* and *police*?

A second difference between derivation and inflection has to do with semantic shift. In inflection, for example when forming the past tense of verbs in English, the meaning is always clear; moreover this meaning is always regular and constant. But in forming new words to expand our vocabulary, this is not necessarily so. Here we often find a narrowing or shift in the meaning of the base word. For example, we use *cooker* for special types of pan or for stoves rather than for a person cooking professionally as you might expect from the *-er* suffix.

A third difference has to do with the order in which morphological processes apply in word formation processes, something which is reflected in the position of affixes within the word as a whole, as illustrated in (45).

(45)	[[pig-]$_N$ let]$_N$ -s	'piglets'
	[[false-]$_N$ hood]$_N$ -s	'falsehoods'
	[[[just-]$_V$ ifi(y)]$_V$ cation-]$_N$ -s	'justifications'

In all three cases in (45) the plural suffix *-s* comes at the end of the word as a whole, after all other, derivational, suffixes. As a general rule, derivational suffixes are closer to the stem than inflectional suffixes. This appears to be the case in all languages. Compare example (46) from Turkish.

Turkish
(46) ev-cik-ler
house-little-*plural*
'houselets'

Here we see exactly the same. The derivational suffix *-cik* 'little' precedes the inflectional plural suffix *-ler*. There may be a few exceptions, but the general rule is that elements that serve to produce new words are closely attached to the stem of the word, whereas inflectional elements are, so to speak, on the edge of the word as a whole.

In sum, we can now say that while the same morphological processes can be used both in inflection and in derivation, there are also a number of significant differences between the two.

12.9 Morphological Differences between Languages

From a morphological point of view, the languages of the world vary tremendously. In this domain the differences between languages are perhaps greater than in any other part of the grammatical system. The differences that exist here may also be quite diverse in character: they may have to do with the complexity of words, with the degree of fusion between their constituent parts, or with the nature of the concepts that are being combined into an individual word. Take, for example, the difference in morphological complexity between the Quechua sentence we saw above in (41), repeated here as (47), and sentence (48) below, from Papiamentu, the creole language spoken in the Dutch Antilles, Aruba, Bonaire and Curaçao.

Quechua
(47) Uqya-naya-chi-wa-nqa-n.
drink-*desiderative-causative-1.singular-past-3*
'It made me feel like drinking.'

Papiamentu
(48) E na laga mira mi e buki.
He *present* let see me the book
'He let me see the book.'

The Quechua sentence consists of one long, complex word *Uqyanayachiwanqan*. The Papiamentu sentence, in contrast, consists of seven short and simple words. But while their morphological structures are very different, in their semantic structure they are very similar. Now, of course Quechua also has short words, and Papiamentu long ones, but still there is a clear difference in the morphological structure of the two languages. A language like Quechua is **morphologically complex**. A language like Papiamentu, the vocabulary of which consists predominantly of internally unstructured words, is known as **morphologically simple** or **isolating**.

Within the category of morphologically complex languages we can make a further distinction which has to do with the degree of fusion between the constituent elements of words. In this respect, we find significant differences between languages. In a language like Turkish, many words consist of little parts, stuck together but not fused; these are known as **agglutinating languages**. A Turkish example is given in (49), where we can see how the complex sentence-word *evciklerimizde* is built.

Turkish
(49) ev-cik-ler-imiz-de
house-*diminutive-plural-1.plural.possessive-locative*
'in our little houses'

Each element of (49) is a separate part that makes an individual contribution to the meaning of the word as a whole. In Tuscarora, on the other hand, a Native American Indian language spoken in New York State and Ontario, we find something quite different (50).

Tuscarora
(50) Kwvhs ara-w-akwahst.
not *irrealis-3.singular.neutral*-good
'That would not be good.'

This sentence is pronounced as *kwvhs a:rvkwahst*, with complete fusion of the morpheme *-w-* and the initial *a* of *-akwahst*, triggered by the presence of the indefinite *ara-*. Languages like these, where the individual parts of a word can melt together, are known as **fusional languages**.

The third dimension along which morphologically complex languages – whether they are fusional or agglutinating – may be different from each other involves the degree of concreteness of the meanings of the constituent elements of the word. This dimension can be exemplified with the use of two languages that are both spoken in North America, English and Fox, a Native American Indian language spoken in the Mississippi Valley. Let us first consider the English form in (51).

(51) $[[[[\text{organ}]_N\text{-is}]_V\text{-ation}]_N\text{-al}]_A$
'concerning the organisation'

This word contains a stem *organ-*, followed by three elements: first *-is*, which turns the stem *organ-* into a verb, then *-ation*, which turns the verb into a noun that represents the completion or result of the implementation of an action, and finally *-al*, which changes the whole thing into an adjective. Only the stem of this word has a more or less concrete meaning. Now compare this with a verb from the Fox language that occurs in a sentence which describes a hunt (52).

Fox
(52) Eh kiwin-a-m-oht-ati-wa-ch(i).
then movement-flee-*causative-reflexive*-each.other-*plural-3.singular*
'Then they chased it with each other and made it flee (for them).'

What is noticeable here is that there is more than one element in the verb that has a concrete meaning: in addition to *kiwin* 'movement' there is also *a* 'flee'. Languages like Fox, in which a single word can contain several elements with a concrete meaning, are known as **polysynthetic languages**.

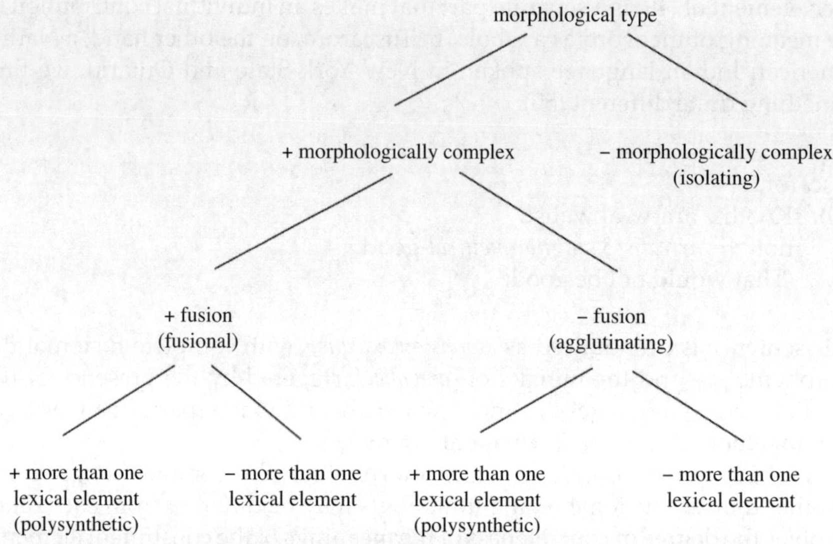

Figure 12.1 Morphological types of languages.

To sum up: there are three dimensions along which languages can be morphologically different. These are:

- the complexity of words (morphologically complex versus morphologically non-complex or isolating languages);
- the degree to which the elements of a word can be fused (fusional versus agglutinating languages);
- the concreteness of the meaning of the various parts of the word (polysynthetic languages, where words contain several elements with concrete meaning, versus languages in which only one element has a concrete meaning).

These dimensions and the morphological typology of languages that is based on them is graphically represented in Figure 12.1.

We have explained the various distinctions in this section using languages that are extreme examples of a certain morphological feature. It is good to remember that very many languages are located somewhere in between these extremes.

Summary

Words often consist of different elements. Words that can be split into smaller parts are called **internally complex**, words that cannot are **internally simple**.

The smallest word element that carries meaning is a **morpheme**, and the discipline which studies the formation of words is known as **morphology**.

Morphology serves two key functions. The first function is **derivation**, which helps to expand the vocabulary of a language. Not every conceivable derivation is always possible; there are often restrictions. The second function is **inflection**, or the grammatical integration of a word into a sentence. The set of word forms that can be produced through inflection from a common **stem** is known as a **paradigm**. In some cases the context may determine the particular inflected form that is required. This is called **contextual inflection**, in contrast to **inherent inflection**.

From an existing word we can make new words in various different ways. In **affixation** a non-lexical element is connected to the stem of a word. Such elements are known as **affixes**, and can occur either at the end (**suffix**), at the beginning (**prefix**), in the middle (**infix**), or at both ends of the word at the same time (**circumfix**). In addition to affixation, some languages also have repetition of a word (**reduplication**). In **conversion** (or transposition) there is a change in word category that is not visible in the morphology. In **suppletion** irregular forms are brought in to make up a full paradigm. Given the principle of compositionality, the structure of a word and its meaning are interconnected.

Productivity plays a major role in the distinction of derivation versus inflection. A second difference has to do with semantic shift, and a third is to do with the placing of affixes. Languages turn out to vary systematically in the complexity they allow in word formation. If a language mostly has internally structured words, it is **morphologically complex**. If not, it is **morphologically simple** or **isolating**. In addition, languages may differ in the degree to which the constituent elements of a word have melted into one (**fusional** languages) or not (**agglutinating** languages), and in the concreteness of the meaning of the various parts of the word: languages with words that contain several morphemes with concrete meanings are known as **polysynthetic** languages, as opposed to languages where only one morpheme has a concrete meaning.

Assignments

1. Which of the following words are internally simple, which are internally complex?
   banana, dangerously, enlarged, door, spinach
2. Which of the following words are multiply complex?
   deliverable, unacceptable, painting, reformation

3. How can you argue that *lover* must be derived from *love*, and not the other way around?
4. What kind of word-category changing derivation do we have in:

   (a) *work* – *working*
   (b) *red* – *redden*
   (c) *lady* – *ladylike*
   (d) *seam* – *seamstress*

5. On the basis of the existing word formation rules of English it is possible to derive the word *presser* from *press*. Native speakers, however, are unlikely to do this. Why do you think that is?
6. What are the morphemes in the following examples, and what do they mean?

   Swahili
   (a) ninasoma 'I read'
   (b) anasoma 'he reads'
   (c) nilisoma 'I read (past)'
   (d) alisoma 'he read'
   (e) alipenda 'he liked'
   (f) aliwapenda 'he liked them'

7. Do the tenses of the verb belong to the inflections of a language?
8. Indicate what types of affixes (prefix, infix, suffix, circumfix) occur in the following examples:

   Hungarian
   (a) level-em
   letter-1*singular*
   'my letter'

   French
   (b) impersonnellement
   'impersonally'

   Chrau (a language from Vietnam)
   (c) voh – v-an-oh
   'know' – 'sensible'

9. How would you characterise, from a morphological point of view and using Figure 12.1, the morphological types of Hungarian, West Greenlandic and Miao?

   Hungarian
   (a) Mari setal-tat-t-a a kutya-m-at.
   Marie walk-*causative-preterit-3singular* the dog-1.singular-accusative.singular
   'Marie walked my dog.'

West-Greenlandic

(b) Tusaa-nngit-su-usaar-tuannar-sinnaa-nngi-vip-puti.
hear-*negation-intransitive.participle*-pretend-all.that.time-can-*negation*-really-*2singular.indicative*
'You really cannot pretend not to listen all that time.'

Miao (a language from China)

(c) Ohov nwg sau lom zen.
nominalisation he write interesting
'What he writes is interesting.'

Test Yourself

1. What is the difference between an internally complex and an internally simple word?
2. What are the most important functions of word formation?
3. Explain what derivation is.
4. Define the term 'inflection'.
5. What is the paradigm of a word?
6. Which two forms of inflection can be distinguished?
7. What is affixation?
8. Which four kinds of affixes can be found in the languages of the world?
9. What happens in reduplication?
10. When do we speak of suppletion?
11. Is productivity the same in derivation and in inflection?
12. What is the difference between a fusional language and an agglutinating one?

Acknowledgments and Further Reading

A good survey of the morphological processes in the languages of the world is given in Sapir (1921), and slightly more comprehensively in Aikhenvald (2007), Bickel & Nichols (2007), and Booij (2007). A generative and theoretical survey is Scalise (1984); a more traditional framework is set out in Matthews (1974). Bybee (1985) gives an analysis of a range of morphological processes from a typological perspective. An introduction to morphology as well as a critical survey of a number of theoretical tendencies is given in Bauer (1995) and in Haspelmath (2002). The Tuscarora example is from Mithun Williams (1976), the ones from Sranan are taken from Wilner (2007). The Swahili examples used in assignment 6 are taken from Cowan & Rakušan (1998), which contains many more exercises.

chapter 13

Compounds and Idiomatic Expressions

13.1 Introduction

Since the second half of the twentieth century, where many roads meet, traffic can cross another road via an *underpass* or *fly-over*. In the late nineties, the British government appointed a *drugs czar* to head its campaign against addictive substances. As internet sites such as Facebook and so have become popular, a verb has been created to cover the breaking of a link with someone – *to defriend.*

For the description of our constantly changing world we constantly need new words. In the last example, *defriend* is the result of derivation (Section 12.4), the prefix *de-* being combined with *friend.* It is also possible to coin new words by combining two existing ones. In the first three examples just given, the new words consist of two parts, each of which is a word in its own right: *drugs* and *czar*, *under* and *pass*, and *fly* and *over*. This type of word is known as a **compound**. In many languages compounds are written as one word, as in German where this can result in extremely lengthy words such as *Dampfschifffahrtgesellschaft* 'steamboat travel company'. English compounds can be written as one word, but also with a hyphen or as two separate words. In the latter case there is only one stress across both words, making it clear that it is a compound, as will be further discussed in Chapter 16.

Speakers of English very regularly make use of this process of compounding in their language; and by coining new compounds they constantly expand

Linguistics, First Edition. Edited by Anne E. Baker and Kees Hengeveld.

their vocabulary. In the last chapter we also discussed derivation, another such vocabulary expansion process. It is interesting to compare the two.

(1)	*Derivation*	*Compounding*
green	green-ish	blue-green
cycle	cycl-ist	cycle shop
swim	bak-er	bakeware
labour	labour-ite	labour union

From the word *cycle* we can derive the noun *cyclist* by adding the non-lexical suffix *-ist* onto the stem *cycl-*. Similar processes produce *greenish*, *baker*, and *labourite*. In compounds, by contrast, we find a different internal structure, since they only take content words as their constituent parts.

The outcome of the derivation process is itself a new word, and this in turn can become part of a compound. In (2), each of the three new compounds is built from two pre-existing words, one of which is itself a derived word taken from (1):

(2) pastry baker, labourite society, cyclist club

As we see, derivations and compounds are different in internal structure, but they serve the same purpose, that is to expand the vocabulary of the language in question.

In Section 13.2 we will discuss the structure and meaning of compounds in more detail. We will explore the word categories from which compounds can be built. We will also consider how, in the type of compound illustrated in (2), there is always one element that serves as its core or head, whereas the other element says something about that head, as we discussed in Section 6.5 for clauses. In Section 13.3 we will discuss the different types of compound, and in Section 13.4 we look in particular at words that incorporate other words, with which they then fuse or merge.

Idiomatic expressions such as *shifting the goal posts* 'changing the aims of a plan', *burning the midnight oil* 'working until very late' and *not being up to scratch* 'being inadequate' are also ways of expanding the vocabulary, since they give new meanings to existing words. Someone who is *shifting the goal posts* is not literally doing that, but only in a figurative way, as a manner of speaking. In Section 13.5 we will explore how 'fixed' such expressions are, and in Section 13.6 we will discuss their meaning.

13.2 Structure and Meaning of Compounds

The order of lexical elements in compounds is variable, as we can see in the examples in (3).

(3) cable TV – TV cable
house boat – boat house
milk chocolate – chocolate milk

A *house boat* is a boat that people use as a home; a *boat house*, on the other hand, is a shed at the edge of a river or lake for housing boats. *Milk chocolate* is chocolate made with milk, but *chocolate milk* is a milk drink that is made by adding chocolate. Clearly, it matters here in which order the two original words are put together in a compound. In the English examples in (3) it is always the last (right-hand) part of the compound that determines the meaning of the whole. A *TV cable* is a kind of cable, and not a kind of TV. The first part of the compound, on the other hand, gives a specification of the second part, and in this respect a compound resembles the order of adjective and noun in English, as in (4).

(4) British TV – long cable
small boat – old house
dark chocolate – hot milk

The parts of a compound belong together and cannot be interrupted by another element. It is not possible, for example, to talk about *a *house small boat*. The adjective *small* must precede the compound *house boat* as a whole.

Given its determining role, the last part of the compound is known as its **head**. It is the head that determines the inflectional properties of the compound as a whole. For instance, if the head has an irregular plural, this plural form will recur in a compound as in (5).

(5) a. house mouse – house mice
b. long-wool sheep – long-wool sheep

Interestingly, in English there is a restriction of having regular plurals in the modifier of the compound, so that (6a to c) are possible but not (6d).

(6) a. mouse catcher
b. mice catcher
c. rat catcher
d. *rats catcher

The position of the head may differ from language to language. Below, we give examples from Hebrew (7), Chamorro (a Polynesian language, 8), and from British Sign Language (BSL, 9).

Hebrew

(7)	eglat-j'ladim	ben-dod
	car-children	son-uncle
	'buggy'	'nephew'

Chamorro

(8)	tronon-niyok	tommon-kanna
	tree-coconut	knee-arm
	'palm tree'	'elbow'

British Sign Language

(9) think-true
'believe'

As we can see, Hebrew, Chamorro and BSL do not put the head at the end of the compound, as in English, but at the beginning. Thus there are two options: the head will either be at the beginning or at the end of the compound.

Young children in the first stages of their language acquisition sometimes make mistakes in the internal order of elements in compounds. When he had just turned three years old, Max used to talk about a *box letter* instead of a *letter box,* and a *house tree* instead of a *tree house.*

Now consider the series of compounds which all have *glass* as their head in (10).

(10) a. flint glass
plate glass
b. sand glass
hour glass
storm glass

In all the compounds of (10a) *glass* is the material glass, in (10b) it means an instrument made to measure. In the compounds in (10a) *flint glass* is a pure lustrous kind of glass, originally made with flint as its main ingredient. *Plate glass,* on the other hand, is a kind of flat glass. In (10b) a *sand glass* uses sand to flow through a glass tube as a measure of time. An *hour glass* is an alternative name for the same instrument but *hour* indicates what is being measured. Similarly, a *storm glass* does not use a storm for measuring but measures storm conditions by indicating atmospheric pressure. These examples demonstrate that the combination of two words in a compound may have very different effects. In (10a) *flint glass* and *plate glass* are kinds of glass but *flint* specifies the main ingredient whereas *plate* indicates the form. In (10b) *sand glass, hour glass* and *storm glass* are instruments for measuring something, but in *sand glass, sand* is the material used in making the measurements, while *hour* and *storm* refer to what is being measured. If you were not familiar with the term, you might think that *sand glass* was a type of glass made primarily of sand. So, while it is true that these are all compounds, each with *glass* as its head and the first element as its modifier, there is at the same time the problem of establishing exactly the relationship between the two parts. It is not quite possible to predict from the combination what the overall meaning of the new word will be.

What can we say about the different parts that can go into a compound? Take the examples in (11).

(11) a. cookbook, swimsuit, runway
b. grandfather, flat pack, high-rise
c. goalpost, shoelace, teacup

Can we establish a pattern in the word categories of the constituent elements in these various compounds? Indeed we can. In (11a) the first part is a verb (V), the second a noun (N). In (11b) the first part is an adjective (Adj), the second a noun. And in (11c) both parts of the compound are nouns. So, in English, compounds may consist of V+N, Adj+N and N+N. In all cases the final N is the head here.

Are there any other possible combinations? Can categories other than N function as the head in a compound in English? Look at the examples in (12).

(12) a. drip-dry, slipshod, stir crazy
b. gluten-free, stone cold, wafer thin
c. sweet natured, blue-green, dark brown

These examples demonstrate that it is possible to produce English compounds that have an adjective as their head. The patterns V+Adj in (12a), N+Adj in (12b) and Adj+Adj in (12c) are parallel to those in (11).

Compounds with a verb as their head – such as *to sweet-talk*, *to undercook* and *to overdo* – also occur in English but relatively speaking they are not so common. Other languages, such as Kayardild, an Australian Aboriginal language, use these quite frequently, as we can see in (13).

Kayardild
(13) a. dul-marutha
ground-lay
'knock to the ground'
b. mibul-barrwaaja
sleep-hinder
'prevent someone from sleeping'
c. birdin-diija
bad-land
'come down in the wrong place'

The process of compounding occurs in many languages. Languages may, however, differ in the extent to which they make use of it and of the different types. In Italian, for example, compounds involving N+N like *capo-treno*, literally chief+train 'head ticket inspector' and *capo-contabile* literally head+accountant 'chief book keeper' do occur, but it is much more common to use prepositions when combining two words in an expression, as in *capo di divisione* 'departmental head' or *capo di famiglia* 'head of the family'. In English, however, compounding is widely used to produce new words such as *resident alien*, *business ethics*, *peace force* and *diet ice cream*. Incidentally, all of these come from a recent list of the top fifty words that appear to contain an internal contradiction in terms of meaning.

13.3 Types of Compounds

So far we have seen that the head of a compound determines important characteristics of the compound as a whole, in particular the word category it belongs to and its inflection, for example plural formation. If the head is a noun, the whole compound is a noun; if the head is an adjective, then the compound as a whole is an adjective. Compare the examples (14a) and (14b).

(14) a. chair [N] - kitchen chair [N] - folding chair [N]
b. brown [Adj] - dark brown [Adj] - light brown [Adj]

This type of compound, in which the properties of the head determine the properties of the compound as a whole, is known as **endocentric compound**. In English, the first part of an endocentric compound normally gives a specification or qualification of the head: a *kitchen chair* is a type of chair, *dark brown* indicates the hue within the category of the colour brown, etc.

There is, however, another type of compound, as we can see in (15).

(15) a. must-have
b. redskin
c. razorback

These words, all nouns, and meaning 'an object you should have' (15a), 'a person characterised by a reddish skin' (15b), and 'a type of hog' (15c), have a different structure from those in (14). We cannot say that (15a) is a kind of *having*, (15b) a kind of *skin*, nor (15c) a kind of *back*. That is, in these compounds, unlike those in (14), it is not the case that the right-hand element is the head. Compounds like those in (15) are known as **exocentric compounds**. We find them in other languages too, as in (16) and (17).

French
(16) a. mille-feuille
thousand-leaf
'tartlet'
b. mange-tout
eat-everything
'kind of pea'

Spanish

(17) a. sobre-mesa
after-table
'dessert'

b. guarda-esquinas
guard-corner
'idler'

13.4 INCORPORATION

In some languages there is a special connection between two forms, different from that in compounding. This can be the case between verbs and some arguments, often the object. It is as if the verb has melted together with its object. When the verb has taken in an argument, this is known as **incorporation**. Such argument incorporations occur in many languages. Compare examples (18a) and (18b) from Nahuatl, a Mexican Indian language:

Nahuatl

(18) a. Ni-k-*qua* in-*nakal.*
I-it-eat the-meat
'I'm eating the meat.'

b. Ni-*naka-qua.*
I-meat-eat
'I eat meat = I'm a carnivore.'

Speakers of Nahuatl may handle the object of *eat* as a separate constituent as in (18a), but they can also incorporate it into the verb as in (18b). This type of object incorporation is a characteristic feature of polysynthetic languages (see Section 12.9). A similar process can be seen in example (19), from Tiwa, a language spoken by Native American Indians living in the southwest of the United States.

Tiwa

(19) a. Seuan-ide ti-mu-ban.
man-*nom.* *1.sing-see-past*
'I saw a/the man.'

b. Ti-seuan-mu-ban.
1.sing-man-see-*past*
'I saw a/the man.'

Sentence (19a) consists of a verb plus an object. In (19b), in contrast, the object is no longer a separate constituent, but has been incorporated into the verb. Similar processes are widely and productively used in many languages, and do not seem to affect the behaviour of the verb. Other languages rarely use this process. In English we have a few such examples, as in *pickpocket* and *scarecrow*, or in German *staubsaugen* 'to hoover', where the object *staub* has become part of the verb. This is evident in the formation of the past participle, which takes the circumfix *ge- -t*, since it is *ge-staubsaug-t* and not *staub-ge-saug-t*.

In many sign languages this process occurs regularly with other word classes, for example between numerals and nouns. Thus in the Indo-Pakistan Sign Language (20) the number three is incorporated into the sign to make one sign meaning 'three years'.

(20) Indopakistan Sign Language

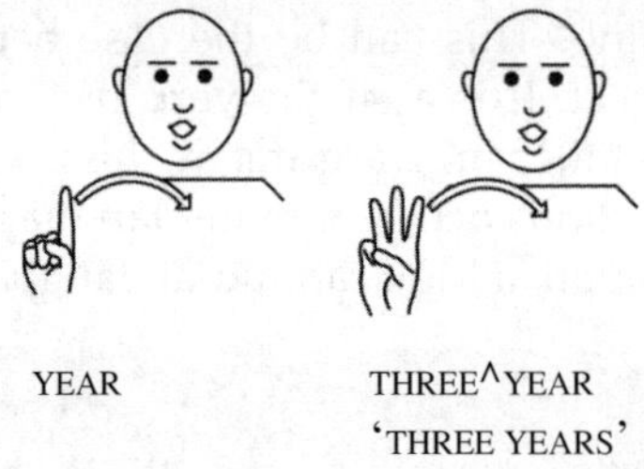

YEAR THREE^YEAR
'THREE YEARS'

13.5 Idiomatic Expressions

Most native speakers of English will have no difficulty in understanding the sentences in (21).

(21) a. His tutor had a sharp tongue and a short fuse.
b. She made too many stupid comments, and I just lost my cool.
c. He's a chip off the old block and will just pull some strings.

What is the matter when someone's tongue is sharp, or when their fuse is short? They talk critically and become angry easily. Can you lose a cool? You cannot literally, since it means to become angry. Being a chip off the old block means being like one of your parents in some aspect of behaviour, and pulling strings means using influence. Once we start thinking about expressions like these, they turn out to be quite complicated. At the same time it seems beside the point to take things literally or to wonder about the grammaticality of *lose my cool*. The sentences in (21) are quite clearly expressions in a class of their own. They are known as **idioms** or **idiomatic expressions**.

It is often said of idioms that they are fixed expressions. What does this term 'fixed' actually mean? Let us first consider some examples involving the expression 'have a short fuse'.

(22) a. John has a short fuse.
'John gets angry very quickly.'
b. John had a short fuse.
c. John has a rather/very/terribly short fuse.
d. *John has a short but reliable fuse.
e. *John received/gave away a short fuse.

The idiom *he has a short fuse* as a whole has one specific meaning: 'he is likely to become angry quickly and often'. The idiom allows some variation, as we can see in (22b), where it can be used in the past tense, and in (22c), where it can be combined with an adverb of degree. But, as the other examples in (22) show, this idiom does not allow further modification: it cannot go with a complex adjectival phrase (24d) and the verb *have* cannot be replaced by other related verbs.

Many idioms are possible only in very restricted tenses (23, 24), although this is by no means always the case (25).

(23) a. Mary will become a millionaire. And pigs will fly.
'Mary becoming a millionaire is impossible'
b. He said that if Mary would become a millionaire, pigs would fly.
c. *Pigs flew

(24) a. If Shaw wrote *Othello*, I'm a Dutchman.
'It cannot be true that Shaw wrote *Othello*.'
b. *If Shaw wrote *Othello*, I was a Dutchman.
c. John said that if Shaw wrote Othello, he was a Dutchman
d. *If Claire will finish that paper, I will be a Dutchman.

(25) a. He was just pulling some strings.
'He was organising through connections'
b. He pulled some strings and we got out of the mess.
c. Oh, he'll just pull some strings.
d. He said he would just pull a few strings.

Modifications are also difficult with idioms, as the examples in (26) show.

(26) a. *And *pink* pigs will fly.
b. *He was just pulling some *yellow* strings.
c. *I'm a lousy Dutchman.

The impossibility of adding anything to the nouns *pigs*, *strings* and *Dutchman* in (26) has to do with the fact that such modifications will activate the literal meaning of the noun and do away with the idiomatic interpretation. In contrast, the addition of a degree adverb like *very* in (22c) is fine, since it does not say anything about the noun *fuse*, but instead specifies the quickness with which John's anger is likely to explode. We conclude that in idioms like those in

(23, 24 and 25), the nouns should not be taken in a literal sense and can therefore not be specified, although in creative writing, for humoristic purposes and in adverts, people do sometimes experiment.

Another aspect of how 'fixed' idiomatic expressions are, is that they quite often do not allow negation (27), nor variation in word order (28, 29), nor the passive form (30).

(27) a. *If Shaw wrote *Othello*, I'm not a Dutchman.
b. *And pigs will not fly.

(28) a. That must have cost an arm and a leg.
'That must have cost a lot'
b. *That must have cost a leg and an arm.

(29) a. She has friends in high places.
'She had friends in influential positions'
b. *In high places she has friends.

(30) a. After the meeting he just hit the ceiling.
'After the meeting he became really angry'
b. *After the meeting the ceiling was hit by him.

The syntactic behaviour we observe in these examples is different from that of non-idiomatic expressions: idioms allow very little syntactic variation. However, this is not an absolute, for there are idioms such as the one in (25) that do allow quite a bit more flexibility. It can, for example, be passivised, as in *some strings were pulled and he was elected*. The answer to our opening question – how 'fixed' are idiomatic expressions? – is therefore that this is a matter of degree.

13.6 The Meaning of Idiomatic Expressions

In the discussion in the previous section we saw that the meaning of some expressions is very far from the literal words used. Let us now consider what meaning they have, and how can we derive the meaning from their constituent elements or from the literal meaning of the idiom in question. We will first consider the examples in (31).

(31) a. going down like a lead balloon
b. putting the cart before the horse

When there is lead, that is, extra weight, in a balloon, it will of course not fly, but come down. Hence, the meaning of this idiom is that something you say or show is not liked at all by your audience. This is actually rather transparent, just as (31b), which means 'doing things in the wrong order'. The idioms in (32), however, are far less transparent.

(32) a. kick the bucket
'to die'
b. pull someone's leg
'to tease someone'
c. be a flash in the pan
'to have no lasting effect'
d. to throw in the sponge
'to admit defeat'

The words in (32) are not difficult to understand, and neither are their combinations. Example (32a) can have a literal meaning, that is, to knock a receptacle for water with your foot. The idiomatic meaning 'to die' appears to be completely unrelated to this literal meaning and its origin is in fact not at all clear. Similarly, the meaning of the idiom in (32b) – 'telling someone something that is not true in order to tease them' – does not follow from the words it contains and, again, its etymology is unclear. These idioms are not transparent at all. Being a flash in the pan comes from the old types of gun on which there was a pan containing some gunpowder that had to ignite the rest. This expression is no longer transparent since this type of gun no longer exists. Throwing in the sponge is also only clear if you are familiar with the world of boxing in which the sponge is thrown into the ring when the contestant wants to retire from the match. Degree of transparency appears to be a variable property of idioms in the same way as the degree of fixedness that we discussed in Section 13.5.

Now what about (33)? Is the idiom transparent?

(33) Arthur seemed to savour every word in his speech.

The answer is yes. Sentence (33) contains familiar words, and it is not difficult to say what it means. But there is something special about this sentence. To savour something is to enjoy and appreciate its taste, in particular in the domain of food and drink. We take a little bite or sip and let this go round in our mouth until we have really tasted it. Now, of course, with words this is not possible, unless of course it is as a figure of speech, a **metaphor**. A metaphor always contains figurative language use based on comparison. The sentence in (33) means that Arthur is choosing his words with great care, as if he is letting each one of them go round in his mouth, assessing its qualities, and only then sharing it with his audience. Such metaphoric language use is one of the most important sources for the creation of idioms. Poets and children often create original metaphors that do not become idioms. To the delight of her parents, Jo (3;6) called cumulus clouds *mashed potato clouds*. Poets such as Reiha Ali or William Wordsworth have also often compared themselves to clouds.

When, as sometimes happens, speakers are unable to find a word they need to describe something, they may resort to using other words or concepts as a metaphor, as for example when a narrowing in the road that causes a traffic jam is called a *bottleneck*. What happens in an idiom is that complete expressions are being used metaphorically, as in *shifting the goalposts, pulling your leg* or *running a tight ship*. When such comparisons appeal to people's imaginations, they catch on and spread throughout the speech community. In this way they may end up as idiomatic expressions. However, not all idioms are based on metaphor; expressions such *out of control* or *bed and breakfast* do not contain comparison or figurative language.

The origin of idiomatic expressions is often obscure, but sometimes we do know a little about their histories and they can be extremely rich and interesting. Take, for example, the idiom *to bite the bullet*, which means 'to make yourself do or accept something difficult or unpleasant'. This idiom has its origin in military and medical history. When army doctors had to perform painful operations, at a time when there were no drugs or painkillers, they gave patients a bullet to put between their teeth so that they could bite firmly and tolerate the pain. Over the years, this expression has become fossilised, and all that matters for the language users of today is its fixed, idiomatic meaning.

When a metaphor is the basis of an idiom, it may occur in more or less the same form in a range of different languages, as we can see in (34).

(34) English: break the ice 'to overcome initial difficulties in a first meeting'
French: briser la glace
German: das Eis brechen
Italian: rompere il ghiaccio
Portugese: quebrar o gelo
Greek: σπάζω τον πάγο

Second language learners are often reluctant to use such expressions, suspecting them of being 'false friends'. From experience they may know that idiomatic expressions very often do not have an exact equivalent in other languages. While an Englishman may tell someone to *go and be hanged* 'go away', the French equivalent is not **allez et soyez pendu*, but rather *va te faire voire*. Sometimes an expression in one language is an exact opposite of the expression in another. In German *über den Berg* means literally 'over the mountain' but the idiom means 'to have overcome difficulties', whereas the related expression in English *over the hill* means 'to be too old'.

With the help of metaphor, language users can expand their vocabulary by assigning new meanings and uses to existing words. The word *bottleneck* already existed, but it acquired a new meaning when it was first used to describe a traffic situation. In this respect, metaphors – like derivations and compounds – serve to expand our vocabulary.

Because idiomatic expressions and metaphors have both a literal and a figurative meaning, speakers have to be aware of possible misinterpretations, just as they do when using words with more than one meaning. When a non-native speaker of English concluded his lecture with the words *I will now jump to my conclusions* he meant to say that he would move on quickly to the conclusions of his talk. However, the expression has a different meaning, namely 'draw rash or unfounded conclusions'. He was not aware of his mistake, but the audience was.

Some metaphors are very common in certain cultures. In many Western languages, for example, the metaphor of sport is common in debate, such as in the expression *we need to start with a level playing field*, meaning that the participants have to start on equal terms, or *he was off in the rough with that point*, referring to a point that was not relevant to the argument. There is considerable discussion about the link between such metaphors and culture but this general point of the relationship between language and culture we will return to in Section 17.4.

Idiomatic expressions and metaphors reflect different styles, just as do individual words. Consider the following example in (35).

(35) a. He made many stupid comments, and I just lost my temper.
b. He made many stupid comments, and I just lost my cool.
c. He shot his mouth off again, and I gave him an earful.

In (35a) the style is fairly neutral, but (35b) and (35c) reflect increasing informality (see Section 5.4).

As we can see, even though many idioms are quite 'fixed' in character, they can be varied according to the demands of the situation or context of language use, including the social status of the speaker. Is it the case that when there is an idiom available, a language no longer needs to have a common, ordinary or neutral way of saying the same thing? Let us take a look at the sentences in (36).

(36) a. He is of considerable means.
He is well-to-do
He is very wealthy
He is rolling in it.
b. I failed to find my way in the city centre
I went wrong in the city centre
I made a big cock-up in the city centre

The meaning of the sentences in (36a) are very similar, in fact the sentences are synonymous. But there is a difference in style. The idiom *He is rolling in it* sounds more vulgar and ostentatious than the non-idiomatic expression *He is very wealthy*, which is more neutral and descriptive. The idiom *He is well-to-do* is quite neutral but the non-idiomatic expression *He is of considerable means* is in a more formal style. In (36b) the idiom *I made a big cock-up* sounds a lot blunter and more judgmental than the neutral, descriptive idiom *I went wrong*. The non-idiomatic expression *failed to find my way* is more formal. As we can see, when idioms and non-idiomatic expressions coexist as alternative ways of saying something, there will usually be a difference in style.

```
This freezer is out
of control
```

Figure 13.1 Mixing metaphors.

One of the tasks facing children in first language acquisition is how to master the meanings of idioms, just as they have to master the different meanings of words. Nick, aged five years, overheard his mother talking about someone as being *very hard-headed* 'stubborn'. His comment was *but we all have hard heads, why is he different?* Children very often take idioms and metaphors literally, until they discover their figurative meaning. This also means that they have problems understanding jokes that depend on the double meaning of words or expressions, at least until they reach the age of seven or eight.

Second language learners also often make mistakes in using idioms and metaphors, as the notice in Figure 13.1 on a freezer in a supermarket exemplifies. Hopefully the freezer was just broken and it was a confusion of the expressions *being out of control* and *being out of order*.

Idioms constitute an intriguing subject in linguistics. Their meanings are often unpredictable and cannot be derived from the constituent words; their syntactic form can be fixed or fossilised. At the same time, since they often originate from metaphors, idioms are intimately involved with language change (see Chapter 19). Consider the examples in (37).

(37) a. So, without further *ado*, let me introduce tonight's speaker.
b. Why can't you let *bygones* be bygones?
c. Someone in the administration was in *cahoots* with the opposition.

Words like *ado*, *bygones* and *cahoots* in (37) used to be used in different contexts but today only occur in these idioms or variants of them such as *with much ado*. This must mean that these idioms are stored in our mental lexicon in their entirety, just as many other fixed and formulaic expressions such as *Good morning, ladies and gentlemen*, or *forever and a day*, etc. Yet, despite the fact that idioms are stored in our minds as complete expressions, we do come across cases where the expressions get mixed, as in (38).

(38) a. Let's take the cow by the horns. (instead of the bull)
b. Carry coals to the Eskimos.
(a mixture of 'Carry coals to Newcastle' and 'Sell refrigerators to the Eskimos')
'doing something that the other person has no need of'
c. His ears fell from his head.
(a mixture of 'He could not believe his ears' and 'The scales fell from his eyes')

Are the sentences in (38) examples of creative innovation, mixed metaphors or just plain wrong? Whatever the answer, they certainly demonstrate that even if idioms are mentally stored as complete, fixed and ready-made wholes, language users can still handle them analytically, that is, they have access to their constituent elements.

Finally, let us look briefly at proverbs. Proverbs are sayings that are completely fixed in form. In contrast to idioms such as *a bright spark* 'an intelligent person' or *to have one's cake and eat it* 'having all the advantages from a situation', a proverb is normally a complete sentence, such as *A woman's strength is in her tongue*, and *Conscience makes cowards of us all*. Proverbs are frozen expressions, often stereotypical and sententious in character, containing traditional lore, beliefs, morality, advice and wisdom. Quotes from well-known speeches or literary works can become proverbs, as in the case of the proverb on conscience taken from Shakespeare's *Hamlet*: *'To be or not to be that is the question . . .'*. They constitute a fascinating domain for anthropological, linguistic and intercultural investigation. We conclude this chapter with some international examples in (39) to (42).

Chinese

(39) Fú wú shuāng zhì, huò bù dānxíng.
Blessing not repeat arrive, misfortune not single.travel
'Fortune seldom repeats; troubles never occur alone.'

French

(40) C'est bonnet blanc en blanc bonnet.
It.is hat white and white hat
'It is all the same.'

Italian

(41) Un caval donato non si guarda in bocca.
A horse given not *refl.* looks in mouth
'Don't look a gift horse in the mouth.'

Yiddish

(42) A goldener shlisl efent ale tirn.
A golden key opens all doors
'A golden key opens all doors.'

Summary

Words can in various ways be connected or enter into a fixed relationship with each other. From a syntactic and semantic point of view, these new units will be more complex than simple, internally unstructured words, though they will be lacking in syntactic flexibility. In **compounds**, the constituent words are closely linked. Many word classes, though by no means all in all languages, are suitable candidates for compounds. As with derivation, compounds serve to expand the vocabulary of a language, but in compounds it is often not easy to predict what the meaning of the newly formed word will be.

The determining part of a compound is known as its **head** and determines the inflectional properties of the compound. This is the case in **endocentric compounds**. In other cases we have to do with **exocentric compounds** that have no head. When a word absorbs another word and the two become one, this is a different process to compounding and is known as **incorporation**.

An important subject in this chapter is that of **idioms** or **idiomatic expressions**. Idioms are usually unpredictable in meaning and somewhat fossilised as to their syntax. They have a stylistic value as do individual words. **Metaphor** is often the basis for idiomatic expressions but not always. Some words occur only in idiomatic expressions, their everyday uses having been lost through language change.

Assignments

1. In the Babungo language we encounter forms such as:

mbii-nii	wee-no
side-house	child-stone
'house wall'	'little stone'

   How would you describe the position of the head in these compounds?
2. In Turkish compounds we find the order Specifier-Head, in Moroccan Arabic the reverse. How could you use this to explain the following compounds in the English spoken by Turkish-speaking immigrants and that of Moroccan immigrants?

English	*Turkish*	*Moroccan*
Tea cup	tea cup	cup tea
Swimming lesson	swimlesson	lesson swim
Biscuit jar	biscuit jar	jar biscuit

3. In a computer exam a student does not understand the term *stand-alone* in the following sentence, and gives the answer in italics.

   Joanna works in an office. Her computer is a stand-alone system. What is a stand-alone computer system?

   It doesn't come with a chair

What class of word is *stand-alone*? And is this an endocentric or an exocentric compound?

4. Think of three different idioms that have each of the following properties.
   (a) is transparent
   (b) contains a word that does not occur independently
   (c) can be used in different tenses
   (d) is based on a metaphor
   (e) is not transparent
   (f) can be further specified
5. After his flying exam a cadet had not found it very easy and commented 'Learning to fly was not a piece of cake. I would give my eye teeth for another try.' What tests can you use to show that *a piece of cake* and *give my eye teeth* are idioms?

Test Yourself

1. Which elements are the building blocks for compounds?
2. What is the definition of the head of a compound?
3. Is it a universal property, shared by all languages, that the second element is always the head of the compound?
4. What is an endocentric compound and what is its opposite?
5. When does incorporation occur?
6. What is an idiomatic expression?
7. Can an idiom show syntactic variation?
8. How important are metaphors for idioms?

Acknowledgments and Further Reading

Aikhenvald (2007) is a useful source on compounds and incorporation. Everaert *et al.* (eds) (1995) contains many articles on idioms. Lakoff and Johnson (1980) wrote a classic on metaphors; a later discussion can be found in Steen (1994). The Kayardild examples are from Evans (1995), the Nahuatl examples from Anderson (1985), and the Tiwa examples from Baker (1988). The Indopakistan Sign Language example is taken from Zeshan (2000).

part V

Speech Sounds

In this part of the book we will take a closer look at the smallest units of linguistic analysis and the ways in which these combine. For spoken languages these are the sounds of speech. In Chapter 14 we will first discuss the speech signal in terms of its physical properties. We will focus in particular on the way in which humans can produce and perceive sounds, and on the various kinds of sounds that can be distinguished in terms of how they are produced in the vocal tract. For instance, some sounds (such as *m*-like and *n*-like sounds) are produced by letting the air escape through the nasal cavity, that is, the nose, while others (such as *p*-like sounds or *r*-like sounds) are produced by letting the air escape through the oral cavity or mouth.

In Chapter 15 we will consider the sound distinctions that are relevant within the system of a spoken language. Here the focus will be on those speech sounds (or phonemes) that are capable of signalling a difference of meaning in the language concerned. These phonemes can be further subdivided on the basis of their distinctive features, such as voiced versus voiceless, as in the last sound of *peas* versus the last sound of *peace*.

Going up from the level of speech sounds it is useful to distinguish larger units. This is what we shall do in Chapter 16, the last chapter of this part. There we will discuss, among other things, the syllabic structure of words – since these can be considered combinations of speech sounds – the way in which stress is assigned to words, and the organisation of sentence intonation.

chapter 14

Speaking and Listening – Speech Sounds

14.1 Introduction

Various software packages are available that make it possible to feed speech into a computer, rather than typing text in. Such software is for instance a useful tool for people who are unable to operate a keyboard or can do so only with great difficulty, as is the case of people with Repetitive Strain Injury (RSI). One of the users of a blog, dedicated to exchanging experiences with such software, wanted to test a new speech recognition program. He reported what happened when, in doing so, he read the following text aloud for storage in his computer.

(1) Bree told me this great story. She was assigned to show around a visiting middleware consultant from France. Nobody was sure if he was gay or not. His name is Serge Duclos – which is sort of funny in itself, because in high school, the fictional guy in my French textbook was Serge Duclos. Everyone my age in my school district has this same Serge Duclos guy in their heads, forever asking where the Métro is.

Linguistics, First Edition. Edited by Anne E. Baker and Kees Hengeveld.

What the computer made of his speech is given in (2).

(2) *Brea* told me this great story. She was assigned to show around a visiting middleware consultant from France. Nobody was sure if he was gay or not. His name is *surge to quote* – which is sort of funny in itself, because in high school, the fictional guy in my French textbook was *searched and quo*. Everyone my age in my school district has the same *surge to call die* in their *ads*, forever asking where the metro is.

The result is remarkably good. Things go wrong as marked in italics when the program does not find words (here the French name *Serge Duclos*) in its dictionary and has to come up with the nearest sound equivalents. The computer also goes wrong in identifying the words *guy* and *heads*, possibly due to a particular pronunciation of this speaker. Only after such new words are added to the software's vocabulary and linked to the corresponding sound strings from the individual speaker does this kind of mix-up stop. As this example indicates, the process of automatic speech recognition requires extensive knowledge of speech.

The **speech signal** can best be understood as part of the **speech chain**. A speaker thinks of something and wants to communicate it; this leads to a series of speech sounds that reaches the ear of the listener, who hears and interprets it. In return this may lead to an utterance from the listener who becomes speaker in turn and keeps the speech chain going (see Section 4.4 on turn-taking in conversations).

Within linguistics there are two sub-disciplines that study the speech signal. The first of these is **phonetics**, which studies the physical process of speaking and listening as well as the physical properties of the speech signal. How are speech sounds produced, what are the properties of the signal, how do we differentiate sounds from each other in perception? In the second sub-discipline, that of phonology (see Chapters 15 and 16), we study sounds as part of the language system. Which sounds serve to differentiate meanings in a particular language, how is the sound system organised, and in what ways can sounds be combined into words and utterances? To differentiate these two perspectives on speech sounds we normally represent sounds between square brackets when we are looking at actual sound realisations from a phonetic perspective, and between slashes when they are represented as phonological abstractions. As a result, there is a principled difference between the phonetic realisation [a] and the phonological abstraction /a/.

In this chapter we will discuss speech sounds from the perspective of phonetics. In Section 14.2 we will consider the way in which the speech signal is produced by the speech organs. In Section 14.3 we will discuss the acoustic properties of the speech signal. The perception of the speech signal is the subject of Section 14.4. Then, in Section 14.5, we will give a systematic description of the phonetic properties of speech sounds. In Section 14.6 we return to the issue of communication with a computer using speech.

14.2 Speaking

We can make all sorts of sounds with our speech organs – clicks, grunts, groans, sighs, screams, and whistles. When young babies begin to babble, they produce the most remarkable sounds, as we showed in Section 3.3. We can also produce the speech sounds of a particular language, English in the case of this chapter. We can chain these sounds together and organise them into words and clauses. We can say the same written clause *I'm going to take you away* in such a way that it is clearly a question, a threat, or an expression of love. So how do humans do this? How do they manage the production of speech sounds and the pronunciation of the words of a language?

When we are speaking, our lungs function as a pair of bellows that expel the air via the windpipe, the vocal folds, and the **pharynx**, shown in Figure 14.1, to the **oral cavity** and the **nasal cavity**. This pathway that the air passes through in speech production is called the **vocal tract**. The air comes out via the mouth and/or the nose, and becomes audible as speech. By exhaling from the lungs with more or less effort, people can vary how loudly they speak. Of course, when we breathe, the lungs also expel air, but we produce almost no

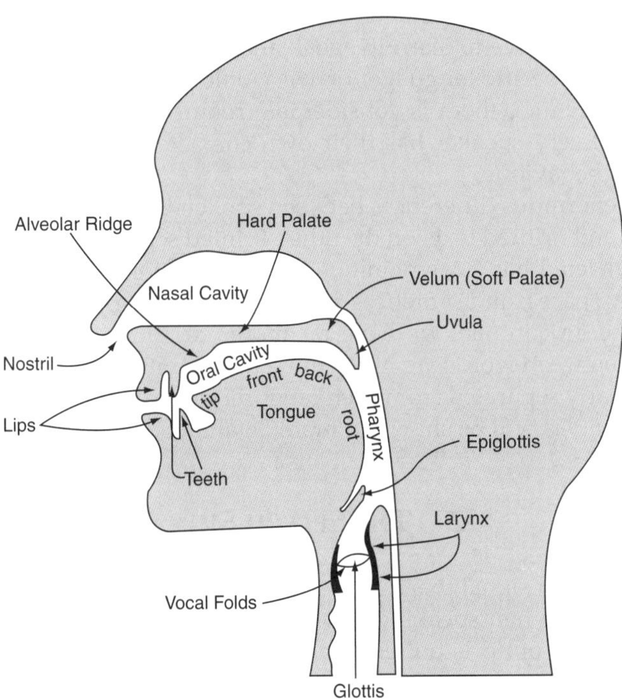

Figure 14.1 Speech organs.

sound. This is because, when breathing, the vocal folds are wide open and the oral cavity is not narrowed at any point. When producing speech, on the other hand, either we bring the **vocal folds** together and allow them to vibrate on the air that is being pushed through, or there is a narrowing somewhere in the vocal tract, created for example by closing the lips or raising the tongue towards the hard palate. Figure 14.1 gives a schematic cross-section of a human head with its various speech organs.

Speech sounds can be made by expelling air through the oral cavity or through the nasal cavity. In producing oral speech sounds the air goes from the lungs via the windpipe through the vocal folds, which can vibrate or not as the case may be, and then out via the oral cavity and the lips. In producing nasal speech sounds the nasal cavity is opened with the back part of the soft palate for the production of nasal sounds like [n] and [m].

Speaking is a largely unconscious, though by no means easy, process. We have to plan what we are going to say, and if there is damage to the relevant areas of the brain (for example in the case of aphasia, see Section 2.5), this planning may not work. People may then produce incomprehensible speech despite the fact that they are still physically capable of making all the necessary individual speech movements. If, for any reason, for example as a result of a tumour, the vocal folds cease to function, then speech becomes impossible. Fortunately there are ways to overcome this specific handicap.

As children we have to learn to speak and to keep to the conventions that apply within a specific language, or we would not be understood in communication. Even so, there is considerable room for variation within those conventions. Every speaker has their own characteristic speaking style and idiosyncratic behaviour.

There are enormous differences between spoken language on the one hand, and written and printed texts on the other. Printed script is in principle unambiguous: each letter has its own unique and constant form; words are normally separated by spaces; and sentences are structured using punctuation. In spoken language, in contrast, we have far more variation: transitions between sounds and between words are much more fluid; units like sounds and words are not as clearly separated from each other, as we argued in Section 2.4.1 and Section 11.2 and as will be shown in more detail in Section 14.3.

14.3 The Speech Signal

Without the speech signal there is no spoken communication. The sound that humans produce when speaking travels as vibrating molecules through the air. The speed of sound is not extremely fast; at 340 metres per second it is much slower than the speed of light. Because of this, if you are standing a few hundred metres away from a road, you will actually *see* two cars colliding before you *hear* the sound of the accident. Sound travels away from its source in

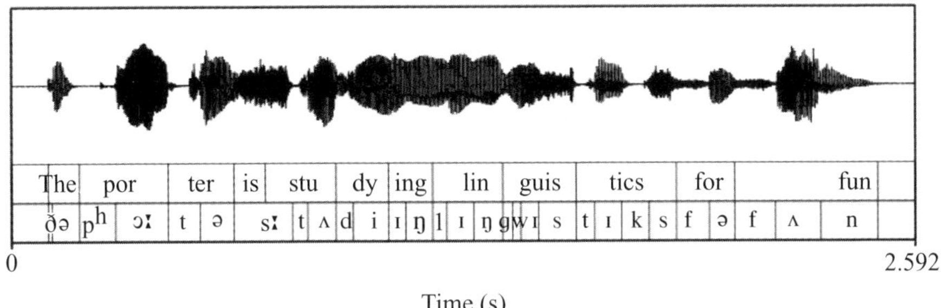

Figure 14.2 Atmospheric pressure produced in the pronunciation of the sentence *the porter is studying linguistics for fun* by an educated female speaker of British English.

all directions, so it has to cover an ever-increasing area. As a result it becomes fainter the farther away it is from the source.

Sound, including speech sounds, can also be transported via other media than air. It can travel from sender to receiver via water, rail tracks or – after conversion – via a telephone cable. Speech sounds can be recorded with a microphone, which converts the sound vibrations into an electric signal that can be stored inside the recorder or in the memory of a computer using an analogue-digital-converter. The recorded sound can then be played and replayed, either as a whole or in short sound stretches. This makes it possible to measure many kinds of properties it may have.

Figure 14.2 represents a piece of a speech signal produced by an educated female speaker of British English. The sentence produced is *the porter is studying linguistics for fun*. The main stress is on the syllable *por* in the word *porter*, indicating the unexpectedness of the porter studying linguistics. The time axis moves from left to right. The diagram consists of three tiers: the top tier shows the changes in atmospheric pressure as measured by a microphone during the pronunciation of the sentence. A thin part of the line indicates little pressure, a thick part strong pressure. The second tier contains the sentence in standard orthography and shows the syllable boundaries. The third tier contains the phonetic transcription (something we will turn to in Section 14.5) and shows the boundaries between individual sounds.

In such a speech signal you can take detailed measurements. For instance, this sentence of twelve syllables lasts 2.592 seconds, so it has a speed of 12 divided by 2.592, that is 4.63 syllables per second, giving an average of 216 milliseconds (msec) per syllable. From measurements taken from other speakers we know that an average speaker of English produces approximately four syllables per second, so the speech recorded here is slightly faster than that.

Comparing the written version of the sentence with the phonetic transcription it is clear that not all sounds that are written are actually pronounced. If you compare the correct written sentence (3) with the string of sounds that are actually realised (4), this becomes obvious.

(3) written: the porter is studying linguistics for fun
(4) realised: thepotestudyinglinguisticsfofun

We can see that both syllable final *r*'s of *porter* and the one of *for* are dropped, that the *i* of *is* is not pronounced, and that the final *s* of *is* and the initial *s* of *studying* melt together in a single *s*. The result is that *porter is studying* is actually realised as *potestudying*.

Already implicit in the previous point is the fact that no word boundaries can be detected in Figure 14.2. There are silent periods, shown by the absence of pressure in Figure 14.2, but the sound curve shows that these silent periods occur just before the sounds [p], [t], and [k]. For all three of these speech sounds speakers use their lips or tongue to close off the oral cavity. This causes a build-up of air pressure inside the mouth, which is then released with a small explosion, resulting in the characteristic sound called plosive. The temporary closure is visible in Figure 14.2 as an (almost) silent break just before each of these sounds (for instance, the [p] of *porter*, the [t] in *studying* and *linguistics*, the [k], written as *c*, in *linguistics*). But there is no necessary silence whatsoever between words.

A final observation with respect to Figure 14.2 is that vowels display the highest degree of pressure: even the unstressed schwa [ə], as in *the*, shows up as the core of the syllable.

Figure 14.3 shows another phonetic aspect of the same sentence, its intonation contour, measured in terms of the frequency in hertz (Hz) with which the vocal folds vibrate during the pronunciation of the sentence.

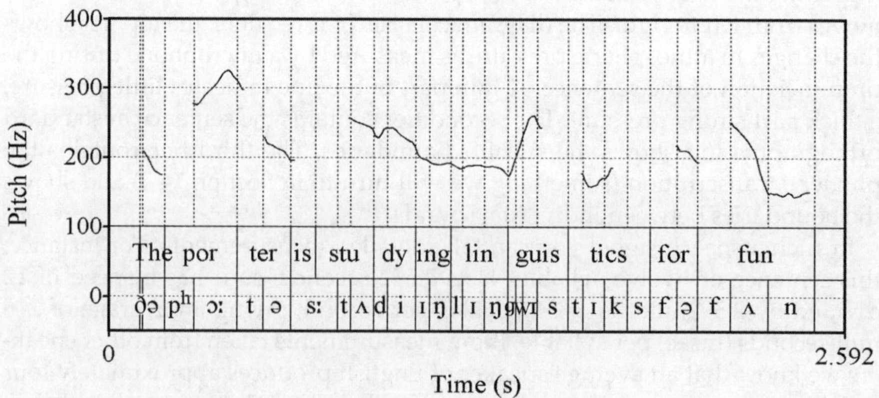

Figure 14.3 Frequency (in Hz) of the sentence *the porter is studying linguistics for fun* pronounced by an educated female speaker of British English.

At some points the curve is interrupted. This happens when the vocal folds are not vibrating because voiceless sounds are being produced. This is for instance the case of the various [s]'s in the sentence. The overall intonation contour is falling, which is common for declarative sentences in English. The contrastive stress on the first syllable of *porter* is also clearly visible in Figure 14.3.

14.4 HEARING AND UNDERSTANDING

How do humans manage to hear and understand speech? What processes are involved? In Chapter 2 this was discussed from the point of view of the different kinds of knowledge involved. Here we will take a look at a few more technical aspects.

In order to be able to hear and understand speech, we will first have to perceive and process the speech signal via the ears (see Figure 14.4). Our external ears or auricles, as part of the **outer ear,** catch the sound vibrations in the air and channel them via the **external auditory canal**. At the end of this canal the vibrations hit the **tympanic membrane**, which passes them on to the **middle ear** with its three hearing bones (**hammer**, **anvil** and **stirrup**). The stirrup conducts the sound vibrations via the **oval window** to the fluid in the **cochlea** in the **inner ear**, where some kind of frequency analysis takes place. The result is conveyed via the **acoustic nerve** to the brain for further interpretation. In order to be able to understand speech we have to be able to hear and listen well; then, secondly, the processing in our brain has to be of good quality; and, thirdly, the various kinds of knowledge mentioned in Chapter 2 are needed if we are to construct a proper interpretation of what we

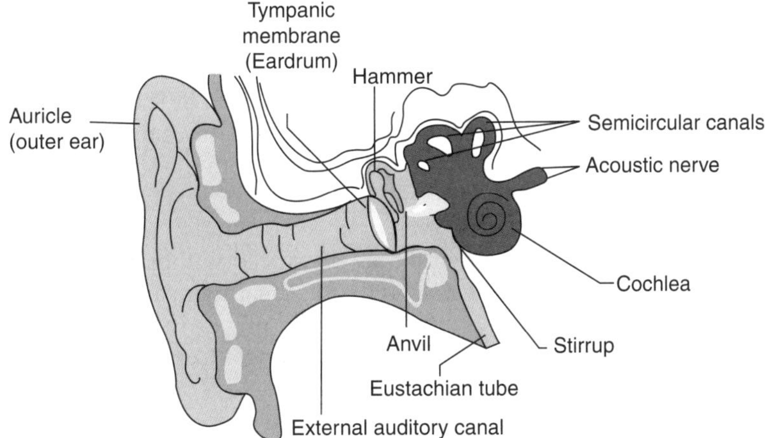

Figure 14.4 Schematic representation of the human ear.

have heard. If something goes wrong at any of these three levels, the process of understanding speech is impaired.

14.5 Speech Sounds

14.5.1 *Introduction*

Whether we study a particular language or investigate spoken languages in general, it is important to have some insight into (the structure of) the speech sounds of the language(s) in question. Which sounds occur in the language under investigation? How are these produced? What properties do they have? And how do we perceive the differences between them?

For the representation of the sounds and sound strings in **phonetic transcriptions** we make use of phonetic symbols that have been rigorously defined in an international standard by the International Phonetics Association (IPA). Figure 14.5 is an adapted and reduced version of a chart published by the IPA. The chart shows the symbols to be used for certain combinations of features that we will discuss below. Many of the symbols given in the chart will be unfamiliar and it may be difficult to imagine what sound they represent. There are many web sites that allow you to listen to the sounds by clicking on the relevant symbol. Listening to the sounds makes it much easier to relate to the explanations given below.

It is important to keep in mind that when studying sounds from the phonetic point of view, that is, when looking at its physical properties, speech is non-discrete. This means that we can measure all kinds of different degrees of certain properties of sounds and will find that they are gradual in nature. It is important to remember this when looking at Figure 14.5. What this chart gives is a number of discrete points in the non-discrete domain of speech sounds. The discrete points that are given are sounds that have been found to be relevant for the analysis of the sound system (see Chapter 15) of at least one language. Empty cells in Figure 14.5 indicate combinations of features that have not been encountered in the sound system of any language, often because they would be difficult or impossible to produce.

There are two important categories of speech sounds: vowels and consonants. **Vowels** are speech sounds that are produced without any substantial narrowing in the vocal tract. The reason that we hear them at all is because the vocal folds are brought together and vibrate on the air that is being pushed through. Vowels may be combined into diphthongs. **Consonants** are speech sounds that are produced by creating a narrowing of some type somewhere in the vocal tract. This narrowing by itself is sufficient to produce a sound, but may be accompanied by vibration of the vocal folds. Most consonants are **pulmonic**, which means that the airstream that is used to pronounce them is produced in the lungs. **Non-pulmonic** consonants are pronounced using an airstream produced by the larynx or the tongue.

We will now look at each of these groups in turn, starting with pulmonic consonants, then non-pulmonic consonants. We then describe vowels, and finally diphthongs, combinations of vowels that form one single sound.

14.5.2 Pulmonic Consonants

Pulmonic consonants (see Figure 14.5) can be further subdivided on the basis of three different features: manner of articulation, place of articulation, and voicing. The **manner of articulation** is given in the leftmost column of the pulmonic consonant table in Figure 14.5. It concerns the degree and nature of the narrowing involved in the production of consonants. The following groups of sounds differ from each other in this respect:

- **plosives** (such as the [p] in *tip* or [k] in *brook*) are produced by building up air pressure inside the mouth through a complete closure. The air is then allowed to escape in one go.
- **fricatives** (such as the [f] in *flat* or [s] in *street*) are produced by an almost complete narrowing of the vocal tract and then an expulsion of the air through the narrow passage.
- **affricates** (such as the [d͡ʒ] in *John* or [t͡ʃ] in *chip*) combine the two previous manners of articulation: they start out as a plosive and end as a fricative.
- **nasals** (such as the [m] in *month* or [n] in *north*) are produced by letting the air escape through the nasal rather than the oral cavity.
- **laterals** (such as the [l] in *long*) are characterised by the fact that the air flows along the sides of the tongue and not across its centre.
- **trills** (such as the [r] in *red* in Scottish English) are produced by vibration of part of the tongue against a place of articulation (see below).
- **taps or flaps** are characterised by a single short closure; they occur in some English dialects but not in others. A good example is the [ɾ] in American English *butter*.
- **approximants** (such as the [j] in *you*) are produced with almost no narrowing of the vocal tract, and thus come close to vowels. This is why they are sometimes called 'semi-consonants' or 'semi-vowels'.

The **place of articulation** of a consonant concerns the part of the roof of the mouth where the narrowing occurs. This narrowing is created by various parts of the tongue, the teeth and/or the lips. Speech sounds such as [p], [t] and [k] are all plosives, that is, they have the same manner of articulation, but they differ in their place of articulation. The [p] is made at the lips, the [t] at the alveolar ridge, and the [k] at the velum (soft palate). You can find these places and others mentioned on page 294 in Figure 14.5. The places of articulation most relevant for dividing consonants are given in the top row of the pulmonic consonant chart in Figure 14.5. Try out these sounds consciously for yourself, and you will immediately notice the differences in the places of contact. They are defined in the following way:

- **bilabial** sounds (such as the [m] in *mouse*) are produced using both lips.
- **labiodental** sounds (such as the [f] in *flat*) are produced by placing the upper teeth against the lower lip.
- **dental** sounds (such as the [ð] in *the*) are produced by placing the tongue against the upper teeth;
- **alveolar** sounds (such as the [s] in *street*) are produced by placing the tongue against the alveolar ridge.
- **postalveolar** sounds (such as the [ʃ] in *show*) are produced by placing the tongue against the area just behind the alveolar ridge.
- **palatal** sounds (such as the [j] in *you*) are produced by placing the tongue against the hard palate.
- **velar** sounds (such as the [ŋ] in *sing*) are produced by placing the tongue against the soft palate.
- **uvular** sounds are produced by placing the tongue against the uvula.
- **pharyngeal** sounds are produced in the pharyngeal cavity.
- **glottal** sounds (such as the [h] in *house*) are pronounced near the glottis.

English has all except uvular and pharyngeal consonants. These are the really 'guttural' sounds particularly common in Arabic.

A third important distinction – after manner and place of articulation – has to do with **voicing**. At the top of the windpipe, in the larynx, are our vocal folds, as we already saw in Figure 14.1. The space between the two vocal folds is known as the **glottis**. The vocal folds can be open (for example while we breathe) or they can be closed (for example when we are lifting very heavy objects). But they can also vibrate, and they then give voice to the so-called voiced sounds. If the vocal folds are open and do not vibrate, we are producing voiceless sounds. **Voiced consonants** are thus consonants produced with vibration of the vocal folds, while **voiceless consonants** are consonants produced without vibration of the vocal folds. Sounds like [p] and [b] are identical as regards their manner of articulation and place of articulation, but they differ in voicing, the [p] being voiceless, and the [b] voiced. Similarly, the [s] is voiceless, but the [z] is voiced, and this is again the only difference between them, since they have the same manner and place of articulation. In each column of the pulmonic consonant chart in Figure 14.5 the voiceless consonant is given to the left and the voiced one to the right. Note that all nasals, laterals, trills, tap or flaps, and approximants are necessarily voiced.

Consonants, pulmonic (voiceless left, voiced right)

	Bilabial		Labio-dental		Dental		Alveolar		Post-alveolar		Palatal		Velar		Uvular		Pharyn-geal		Glottal	
Plosive	p	b					t	d			c	ɟ	k	g	q	ɢ			ʔ	
Fricative	ɸ	β	f	v	θ	ð	s	z	ʃ	ʒ	ç	ʝ	x	ɣ	χ	ʁ	ħ	ʕ	h	ɦ
Affricate			p͡f	b͡v			t͡s	d͡z	t͡ʃ	d͡ʒ	c͡ç	ɟ͡ʝ	k͡x		q͡χ					
Nasal		m		ɱ				n				ɲ		ŋ		ɴ				
Lateral								l				ʎ		ʟ						
Trill		ʙ						r								ʀ				
Tap or Flap								ɾ												
Approximant		w		ʋ				ɹ				j		ɰ						

Vowels (unrounded left, rounded right)

	Front		Central		Back	
Close	i	y	ɨ	ʉ	ɯ	u
	ɪ	ʏ				ʊ
Close-mid	e	ø	ɘ	ɵ	ɤ	o
			ə			
Open-mid	ɛ	œ	ɜ	ɞ	ʌ	ɔ
	æ		ɐ			
Open			a	ɶ	ɑ	ɒ

Consonants, non-pulmonic

Clicks		Voiced implosives		Ejectives	
ʘ	Bilabial	ɓ	Bilabial	p'	Bilabial
ǀ	Dental	ɗ	Dental/alveolar	t'	Dental/alveolar
ǃ	Alveolar	ʄ	Palatal	s'	Alveolar fricative
ǂ	Palatal	ɠ	Velar	k'	Velar
ǁ	Lateral	ʛ	Uvular	q'	Uvular

Figure 14.5 International phonetic alphabet (adapted from IPA 2005 revision).

14.5.3 *Non-pulmonic Consonants*

The long list of possible consonants given in Section 14.5.2 does not exhaust the possibilities that languages can make use of. So far we have only considered the pulmonic type, but there are also consonants of the non-pulmonic type. Non-pulmonic consonants are produced by an airstream that does not originate in the lungs. They are rather less frequent than pulmonic consonants, and so are most likely to be unknown to you and require more of your imagination. In the non-pulmonic consonant chart in Figure 14.5 three types are distinguished:

- **clicks** are sounds that are produced by sucking air into the mouth; they are not part of the sound system of English, but English speakers do produce them. One type occurs when trying to get a horse moving forward, another when imitating the sound of a kiss.
- **voiced implosives** are sounds that are produced by combining a closure of the vocal tract with lowering the larynx. This creates low pressure in the oral cavity, with the result that upon release of the closure air moves into the mouth. This is the opposite of what happens with plosives, hence the name 'implosives'.
- **ejectives** are sounds that are produced by combining a closure of the vocal tract with rapid raising of the larynx. This produces high pressure in the oral cavity, with the result that upon release of the closure air moves out of the mouth. These consonants thus differ from plosives in that the pressure originates in the larynx rather than the lungs.

14.5.4 *Vowels*

As indicated in Section 14.5.1, vowels are speech sounds that are produced without substantial narrowing in the vocal tract. The reason that we can hear them is that the vocal folds vibrate when vowels are produced. The quality of the vowel may be changed, among other things, by changing the position of the tongue (see Figure 14.1) or by changing the form of the mouth. Correspondingly, as shown in the bottom left chart of Figure 14.5, vowels may be distinguished among themselves in terms of their place of articulation (for vowels defined in terms of the position of the tongue root), and rounding, defined in terms of the form of the lips. The place of articulation is described in terms of the position of the tongue root along both the horizontal and the vertical dimension. Along the horizontal dimension, moving the tongue root from the front to the back of the oral cavity, the following classes of vowels occur:

- **front** vowels (such as the [i] in *beat*) are produced with the tongue root in the front part of the oral cavity.

- **central** vowels (such as the [ə] in *about*) are produced with the tongue root in the centre part of the oral cavity.
- **back** vowels (such as the [ɑ] in *father*) are produced with the tongue root in the back part of the oral cavity.

Along the vertical dimension, moving the tongue root from a high to a low position, the following classes of vowels can be distinguished:

- **close** vowels (such as the [ʊ] in *put*) are produced with the tongue root in the highest position.
- **close-mid** vowels (such as the [e] in French *santé* 'health') are produced with the tongue root just below the highest position.
- **mid** vowels (such as the [ə] in *about*) are produced with the tongue root in the middle position.
- **open-mid** vowels (such as the [ʌ] in *cut*) are produced with the tongue root just above the lowest position.
- **open** vowels (such as the [ɒ] in *body*) are produced with the tongue root in the lowest position.

As shown in Figure 14.5, the sounds [ʌ] (as in *run*) and [ɔ] (as in *sort*) are both open-mid back vowels, that is their place of articulation is identical as regards both the horizontal (back) and the vertical (open-mid) dimensions. The difference between them is due to the fact that [ɔ] is pronounced with rounded lips, while [ʌ] is not. With **rounding** many pairs of vowels can be produced that differ only with respect to the rounded versus non-rounded shape of the lips. In every column of the vowel chart in Figure 14.5 the non-rounded vowels are given at the left, and their rounded counterparts on the right.

14.5.5 Diphthongs

A last group of sounds to be discussed here can be described as the combination of two vowels and are called **diphthongs**. Some examples of diphthongs are [aɪ] in *mine*, [ɔɪ] in *joy*, and [aʊ] in *now*. What is special about these sounds is that they start out as one vowel and end up as another. So, in the case of *mine*, the vocalic part starts out as an [a] and ends up as an [ɪ]. This effect is achieved by adjusting the tongue and the lips during pronunciation so that the two vowels are pronounced in a single flowing movement. There are many combinations of vowels that together may form a diphthong. Various examples will be given in Chapter 15.

14.5.6 *Further Features*

What we have presented in Sections 14.5.2 to 14.5.5 are the major features along which speech sounds can be distinguished from one another. Further features, often referred to as secondary articulations, can be superimposed on the classification given in Figure 14.5. Two of these are already illustrated in Figure 14.2 in the transcription of the word *porter* as [pʰɔːtə]. The ʰ following the p shows that the consonant is aspirated, that is, followed by a kind of a hissing sound. The ː following the ɔ indicates that the vowel is lengthened in pronunciation. Another example of a secondary articulation is the nasalisation of vowels. The French word *vin* 'wine' is phonetically realised as [vɪ̃], in which the symbol ~ across the vowel indicates nasalisation. These are just a few examples of secondary articulations.

14.6 Speech Synthesis and Speech Recognition

In the preceding sections we explained how humans produce and recognise speech sounds. Is this a uniquely human ability or can we get computers to produce and recognise understandable speech? One option is to imitate human articulation in every detail, but this turns out to be vastly complicated. Another extreme would be to use the computer as a tape recorder with knobs on. In this case we would have to pre-record all possible words and utterances, and once this is done, we could call them up whenever necessary and string them together in speech production. However, when text and speaking style are changing all the time, and when the numbers of words and sentences become very large, this is no longer an efficient solution. But in specific applications with a limited style and vocabulary, such as bus stop or underground announcements in public transport, or voicemail or a speaking clock, it is an excellent technique.

Another option would be to construct the speech we want to produce, starting from smaller pieces of natural speech, such as single speech sounds or combinations of two speech sounds, or half syllables. A very popular approach is to use units the size of two half sounds, or **diphones**. A word like *extra* requires the following seven such diphones: [#ɛ], [ɛk], [ks], [st], [tr], [rə] and [ə#], where # represents the silence before and after the word. The transition from one sound to the next has here been incorporated into the diphone elements themselves, and this turns out to greatly enhance the quality of the synthesis. For a language like English, with some 40 relevant speech sounds, we will need 40 x 40 = about 1600 diphones. But do we really need all those combinations? After all, many combinations are excluded in English, an example being the sequence [tk]. Yes, we indeed really need them, for we will also need to be able to make phoneme combinations across syllable- and word-boundaries, and then those seemingly excluded combinations do occur, for example in *Atkinson* or *hot coffee*.

Simply putting diphones together one after another does not yet produce speech that sounds natural. For this we will also need to adapt loudness, phoneme length and pitch to the desired prosodic structure or melody of the sentence. In a question sentence, for example, pitch needs to rise towards the end of the sentence. Equally, a stressed syllable will need to sound louder and longer than an unstressed syllable (see Chapter 16).

The most flexible, though also most difficult, form of **speech synthesis** is the one where the complete generation or production of sounds, including the transitions between phonemes, is guided by a set of rules. These rules are deduced from detailed investigations of the production and perception of natural speech and its regularities.

So far we have tacitly assumed that a phonetic transcription of the text is available, which indicates for example that the word *extra* needs to be pronounced as [ɛkstrə]. Similarly, at some level of representation it should be known that the two occurrences of 'o' in *photographer* have to be pronounced [ə] and [ɒ] respectively. This aspect of text interpretation, the conversion of text symbols (graphemes) into sound symbols (phonemes), is known as **grapheme-to-phoneme conversion**. We will come back in Chapter 15 to the relation between speech and script.

As we saw in the introduction of this chapter, a great deal of linguistic and technical knowledge is also needed for **automatic speech recognition**. First we need an analysis of the speech signal that has been recorded. The results of this analysis are then used to compare the pattern of all spoken words in the sentence (in bits of 10msec, or per phoneme, or per word) to the previously trained patterns for all phonemes and words. The best fit will then hopefully lead to a correct identification. For some applications it is sufficient if a limited set of separate words or short commands from a specific individual speaker are correctly recognised. But for other applications, for example a system that provides information, it is important that a sentence spoken by any speaker is at least partially recognised. Through this recognition the customer, via a question-and-answer routine, will then receive the right information as quickly as possible. We can think here of information retrieval over the telephone about train departure times. The speech recogniser will then have to be able to hear and understand rather complex sentences like 'If I want to be in Oxford at noon tomorrow, which train should I take from Victoria Station?'

SUMMARY

Spoken language is the most natural form of communication between humans, and in the future perhaps also between humans and machines. In

phonetics we study the physical process of speaking and hearing, paying particular attention to the interaction between speaker and listener (the **speech chain**) and the role of the **speech signal** in that interaction. When producing speech sounds, speakers make use of their speech organs in the **vocal tract**, which consists of the **vocal folds**, the **pharynx**, the **oral cavity** and the **nasal cavity**.

In processing speech, the speech signal caught by the auricles, which are part of the **outer ear**, passes through the **external auditory canal**. At the end of this canal they hit the **tympanic membrane**, which passes them on to the **middle ear** with its three hearing bones (**hammer**, **anvil** and **stirrup**). The stirrup conducts the sound vibrations via the **oval window** to the fluid in the **cochlea** in the **inner ear**, where the sounds are physically analysed. The result is conveyed via the **acoustic nerve** to the brain for further interpretation.

Speech sounds are often shown in a **phonetic transcription**. Within the sound system we can distinguish **vowels** and **consonants**, the latter being divided into **pulmonic** and **non-pulmonic**.

Pulmonic consonants may be further subdivided according to **manner** and **place of articulation** and **voicing**. According to manner of articulation we can distinguish eight categories of consonants: **plosives**, **fricatives**, **affricates**, **nasals**, **laterals**, **trills**, **taps or flaps**, and **approximants**. According to place of articulation we can distinguish **bilabial**, **labiodental**, **dental**, **alveolar**, **postalveolar**, **palatal**, **velar**, **uvular**, **pharyngeal**, and **glottal** sounds. Whether a sound is **voiced** or **voiceless** depends on whether the vocal folds in the larynx vibrate or not. The space between the two vocal folds is known as the **glottis**.

Non-pulmonic consonants are produced by an airstream that does not originate in the lungs. They are subdivided into **clicks**, **voiced implosives**, and **ejectives**.

Vowels are subdivided according to the place of articulation and according to **rounding**. In the case of vowels the place of articulation concerns the position of the tongue root along the horizontal and the vertical dimension. Along the horizontal dimension **front**, **central**, and **back** vowels are distinguished; along the vertical dimension **close**, **close-mid**, **open-mid** and **open** vowels. Rounding refers to the shape of the lips when producing a vowel; vowels may correspondingly be divided into rounded and non-rounded vowels. **Diphthongs** are combinations of vowels.

In this technical age machine speech is also being considered. When speech is generated by a computer (**speech synthesis**), written text has to be converted into speech sounds (**grapheme-to-phoneme conversion**). Here **diphones** (combinations of two successive half phonemes) are often used as speech units to be strung together. In addition to the production of machine speech there is also **automatic speech recognition**: involving the interpretation of spoken text by a computer.

Assignments

1. An interesting way to test the speech sounds of your language is to sit with a group in a circle. The first speaker whispers a few sentences into his or her neighbour's ear, who passes it on in the same way to the next person, etc., until it has come full circle. Then you check what is left of the original sentences and discuss which aspect of the sentence have survived this whispering chain.
2. Reiterant speech is speech in which all syllables in a sentence are replaced by, for example, *ma-ma-ma-ma-ma*. All other properties of the speech signal (pauses, syllable length, sentence rhythm, etc.) stay the same. Do this for the sentence *Shall we go swimming?* by saying it aloud. Then check whether you can still hear the word boundaries, the stressed syllables, and a rising question intonation pattern.
3. Consonants [p], [t], [f] and [s] are voiceless. Which four voiced consonants can be paired with them?
4. Two words that are written almost the same are sometimes pronounced very differently (*lead* (noun) versus *lead* (verb), *tough* versus *dough*, *peace* versus *peas*). Their meanings, too, may change when the pronunciation changes (*permit*, *row*, *desert*). Could you think of more examples of this in English or in another language you know well?
5. Give a phonetic transcription (using Figure 14.5) of your pronunciation of the following words: *reuse* (V), *banana*, *Royal Navy* and *298*.
6. Locate a text-to-speech synthesis system via the internet. Try to synthesize a few of your own texts, both in the language of the synthesizer and in a different one, and see where the synthesizing program goes wrong.
7. In diphone synthesis sound transitions are used as building blocks. How many diphones are necessary to generate the word *tomato*?
8. Which problem do you encounter in the grapheme-phoneme conversion of the pairs *not* and *knot*, and *sin* and *cinema*?

Test Yourself

1. What is meant by the term 'speech chain'?
2. What is the difference between the disciplines of phonetics and phonology?
3. What is the difference between vowels and consonants?
4. Give an example off a lateral speech sound.

5. What is an alveolar sound?
6. What is the difference between pulmonic and non-pulmonic consonants?
7. Which two dimensions are used to describe the articulation of vowels?
8. What is a secondary articulation?
9. What is grapheme-phoneme-conversion?
10. What is a diphone?

Acknowledgments and Further Reading

An excellent introduction to the field of phonetics is Ladefoged (2001), which is accompanied by a CD that allows you to listen to the sounds discussed in this chapter. A more advanced treatment is given in Ladefoged and Maddieson (1996). Pullum and Ladusaw (1986) is a very useful guide for the use of phonetic symbols. The International Phonetics Association publishes an International Phonetic Alphabet that is regularly updated. For this chapter we have used the 2005 revision. The phonetic analyses given in Figure 14.2 and Figure 14.3 were made using the Praat programme, described in Boersma and Weenink (2005). The picture of the human ear is from www.scienceclarified.com.

chapter 15

Sound Systems and Phonological Processes

15.1 Introduction

When Spanish people start to learn English as a second language, it is quite possible they will pronounce the word *live* as in (1) instead of the correct form in (2).

(1) I want to leave [li:v].
(2) I want to live [lɪv].

The reason for this pronunciation error is that the sound system of Spanish does not distinguish between the close front vowel [i] and the near-close front vowel [ɪ]. As a consequence it is difficult for a Spaniard to hear, let alone produce, the difference between these two vowels. The intended verb *live* ends up sounding in fact like *leave*.

In the previous chapter we discussed differences between speech sounds from the point of view of phonetics, with particular attention to the production of these sounds and their physical properties. In this chapter we will take a look at sounds in as far as they are relevant as units of a language system. This is the domain of **phonology**. From (1) and (2) it should be clear that for a proper understanding of Spanish the distinction between a close and a near-close vowel is irrelevant, whereas for English it is relevant. We will discuss

Linguistics, First Edition. Edited by Anne E. Baker and Kees Hengeveld.

the role of such sound distinctions within a language system in Section 15.2. Once we have established all the relevant distinctions of a particular language, we can establish the scope and structure of its sound system. This will be the subject of Section 15.3.

For a systematic description of a sound system it is useful to distinguish the basic properties of speech sounds. The pronunciation error in (1) has to do with vowel height. The basic feature 'height' is an example of a feature that may help us to group speech sounds together into categories. In Section 15.4 we will further discuss these and other basic features. Then in Section 15.5 we will demonstrate how such features can be used to formulate regularities that can account for the varying pronunciation of words.

15.2 Distinctiveness

An essential notion in phonology is that of **distinctiveness**, that is, the property that makes it possible to distinguish between words. Distinctiveness here means specifically the ability of sounds to distinguish words with different meanings. Meaning, in particular the transmission of meaningful messages, is after all the key reason why people use language, and when they use a spoken language, they use sounds to get their message across.

In English the *b* differs from the *m*, since by means of these two different sounds we can distinguish the different words *bark* and *mark* and *bad* and *mad*. This may seem self-evident, perhaps even trivial. Don't all languages have the sounds *b* and *m*, and are these not used everywhere to mark the difference between words? It is true that this is the case in many of the world's languages, for example in French, Turkish, and Arabic, to name but a few. In all these languages the *b* and the *m* are used, just as in English, to distinguish words from each other. But there are actually quite a few languages that do not have this difference. Tahitian and North-American Yuma, for example, do not have a /b/, and North-American Tlingit and Arapaho do not have an /m/.

In English [b] and [m] are different, or rather distinctive, speech sounds, since, as we have said, the two can be used to differentiate words in English. This can be shown by identifying pairs of words that are different in one respect only, that is, one member has a [b] where the other has an [m]. For this reason such word pairs are known as **minimal pairs**. Some examples from English are in (3).

(3) **m**all **b**all
merry **b**erry
mo**b** mo**m**
gra**b** gra**m**

The technical term for a meaning-distinguishing speech sound is **phoneme**. The phonemes of a language are graphically represented between slashes to distinguish them from speech sounds as studied from the phonetic perspective, which are represented between square brackets. We can thus say that /b/ and /m/ are phonemes of English. But this does not mean that English must always have a word with /m/ whenever it has a word with /b/, as we can see from (4).

(4) /bɒnət/ 'bonnet' /*mɒnət/ 'monnet'

Now there is nothing wrong with the sound structure of the asterisked word /*mɒnət/; it just happens not to exist in English. It could though, in principle, be a word of English. This is not the case for the example in (5).

(5) /brʊk/ 'brook' /*mrʊk/ 'mrook'

The word /*mruk/ does not exist in English, and it could not exist since words are not allowed to begin with the consonant combination /mr/ in English. In other words, in English, /b/ can be combined with a different range of other phonemes than /m/. This is not a rule that holds true for all the world's languages. The combination /mr/ at the beginning of a word does occur in Scottish Gaelic, for example, as in *mnatha* /mraha/ 'woman.*genitive.singular*'. Such differences between languages in terms of the combinatorial possibilities of phonemes will be further discussed in Chapter 16.

Not all languages have the same sort of distinctions as English. In Section 15.1 we saw that Spanish does not distinguish between, for example, /i/ and /ɪ/. Thus, where English has two different phonemes, as in the minimal pair *leave* and *live*, Spanish has a single phoneme. This may be pronounced in different ways, but the key point is that these different realisations do not signal a difference in meaning in Spanish, as we see in (6).

(6)

Spelling	*Meaning*	*Phoneme*	*Pronunciation*
rincón	'corner'	/i/	[ɪ]
dinero	'money'	/i/	[i]

In (6) the Spanish vowel *i* is given with both a phonological (between slashes) and a phonetic (between square brackets) transcription. The phonetic transcription is much closer to the actual pronunciation, and contains different realisations of the same phoneme. These variants are known as **allophones**. The Spanish allophones [i] and [ɪ] are two possible realisations of the single phoneme /i/.

In English we do not have two allophones but two different phonemes /i/ and /ɪ/, given the existence of minimal pairs like *leave* and *live*. These two

English words differ in meaning, and the meaning difference is signalled by the difference in sound. In contrast, Spanish may have two sounds that resemble the English phonemes, but there are no minimal pairs of words that are differentiated by this sound difference alone. These sounds lack distinctiveness in Spanish, and are therefore not phonemes, but allophones of one single phoneme.

English also fails to make distinctions that are important in other languages. Aspirated and non-aspirated sounds such as [kʰ] and [k] can never be used to create meaning oppositions in English, although both are produced in English words as in [kʰɪn] *kin* and [skɪn] *skin*. These sounds lack distinctiveness in English. In a language like Hindi, on the other hand, they can be used to distinguish between words such as /kaːn/ *ear* and /kʰaːn/ *mine*. In Hindi we thus have two phonemes /kʰ/ and /k/, while in English we have one phoneme /k/ with the two allophones [kʰ] and [k].

Which allophone of a particular phoneme is chosen has to do with the environment in which the phoneme occurs. For instance, English voiceless plosive consonants are aspirated at the beginning of a word or of a stressed syllable; in other circumstances aspiration does not occur. Similarly, the Spanish vowel /i/ illustrated in (6) is realised as an [i] in an open syllable, that is, when it is not followed by a consonant within the same syllable. Alternatively it is realised as an [ɪ] in a closed syllable, i.e. when it is followed by a consonant within the same syllable.

After children have learned to babble (Section 3.3), they start to produce words and are busy learning the properties of their language, including the distinctiveness of sounds. In the early stages they may fail to distinguish phonemes that are important in the adult system. Kate, at one and a half years, does not yet distinguish /t/ from /k/ nor /d/ from /g/, as we see in (7).

Kate (1;6)

(7) [ta] or [ka] for 'car' [to] for 'toe'
[do] or [go] for 'go' [dada] for 'daddy'
[bæk] for 'back' [tɪk] for 'stick'

Kate does not distinguish the dental plosives from the velar plosives. She produces some velar plosives but often replaces these with dental plosives even in the same word. The acquisition of the distinctive sounds or phonemes for the first language is more or less complete, though, by age four. Second language learners, as we saw at the beginning of this chapter with the Spanish example, can have far more difficulty in learning distinctive sounds that are not distinctive in their first language. In Chinese the English phonemes /l/ and /r/ are not distinguished and hence the common pronunciation by Chinese speakers of *flied lice* for 'fried rice'. It can take second language learners a considerable amount of time to acquire some distinctive sounds; their pronunciation may even become fossilised (Section 3.5).

15.3 Sound Systems

The set of all phonemes of a language constitutes its **sound system**. The large majority of languages in the world have a sound system with between 20 and 40 phonemes. English is an average language in this respect, having 36. In Figure 15.1 we give the consonant and vowel inventory of the variety of Standard British English. Note that this and following figures concerning sound systems make use of the IPA chart we presented in Chapter 14. The possible sounds according to this chart are printed in grey, while the sounds with phonemic status in the language concerned are printed in black. The smallest number of phonemes found in any language to date is 11. Such a sound system has been attested in the Rotokas language, spoken on the island of Bougainville in Papua New Guinea. The sound system of this language is given in Figure 15.2.

In addition to the number of sounds in a language, what also matters is the nature of these sound distinctions. The first thing to note here is that all languages have plosives and vowels. The other manners of articulation are not used in every language in the world. The second common point is that languages never have more vowels than consonants. The Rotokas language illustrates both these points, since it has a rather simple sound system, with six plosives and five vowels. The phonemes /b/, /d/ and /g/ in this language have various allophones. The plosive [b] and the nasal [m] are allophones of the same phoneme /b/, but this phoneme also has allophones in which the mouth is not completely closed, such as fricatives and liquids. Similarly [d] and [n] are allophones of the phoneme /d/, and [g] and [ŋ] of the phoneme /g/, and these have further allophones as well. Because the language has so few phonemes, there is ample space for allophonic variation.

Another rather extreme language is Danish. This language has almost as many vowels as it has consonants, as shown in Figure 15.3 as well as 18 consonants there are 16 vowels. This language also further illustrates what we have referred to as secondary articulations in Section 14.5. Various cells in the vowel table in Figure 15.3 contain two elements. These are distinguished from one another by length, a secondary articulation that languages use to create sound oppositions. A vowel followed by the symbol 'ː' is the long variant of that vowel.

A special kind of phoneme can be found in so-called tone languages. In this type of language the tone with which a sound is pronounced has a meaning-distinguishing function, and is therefore phonologically relevant. A good example of a tone language is Mandarin Chinese, as we briefly mentioned in Section 1.2.

Consonants, pulmonic (voiceless left, voiced right)

	Bilabial		Labio-dental		Dental		Alveolar		Post-alveolar		Palatal		Velar		Uvular		Pharyn-geal		Glottal	
Plosive	**p**	**b**					**t**	**d**			c	ɟ	**k**	**g**	q	ɢ			ʔ	
Fricative	ɸ	β	**f**	**v**	**θ**	**ð**	**s**	**z**	**ʃ**	**ʒ**	ç	ʝ	x	ɣ	χ	ʁ	ħ	ʕ	**h**	ɦ
Affricate			p͡f	b͡v			t͡s	d͡z	**t͡ʃ**	**d͡ʒ**	c͡ç	ɟ͡ʝ	k͡x		q͡χ					
Nasal		**m**		ɱ				**n**				ɲ		**ŋ**		ɴ				
Lateral								**l**				ʎ		ʟ						
Trill		ʙ						**r**								ʀ				
Tap or Flap								ɾ												
Approximant		**w**		ʋ				ɹ				**j**		ɰ						

Vowels (unrounded left, rounded right)

	Front		Central		Back	
Close	**i**	y	ɨ	ʉ	ɯ	**u**
	ɪ	ʏ				**ʊ**
Close-mid	e	ø	ɘ	ɵ	ɤ	o
			ə			
Open-mid	**ɛ**	œ	**ɜ**	ɞ	**ʌ**	**ɔ**
	æ		ɐ			
Open			a	ɶ	**ɑ**	**ɒ**

Consonants, non-pulmonic

Clicks		Voiced implosives		Ejectives	
ʘ	Bilabial	ɓ	Bilabial	p’	Bilabial
ǀ	Dental	ɗ	Dental/alveolar	t’	Dental/alveolar
ǃ	Alveolar	ʄ	Palatal	s’	Alveolar fricative
ǂ	Palatal	ɠ	Velar	k’	Velar
ǁ	Lateral	ʛ	Uvular	q’	Uvular

Figure 15.1 The sound system of Standard British English. The characters printed in black are the phonemes of this language.

Consonants, pulmonic (voiceless left, voiced right)

	Bilabial		Labio-dental		Dental		Alveolar		Post-alveolar		Palatal		Velar		Uvular		Pharyn-geal		Glottal	
Plosive	**p**	**b**					**t**	**d**			c	ɟ	**k**	**g**	q	ɢ			ʔ	
Fricative	ɸ	β	f	v	θ	ð	s	z	ʃ	ʒ	ç	ʝ	x	ɣ	χ	ʁ	ħ	ʕ	h	ɦ
Affricate			p͡f	b͡v			t͡s	d͡z	t͡ʃ	d͡ʒ	c͡ç	ɟ͡ʝ	k͡x		q͡χ					
Nasal		m		ɱ				n				ɲ		ŋ		ɴ				
Lateral								l				ʎ		ʟ						
Trill		ʙ						r								ʀ				
Tap or Flap								ɾ												
Approximant		w		ʋ				ɹ				j		ɰ						

Vowels (unrounded left, rounded right)

	Front		Central		Back	
Close	**i**	y	ɨ	ʉ	ɯ	**u**
	ɪ	ʏ				ʊ
Close-mid	**e**	ø	ɘ	ɵ	ɤ	**o**
			ə			
Open-mid	ɛ	œ	ɜ	ɞ	ʌ	ɔ
	æ		ɐ			
Open			**a**	ɶ	ɑ	ɒ

Consonants, non-pulmonic

Clicks		Voiced implosives		Ejectives	
ʘ	Bilabial	ɓ	Bilabial	p'	Bilabial
ǀ	Dental	ɗ	Dental/alveolar	t'	Dental/alveolar
!	Alveolar	ʄ	Palatal	s'	Alveolar fricative
ǂ	Palatal	ɠ	Velar	k'	Velar
ǁ	Lateral	ʛ	Uvular	q'	Uvular

Figure 15.2 The sound system of Rotokas. The characters printed in black are the phonemes of this language.

Consonants, pulmonic (voiceless left, voiced right)

	Bilabial		Labio-dental		Dental		Alveolar		Post-alveolar		Palatal		Velar		Uvular		Pharyn-geal		Glottal	
Plosive	**p**	**b**					**t**	**d**			c	ɟ	**k**	**g**	q	ɢ			ʔ	
Fricative	ɸ	β	**f**	**v**	θ	**ð**	**s**	z	**ʃ**	ʒ	ç	ʝ	x	ɣ	χ	ʁ	ħ	ʕ	**h**	ɦ
Affricate			p͡f	b͡v			t͡s	d͡z	t͡ʃ	d͡ʒ	c͡ç	ɟ͡ʝ	k͡x		q͡χ					
Nasal		**m**		ɱ				**n**				ɲ		**ŋ**		ɴ				
Lateral								**l**				ʎ		ʟ						
Trill		ʙ						**r**								ʀ				
Tap or Flap								ɾ												
Approximant		w		ʋ				ɹ				**j**		ɰ						

Vowels (unrounded left, rounded right)

	Front		Central		Back	
Close	**i**	**y**	ɨ	ʉ	ɯ	**u**
	ɪ	ʏ				ʊ
Close-mid	**e**	**ø**	ɘ	ɵ	ɤ	**o**
			ə			
Open-mid	**ɛ**	**œ**	ɜ	ɞ	ʌ	**ɔ ɔː**
	æ		**ɐ**			
Open			**a aː**	ɶ	**ɑ**	**ɒ**

Consonants, non-pulmonic

Clicks		Voiced implosives		Ejectives	
ʘ	Bilabial	ɓ	Bilabial	p’	Bilabial
ǀ	Dental	ɗ	Dental/ alveolar	t’	Dental/ alveolar
ǃ	Alveolar	ʄ	Palatal	s’	Alveolar fricative
ǂ	Palatal	ɠ	Velar	k’	Velar
ǁ	Lateral	ʛ	Uvular	q’	Uvular

Figure 15.3 The sound system of Danish. The characters printed in black are the phonemes of this language.

Mandarin Chinese

(8) bāo - flat tone
'to pack'
báo - rising tone
'thin'
bào - falling tone
'newspaper'
bǎo - falling-rising tone
'full'

As we see from (8), the different tones serve to distinguish words in Chinese. We know, therefore, that they are phonemically relevant. Such tone distinctions are also known as 'tonemes'.

Speakers of languages that do not distinguish tones often think that tonal languages are particularly difficult to learn. They are difficult for such speakers as a second language, but children learn them really quickly.

15.4 DISTINCTIVE FEATURES

A characteristic feature of English is that the plural suffix /z/ becomes /s/ when it follows a certain group of voiceless consonants. Thus we see the pattern in (9).

(9) a. knives [naɪvz]
b. beans [biːnz]
c. taboos [təbuːz]
d. rats [ræts]
e. pdfs [pidiɛfs]
f. decks [dɛks]

The consonants /v/ and /n/ in (9a and b) and the vowel /u/ in (9c) trigger the phonetic realisation [z] in the plural suffix; the consonants /s/, /f/ and /k/ in (9d to f) require the phonetic realisation [s] of the plural suffix. The differences in (9) are not a random collection: they are systematically related by a general rule. We will refine this rule below, but for now we may simplify a little bit by saying that, if the suffix follows a voiced sound, it takes the voiced form [z], but if it follows a voiceless sound, it takes the voiceless form [s]. So when describing this phenomenon in English, it is not necessary to discuss each of these differences individually. We can give a systematic description by using the feature voice.

Thus, the sound systems of languages are not unordered collections of phonemes. On the contrary, they can be subdivided in various smaller constituent sets and each set can be defined in terms of a small number of phonetic features. Voice is one example of such a feature, nasality is another. If you try pronouncing the phonemes /b/ and /m/ straight after one another, then you see that there is a clear resemblance between the two: both are bilabial and voiced. Where they differ is in their nasality: /b/ is not nasal, whereas /m/ is. Phonemes are thus built up from a limited number of phonetic features, also known as **distinctive features**. The phonemes /b/ and /m/ are different in terms of the distinctive feature [nasal]; /d/ and /t/ differ in the distinctive feature [voice].

It is not only the /b/ and the /m/ that can be distinguished in terms of the distinctive feature [nasal], but also /d/ versus /n/, and /g/ versus /ŋ/. These various pairs of speech sounds all differ in terms of nasality. In this sense, the difference between /b/ and /m/ is identical to that between /d/ and /n/, and /g/ and /ŋ/. This is represented in (10), where we also see that the three voiced plosives /b/, /d/ and /g/ have the same place of articulation as the three (voiced) nasals /m/, /n/, /ŋ/: /b/ and /m/ are both bilabial; /d/ and /n/ are both alveolar; and /g/ and /ŋ/ are both velar:

(10)

Bilabial	*Alveolar*	*Velar*
/b/	/d/	/g/
/m/	/n/	/ŋ/

The distinctive feature [nasality] refers to the manner of articulation of speech sounds. It is a rather specific feature. There are also a number of more comprehensive features which can help to characterise manners of articulation. For example, all speech sounds, except vowels and approximants, share the feature [consonant], which means they are produced with closure of the oral cavity. Similarly, all speech sounds, except plosives, fricatives, and affricates have the feature [sonorant]. They are similar in that they are produced without turbulence in the vocal tract. Sonorant consonants are thus nasals, laterals, and approximants.

Coming back to the formation of English plurals illustrated in (9), we note that apart from with [s] and [z] the plural can also be formed with [ɪz], as in *crutch-crutches*, *kiss-kisses*, and *ridg(e)-ridges*. It turns out that we can generalise across these cases using two features; [coronal] and [strident]. Coronal sounds are those that are produced with the tip or the blade of the tongue, strident sounds are those that are produced with rather strong friction. Nouns that end in a phoneme that combines exactly these features such as /s/ require the ending [ɪz] to form a plural.

For vowels we also need distinctive features. As we have seen, there are a number of features that refer to the place in the mouth where the vowel sound is produced in terms of the relative position of the tongue in the oral cavity. The features reflect the extreme positions on the horizontal and vertical axes in the mouth, as in (11).

(11) [high] the tongue is high in the mouth
[low] the tongue is low in the mouth
[front] the tongue is at the front of the mouth
[back] the tongue is at the back of the mouth

With these four features we can analyse the five-vowel system of Spanish as in (12).

(12)
```
              high
       i              u
front    e          o    back
              a
             low
```

This five-vowel system in fact occurs quite frequently in the languages of the world. The full specification for each of these five vowels individually is set out in (13).

(13) *The full specification of the vowels of Spanish*
/i/ [+high, -low, +front, -back]
/e/ [-high, -low, +front, -back]
/a/ [-high, +low, -front, -back]
/o/ [-high, -low, -front, +back]
/u/ [+high, -low, -front, +back]

With these vowel specifications we can now demonstrate another property of distinctive features in phonology. As we can see in (12), there is a degree of redundancy in the Spanish vowel specifications. For the vowel /a/, for example, the features [front] and [back] are not relevant, since there is no contrast between low front vowels and low back vowels in Spanish. Similarly, for vowels that are [+high], it follows automatically that they are [-low]; if they are [+front] they are [-back], and vice versa. Eliminating this redundancy, it is sufficient to have the specifications in (14) to describe the Spanish vowel system.

(14) *The vowels of Spanish without redundancy*
/i/ [+high, -back]
/e/ [-high, -low, -back]
/a/ [-high, +low]
/o/ [-high, -low, +back]
/u/ [+high, +back]

In phonology, specifications like (14) are more common than those given in (13), because in phonology we need to specify fewer details than in phonetics. Many phonetic details are superfluous or even irrelevant when we aim to characterise phonemic differences within a sound system. For this reason, not all phonetic categories correspond to phonological distinctive features.

15.5 Morphophonological Processes

Distinctive features are useful tools for the description of processes that occur when we chain morphemes together. Consider the examples from Dutch in (15).

Dutch

(15) (a) voet-zoek-er: /vut/ + /zukər/ → [vut**s**ukər]
foot-search-er
'a fire cracker'

(b) plat-voet-en: /plɑt/ + /vutən/ → [plɑt**f**utə]
flat-foot-*plural*
'flat feet'

(c) op-zadel-en /ɔp/ + /zadələn/ → [ɔp**s**a:dələ]
up-saddle-*infinitive*
'to saddle'

What happens here is that, in compounds, the last phoneme of one morpheme influences the form of the first phoneme of the next morpheme, such that these phonemes become more alike. In this case, the result of the process is that the two phonemes have the same value for the feature [voice] that we saw in Section 15.4. Thus, as marked in bold face in (15), the /z/ becomes a voiceless [s] and the /v/ a voiceless [f]. This process in which phonemes are adapted to become more similar to one another is known as **assimilation**.

The processes of sound adaptation that occur when morphemes are linked together are the subject of **morphophonology**. Morphophonological phenomena are often described in terms of formal rules and processes, on the model of a general rule pattern (16).

(16) Sound A becomes sound B in the context of sound C.

The examples of assimilation given in (15) can be described as in (17).

(17) /z/ becomes [s] in the context of a preceding /t/
/v/ becomes [f] in the context of a preceding /t/
/z/ becomes [s] in the context of a preceding /p/

This can be further applied to other pairs. But now we are missing an important generalisation. On closer inspection, it turns out that the rule of devoicing happens to apply to all cases in which a voiced fricative follows a voiceless plosive or fricative in compound words. Using the rule pattern of (16) we can now write this up in general terms as in (18).

(18) [+voice] fricative becomes [-voice] fricative in the context of a preceding [-voice] plosive/fricative

If we now go on to describe the process in a rule that uses only those distinctive features that are relevant, we can arrive at the essence of the process (19).

(19) [+fricative] → [-voice] / [-son] ___________
[+ voice] [-voice]

The first part in (19), left of the arrow, describes the phoneme that needs to be adapted to the context. This phoneme is characterised as a voiced [+voice] fricative [+fricative]. The arrow means 'acquires the value of'. To the right of the arrow we first see the distinctive feature of the phoneme specified to the left of the arrow that needs to be adapted. In this case it is the feature [+voice] that has to be changed into [-voice]. The next element in the formula, the slash (/), means 'in the context of'. This context is then specified by the underlining which indicates the position of the sound that needs to change relative to the other sounds that are involved in the process. Here the underlining is to the right of the phoneme specification [-son][-voice], that is, the non-sonorant, voiceless speech sounds. In Section 15.4 we mentioned that non-sonorant sounds are those that are produced with turbulence in the vocal tract. This holds for plosives and fricatives, and that is precisely the category of sounds we want to specify here.

The analysis and discussion above introduced the notion of 'phonological rule'. Before we continue, let us step back and have one more look at what these rules actually do. Rule (19) literally has the function to make a voiced fricative voiceless under certain conditions. But although this is its literal function, it is not the case that the rule works on sounds in isolation. It applies rather to morphemes. This means that a particular morpheme can have more than one form, depending on the context in which it appears. When this happens, each of these forms is known as an **allomorph**. Just as we made a distinction, earlier on, between a phoneme and an allophone, we are now looking at the difference between a morpheme and an allomorph. In both cases, the allophones and the allomorphs correspond to the actual forms we hear, whereas the phonemes and the morphemes are the abstract, meaningful units from which the actual forms are derived. This can be illustrated with the examples given in (15), where the morphemes we discussed all had two different realisations (20).

Dutch
(20) zoek /zuk/ → [zuk], [suk]
voet /vut/ → [vut], [fut]
zadel /zadəl/ → [za:dəl], [sa:dəl]

Between slashes the underlying phonological representation of the morphemes concerned is given, before rule (19) is applied to them. Then, between brackets, we have the two different audible forms, or allomorphs, that may result from that rule.

It is not always possible to reduce all different appearances of a morpheme to one single, unique base form, but we do work on the assumption that this is usually the case. Some morphemes just happen to be irregular, and in that case we have no option but to posit two different base forms. A simple English example is the verb *have*. Here we have to assume two present tense morphemes, *have* /hæv/ and *has* /hæz/, respectively, plus an irregular past tense form *had* /hæd/. This phenomenon is known as suppletion, and was discussed in Section 12.6.

In this chapter we discussed how individual phonemes are distinctive, and how they combine. The morphemes produced in this way are not pronounced as unstructured series of phonemes. On the contrary, such a phoneme series constitutes a highly hierarchical structure, as we shall see in Chapter 16.

15.6 Graphemes and Phonemes

Many spoken languages do not have a written form. Even when they do, it remains a problem as to how to represent speech in graphic form. A common **writing system** is one in which the key principle is that each individual speech sound is represented by a separate letter symbol. This type of system is called **alphabetic**. In this type of writing you would in principle need just as many letter symbols as there are phonemes in the language. The main advantage of this system is that any word can, in theory at least, be written down quite easily, even if you have never seen or read it before. This would be the case if everyone used the International Phonetic Alphabet. But in many alphabetic writing systems the central principle of one sound-one symbol has been compromised. English is notorious in this respect. As George Bernard Shaw is supposed to have pointed out, a written form in English like *ghoti* could in fact be pronounced as *fish (gh* as in *enough*, *o* as in *women*, *ti* as in *nation*). A single English speech sound can be represented by a range of different symbols or symbol combinations, as in the case of the long /i/ of *team*, *tangerine*, *steep* and *theme*. Conversely, letters may represent different speech sounds: the letter *o* can be pronounced as [ɑː] as in *body*; [ɪ] as in *women*; or [ɒ] as in *hot*. These many possibilities lead to unusual pronunciations of foreign words. The name Van Gogh, for example, that should have the [x] sound of Scottish *loch* is pronounced by English speakers in various ways: as if rhyming with *toff*, or with *blow*, or with *bog*. Since English today continues to be written as it was in the time of Shakespeare, the gap between spoken and written language is now at times so extreme that the basic principle of alphabetic writing breaks down. You simply have to learn to write each individual word as it comes, in its own unique and arbitrary way. These difficulties have led to suggestions for spelling reform in English to bring it closer to the basic alphabetic principle of 'one sound-one symbol'. Such spelling reforms have been proposed for many languages using an alphabetic system, and some have been implemented, for example in Germany in the 1990s and in The Netherlands in the 1950s, but with varying success rates. In the English-speaking world, the issue is continually debated but as yet no concrete steps have been taken.

Summary

Phonology is the study of speech sounds as relevant units within a language system. Sounds are relevant when they serve to distinguish meanings, that is, have **distinctiveness**. Sounds that distinguish meanings are known as **phonemes**. The test to decide whether a particular speech sound is a phoneme is to take a **minimal pair**, that is, two words of the same language which only differ in one speech sound. If the two words are different in meaning, the two sounds are phonemes. If not, we have two **allophones**, that is, sounds that are different but do not distinguish meanings. The set of phonemes of a language constitutes its **sound system**.

Phonemes are built from smaller elements: the **distinctive features**, which broadly correspond to the phonetic properties of speech sounds. Distinctive features play an important role in the description of the sound adaptations that occur when morphemes are being chained together. This subfield of phonology is known as **morphophonology**. An example of a morphophonological process is **assimilation**, where two adjacent sounds come to resemble each other in respect of one of their distinctive features. In describing such processes, the assumption is that there is an underlying morpheme that can be expressed or realised in different phonetic forms. Such alternative forms of one single morpheme are known as **allomorphs**.

Many **writing systems**, called **alphabetic**, are based on the principle that each individual speech sound is represented by a separate letter symbol. This ideal situation hardly ever lasts, for instance when pronunciation changes with time.

Assignments

1. If a language does not have a /b/-phoneme, what could happen to loan words from English that contain a /b/-phoneme such as *boat*?
2. In Yoruba we find the word pair [dá] 'to be rare' and [dã́] 'to polish'. You can ignore the symbol ´ that indicates tone. Are [a] and [ã] phonemes in Yoruba?'

3. In English the sound æ is pronounced as [æ] in *bad* but as [æ̃] in *man*. The symbol '~' indicates nasalisation. Are the sounds [æ] and [æ̃] phonemes in English?
4. Compare the sound system of Standard English (Fig. 15.1) with that of another language you know well. Where are the differences in the phoneme inventory of the two languages? Are there also differences in the allophones where the two languages have the same phoneme?
5. Which distinctive features do you need to distinguish the following phonemes: /b/, /d/, /n/, /z/ and /m/?
6. The negative prefix in Latin-based adjectives has different forms in English. They are written as *im-* as in *impossible* and *immovable* or as *in-* as in *intolerable* and *incontinent*. Firstly transcribe these forms as they occur in the words above. Secondly specify the phonological context for each of these forms. Do the same for *un-* in *uncool* and *unwitting* versus *unbecoming* and *unpatriotic*. What is the phonological rule here?
7. Examine the following set of data in Finnish.

[kuːzil] 'six'	[liːsɑ] 'Lisa'
[kɑːdot] 'failures'	[mɑːdon] 'of a worm'
[kɑːte] 'cover'	[mɑːton] 'of a rug'
[kɑːtot] 'roof'	[rɑːtɑːs] 'wheel'
[kɑːde] 'envious'	[liːzɑ] 'Lisa'
[kuːsi] 'six'	[rɑːdɑn] 'of a track'

   On the basis of this data set are the [s] and [z] phonemes? And the [d] and [t]?
8. Tim (1;9) produces the following forms for adult words:

[siːp] 'sleep'	[tæm] 'stamp'
[puːn] 'spoon'	[soː] 'slow'
[tɒp] 'stop'	[wɪŋ] 'swing'

   Can you formulate the phonological rule that applies to his production at this age?

TEST YOURSELF

1. What is a phoneme, what is an allophone?
2. Give an example of a minimal pair.
3. Do all phonemes occur with equal frequency?
4. What is the maximum size of a system of speech sounds?
5. Give three examples of distinctive features.

6. Which processes are being studied in morphophonology?
7. What is assimilation?
8. What is the difference between an allophone and an allomorph?

ACKNOWLEDGMENTS AND FURTHER READING

Accessible introductions to the field of phonology are Spencer (1996) and Smith (in preparation). The chart showing the sound system of British English is based on Ladefoged (2001), the one for Danish is based on Basbøll (2005). Some further examples of sound systems given here were taken from SPIN (Smith's Phoneme Inventories), made accessible through the Typological Database System (http://languagelink.let.uu.nl/tds/index.html).

chapter 16

Syllables, Stress and Intonation

16.1 Introduction

In Chapter 15 we discussed two phonological aspects that learners of English as a second language will have to master. They have to acquire the phonemes of English and their distinctive features, and they have to learn when to use the various allophones when stringing their sounds together. Let us imagine that the Spanish learners of English we mentioned at the beginning of the previous chapter have mastered these two aspects of English phonology. Nevertheless they may produce sentence (1) as (2) instead of the correct form in (3). The symbol ' indicates that stress is on the syllable following it. The line above the sentence roughly indicates the intonation contour.

(1) Could you put the rubbish bin on the street?

(2) Could you put the rub'bish bin on the estreet?

(3) Could you put the 'rubbish bin on the street?

The pronunciation in (2) is correct in many respects, but it does not sound like the version a native speaker of English would produce. It contains in fact

Linguistics, First Edition. Edited by Anne E. Baker and Kees Hengeveld.

three errors, which have to do with the way in which strings of phonemes are organised into larger units: syllables, words and sentences.

The first error in (2) is that *street* is pronounced as *estreet*. The Spanish learner has turned a word consisting of one syllable into a word containing two and in this way has broken up the consonant cluster *str*. This change in the syllable structure of the word is the result of the fact that the combination *str* is not allowed in syllable initial position in Spanish. The ways in which syllables can be built up from strings of phonemes are studied in the sub-discipline of **phonotactics** (Section 16.2).

The second error in (2) occurs at the word level. Words have a main stress that has to fall on one particular syllable. In Spanish this often falls on the ultimate or penultimate syllable, whereas English words often have initial stress. The notion of stress will be discussed in Section 16.3.

The last error in (2) has nothing to do with the Spanish mother tongue of the speaker involved. The error is that the sentence is pronounced with the intonation pattern of a statement where a question was intended. This error has to do with the phonological organisation of the sentence as a whole. This topic will be further discussed in Section 16.4.

In the final section of this chapter we will briefly discuss the notion of rhythm.

16.2 The Syllable: Phonotactics

Words can be subdivided into syllables. A **syllable** is a small group of phonemes that normally contains one vowel. For speakers of most languages, once they know how the vowels are distributed, they can tell the number of syllables a word has. The process of grouping phonemes into syllables is known as syllabification.

It is important to note straight away that the principles of syllabification have no direct relation with the orthographic rules for dividing a word at the end of a line, which you find in many dictionaries, style books and hyphenation modules of word processors. Take, for example, the English word *shoving*. Orthographically this word is divided as *shov-ing*, but phonologically this word is divided into the syllables /ʃʌ-vɪŋ/. If you try to say this word loudly and make it last as long as possible, the natural break between the syllables becomes clear.

(5) /ʃʌ..............................- vɪŋ................................/ !!!

Another important distinction is that the syllable structure of a word is clearly different from its morphological structure. Take again the word *shoving*. This consists of two morphemes, the lexical stem /ʃʌv-/ and the suffix /-ɪŋ/, but its syllabification in phonology is /ʃʌ-vɪŋ/. Phonology (syllable structure) and morphology (morphemes) may thus lead to different ways of dividing the word into its component parts. Some further examples of this are given in (6).

(6)	*readable*	*kings*	*important*
Phonology:	/riː-də-bəl/	/kɪŋz/	/ɪm-pɔː-tənt/
Morphology:	/riːd-əbəl/	/kɪŋ-z/	/ɪmpɔːtənt/

Orthographic rules are language specific. The rules for hyphenating words in English spelling follow for the most part the morphological structure (and the etymology) of the word. In some other languages the orthographic rules follow the phonology quite closely, but in others they may follow neither or even both. From here on, we will only be concerned with phonological syllabification.

There are many language games in which syllables play an important role. For instance, in French *Verlan* speech syllables are shifted around, such that for instance *tomber* 'to fall', pronounced *tõ-bé*, becomes *bé-tõ*; in English *Pig Latin* speech the consonants at the beginning of a word are placed at the end of that word, followed by *-ay*, such that *ba-na-na* becomes *a-na-na-bay*.

The way in which syllables can be built from strings of phonemes varies a great deal between languages. For our description and discussion of phonotactic rules it is necessary to take a closer look at the syllable as a unit. How is it structured? Does a syllable in languages in general have a simple, flat, linear structure, or is its structure hierarchical? Which of the three diagrams in (7) gives the best representation of the monosyllabic word *man*? In these and following representations the symbol σ is used for syllables.

(7)
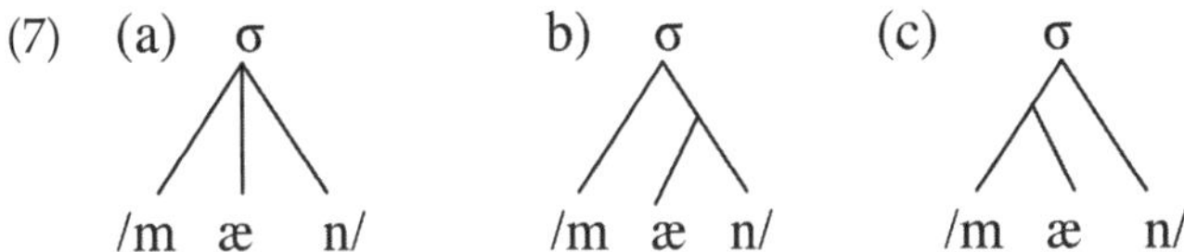

The diagram in (7a) represents the view that the three phonemes /m, æ, n/ belong to the same syllable, and that that is all there is to it. In (7b) the syllable consists of two parts, a beginning /m/, and the rest, which consists of /æ/ and /n/. In (7c), in contrast, the /m/ and /æ/ are grouped together, and stand apart from /n/.

The correct one is the diagram in (7b).The relationship between the vowel and the final consonant seems to be closer than between the initial consonant and the vowel. We see this in the fact that in many languages there are clear restrictions on the combination of a vowel and what can follow it, but not on the combination of a vowel and what can precede it. For instance, in English the nasal consonant /ŋ/ can be preceded by some vowels, such as /æ/ in *bang* and /ɪ/ in *sing*, but not by other vowels: there are no words with a syllable ending in /iŋ/ (orthographic *eang*) or in /uŋ/ (orthographic *oong*). We do not find similar restrictions for the combination of initial consonants and vowels. One way to account for this difference in the structure of the syllable is to treat the vowel and what follows it as a separate element of the syllable as in diagram (7b). Within each of the elements or constituents of the syllable we can then describe the relevant restrictions on the combination of phonemes. In this analysis, the initial consonant does not have a direct relation with the vowel, but with the vowel and what follows it.

This is sufficient reason to prefer the syllable model represented in (7b). To make further discussion easier it is useful here to introduce a number of technical terms. The beginning of the syllable is known as the **onset**. The onset contains all sounds that precede the vowel in the syllable. The rest of the syllable, that is the vowel and everything that follows, is known as the **rhyme**. The examples in (8) illustrate this.

(8)

Syllable	*Onset*	*Rhyme*
tip	/t/	/ɪp/
trip	/tr/	/ɪp/
strip	/str/	/ɪp/
string	/str/	/ɪŋ/

The term 'rhyme' reflects the fact that the last part of the syllable provides the end rhyme as in *t-ip, tr-ip, str-ip* (8), or *d-own, g-own, fr-own, cl-own*.

The rhyme itself contains two parts, as we can see in (7b), here repeated as (9).

(9)

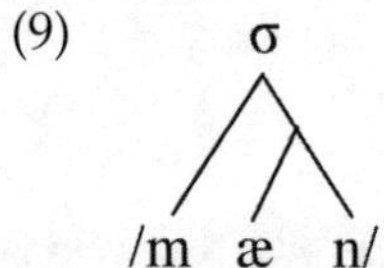

The two parts of the rhyme are known as **nucleus** and **coda** respectively. The overall structure of the syllable can be represented as in (10).

(10)

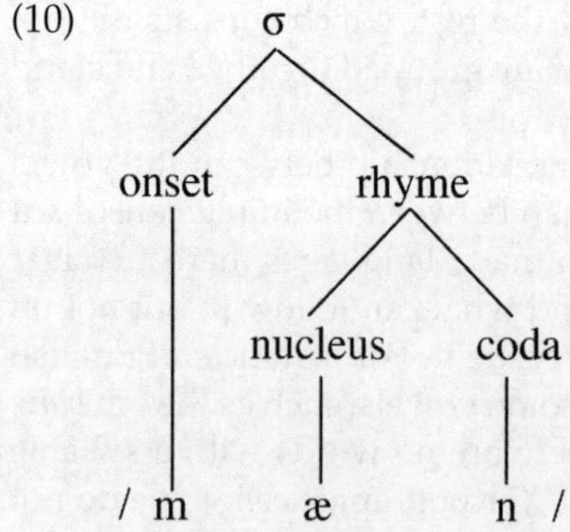

The nucleus is obligatory and in most languages contains a vowel. A syllable can consist of a nucleus only, for instance in English the letter *i* corresponds to a syllable in words like *I*, *ideal*, and *Ivanhoe*. If present, onset and coda consist of consonants. The syllables in (8) can thus be further subdivided as in (11).

(11)

Syllable	*Onset*	*Nucleus*	*Coda*
tip	/t/	/ɪ/	/p/
trip	/tr/	/ɪ/	/p/
strip	/str/	/ɪ/	/p/
string	/str/	/ɪ/	/ŋ/

Some further examples of subdivisions of syllables are given in (12).

(12)

Syllable	*Onset*	*Nucleus*	*Coda*
see	/s/	/iː/	-
ask	-	/a/	/sk/
soon	/s/	/u/	/n/
egg	-	/ɛ/	/g/
you	/j/	/u/	-
strengths	/str/	/ɛ/	/ŋθs/

After this brief detour into the structure of the syllable, we now return to phonotactics, that is, to the rules that govern the construction of syllables in different languages. The examples we will use below follow the order in which a syllable is put together: first the onset, then the nucleus, finally the coda.

There is great variation between languages in the possibilities they have for filling in the onset. A language that allows very complex consonant clusters in the onset is, for example, Russian. It has syllables with onsets consisting of four consonants, as in the first syllable of *vstréča* 'meeting'. Other languages allow only one consonant in onset position, for example Bahasa Indonesia. Dutch loan words in Indonesian are adapted to this requirement. So Dutch *griffier* 'clerk of the court' becomes *gə-ri-pir.* The consonant cluster /xr/ has been broken up by schwa (ə) insertion. Similarly *station* 'station' becomes *setasiun* and *strijken* 'to iron' becomes *seterika*. In the latter example all three onset consonants *str* of the Dutch word *strijken* have become the single onset consonants of the separate syllables *se*, *te* and *re* of the Bahasa Indonesian word *seterika* (see Section 20.6 for more on loan words).

The nucleus, as have said, is the only part of the syllable that is obligatory in all languages. But there are languages that do not allow a syllable to consist of just a nucleus. In Hawaiian, for instance, every syllable must have a single consonant in onset position followed by a vowel, as we see in place names such as *Honolulu*. In other languages syllables consisting of just a vowel may be restricted as to their possible position within the word. For instance, the three examples of a syllable consisting of just the diphthong /aɪ/ in English, *I*, *ideal*, and *Ivanhoe*, all occur in word-initial position. This is also the case with the *o* in words like *oblique*, *overt*, and *opera*. In Danish this is quite different. Here we can find words in which all syllables, whatever their position, can consist of a nucleus only. An extreme example is (13), a sentence which consists exclusively of vowels, from a Jutland dialect. Note that there is considerable difference between the written form of the Danish sentence and its pronunciation.

Danish (Jutland dialect)

(13) [ɑɛuːɔɛø'iɛɔ']
Jeg er ude på ø-en i a-en.
I am outside on island-*definite* in river-*definite*
'I am outside on the island in the river.'

Finally, in coda position there is also considerable variation between languages. A considerable number of languages, for example in the Pacific area, do not allow syllables with a coda, as we saw in the Hawaiian example. At the other extreme there are languages with very complex codas. English is a good example, with codas that run easily up to three consonants, as in *pants*, and sometimes have four, as in /tɛksts/ *texts*. Note that these combinations of consonants can only occur in coda position and never in the onset. There are no words in English that have /ksts/ or /nts/ as their onset.

Sometimes there are very specific restrictions on syllables that occur at the beginning or the end of a word. We saw above examples of English syllables consisting of just a vowel that can only occur at the beginning of a word. Another example comes from Spanish: in this language the last syllable of a word cannot end in the phoneme /m/, although syllables in other positions may. Thus we find words like *em-ba-ja-da* 'embassy', but the last syllable of a place name like Birmingham is pronounced by Spanish speakers as Birminghan with a word-final [n] rather than [m].

The writing system of several languages is based on syllable structure. In such **syllabic** writing systems each syllable – such as, for example, ba-be-bi-bo-bu, or ta-te-ti-to-tu – has its own written symbol. Contemporary Japanese has such a system of syllabic writing: the name *Hiroshima* is thus written with four different symbols as in (14).

(14) Hi-ro-shi-ma: ひろしま

In Japanese there are severe phonotactic restrictions. A syllable may either consist of a consonant and a vowel, or just a vowel. Furthermore, Japanese has a fairly small inventory of consonants and vowels. The number of possible syllables is therefore limited, and the syllabic writing system consists of about 50 symbols.

16.3 The Word: Stress

In all English words there will be at least one syllable that carries **stress**. The only exception to this rule is a small group of monosyllabic function words or clitics (such as *'m* in *I'm* and *'s* in *John's*, see Section 11.2). A stressed syllable is marked by a higher tone, increased volume and/or a greater length than comparable unstressed syllables. Longer words may contain several stressed syllables, but there will always be one syllable that carries the main stress, whereas other stressed syllables carry secondary stress. In this section we will only be concerned with the main stress of a word.

Could every syllable carry stress, in principle? Try and pronounce the nonsense words in (15) as if they were English words. Where would you put the stress?

(15) a. frezomatodee
b. stripalontak
c. kapatornitan

Speakers of English, using their unconscious linguistic competence (see Section 2.2), and without ever having seen these words, would probably put the stresses as shown in (16).

(16) a. frezo'matodee
b. stripa'lontak
c. kapa'tornitan

Without going into the highly specific rules that govern stress assignment in English, these examples show that stress assignment is usually not random, but is governed by rules of the language.

In (16b) the stress is on the penultimate (one before last) syllable; in (16a) and (16c) it is on the antepenultimate (two before last) syllable. This shows that in English there is variation with respect to the position of the stressed syllable within the word. In many other languages the position of the stressed syllable is fixed. Table 16.1 gives a few examples of languages with different fixed stress positions.

Table 16.1: Fixed stress positions with examples

Stressed syllable	*Language*	*Examples*	
initial	Cahuilla (United States)	*'ña?a,čeh* 'sit down'	*'neñukum* 'female cousins'
second	Mapudungun (Chile)	*t̪i'panto* 'year'	*e'lumu,yu* 'give us'
third	Winnebago (United States)	*hochi'chinik* 'boy'	*waghi'ghi* 'ball'
antepenultimate	Paumarí (Brazil)	*ra'bodiki* 'wide'	*oni'manari* 'seagull'
penultimate	Djingili (Australia)	*bi'aŋga* 'later'	*ŋuru'ala* 'we all'
ultimate	Weri (Papua New Guinea)	*u'lua,mit* 'mist'	*aku'nete,pal* 'times'

Among fixed stress languages the antepenultimate type of stress is most frequent, followed by languages in which stress is in the initial and the ultimate syllable respectively. The other types are much less frequent, as Figure 16.1 shows.

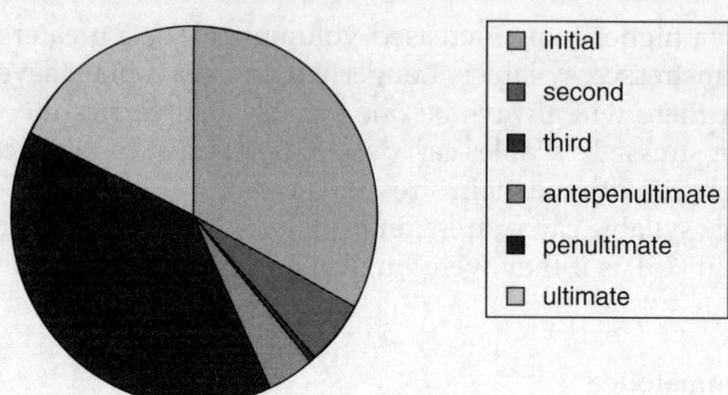

Figure 16.1 Distribution of fixed stress positions in a sample of 281 languages.

In languages with variable stress position the position of the stress may even vary in words based on the same stem when combined with other morphemes. Examples (17) and (18) show this for English.

(17)	'stupid	'stupidness	stu'pidity
	'rigid	'rigidness	ri'gidity
	in'trepid	in'trepidness	intre'pidity

(18)	col'laborate	col'laborator	collabo'ration
	in'vestigate	in'vestigator	investi'gation
	'aggregate	'aggregator	aggre'gation

In (17) the addition of the derivational suffix *-ness* forms the abstract noun from the adjectives in the first column. Its addition does not affect stress assignment, whereas the suffix *-ity* that has the same function causes the stress to shift to the final syllable of the stem. In (18) the addition of the suffix *-or*, forming the agent from the verbs in the first column, leaves stress placement unaffected but the suffix *-ion* to make the abstract noun causes the stress to shift to the right. In other words, there are two different kinds of suffixes, those that causes stress shift and those that do not. Second language learners of English find such variation quite difficult to master.

16.4 The Sentence: Intonation

Many languages use intonation to express certain distinctions related to the speech act expressed by the sentence (see Chapter 5). To explain this, we will take a closer look at the simple sentence in (19).

(19) There's a bull in the field.

This sentence could be used simply to announce the presence of a bull in a field, but it could also be used as a warning. The following two contexts disambiguate these two readings (20).

(20) a. How interesting! There's a bull in the field.
b. Watch out! There's a bull in the field!

But even without these disambiguating contexts, (19) would not be ambiguous in spoken language. The intonation patterns associated with the two readings are very different, as you will notice when you say (20a) and (20b) out loud.

In (19) it is only the difference in intonation that marks the difference between the speech acts of a statement and a warning: the words and word order may remain completely unchanged. It is, of course, also possible to mark the differences between the speech acts using both intonation and a change in word order. Comparing the question in (21) with the statement in (22) we see a difference in word order but also in intonation.

(21) Is Robert walking home? (rising intonation towards the end of the sentence)
(22) Robert is walking home. (falling intonation towards the end of the sentence)

Children learn the intonation patterns of their first language very quickly Even in the one-word stage they can make it clear if their one-word utterances are questions or not, as we see in examples from Kate in (23).

(23) Kate (1;6)
/bɒ/ (rising intonation) when she wants to know where the ball is
/mɑma/ (falling intonation) when she is naming her mother

In addition to speech act distinctions, intonation also serves to express certain emotions, such as astonishment, irritation, and irony.

An aspect of grammar often expressed through intonation is the information status of constituents. If you say a sentence such as (21) out loud, you immediately notice that at least one word gets more emphasis than the rest. This is the word that carries **sentence stress**, here indicated with capital letters on its most prominent syllable. This syllable is also the location for the most important pitch movements in the sentence, as illustrated in Figure 14.3 (See Chapter 14). In the interrogative sentence (21), for instance, sentence stress could be placed on three different words, as indicated in (24).

(24) a. Is RObert walking home?
b. Is Robert WALking home?
c. Is Robert walking HOME?

The sentences in (24) give special prominence or focus (see Section 5.3) to the words *Robert, walking*, or *home*. These are the words that present new or special information, as would occur in the contexts in (25).

(25) a. Is RObert walking home? I thought it was PEter.
b. Is Robert WALking home? He normally takes the BUS.
c. Is Robert walking HOME? At this time he is normally on his way to WORK.

In this example we have talked about words but in fact in this case each word is a constituent. If you replace some of the words in (21) with more complex constituents, as in (26), the sentence stress may fall on multiple syllables.

(26) a. Is the QUEEN of ENGland walking to Buckingham Palace?
b. Is the Queen of England TAking the BUS to Buckingham Palace?
c. Is the Queen of England walking to BUckingham PAlace?

16.5 RHYTHM

The rhythm with which words and sentences are produced is the last aspect of the organisation of phoneme strings into larger units that we shall discuss here. Rhythmic patterns are formed by combining syllables, often across word boundaries. A single stressed syllable, or a pair consisting of a stressed and one or two unstressed syllables, constitutes a rhythmic unit, known as a **foot**, a term borrowed from poetics. We will use a traditional nursery rhyme to illustrate the notion of 'foot' (27). The divisions between feet are indicated by slanting lines. Try clapping out the rhythm to get a feel for the pattern.

(27) ˈbarber / ˈbarber / ˈshave a / ˈpig!
ˈhow many / ˈhairs to / ˈmake a / ˈwig?
ˈfour and / ˈtwenty / ˈthat's e-/ˈnough!
ˈgive the / ˈbarber a / ˈpinch of / ˈsnuff.

In this short rhyme each combination of a stressed and an unstressed syllable, such as *ˈbarber* or *ˈshave a* or *ˈthat's e-* constitutes a foot. The last foot of each line consists of only one single stressed syllable. Note that foot structure does not respect word boundaries, as shown by the fact that the two syllables of *enough* are divided over two feet. The key criterion for a foot is the presence of a single stress. In the first three feet of each line in (27) we find a bi-syllabic foot, i.e. a foot with two syllables, the first of which is stressed, while the second is unstressed. This is called a **trochee**.

Longer words can also contain feet. The hierarchical structure of the word *Honolulu*, for example, can be represented as in (28).

(28)
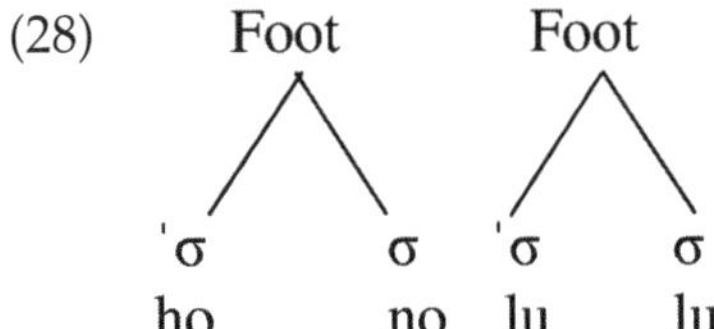

The word Honolulu is a good example of a word with two stress positions, primary stress on the third syllable and secondary stress on the first syllable. The word clearly consists of two feet, each of which contains one stressed syllable and an unstressed syllable. Both feet are bi-syllabic feet, with the first syllable stressed and the second unstressed. So *Honolulu* consists of two trochees.

A foot in which the first syllable is unstressed and the second syllable stressed, the mirror image of the trochee, is called an **iamb**. Its form is represented in (29).

(29)
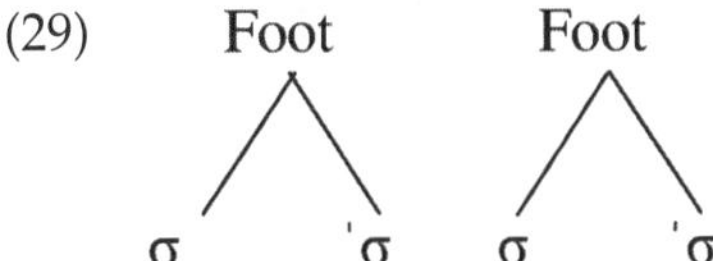

A language that has mostly iambic feet is Sierra Miwok, from South California. The sentence in (30) shows how this works in this language.

Sierra Miwok
(30)
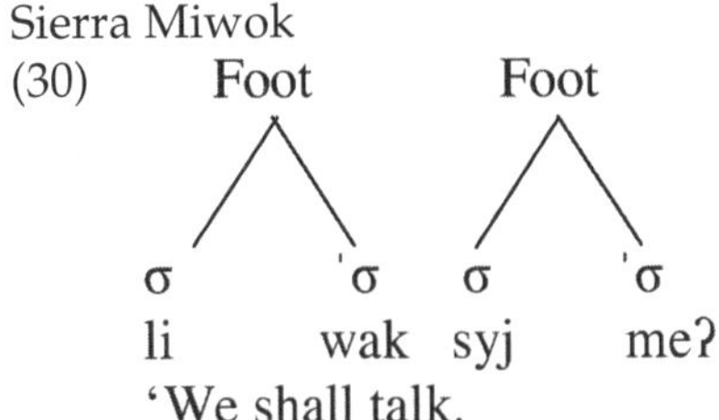

Summary

This chapter deals with the different ways in which series of phonemes can be organised into larger wholes: syllables, words and sentences. **Syllables** are small groups of phonemes which normally contain at least one vowel. Languages have restrictions on the phonemes that can be combined in syllables (**phonotactics**). The syllable has an internal structure and can be divided into **onset** (everything that comes before the vowel) and **rhyme** (the vowel and everything that follows it). The rhyme can be further subdivided into the **nucleus** (the vowel) and the **coda** (what follows after the vowel). Some languages use the syllable as the basis for their **syllabic** writing system.

Almost all words contain one or more syllables that carry **stress**. Stress placement is fixed in some languages, and variable in others, but even if it is variable it is often highly predictable on the basis of the syllabic structure of the word.

At the sentence level various different speech act distinctions and emotions can be expressed through intonation. Usually a sentence contains at least one word that has greater prominence than the rest. This word carries **sentence stress**, which in many languages can be used to mark focus.

Independently from word boundaries, syllables can be subdivided into **feet**, which determine the rhythmic structure of words and sentences. The foot is a unit of one or two syllables which always contains a stress. Two types of feet are distinguished here: the **trochee** (pattern: stressed-unstressed), and the **iamb** (pattern: unstressed-stressed).

ASSIGNMENTS

1. How many phonological syllables do the following words have? Transcribe these words and then mark the boundaries.
   (a) bewitching
   (b) photography
   (c) alabaster
   (d) prognosis
2. English is a language that allows codas, Hawaiian does not. English loan words are usually adapted to the syllable-structure of Hawaiian. How would a Hawaiian speaker most likely pronounce the word *prognosis*?
3. When we consider the suffixation in the following Hebrew words, what conclusion can we draw about the suffixes involved? Are these suffixes stress-shifting or stress-neutral? Compare examples (17) and (18) in Section 16.3.
   Hebrew
   (a) 'telefon 'telephone' tele'fonim 'telephones'
   (b) 'ʔalkohol 'alcohol' ʔalko'holit 'female alcoholic'
4. As we saw in Chapter 2, speakers sometimes produce slips-of-the-tongue where the onset consonants in adjacent words are exchanged. Instead of saying *Let us pray to our loving shepherd* they may produce the following:
   (a) Let us pray to our shoving leopard.
   Why is it far less likely that people will say something like (b) or (c)?
   (b) Let us pray to our loving peshard.
   (c) Let us pray to our loping shevard.

5. Say the following sentence out loud, once with a relieved intonation and again with an angry intonation. Mark in each case where the rise and fall in intonation occurs and which word gets the main stress.
   (a) The milk is finished.
6. Indicate the stresses and feet in the following verse. Identify the bisyllabic feet as trochees or iambs.
   To bed, says sleepy head,
   Tarry a while, says slow,
   Put on the pot, says greedy gut,
   We'll sup before we go.

TEST YOURSELF

1. What is syllabification?
2. What is a coda?
3. Which part of a syllable is obligatory?
4. Which intonation patterns do declarative sentences have in English?
5. What is the difference between word stress and sentence stress?
6. What is the difference between an iamb and a trochee?

ACKNOWLEDGMENTS AND FURTHER READING

Spencer (1996) and Smith (in preparation) were mentioned in relation to Chapter 15 and are also good introductions to the topics dealt with in this chapter. The data on and examples from languages with fixed stress positions were taken from Goedemans & van der Hulst (2005). The Hebrew examples are from Bat-El (1993).

part VI

Languages and Communities

In Parts II to V we discussed the various units of linguistic analysis, going from large to small. In this final part of the book we will look at four thematic subfields of linguistics. This means that the discussion will not be restricted to a particular level of linguistic analysis, such as for example sentence structure. In principle, all levels of analysis may be involved here.

In Chapter 1 we briefly mentioned the differences and similarities existing between languages. We will explore this theme in more depth in Chapter 17. Family relationships between languages such as in the Germanic language family will be discussed. Languages are always used to express aspects of culture – this relationship will also be examined in Chapter 17.

Native speakers of a language may differ considerably from each other in the way they use their language. That is, a language is not homogeneous, but full of variation. This variation will be the subject of Chapter 18, which also considers the link between linguistic differences and social factors.

Languages can be full of variation at any one time but they can also change over time. If you read a sixteenth-century play such as William Shakespeare's *Midsummer Night's Dream*, or even a nineteenth-century novel from Charles Dickens, you cannot fail to notice that their language is different from our contemporary English. Language change is the central theme of Chapter 19. Here we will look at both ongoing changes in the contemporary form of languages and also changes that occurred in the past, the domain of historical linguistics.

In many language communities in the world it is absolutely normal for people to speak two (or more) languages in their daily life. Chapter 20 will discuss various aspects of bilingualism, such as the influence of bilingualism on the development of children, expanding the discussion from Section 3.6, and the possibility of language mixing in the speech of bilinguals. This chapter, and the book as a whole, closes with a section on the creation of new languages in bilingual situations.

chapter 17

Differences and Similarities between Languages

17.1 Introduction

From the discussion in the previous chapters we have seen how diverse the languages of the world can be at the different linguistic levels: sound system, word and sentence structure, lexicon, and pragmatics. When you learn a new language, these differences really become apparent. French students learning English, for example, will have to tackle the two sounds written as *th as* in *thick* or *there,* since they do not exist in French. English students learning French, on the other hand, will have to get used to pronouncing the *é* of French *mangé* that does not occur in English. There are also different groups of verbs with all different endings such as *manger* 'to eat', *punir* 'to punish' and *prendre* 'to take'. French compounds such as *table à manger* 'dining table' are also formed in quite a different way. In sentence structure, as we saw in Chapters 6 to 10, languages can be very different. In Italian, for example, you can leave out the subject of the sentence and it will still be grammatically correct: *mangia* means 'he/she is eating'. In a language like German this is out of the question: **isst* 'eats' is ungrammatical without the subject *er* 'he'. Word order, too, can be quite different from one language to the next. In Spanish, for example, the main verb can occupy the first position in the sentence, as in *ha llegado mi tio* (literally: has arrived my uncle), meaning 'my uncle has arrived'. As we saw in Chapter 7,

Linguistics, First Edition. Edited by Anne E. Baker and Kees Hengeveld.

the direct object and verb can vary in position in some languages and not in others. In German the verb can follow the direct object in an embedded clause as in (1), whereas in Spanish this is not possible (2). The object must follow the verb in Spanish.

German

(1) ... als Maria den Vogel sah
... when Maria the.*accusative* bird saw
'... when Mary saw the bird'

Spanish

(2) *... cuando Maria el pájaro vio.
... when Maria the bird saw
'... when Mary saw the bird'

Another well-known difference between languages is the way in which the lexicon varies. For example, the French word *professeur* can mean both 'secondary school teacher' and 'university professor' whereas many languages label these distinctly as in English. French, on the other hand, does not have a word for English *sibling*. Languages also differ in the way they express certain meanings. In French it is common to say *elle n'arrive qu'avant huit heures* meaning 'she won't get here till eight o'clock', but in English you cannot express it this way **she does not arrive but before eight o'clock.*

In the previous chapters we have looked at the possible differences between languages, and we have considered many different types of languages. The examples just discussed come from relatively well-known and closely related European languages, but looking at languages from very different parts of the world, as we have done in the previous chapters, gives us even more insight into language as a whole. The point is that if we want to come to a better understanding of what is a human language, it is essential to compare languages. From such comparisons we can draw several conclusions:

- Differences between languages can be found in every single part of the linguistic system, ranging from sounds to language use in conversation and longer texts.
- Differences between languages can be quite considerable.
- Apart from differences, there are also certain constants or universals (see Section 1.2).

In all spoken languages we find vowels and consonants, even though their number and nature may vary considerably. Sign languages do not have vowels and consonants, of course, but signs do have structure. Both spoken and sign languages share the property that meaning is expressed by linking predicates (*to see, to hit, to walk*) with one or more arguments (*Mary, you, the neighbour, each other*).

Languages differ from each other but there are limitations on the possible variation, and it is interesting to try and determine what those limitations are. Our knowledge of languages from many different parts of the world is rapidly increasing, and our insight into what constitutes a human language and how languages can or cannot be organised is constantly expanding.

In Section 17.2 we will first consider the similarities we find between languages, and the varying origins of those similarities. One of these background factors, that is, the genetic relationship or possible family connections between languages, will be discussed in more depth in Section 17.3, including the methods used by linguists to map out these various kinds of relations between languages.

Languages originate in a specific environment, in a particular culture, and it is an intriguing question to what extent linguistic differences can be correlated with cultural differences (Section 17.4). In the last section, Section 17.5, we will discuss one particular view of the relationship between language and culture, the so-called Sapir-Whorf Hypothesis, which claims that the languages people use will influence, or even determine, the way they think.

17.2 Similarities between Languages

In addition to universal features that are shared by all languages, there may also be specific similarities between particular groups of languages. These similarities can have different origins. Similarities that are the result of a family relationship between languages can be observed between German and English. At the level of words, first of all, we find pairs of similar words across the whole system of language, such as *house-Haus* (Noun), *five-fünf* (Numeral), *blue-blau* (Adjective), *the-der* (Article), *we-wir* (Pronoun), *now-nun* (Adverb), *in-in* (Preposition), *think-denken* (Verb), *before-bevor* (Conjunction) and *yeah-ja* (Interjection). Secondly, at the level of grammar, we see that in both languages – compare (3) with (4) – adpositions occur before the noun, that is both languages have prepositions (*mit* and *in*) and not postpositions.

German

(3) Das Buch kam mit der Post
    the book came with the post
    'The book came in the post.'

English

(4) The book came in the post

At the phonological level, finally, German and English share a wide range of vowels and consonants, but with a few and very notable exceptions such as English /θ/ as in *thin* and German /x/ in *lachen* 'laugh' and /y/ in *grün* 'green'. The different kinds of similarities found between English and German are due to a close family relationship between the two languages: they have a common ancestor.

This type of **genetic relationship** has been known since the early Renaissance, when Dante in his *De vulgari eloquentia*, published in 1305, made a plea for the use of the vulgar tongue instead of Latin. He described what he knew of the relationship between languages, distinguishing three large language families in Europe: Germanic in the north, Latin in the south, and Greek in the border area between Europe and Asia. Using the word for 'yes' as a criterion he distinguished between the Germanic languages that say *ja* or *io*, Greek with *ne*, and the Latin languages, with *si* in Italian, *oc* in the south of France and *oil* in northern France (which later developed into today's *oui*). In fact, ever since Dante, a distinction has been made between the *Langue d'oc* (Occitan) and the *Langue d'oil* (French). In Section 17.3 we will return to genetic relations in more detail.

A second type of similarity can be illustrated with examples from Basque, Turkish and Quechua. These languages show remarkable parallels in structure, as we can see in sentences (5), (6) and (7).

Basque

(5)	Zu-k	ni-ri	etxe-a	eman	d	-i	-da	-zu.
	You-*ergative*	I-*dative*	house-*definite*	give	*3.sing*	*-aux*	*-1.sing*	*-2.sing*

'You gave me the house.'

Turkish

(6)	Sen	ban-a	ev-i	ver-din.
	you	I-dative	house-*accusative*	give-*past.2.sing*

'You gave me the house.'

Quechua

(7)	Qan	ñuqua-man	wasi-ta-n	qu-wa-rqa-rki.
	you	I-*dative*	house-*accusative-modality*	give-*1.sing-past-2.sing*

'You gave me the house.'

All three languages have the possibility to make very complex words; verbs are placed at the end of the sentence; verbs are conjugated to indicate tense and person; nouns carry case markings, etc. Also, words like *zuk*, *sen* and *qan*, which indicate the subject of the sentence, can be left out, just as in Spanish and Italian. Still, as far as we know, Basque, Turkish and Quechua are not genetically related. The remarkable similarities in their structure are due to the fact that they are languages of the same type and are built according to the same principles. The languages are **typologically** similar. Typological similarities occur when languages select the same structural 'options'. An important point here is that such options are logically related: complex verb forms, for example, often co-occur with an elaborate case system and with sentence-final verb position.

A totally different set of choices can be observed in Mandarin Chinese and Saramaccan, the language of escaped slaves in Surinam. Consider the following two examples in (8) and (9). Note that the label *class* in the word-by-word rendition of (8) reflects the fact that in Mandarin Chinese nouns are marked for their class.

Mandarin Chinese
(8) wǒ sòng yì-běn shū gěi nǐ.
I give a-*class* book give you
'I give a book to you.'

Saramaccan
(9) mi bái di wósu dá i.
I buy the house give you
'I buy the house for you.'

One of the common structural features of these two languages is that actions are often referred to with a chain of different verbs, in (8) with *sòng...gěi* ('give...give'), and in (9) with *bái*...dá ('buy...give'). But does this mean that Mandarin Chinese and Saramaccan are genetically related languages, like English and German? No, it does not, but they do belong to a particular type of language.

Not every language belongs clearly to a particular 'type'. Many languages have a typologically mixed character. And there is no standard list of language types on which all linguists agree. Nevertheless, it is important to consider typological similarities when comparing languages, if only to reduce the risk of jumping to the conclusion that languages, simply because they are similar, must therefore be genetically related.

To complicate things even further, languages that are not genetically related can often display all kinds of similarities if they are spoken in the same area. Intensive bilingualism over a long period can have the effect that languages begin to converge and develop **areal** similarities. This can be illustrated by considering the Balkans. The languages Albanian, Romanian, Bulgarian and Greek are similar in many ways. For example, various Balkan languages have the definiteness marker *after* instead of *before* the noun as we see in (10), where the marker is printed in boldface. This grammatical feature was not present in earlier forms of these languages and it is also not found in other related languages.

(10) Albanian: qiell-**i** lul-**ja**
Bulgarian: nebe-**to** cwet-**jat**
Rumanian: cer-**ul** floar-**ea**
'the sky' 'the flower'

Many of the similarities observed today between these languages are due to influences from contact rather than genetic influence.

A second example from the same area is that of the replacement of the infinitive by a finite construction. Unlike the English infinitive construction *I want to leave,* the Balkan languages use a construction that literally translates as *I want that I leave* as in (11).

(11)

Albanian:	due	te	shkue
Bulgarian:	iskam	da	otida
Rumanian:	veau	sa	plec
Greek:	thelo	na	pao
	want.*1.sing*	to	leave.*1.sing*
	'I want to leave.'		

The verb that follows after the conjunction, like *shkue* after *te* in Albanian, is in the present tense and has the same person and number as the main verb *due*, that is first person singular. It is likely that this construction was adopted from one language into another, but we do not know for certain.

An area like the Balkans, where different languages have acquired a number of similar features, is known as a **Sprachbund**. Another Sprachbund is found in the area around the Baltic Sea, involving languages as different as Swedish, Norwegian (except its northwestern dialects), most dialects of Danish, some dialects of northern German and North Cashubic (a slavonic language in north Poland), Estonian, Latvian and Lithuanian.

In some cases similarities between languages may be purely coincidental. In Swahili, for example, the word *pashwa* 'it has to be' is very close to spoken French *il n'y a pas de choix* [ilɲapadʃwa] 'there is no choice'. Similarly, Basque *elkar* happens to have the same sound and meaning as Dutch *elkaar* 'each other', although these languages are not genetically related and not in regular contact.

17.3 Genetic Relations

If we go back in time, we will eventually come to a point when there was no English language as such, or at least there was no separate language that was identifiable as English. English has grown out of an earlier ancestor language, which has also given rise to German, Danish and several other languages. This family relationship has a certain immediate, intuitive plausibility and this becomes more evident when we take a look at the English and German words in (12).

(12)

English	*Danish*	*German*
house	hus	Haus
brown	brun	braun
out	udenfor	aus
thousand	tusinde	tausend

There is a systematic correspondence here between the sound shapes of a range of words from the three languages. Put simply, Danish /u/ corresponds systematically to English and German /au/, and this in turn suggests a close family relationship, a common historical ancestor.

How can we find out about older forms of languages, even though the speakers are long dead and buried? Ever since the Renaissance, there have been many generations of linguists who have carried out research. They developed a range of research techniques and explored all kinds of language data. For languages still in use at that time they engaged in fieldwork, making notes on the indigenous languages. Missionaries often wrote descriptions of the languages with which they came into contact. In Figure 17.1 this grammar describes the Arabic dialect spoken in Damascus and written by a Spanish Franciscan priest, Lucas Cauallero, in 1709.

Interestingly, in the first words of the text Cauallero compares the differences between Latin and Castilian Spanish, which was then often seen as a kind of corrupt Latin, to the great differences between literary Arabic and the spoken Arabic of Damascus. These kinds of descriptions provide invaluable information on the languages as actually spoken at the time, since the literary language was hardly changing.

In areas settled by European migrants in colonial times, most of the indigenous languages vanished long ago, for example in the eastern parts of the United States, so that we have to rely on incomplete records. As a consequence we are not in a position to describe the linguistic history of these areas with any degree of precision.

For the so-called 'dead languages', such as Hittite and Sumerian, we can use, if we are lucky, written sources, often in a different script than that used today. Without Mesopotamian clay tablets with cuneiform writing, or papyrus scrolls with Egyptian hieroglyphics, it would be far more difficult to reconstruct the linguistic history of the Ancient Middle East. In addition to written sources we do sometimes have access to early sound recordings of languages. There are, for example, nineteenthth-century recordings of remote Siberian languages on wax rolls, and for some Native American languages on audio-cassettes with spoken texts and conversation. When describing the early history of sign

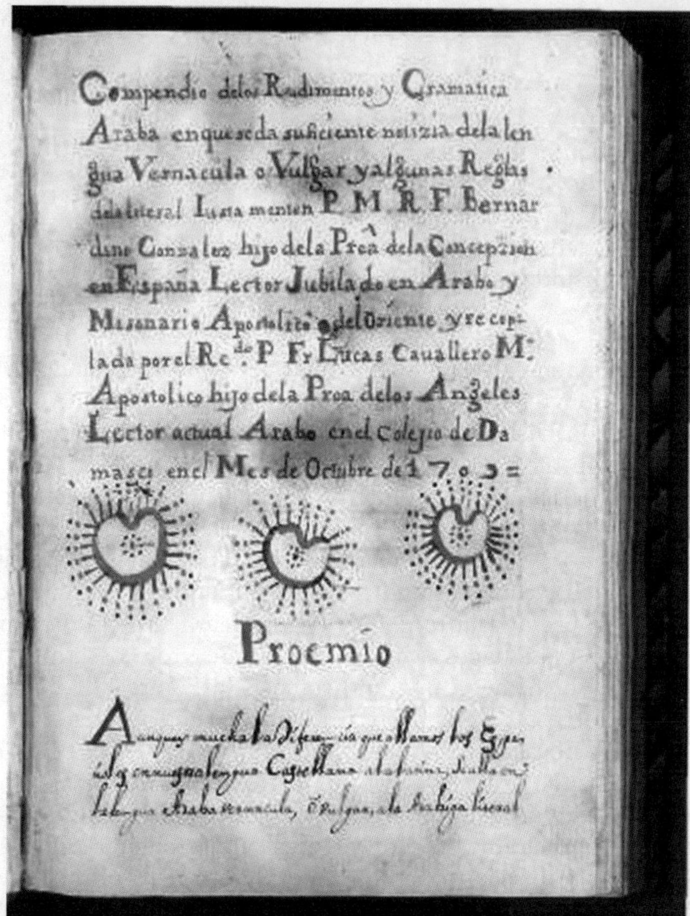

Compendio delos Rudimentos y Gramatica
Araba enque se da suficiente noticia dela len
gua Vernacula o Vulgar yalgunas Reglas
dela literal Lusta menten P. M. R. F. Bernar
dino Gonzalez hijo dela Prov.a dela Concepcion
en España Lector Jubilado en Arabe y
Misionario Apostolico del Oriente y recop
ilada por el Re.do P. Fr. Lucas Cauallero M.
Apostolico hijo dela Prov.a delos Angeles
Lector actual Arabo enel Colegio de Da
masco enel Mes de Octubre de 1709 =

Proemio

Figure 17.1 Cover of the grammar of an Arabic dialect written by Lucas Cauallero in 1709. Otto Zwartjes.

languages we are in a far worse position, since visual recording techniques were only available at the end of the nineteenth century.

The history of a language, whether it is still in use or not, is also reflected in the spread and distribution of place names and surnames. We know that the area of diffusion of Basque in the north of Spain must have been far larger in the past, because there are Basque names of villages and families still to be found in areas that have since become completely Spanish speaking. The study of place names is known as **toponymics**.

In addition there are different types of secondary sources about languages. In about AD 40, for example, the Roman historian Tacitus wrote his book *Germania*, which contains a vast amount of information on the Germanic tribes living across the river Rhine, on the periphery of the Roman Empire. Archaeology also provides us with indirect evidence. If, for example, a specific tool or object is found in neighbouring areas where today different languages are spoken, it is plausible that in the past the producers and users of the object were in contact and may have used a common language.

In principle, then, it is possible to go back in time, and to investigate from what common ancestor language the three languages in (12) are descended. In historical-comparative linguistics the main aim is to describe and explain the development of language families, the relations between languages within a particular family, and the way in which these languages have grown apart from each other. The basic approach in this field consists of a systematic comparison of different languages at different historical stages, a procedure we can illustrate with the following case of words for small numbers. In (13) we give a survey of the number words for *three*, *four* and *five* in a range of languages. Note that the transcription here is orthographic, and not phonetic; Old Church Slavonic Ъ represents the sound [ɪ] as in *pit*; and ę represents the nasalised sound [ɛ̃], as in French *peintre*:

(13)				
	English	three	four	five
	Frisian	trije	fjouwer	fiif
	German	drei	vier	funf
	Dutch	drie	vier	vijf
	Gothic	threis	fidwor	fimf
	French	trois	quatre	cinq
	Spanish	tres	cuatro	cinco
	Latin	tres	quattuor	quinque
	Greek	treis	tetra-	penta
	Serbian	tri	četiri	pet
	Old Church Slavonic	trЪe	četyre	pętЪ
	Sanskrit	trayas	catvaras	pañca
	Hindi	tina	cara	panca
	Lithuanian	trys	ketri	penki

At a glance you can see that all the words for THREE are clearly related. It is possible on the basis of these forms to suggest a word from which all the forms listed in (13) could be derived. For THREE the reconstructed form that has been proposed is **treyes*. In historical linguistics the *sign indicates that we have to do with a reconstructed form that has not been attested in the historical record of the language(s) in question. Note that this is in contrast to other subfields of linguistics where the *sign is used to mark forms as ungrammatical. This procedure of creating a common form from which others could be derived is known as **comparative reconstruction**. The aim is to find a form from which other forms can be derived with the minimum number of

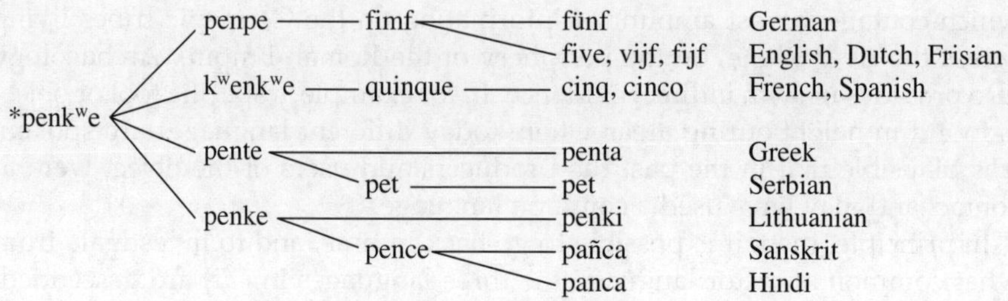

Figure 17.2 Relationships between some Indo-European languages.

phonologically plausible sound changes. In the case of (13) most of the words for THREE start with [tr], end with [s], and have vowels in the vicinity of [e]. Languages that share such a word for THREE (and many other similarities as well) belong to the so-called Indo-European **language family**. This family comprises a large collection of languages, though by no means all, from Europe and India, as was first demonstrated by Sir William Jones in 1786.

The words for the number FOUR show that such a family relationship is not always immediately evident. German *vier* and Serbian *četiri* do not seem to be related. The Gothic *fidwor* and Old Church Slavonic *četyre*, that is, forms from older languages that are related to German and Serbian respectively, are already a little bit closer; for example Gothic FOUR consisted of two syllables as did Old Church Slavonic. Continuing in this vein, it has been possible to reconstruct an Indo-European proto form $^*k^wet^wores$, from which all others can be derived. Note that the sounds k^w and t^w are labialised sounds. Labialisation is a secondary articulation that involves the lips. Applying the same procedure to the words for FIVE has led to an Indo-European **proto-form** $^*penk^we$. The diagram in Figure 17.2 gives an idea of how existing forms in various languages are derived from this proto-form.

What do the forms in Figure 17.2 illustrate? Taken together with other evidence, we can in fact distinguish various subfamilies within the large Indo-European language family. English, German, Gothic, Dutch and Frisian belong to the Germanic family. The fourth-century Gothic *fimf* is the oldest recorded form we have of this numeral. French and Spanish belong to the Romance languages, which both derive from Latin. Serbian and Old Church Slavonic belong to the Slavonic family, Lithuanian is Baltic. Hindi and Sanskrit belong to branches that split off earlier. Obviously this picture of the Indo-European language family and its internal structure is a highly simplified one; for a full survey we refer to the literature at the end of the chapter.

Once enough proto-forms have been reconstructed, we can establish the **proto-language**, like for example Proto-Germanic or Proto-Indo-European. It is not at all certain what these languages actually sounded like. A proto-language is no more than the sum of all hypothetical, reconstructed proto-forms within a certain language family. Proto-forms remain hypothetical until they have been attested; and as long as the actual, historical form is not known, the proto-form is no more – but also no less – than the most likely candidate.

In their analysis of the relationship between different languages, historical linguists have managed to establish rules expressing systematic correspondences between languages. Initially the rules only involved speech sounds. Typically, a correspondence was established between sound 'X' in certain positions in language A and sound 'Y' in the same positions in the word forms of language B. Such rules are known as **sound laws**. An example is the relation between the /p/ of Proto-Indo-European and the /f/ in Proto-Germanic: wherever Proto-Indo-European has /p/, Proto-Germanic has /f/, as we can see in for example Latin *pater* and English *father*, but also in *penk^{w}e* and *fimf* in Figure 17.2. This /p/↔/f/ relation is one of a whole series of such correspondences. Sound laws do not just involve individual sounds, but the sound system as a whole. The /p/↔/f/ sound law, for example, runs in parallel with the /t/↔/θ/ sound law (θ as in *thick*), which connects Gothic *threis* with Proto-Indo-European **treyes*. In both sound laws there is a correspondence between a plosive (/p/, /t/) and a fricative (/f/, /θ/). (For an explanation of these terms see Section 14.5.2). In the nineteenth century much emphasis was placed on such laws, especially by the German school of historical linguistics known as the Neogrammarians. The reality is in fact more complex.

Sometimes in the same language we find different forms of a rule. Let us take the example of the English past tense, which we already discussed in Section 12.8.

(14)

Regular *stem*	Past *past*	Irregular *stem*	Past *past*
vote	voted	meet	met
wait	waited	cut	cut
regret	regretted	put	put
mend	mended	rid	rid
grade	graded	bleed	bled
found	founded	shed	shed

If we look at the list of verbs in (14) we see two types – those verbs that form the past tense in /əd/ on the left and those that seem to have no ending on the right. Most English verbs form their past with /d/ or /t/ like *seem- seem/d/* or *link- link/t/*. Why do the words in (14) behave differently and why are there two groups? All the verb stems in (14) end in a /d/ or /t/, since the letter *e* in a verb such as *grade* is not pronounced. This makes these different from other verbs in English. But this does not explain why there are two groups in (14). The verbs on the right are from the basic vocabulary of English (see Section 11.10), but so are some words on the right. Verbs on the left contain verbs derived from Latin or French whereas these do not occur on the right. These are older Germanic verbs. This suggests that the past tense forms on the right are in fact the older forms. That is, in verbs ending in /d/ or /t/ the past tense ending has been absorbed into the stem. In later forms this has not happened. This explanation is supported by imagining a novel verb like *drad* – most speakers would agree that the past tense of this would be *dradded*. This line of reasoning is an example of how we may use data from one single language in an attempt to determine what was the original form or rule in that language. This is also a form of reconstruction, but in this example there is no comparative element. But in many instances evidence from one language is not sufficient to enable a satisfactory reconstruction. In such instances the method of comparative reconstruction is used.

As a result of research into the genetic links between all kinds of languages a number of large language families have been identified. The best-known, at least from a European perspective, is the Indo-European language family mentioned above. This family consists of at least 150 languages, grouped into ten sub-families. The most important other language family in Europe is the Finno-Ugric family, comprising Hungarian, Finnish and a number of smaller languages from Russia and surrounding countries. The Semitic languages, such as Arabic and Hebrew, belong, together with the Berber languages, to the so-called Afro-Asiatic languages. Turkish is a member of the Altaic language family, together with several languages spoken in Asia. In the rest of the world many other language families have been discovered. Some may cover a whole continent, like the Australian language family, others only a small and remote part of a continent, like the Inuit (Eskimo) language family. There is still much to discover in this field. Thus, for example, it has proved impossible, despite many efforts, to place Basque in a larger language family; it appears to be a family on its own.

In (15), (this page and page 347), we give an example of a language family, the Uralic and Yukaghir language family. The languages belonging to this family are, with the exception of Hungarian, spoken in parts of Northern Europe and Siberia. This family has two sub-families, one of which – the Uralic languages – is subdivided again. The names of the languages are printed in normal case, those of the (sub-)families in italics. Some of the languages, such as Chuvantsy, are no longer spoken. The Sami languages (North Finnish) are also called 'Lappish'.

(15) *Uralic-Yukaghir*
- I *Yukaghir*: Yukaghir, Chuvantsy, Omok
- II *Uralic*:
  - A. *Samojedic*:
    - (1) *North*: Nenets, Enets, Nganasan
    - (2) *South*: Selkup, Kamas

B. *Finnish-Ugric*:
  (1) *Ugric*:
    (a) *Hungarian*: Hungarian
    (b) *Ob-Ugric*: Xanty, Mansi
  (2) *Finnish*:
    (a) *Permic*: Udmurt, Komi
    (b) *Volgaic*: Mari, Mordvinic
    (c) *North-Finnish*:
      (i) *Sami*: North-Sami, East-Sami, South-Sami
      (ii) *Baltic Finnish*: Finnish, Ingric, Karelic, Olonets, Ludic, Vepsic, Votic, Estonian, Livonian

This discussion of language families and the genetic relations between languages naturally leads to the question of the origin of language. Was there perhaps in the beginning one Proto-World language? If so, this would have to be placed at the very top of the pedigree of all the languages of the world. More than this we cannot say with any degree of certainty. Some researchers think that the predecessor of our own species of *homo sapiens*, the *homo erectus* who lived about two million years ago, had an elaborate and complex system for communication, perhaps some form of signing. From paleo-anatomical research it is plausible that the latest common ancestor of Neanderthals and *homo sapiens*, who lived about 400,000 years ago, was using some form of speech.

17.4 Language and Culture

Differences between languages can be related to differences between cultures. But before we discuss this in further detail, we must first define the notion of culture. **Culture**, as we will use the notion here, consists of what is usually called 'high culture': literature, music, painting, etc., but also the much wider domain of values, norms and customs of a society. This includes views on what is right and wrong, ideas about the education of children, and, wider still, the domain of 'material culture', that is, everything around us, both nature and all man-made products. Both rain and thunder on the one hand and tea and crumpets on the other form part of the British culture.

That there is a relation between language and culture becomes apparent the moment we take a look at the vocabulary of a language. Let us look at a few examples. First, Inuit, the language of the Inuktitut in Northern Canada, has a large number of separate words for different kinds of seal in different kinds of situations, words that we could translate as 'young, spotted seal' and 'male, swimming seal'. The Dutch, on the other hand, have traditionally had a large number of mills, for which they use different words such as *meelmolen* 'flour mill', *windmolen* 'wind mill', *watermolen* 'water mill', and, by extension, *koffiemolen* 'coffee grinder' and *snijbonenmolen* 'bean cutter'. In British conversation, unlike for example in Indonesia, the weather has always been an important social topic, hence the large number of expressions (Section 13.5) and rhymes about the weather, some of which are illustrated in (16).

English
(16) a. Red sky at night, a shepherd's delight
Sky red in the morning, a sailor's sure warning
b. The morning sun never lasts a day
c. Make hay while the sun shines
d. It's raining cats and dogs

Now that shepherds and sailors are no longer as common in the English-speaking world as they once were, some of these expressions are going out of fashion.

Words that refer to speech and ways of speaking can tell us something about how a culture sees language and language use. Take, for example, the Tzeltal language, spoken by the inhabitants of Tenejapa in the central highlands of Mexico. Talking, and the many different ways in which this can be done, plus the situations surrounding all that talk, are of great interest to the Tenyupan people. In other words, it is an important part of their culture. The Tenyupan people not only talk a lot, but they also spend a lot of time repeating what someone has said, appreciating and commenting on it, making jokes and having fun at the expense of the speaker, and so on. For this purpose, the Tzeltal language has hundreds of words to refer to the many different kinds of monologues, conversations, etc., that may take place. All these words have the form *X + k'op* 'talk/speak' (17).

Tzeltal
(17) a. *yom k'op*: 'discussion between various people who have come together to take a decision'.
b. *c'ayem k'op*: 'conversation that was audible, but slowly becomes inaudible because the speakers are moving out of ear-shot'.
c. *lukul k'op*: 'talk by someone who is lying down'.

Another area in which we can see the relation between language and culture is the area of kinship systems, the systems of terms with which we refer to family relations. For the English, as for many European languages, it goes without saying that 'father of someone's father' and father of someone's mother' are referred to with the single word *grandfather*. But in other languages this is by no means self-evident. In the Njamal language, for example, an Aboriginal language spoken in Australia, the word for 'father's father' is *maili*, and for 'mother's father' *mabidi*. In the case of such languages it could be that this is culturally determined – in the sense that the grandfather on the mother's side has a different role in the family to that of the grandfather on the father's side.

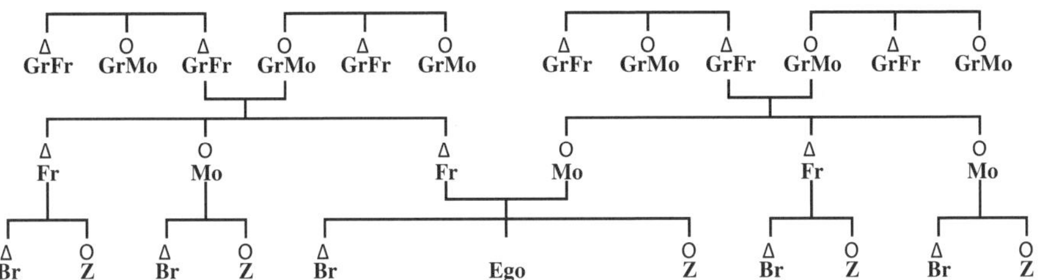

Figure 17.3 Hawaiian kinship system.

The organisation of kinship terms into kinship term systems can often be seen as the reflection of the, perhaps only historical, views on family relationships within a certain community. A further example of a kinship term system, that of Hawaiian, is given in Figure 17.3. In that figure the Ego represents the person from whose perspective the relations are named. Circles indicate females and triangles males. The diagram shows that the same term indicated as Fr is used for both the direct male parent and uncles, and the same term marked as Mo is used for the female parent and aunts. Similarly, the term indicated as Br is used for brothers and male cousins, while the term marked as Z is used for both sisters and female cousins. Finally, the term marked GrFr is used for grandfathers and great-uncles, while the term marked as GrMr is used for grandmothers and great-aunts.

So we see that in the Hawaiian system of kinship terms, the same terms are used for collateral relatives within the same generation. Words like *makua kāne* may be both 'father' and 'uncle', *makuahine* both 'mother' and 'aunt', *kaikunāne* 'brother' and 'male cousin', and *kaikuahine* 'sister' and 'female cousin'. Such a system, known as a 'generational system', reflects a cultural organisation in which the task of bringing up children is shared between the members of the entire generation to which the biological father and mother belong. Let us stress here that there is certainly not a direct relationship between culture and language, as a linguistic system of classification may persist long after the cultural triggers for it have disappeared.

The forms and rules for addressing people in a particular language community often also reflect its social structure and cultural conventions. In Section 5.4 we briefly looked at forms of address in Japanese. The way these forms are used reflects a set of culturally important distinctions in Japanese society. The same is true for languages such as German, French, and Italian where the distinction between formal and informal – German *du* and *Sie*, French *tu* and *vous*, Italian *ti* and *Lei* – reflects important social distinctions and relations. These were discussed in Section 5.4 in relation to pragmatic appropriateness of language use. What is appropriate is culturally determined and forms an important aspect of culture.

The important role of cultural factors in language use also becomes obvious when we look at the rules for language use in conversations. When a Japanese man introduces himself, he will often say straight away for which company he works and what his function is. And he will expect his conversation partner to do the same. For the Japanese this is of great importance, because status plays an essential role in their social relations. You need to be able immediately to place your conversation partner, and this will have consequences for the ensuing communication, for example in the choice of forms of address. Another important feature of Japanese culture is that the personal and individual is by and large subordinated to the general and collective. So the Japanese will not readily give their personal opinion. Rather, they will tend to avoid expressions like *I believe...*, *In my opinion...* or *If you ask me....* Such cultural characteristics are often misunderstood by Westerners.

Linguistic anthropology is a treasure trove of examples of language use that are typical for specific cultures and communities, particularly in non-western societies. A famous case was reported in an article entitled 'How to ask for a drink in Subanun'. Subanan is a language of the Philippines. As it turns out, it is not enough to be able to produce a grammatically correct sentence in Subanun, more or less as a translation of the same request in English. According to the author of the article, the speaker might then perhaps be complimented on his proficiency in Subanun, but he is not very likely to get a drink. Grammatical competence in a language is not enough for adequate communication. You also have to know the rules for using that language in specific situations; that is, communicative competence (see Section 2.2 and Chapters 4 and 5).

These examples may give the impression that culture is expressed completely in language, and that language directly reflects culture. But this is certainly not the case. Languages can differ from one another in many ways, without this having anything to do with cultural differences. Take again, for example, the forms of address in different languages. As we have mentioned, many languages make a distinction between formal and informal second person pronouns, but not present-day English, where there is only the single form *you*. The eighteenth-century French philosopher Voltaire discovered this to his horror when he first arrived in London and felt socially inhibited. Now does this mean that the social factors of 'status' and 'solidarity', which play a key role in the choice between *tu* and *vous*, are not important in English-speaking communities? No, of course not. These factors are important, but the way they are expressed in language is different, for example in the use of forms of address such as *Margaret* or *Mrs Thomson*. It makes a world of difference in British English whether you address a person as *Winston*, or *Churchill*, *Mr Churchill*, *My Right Honourable Friend* or *Prime Minister*. In multilingual India, where English is one of the official and widely used languages, it would be nonsense to think that such social distinctions do not matter to Indians when they speak English, but that they do as soon as they switch over to another language such as Hindi or Marathi.

There are in fact many aspects of language structure that do not appear to be related to culture. In the Kiwai language, for example, spoken in Papua New Guinea, we find a system of personal pronouns that differs significantly from the systems commonly used in western languages. In addition to the personal pronouns for singular and plural, Kiwai has three additional distinctions in the plural: between a plural of two people (*dualis*), a plural of three (*trialis*) and a group of more than three people. That is, for the first person plural, where English has only *we*, Kiwai has three separate forms: *nimoto* 'we two', *nimoibi* 'we three' and *nimo* 'all of us (more than three)'. But as far as we know, this grammatical system is unrelated to cultural distinctions. It is not the case that groups of two, three or more people are in any way important in Kiwai culture. Furthermore, it is striking that Kiwai does not even have a word for THREE; this concept is expressed by a combination of the words for 'one' and 'two'. This makes it even less likely that the Kiwai pronominal system with its *dualis* and *trialis* really has a cultural basis.

In English the finite form of the verb indicates when a particular action or event took place, is or will be taking take place. In other languages different factors influence the form of the verb, and the tenses may be organised quite differently from the English system. In the Kewa language, for example, also spoken in Papua New Guinea, speakers must always indicate whether they themselves have actually witnessed the event or action they are talking about. This difference is expressed in two Kewa sentences in (19), each consisting of one single, complex word.

Kewa

(18) (a) Ira-a-ha.
cook-*past.3.sing-visual*
'He/she cooked (and I saw it myself).'

(b) Ira-a-ya.
cook-*past.3.sing-nonvisual*
'He/she cooked (but I did not see it myself).'

We say that the feature 'visual/non-visual' must be expressed grammatically in Kewa. The grammar forces the speaker to make a choice at this point. Such a difference can, of course, also be expressed in other languages. In English, for example, it is perfectly possible to say *I saw him cooking*. However, in English one does not *always* have to say whether one has seen something for oneself or not, whereas in Kewa one does. In the same way, in English grammar you have to express, in the finite form of the verb, when exactly something happened or will happen.

Could it be that such properties of grammar have a cultural basis or origin? Could it be that in the Kewa community lack of trust plays a greater role than in communities where speakers are not forced by their grammars to indicate with so many words whether they have actually witnessed what they are reporting?

This is possible, though some will think improbable. But the question remains – why do Kewa, Turkish and Korean have such a system, whereas English, Italian and Farsi do not? Why is the grammar of one language so completely different from that of another? We cannot answer these questions fully, but, from comparative linguistic research, we do know that the range and number of distinctions that can be expressed in verb forms is limited. That is, the possible variation between languages is restricted, as we saw in Chapter 9.

17.5 Language and Thought: the Sapir-Whorf Hypothesis

In the previous section we discussed the question to what extent language use is culturally determined. Here we will change perspective and ask whether languages influence the way their speakers think. Do languages control the perception and interpretation of reality? These questions received a cautiously positive answer from the proponents of the so-called **Sapir-Whorf Hypothesis**, named after two American linguists, Edward Sapir and his student, Benjamin Lee Whorf, who further developed Sapir's views. Sapir's premise was: 'We see and hear and otherwise experience very largely as we do because the language habits of our community predispose certain choices of interpretation.' Whorf's main idea was that the system or grammar of any language is not just an instrument for the representation of ideas, but that it creates new ideas. He saw it as the program and guide for speakers' mental activity, for the analysis of impressions, for the synthesis of what they have in their head.

According to these views, language plays a large part in the 'processing' of impressions, the interpretation of reality, and the organisation of thought. Language, it is claimed, acts as a filter on reality. In this way language influences the worldview of the individual speaker. Sapir and Whorf developed these ideas on the basis of their research into Native American Indian languages, which turned out to have a totally different structure than the more widely studied Indo-European languages. When studying the grammatical structure of Navaho, you could say that in this language actions are seen as classes of separate elements. People who carry out a particular action are not seen in this language as 'initiators' or 'agents', but rather as involved in an action, which already exists outside of them. In Navaho you say something like 'The hunting takes place with White Feather', instead of 'White Feather is hunting'. According to the Sapir-Whorf Hypothesis, the Navaho language thus guides its speakers in the interpretation of reality. When they see a person X carrying out an action, they will consider this action as something that 'happens to' X; X is taking part in something that is already preordained, X is not acting independently.

Before we go to examine more closely the merit of the Sapir-Whorf Hypothesis, it is necessary to formulate it in a more systematic way. We need to distinguish between the vocabulary of a language and its grammar. It is quite plausible that the words speakers have at their disposal will, one way or another, have an important influence on the way they think. It is, after all, with those words that we describe the reality around us. If you do not have the various different words for SEAL that the Inuit have in their language, it is not so easy to perceive the different kinds of seal in different situations. Speakers of Inuit, on the other hand, are forced by their language to name each of these different types of seal, and the mental effect this has is that they are more likely to think about seals in terms of those different types. For Sapir and Whorf, however, this lexical interpretation of their hypothesis, the impact of vocabulary on thought, was always less important than the structural-grammatical interpretation reflected in the quote from Sapir's work above.

We also need to distinguish 'influencing' from 'determining'. In some of their writings it seems as if Sapir and Whorf take the view that the way people think and view the world is *determined* by the language they speak: the language in question is controlling its users, and it is impossible to escape. In other passages they formulate their views less extremely, namely that thought is largely *influenced* by language, in which case the role of language is not as dominant as we first thought.

The question now is: where lies the truth? Let us first take the issue of 'influencing' versus 'determining'. This makes it necessary to say something more general about the relationship between language and thought, a problem that has occupied generations of scholars from many different disciplines, and one which is far from being resolved. Although there are still many points of disagreement, it is today generally accepted that thought is to some extent non-verbal in nature. The evidence for this comes from people with severe language impairment: they have major damage to their linguistic competence, but can think in a normal way (see Section 2.3). Many mental activities are in fact non-verbal in character, for example, those involved in artistic endeavours such as painting and composing music. Similarly, solving difficult mathematical puzzles can often be done without recourse to verbal reasoning.

All this implies that it is really not possible to claim that language 'determines' thought. At most we can speak of the 'influence' of language. This view can be supported with a second argument. A concept for which there is a separate word in language A can always be described by a paraphrase in language B. Take, for example, the British English word *fortnight* meaning a period of two weeks. French and German, for example, do not have a separate word for this concept. So in these languages the notion FORTNIGHT will have to be expressed in a paraphrase: in German *zwei Wochen* 'two weeks' or in French *quinze jours* 'fifteen days'. Speakers of these languages can obviously perceive and think about this unit of time, but when they speak their own language, they do not have one single word at their disposal with which to refer to it.

English	red	yellow	blue	green	black
Language X	colour 1		colour 2		

Figure 17.4 Schematic view of division of the colour spectrum in a language.

In other words, they may have the notion or the concept but not a one-word equivalent. In more technical terms, we would say that the notion *fortnight* has been lexicalised in British English, but not in French, German, Italian or even American English. In the same way the notion MALE SWIMMING SEAL has been lexicalised in Inuit, but not in English.

The same holds true at the grammatical level. Think, for example, of the case mentioned in Section 17.4, of the Kewa language, in which speakers are obliged to indicate whether they have personally witnessed a certain action or not. In a language like English it is quite possible to express this in the form of a paraphrase, as in *I saw him cooking* in contrast to *he did the cooking, but I didn't see it myself*. We can thus conclude that anything can be expressed in any language, but that in some languages some things *have* to be expressed and that certain distinctions must be made.

So far we have not presented any hard evidence for or against the Sapir-Whorf Hypothesis. It is not easy to obtain that kind of evidence through linguistic research, but it has been attempted. One experiment looked at vocabulary, in particular colour terms. We have known for a long time that the number of colour terms differs between languages, just as the distribution of colour terms over the spectrum is not the same in all languages. Language X could therefore well be different from English in the way indicated schematically in Figure 17.4. Now, if it is the case that language has a strong influence on perception and thought, then speakers of English and X, respectively, must differ from each other in the way they carry out tasks involving colour perception.

To test this hypothesis, English-speaking subjects were given two types of cards to name: (i) cards of a colour that could be named with a single colour term in English, for example *blue*, and (ii) cards where the colour had to be named with a combination of two colour words, for example *blue-green*. After then doing an unrelated task as a kind of diversion, the subjects were asked to select the original cards from a large collection of cards. It turned out that cards of type (i) were more easily retrieved than those of type (ii). The explanation for this is that the difference in lexicalisation had influenced the search procedures of these subjects: since *blue-green* is not lexicalised, a circumlocution is necessary here, whereas for *blue* this is not the case. This result appears to offer support for the Sapir-Whorf Hypothesis.

On the other hand, although the boundaries between the various colour terms may be drawn differently in different languages, it turns out that the *focus* or *centre* of colour terms is the same for speakers of different languages.

When asked to point out the 'truest' red or blue, they will point to the same colour, regardless of their language. They do this independently of the way the colour spectrum is divided in the language they happen to speak.

In addition, there are some languages where the colour spectrum is divided in two, with words only for BLACK and WHITE (or DARK and LIGHT). According to the Sapir-Whorf Hypothesis, speakers of those languages should have greater difficulty in recognising other colours than the two for which they have words. This has been investigated with the speakers of Dani, a language of Irian Jaya (Indonesian New Guinea), which indeed only has words for DARK and LIGHT. When the Dani speakers were asked to do the same experiment as the English speakers, they too recognised colours of type (i) far more easily than those of type (ii). The conclusion drawn from this experiment was that in general language does *not* have a strong influence on the recognition of colours, and that everyone, whatever the colour system in their language, recognises some colours more easily than others, because they are visually more striking. We may deduce from this that it is the human perception system that determines which colours people recognise more easily, and that the colours that are most easily recognised are most likely to be lexicalised. If a particular language divides the colour spectrum in three (instead of two, as with the Dani), the third colour term, after 'black' and 'white' will always be 'red', because that colour is always best recognised and perceived most quickly.

Linguistic research thus indicates that the Sapir-Whorf Hypothesis has to be moderated. Language seems to have some influence on the mental activities of humans. But if members of a community share certain ideas and views, or if they perceive and interpret their environment in a particular way, this is mostly due to the culture they have grown up in. When in a certain culture the attitude towards the 'aunt who is the sister of the father' is different from the attitude towards the 'aunt who is the sister of the mother' this is more likely to be due to the fact that these two different sorts of aunts occupy different positions within the social system of the family, rather than to the fact that they are named using different words, as for example in Turkish with *hala* 'father's sister' and *teyze* 'mother's sister'. Language does not force people to think in certain ways, but it has an influence on our perception and interpretation of the world.

Summary

This chapter focuses on the question of how differences and similarities between languages can be analysed and explained. There are three kinds of possible similarities between languages: **genetic** (e.g. amongst the Romance languages), **typological** (e.g. Turkish, Japanese and Quechua), and **areal** (e.g. the languages spoken in the Balkan). An area where languages show similarities because of a history of shared contact is called a **Sprachbund**.

Languages with genetic similarities are part of a **language family**: they have a common ancestor. The method of **comparative reconstruction** is used to recover former phases of a language: **proto-forms** and **proto-languages** can be derived through **sound laws**. There are a number of large language families in the world, such as the Indo-European language family. There are also isolated languages, like Basque, that appear to form a language family of their own. Information about language families can be gathered through fieldwork, through the study of written sources, and from place names and surnames. This last sub-discipline, also known as **toponymics**, can, for example, shed light on the geographical distribution of a language like Basque.

The last part of this chapter is concerned with the relation between language and **culture**, that is, between a language and the total set of norms and values of a particular society. By way of example, we looked into the system of kinship and colour terms, and what these can tell us about the **Sapir-Whorf Hypothesis**, which postulates a strongly determining influence of language on thought.

ASSIGNMENTS

1. Identify five grammatical similarities between English and another language that you know well. Then try to identify five differences in grammar between the two languages.
2. Consider the following two groups of three words in Frisian, Dutch and English, with the pronunciation given between square brackets. What regularity can you observe?

Frisian	*Dutch*	*English*
dyk [dik]	dijk [dɛik]	dike [daɪk]
wyn [vin]	wijn [ʋɛin]	wine [waɪn]

3. In an experiment, German and English adults were asked to assign a name to a set of toys, some representing animals and others objects. The toys were all characters in a children's story. The adults were then asked to say whether the character was male or female. Thus a clock (*die Uhr*, feminine gender in German) was made into a female character 80% of the time by the German subjects compared to only 8% in the English subjects; the ball (*der Ball*, masculine gender in German) was male 84% of the time for the German subjects and 71% for the English subjects. The German adults were strongly influenced by the grammatical gender of the noun in German. The

English subjects showed a general tendency to make the characters male. Discuss how these findings relate to the Sapir-Whorf hypothesis.

4. Give three examples of differences in vocabulary between English and another language you know well, where you think that the lexical difference reflects a cultural difference. Describe as precisely as possible the cultural differences involved.
5. In the following letter to the editor of a national newspaper the journalist who had written a previously published article is criticised for his choice of words:

   'In the article "Former group leader of mentally handicapped convicted of indecent assault", the people living in this institution are referred to as "patients". By using this term you unnecessarily evoke an incorrect and negative image of the mentally handicapped. It would have been better to speak of "inhabitants".'

   Which view of the relationship between language and thought underlies the claims in this letter?
6. In the Native American Indian Language, Yuchi, there is a distinction between verb forms used by men and by women. What might you conclude from this about the relationship between language and culture?

Test Yourself

1. Name the three different possible explanations for similarities between languages.
2. What is the difference between comparative and internal reconstruction?
3. What is a proto-form?
4. What is a sound law?
5. Can all differences between languages be reduced to cultural differences?
6. What claim does the Sapir-Whorf Hypothesis make about the relationship of language to thought?

Acknowledgments and Further Reading

Introductions to language typology are available in Comrie (1989) and Croft (1993). Thomason & Kaufmann (1988) present a study of areal features and Sprachbund-phenomena. For an introduction to the comparative-historical study of Indo-European languages see Beekes (1995). The data from the missionary grammar on Damascan Arabic by Cauallero are discussed in

Zwartjes (2007). In Foley (1997) we find an extensive discussion of the cultural dimension of language. Wardhaugh (1986) contains a thorough review of the Sapir-Whorf Hypothesis. Everett (2008) and Deutscher (2011) provide a very readable discussion of many of the language-culture issues. The quote from Sapir comes from Sapir (1929). Colour terms have been investigated by Berlin & Kay (1969). Reports of research into non-western communities regularly appear in the journal *Anthropological Linguistics*. A discussion of the evolution of speech is taken from Martínez *et al.* (2008). The example from Hawaiian is taken from Elbert & Pukui (1979). The information on Tzeltal is taken from Stross (1974), on Subanun from Frake (1964). The gender experiment is taken from Mills (1985). The discussion of Yuchi comes from Abley (2003), a very accessible book on endangered languages.

chapter 18

Language Variation

18.1 Introduction

In this book we have often used expressions such as 'English', 'Farsi' and 'Turkish', terms which suggest that languages can be precisely defined and that they are homogeneous units. But is this really the case? Take for example the texts in (1).

English
(1) a. Ye ar the licht o the warld. A toun biggit on a hill-tap canna be hoddit.
    b. You are the light of the world. A city set on a hill cannot be hidden.
    c. Ye are the light of the world. A city that is set on an hill cannot be hid.

We can recognise (1b) as being what we might call Standard English. But (1a) and (1c) are different. (1c) is the same Bible verse but in the King James version, reflecting English of the seventeenth century. (1a) is a modern-day translation into Scots English. Languages, as we have repeatedly seen in this book, do not only differ from one another; we also find differences within one language. Languages change over time and those differences will be the topic of the following chapter. Languages also differ at any one point in time and we then talk of **language variation**.

Linguistics, First Edition. Edited by Anne E. Baker and Kees Hengeveld.

In this chapter we will discuss this variation. However, before we do this, we will first, in Section 18.2, discuss the question of what constitutes a language. What criteria do we use? The next question is how we can define and delineate dialects such as Scots English in (1a). This question will be discussed in Section 18.3.

Variation occurs in every language. What language variation is and how it is studied will be explained in Section 18.4. Language variation is to be found everywhere, but this does not mean that people's language use is totally arbitrary. Whether people say *daddy* or *da* for 'father' depends on the region they come from or where they live. Equally, people from a lower social class are more likely to say *innit?* than people from a higher social class who usually say *isn't it?* In other words, language variation can be related to the origin or social position of speakers; this relationship will be discussed in Section 18.5. The particular choice of language forms by speakers is, however, not only dependent on their (social) background but also on the situation in which language is used. This point will be further discussed in Section 18.6. A speaker who says *Yo look at my new car innit!* is often judged differently from a speaker who says *Just look at my new car!* Different language forms are subject to different (social) evaluations, and this social meaning of language variation will be discussed in the closing section of this chapter (Section 18.7).

Language variation is studied within the subfield of linguistics called **sociolinguistics**, which is concerned with the relationship between language and a variety of social factors. On the one hand the influence of social factors on language and language use is important, but equally important is the influence of language on society.

18.2 What is a Language?

Compare the following two sentences, in Danish (2) and in Norwegian (3).

Danish
(2) Jeg vil ikke have det
I want not have that
'I don't want to have that.'

Norwegian (Bokmål)
(3) Jeg vil ikke ha det
I want not have that
'I don't want to have that.'

There is very little difference between the two; people who speak Danish will not have much difficulty with the Norwegian, and vice versa. Yet nobody assumes officially that we are talking about one language here which we might call DaNo, with one 'Danish dialect' and another 'Norwegian dialect'. Norway does in fact have two standard languages, Bokmål and Nynorsk – a situation that arose in 1814, when centuries of Danish rule over Norway came to an end. Bokmål can be considered to be Norwegian with a strong Danish element. Nevertheless, it remains officially a separate language within Norway.

The differences between Danish and Norwegian are relatively small, and in any case a lot smaller than those between Scots English and, for example, New York City English. In contrast to Danish and Norwegian, however, Scots English and New York City English are, in fact, considered to be two dialects of one language, English. This has partly to do with the fact that the speakers of these dialects themselves feel they are speaking a form of English. In different situations speakers may move in the direction of the standard language, for example when they are seeing their doctor. A New York City speaker would then move towards Standard American English; a Scots English speaker more towards Standard British English.

Another example of large differences within one language comes from Sranan, the creole language of Surinam. Examples (4), (5) and (6) show the different forms of the relative clause *with whom I am going to the cinema* attached to the noun *man*.

Sranan

(4)	a	man	[di	mi	go	luku	a	kino	nanga]
	the	man	[*rel. pronoun*	I	go	look	the	cinema	with]
(5)	a	man	[di	mi	go	luku	a	kino	nanga en]
	the	man	[*rel. pronoun*	I	go	look	the	cinema	with him]
(6)	a	man	[nanga suma	mi	go	luku	a	kino]	
	the	man	[with *rel. pronoun*	I	go	look	the	cinema]	

'The man with whom I am going to the cinema.'

In (4) the bare preposition *nanga* 'with' occupies the last position in the sentence; in (5) this preposition is followed by a pronoun: *nanga en* 'with him'; in (6) we find the preposition, together with a pronoun, at the beginning of the relative clause: *nanga suma* 'with whom'. Despite these grammatical differences, Sranan – in contrast to Danish and Norwegian – is considered to be one single language.

In the discussion about what is or is not one language, Hindi and Urdu, two important languages of India and Pakistan, serve as a good example. The two languages are very similar, they are mutually intelligible, and some linguists actually refer to 'Hindi–Urdu' when they are discussing the properties of this language/these languages. Yet without doubt many people in India see these two languages as different, because Hindi, which is written in the Devanagari script, is linked with the Hindu religion, whereas Urdu, which is written in Persian script, is the language of Islamic people. Religion is also the main cause of the differences between the two languages, for, unlike Hindi, Urdu has borrowed quite a few words from Arabic.

When deciding what constitutes a language or what differentiates two languages, we do not really rely on linguistic arguments such as the number of linguistic differences between them or the size of these differences. Of far greater importance are non-linguistic arguments such as the judgment and behaviour of speakers, or the political situation in the area. In fact, a definition of a language has been proffered that makes the political element very clear: a language is a dialect with an army. In Europe, for example, the fact that from the seventeenth century onwards certain dialects have been adopted as the national languages of the various European states, has definitely had consequences for those languages: within these states we find linguistic unification and standardisation, and at their borders we find more sharply defined linguistic transitions. Some countries, on the other hand, have very many languages and dialects. An extreme example is India, with more than 1500 language varieties; this raises in turn many political and social issues such as the choice of the language of education.

18.3 What is a Dialect?

So far the notion of **dialect** has been used to refer to forms of language used in certain areas or communities. It would be easy if a language could be divided into a number of dialects. In Britain, for example, where we find the dialects of Scottish English, Lancashire, Welsh English, Cornish, etc., the English language would then be the sum total of all these dialects. But is it clear what constitutes a dialect? Within Lancashire in Britain, for example, there is also variation: in Wigan the word *moggy* means 'a small mouse' or 'insect' but in other parts of Lancashire it means 'cat'. Pronunciation varies also. So, dialects themselves are not homogeneous either. Within what is considered a dialect, we find, yet again, variation.

Furthermore, it is impossible to determine exactly which language forms belong to a certain dialect and which do not. Should all speakers of a particular dialect actually use the language form in question? The question can be put more precisely when we take a look at Texas. Some people who are considered to be speakers of Southern American English will say *snap bean* instead of *green bean*. Is using *snap bean* a feature of the Southern American dialect? Can we establish a series of features that define this dialect? The answer is no, because there are people in Texas who do not pronounce the /r/ in *forty* (unlike other American dialects that do pronounce it), but who do not say *snap bean*. It would not make much sense to say that these people do not speak the Southern American dialect. In addition, we find that individual speakers are often not consistent in their use of a particular language form. For example, in Dorset in Britain speakers can use special forms of the verb *to be*: *he be*, *I be* and *thee bist*. But they do not always use these forms.

The more we look into these problems – all to do with defining what is a dialect – the more the definition seems to elude us. What are we to do if we cannot even give a proper definition of the notion 'dialect'? Does this mean that anyone can actually say anything, and there is no real system in all this variation? Such a negative conclusion would go too far. Our discussion of the notion of 'dialect' has thrown up a number of phenomena that have to do with the fact that language communities are not homogeneous but heterogeneous, and it is these phenomena that will be discussed in this chapter. Though it may be difficult to define, we can still use the term 'dialect' as a practical notion for the study of certain kinds of variation in a language community. We use it, first of all, for regional variation, as for example when we speak of the dialects of regions such as Lancashire or Dorset in Britain or of cities such as New York or London. But language variation is a much broader phenomenon. A particular feature may occur in the speech of all kinds of speakers, regardless of where they come from. An example is sentence (7).

(7) Me and him have bought that car I told you about.

The forms *me* and *him* used here are an alternative for the more standard forms *I* and *he* in subject position. The variation between *me* and *I*, *him* and *he* is not regional, and so not part of a dialect. For the description of all kinds of variation we will use the notion of **language variety**. Dialects are then a regional variety. In Section 18.5 we will further discuss different types of language variety.

Language varieties can be different on different linguistic levels, such as sounds, words and word formation (see Section 18.4). Some forms of language use can be distinguished solely on the basis of differences in pronunciation. For example, we can say that someone speaks English with an Australian or Indian accent. The different sounds mark that person's regional origin, but otherwise they share the same grammatical and lexical features in their speech. For this kind of variety we use the notion **accent**.

Before we go into more detail on the kinds of variety that may exist in a language community, we should first mention the difference between standard and non-standard language. Many languages in the world have a standard form, that is a form that has been described or recorded in a grammar and a dictionary, as we discussed in Section 1.6 and Section 11.7. This allows us to speak, for example, of Standard British English. But it is quite possible to see the standard itself as one of the many varieties of a particular language. Standard British English, for example, is based on the dialect of the South East, in particular London, as a result of the influence of the royal court and governmental power.

People sometimes believe that a standard language is central and that dialects are derived from it. This is incorrect. It is, however, the case that non-standard varieties often have lower prestige. Often, the standard language is associated with social success and progress, and this may result in a negative attitude towards dialects, as if these are not quite good enough. But just as languages are equal, so are language varieties: the standard is no more (or less) complex than other dialects. The difference in status is due not to linguistic but social factors. We will say more about this in Section 18.6.

Our final question here is when or how a particular dialect can become a language. In Section 18.2 we stated that it is impossible to decide what is a language solely on the basis of linguistic criteria. The same argument applies to dialects. Speakers of a variety sometimes want to see its status raised to that of a 'language'. Kven, which is spoken in Northern Norway, has acquired this status, just as have Catalan in Spain and Limburgian in the Netherlands, but Occitan in France failed in its attempt to get recognition. In Europe these have been political decisions under the European Charter for Regional or Minority Languages of 1998, which applies the following criteria to a language variety for it to be recognised as a language. The variety should:

- have gone through a development of its own;
- be sufficiently different from the standard language;
- have the social and cultural support of a broad group of people.

It is clear that these criteria are exceedingly vague, and that it is a matter of opinion as to when you can say that a language variety is 'sufficiently different' or has gone through a 'development of its own'. Interestingly, this Charter forgot to include sign languages for official recognition

18.4 The Study of Language Variation

Almost all native speakers of any language know that they do not always speak the same variant of the language as other people. Some German speakers say the word *strand* 'beach' pronouncing the first sound as a [ʃ] as in English *sugar*, other speakers of German say [s]. These options are called **(language-) variants**, and together they constitute the **linguistic variable** that we could give the name 'alveolar fricatives in clusters'. Speakers of German may say [s]trand or [ʃ]trand, [s]piel or [ʃ]piel, etc. We can investigate what factors are involved in the choice between these variants. In the last section we saw that dialects are often hard to delimit. For that reason the study of variation in a language community is often focused on specific language forms that vary in actual usage, that is, on linguistic variables.

Yet another example is that in (8), taken from Italian: compare the paradigms of the verb *mangiare* 'to eat' in the Abruzzese dialect of Italian and Standard Italian.

Italian

(8) Abruzzese		Standard Italian		
magne	/maɲə/	mangio	/mand͡ʒo/	'I eat'
magne	/maɲə/	mangi	/mand͡ʒi/	'you (sing.) eat'
magne	/maɲə/	mangia	/mand͡ʒa/	'he/she eats'
magneme	/maɲamə/	mangiamo	/mand͡ʒamo/	'we eat'
magnete	/maɲatə/	mangiate	/mand͡ʒate/	'you (pl.) eat'
magnano	/maɲanə/	mangiano	/mand͡ʒano/	'they eat'

As we see here, a linguistic variable is a linguistic unit that can be expressed quite differently by its variants. This variable is phonological.

Another example of language variation is given in (9). What is the difference between the pairs of sentences in (9a) and (9b)? What is the linguistic variable in this case?

(9) a. They ask him yesterday
They asked him yesterday
b. He move last week.
He moved last week.

Here we see that the past tense of the verb is not marked explicitly in the first of each pair of sentences (stem+ Ø) and in the second sentence it is (stem+/d/). The second sentences are from Standard English and the first from a London dialect. The linguistic variable here is the 'past tense'. This variable is taken from the area of morphology, in contrast to the two previous examples, which were taken from phonology.

What can we see in (10)?

(10) a. One swallow does not a summer make.
b. One swallow does not make a summer.

The difference here is in the word order. The variable is 'the relative order of the object and main verb'. The two variants are: (10a) with the main verb in final position after the object, and (10b) with the main verb before the object. The order in (10a) is stylistically marked, being more poetic in nature.

In the case of the pronunciation of German we talked about the variable 'alveolar fricatives in clusters'. This is not to say, however, that everyone should really be using a [ʃ], and that the other forms are deviant. This would mean that the standard language is the starting point for describing all other varieties. Likewise, it would be incorrect to say that the verb form in the second sentences in (9) is correct or that the word order of (10b) is the right one. It is merely the norm of the standard language. The labels we use for a particular linguistic variable should really be neutral with respect to the variants involved, although this may sometimes be hard to achieve. The key point here is that in the study of language variation no single variant is 'better' than another; the investigation is not prescriptive or normative but descriptive in character (see also Section 1.6 for these notions).

We have given examples of **phonological**, **morphological** and **syntactic variation**, in that order, that is to say, variation at the level of pronunciation, word formation and sentence structure. Is there variation at other linguistic levels too? There is, of course, **lexical variation**, when two or more different words refer to the same object. In British English, for example, *pavement* is used but in American English the equivalent is *sidewalk* or *walkway*. In Canadian French *noirceur* 'darkness' is used where Standard French uses *obscurité*. Arabic has many different variants for the concept NOTHING as in shown in (11).

Arabic

(11)	Moroccan	wálu	'nothing'
	Libyan	kān lbarka	'nothing'
	Algerian	ši	'nothing'
	Tunisian	šay	'nothing'

In the domain of body parts, for example, we find in English the standard form *head*, but also *noodle*, *bean*, *pate* or *block*. As well as the standard *hand*, *mitt* or *paw* are also used. These are all stylistic variants. Taboo words, especially in the domain of sexuality, may also have a wide range of variants.

Lexical variation refers to different forms used for the same concept. There is also **semantic variation**, when the same word is used in different language varieties to refer to (partially) different concepts. In Standard German *schmecken* means 'taste' but in Southern German dialects it also means 'smell'. In Russian the verb *guljat'* means 'to go for a walk' but in South Russian dialects that meaning changes to 'to play'. In Westfrisian Dutch the verb *kreuken* not only means 'to crumple', as in other dialects, but also, surprisingly, 'to fold neatly'.

Finally, there is **pragmatic variation**. In English, there are great differences in the way people answer the phone, ranging from *This is 360013* or *This is Catherine Brown speaking* to just *Hallo!* or *Yes?*. The first two examples are both more formal than the second two. This is related to the notion of pragmatic appropriateness discussed in Section 5.4. Certain language forms may be appropriate in one situation but not in another. At the end of a job interview, for instance, it is not advisable for the applicant to say *Cheerio then* or *Seeya*.

In general, variation in a language community occurs most prominently on the phonological and lexical levels. It is at these levels in particular that dialects differ from each other. Very often, different forms of variation occur together in a single utterance. In Yorkshire a child may put the question in (12) to another child.

(12) [kʊmɪŋaʊtəlɑːk] coming out to lark?
'(Are you) coming out to play?'

In this example, we can see:

- pragmatic variation: an informal question that would only be addressed to a peer;
- lexical variation: *lark* for *play*;
- phonological variation: /kʊmɪŋ/ for /kʌmɪŋ/; and
- syntactic variation: the auxiliary is not used.

18.5 Language Variation and Social Factors

So far we have established that in any language there are many variants. This could lead us to think of language as a huge sack containing all kinds of elements from which people just pick and choose what they need. The use of certain variants would then be purely coincidental. But is this really the case? Do people just say whatever they like? Do they choose [kʊmɪngaʊtəlɑrk] or *coming out to play?* without following any clear system? This does not appear to be the case. Some people clearly use one variant more often than others; other people may have different preferences. The pronunciation of *strand* 'beach' in German with a [s] does not occur in the speech of a Southern German speaker, only in the speech of someone from the North. Someone from a lower class background is more likely to say *block* for *head*, whereas a language user from a higher social class will use more standard variants.

Why are there so many differences within a language community? What is at the root of all this variation? The origin as well as the perpetuation of variation within a language community lies in the social differences in that community. People tend to express these differences in many ways, for example through clothing but also in speech. They can wear jeans or a suit, just as they can say either *Me and Anita* or *Anita and I*. In both cases they signal which group in society they belong to or want to belong to. Interestingly, research has shown that children will choose to play with other children who speak the same way rather than to play with other children who look the same. The choice of a certain language variant is probably less conscious, though, than the choice of a clothing style.

The distribution of language variants across a society can be related to all kinds of social factors. In general, you can say that the study of language variation concentrates on the following social factors: region, socio-economic class, ethnic group, sex and age. In Sections 18.5.1 to 18.5.5 we will discuss these five factors.

18.5.1 Region

The investigation of language variation has traditionally been the domain of dialectologists. They study **regional varieties** or dialects and focus in particular on the geographical distribution of language variation. Dialectologists are especially interested in language forms that deviate from the standard language. We may roughly distinguish two kinds of traditional dialect research: (a) dialect description, and (b) dialect geography.

When dialectologists want to describe a dialect, they investigate the special features of that particular dialect. In several dialects of the North of England, for example, there is a different rule for the inflection of the present tense in the verb. Very generally, the rule for Northern varieties states that every person of the verb in the present tense can take an *-s* ending, unless it is directly adjacent to a personal pronoun. In (13) we see the Standard English form and the Northern dialect form.

(13)	Standard English	Northern varieties
	a. John and I say...	Me and John says...
	b. They think and strongly believe	They think and strongly believes

Through fieldwork, the frequency of occurrence of the form being studied can be plotted on a map as in Figure 18.1. Here we see that the most occurrences of the Northern variety were found in the middle part of Northern England. It is the general goal of dialect geography to produce a linguistic map of a certain area. The investigation focuses on the geographical distribution of variants, and the results are displayed in detail on a map, as in Figure 18.1. The feature at issue here is a verb inflection, so we are looking at a morphological variable.

Dialectologists can produce their maps in a different way, namely by drawing boundaries on the basis of the frequencies in the map. Such a boundary between areas is called an **isogloss**. Isoglosses show the division between areas where a particular pronunciation, form or construction occurs and does not or rarely occurs. In British English, we find isoglosses for the pronunciation of certain vowels and these are shown in Figure 18.2 (for England only). The black circles indicate a pronunciation of /ʌ/ and the crosses a pronunciation of /ʊ/. The isogloss for the /ʌ/ vs /ʊ/ distinction is then constructed and indicated in the figure by the solid line. It runs horizontally across England.

Isoglosses can also be drawn for lexical variables. In Poland, for example, the expressions *na polu* and *na dworze* vary in meaning. In the North of Poland *na polu* means 'in the field' but in the South and South Eastern regions it also means 'outside'. Conversely, *na dworze* means 'outside' and 'in the yard' in the North, but only 'in the yard' in the South and South East.

Regional dialect variation can also be found in sign languages. Research on American Sign Language (ASL) has found lexical variation, and the same is the case for British Sign Language (BSL). Australian Sign Language (Auslan)

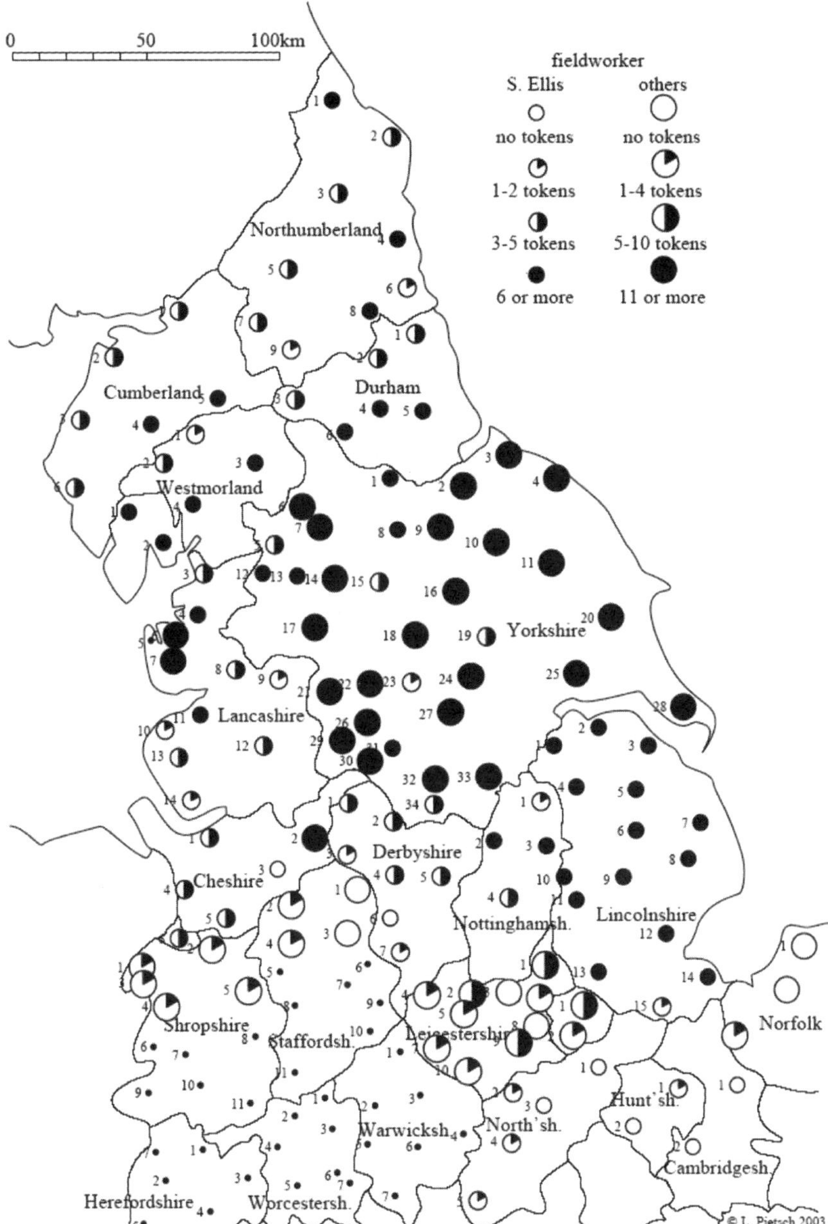

Figure 18.1 The generalised occurrence of the use of *-s* in the present tense in the English of England. Pietsch, L. (2005) Some do and some doesn't: verbal concord variation in the north of the British Isles, in Kortmann, B., Herrmann, T., Pietsch, L. and Wagner, S. (eds) *A Comparative Grammar of British English Dialects: Agreement, Gender, Relative Clauses* (Topics in English Linguistics, 50.1), Berlin & New York: Mouton de Gruyter, pp. 125–209.

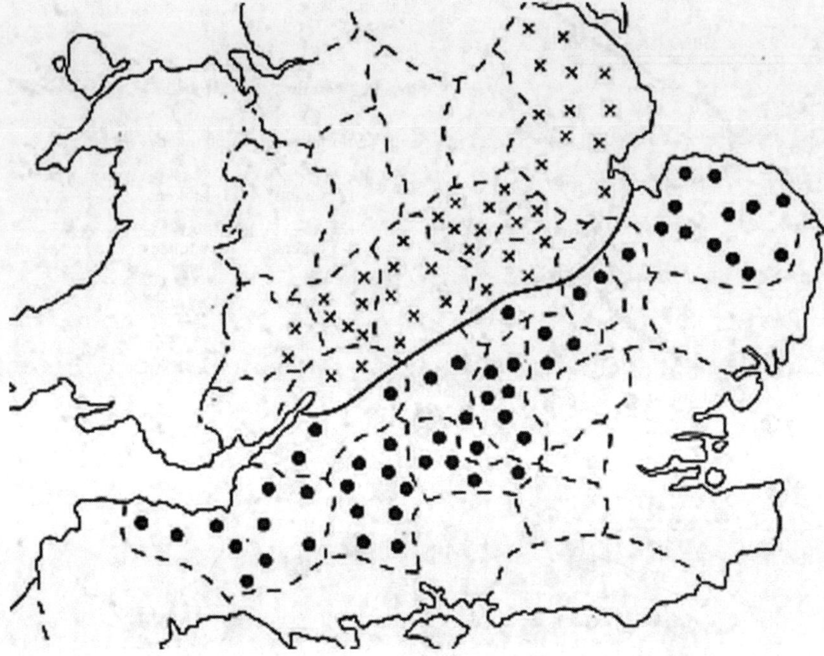

Figure 18.2 The isogloss indicating the phonological variables Southern /ʌ/ vs the Northern /u/ (solid line). The circles indicate /ʌ/ and the crosses /ʊ/. Laver, J., (1994) *Principles of Phonetics*, Cambridge: Cambridge University Press.

is historically derived from British Sign Language and some would argue that it is a dialect of BSL. The Swadesh list introduced in Section 11.10 shows quite a percentage of overlap in the signs from BSL and Auslan.

Dialect research usually gives a pretty good idea of the range of variants of language that are used. But it often does not tell us about the type of speakers who frequently use a particular variant. But then, that is invariably not the aim of this kind of investigation. The particular variant people use often turns out to be strongly dependent on the social class to which they belong.

18.5.2 Social Class

In Section 18.4 we mentioned that not all speakers in an area will use the local dialect, even if they were born and bred there. This has to do with social class. Differences in language may reflect differences in region and origin, but they may also express differences in social class. In general, the speech of manual workers is different from that of academics; the two groups use different language forms. In other words, we can distinguish different social varieties of language. These are called **sociolects**. Often dialect research includes the study

Table 18.1 Scores for the variable 'verbal morpheme -*ing*' across five social groups in Norwich (Britain)

Low 1	98
Low 2	88
Middle 1	74
Middle 2	15
High	3

of social factors. Here we move into the field of socio-dialectology, where researchers study the social distribution of language variants, in this case regional variants. The aim is not to give a complete description of the dialects in question, be it Swabian (German), Yorkshire (British English) or Moroccan (Arabic). The question is rather: Who uses a particular Yorkshire variant (such as the /ʊ/ in *cup*), under which circumstances and how often?

An example that has been well studied is the pronunciation of the suffix -*ing* in present participles such as *talking* and *writing* in the city of Norwich. The variable 'verbal morpheme -*ing*' has two variant pronunciations of the final consonant: the standard form [ɪŋ], as in *talking*, and the non-standard form [ɪn] as in *talkin'*. In the Norwich investigation a numerical score of 100 was given to someone who consistently used the non-standard form in a number of different tasks, and a score of 0 to someone who consistently used the standard form. Table 18.1 gives the actual scores for the five social groups that were distinguished in this project, indicated here as Low-1, Low-2, Middle-1, Middle-2 and High.

As we see here, again, certain variants are not used exclusively by certain groups. In other words, it is not the case that a variant like [ɪn] only occurs in the speech of the lower social classes in Norwich. Even the highest social group still has a score of 3. So, both variants occur in all social classes, but not at the same rate: the higher the social class, the less likely the speaker is to use the non-standard form. Thus, there is only a difference of degree between the sociolects; the difference is not absolute.

Differences of this type occur in many languages and in all aspects of language. So, for example, in Russian the verb *čujat'* means 'to smell (of animals)' for speakers of the middle social groups, but in lower groups it means 'to feel' and in even lower social groups 'to understand'.

Using the neuro-imaging techniques we discussed in Section 2.3, experiments have been carried out that show the effect of sociolect. Speakers with upper class voices and lower class voices, that is, voices reflecting these sociolects, were asked to produce specific sentences. These sentences were played to other speakers and their brain activity was then measured. The content of some sentences was perceived as not matching the social class of the speaker. For example, the sentence *I have a large tattoo on my back* spoken in an upper class sociolect was perceived as inappropriate. This shows how features of a sociolect are used by listeners to immediately place someone in a social class and that this perception can in turn affect the perception of the content.

18.5.3 *Ethnic Group*

Many people with African ancestry living in the United States speak a kind of American English that deviates from Standard American English as well as from other social and regional dialects. Speakers often express their allegiance to a particular ethnic group through their use of language. They use an **ethnic variety** or **ethnolect**, such as Black English in the United States, Indian English spoken in India and Britain, or Surinamese Dutch spoken in Suriname and the Netherlands. Next to social class we can thus identify 'ethnic group' as a factor involved in language variation. Interest in this ethnic factor increased in the sixties, when there were fiery debates in the United States on the question whether Black English was 'correct' or perhaps a reduced, bastardised form of the standard language. This debate was triggered in particular by the disappointing achievements of black children in education. Further investigation has made it clear that the variety in question, which is now often referred to as African American Vernacular English (AAVE), should have the same linguistic status as other dialects. AAVE is an ethnic variety in which there are variants on all different linguistic levels. For example, double negation is often used, as in *He ain't got no book*. This has been criticised as an illogical form of language use, but linguistically this is not the case. Double negation is one way of expressing negation. It is a normal phenomenon in all kinds of language varieties, both standard and non-standard.

For variants that are typical of the language of ethnic groups we find, again, that members of the group do not always produce that variant, nor does every member of the group use the variant. Asian speakers of English, in particular those from India and Pakistan, use the tag question *innit?* in a way that Standard British English does not, as in *we need to decide about that now innit?*. More educated speakers within this group use this variant far less often. A Surinamese–Dutch variant consists of using [w] instead of [ʋ], and it is often used to typify, stereotype or parody the language use of Surinamese people in the Netherlands. This feature is used much less by Surinamese people in the Netherlands who have had a high level of education.

18.5.4 *Age*

Another factor that can influence linguistic differences in a particular community is age. Older people often speak in a way that is different from the younger generation. Age differences may reflect an ongoing process of language change (see Chapter 19), but they may also just be age-related forms of language behaviour. Lexical differences are very common here. Some words may be age-related, such as the English expression *cool* for all kinds of superlative properties or situations in the 1960s. In modern Russian young people use the verb *zadrat'* to mean 'to rip apart' whereas for older people it means 'to lift up'. Young people regularly introduce new, fashionable words. Some gain linguistic currency when they are adopted by an increasing number of speakers, young and old, as has in fact happened with *cool*. Other new words are only used for a short time. Youth movements like hip hop spawn many new words such as *crunk* 'to act naturally' or even morphological formations such as the addition of *-izzle* in *faw shizzle* 'for sure'. Words or processes like these are likely to disappear again from the vocabulary of young people, but time will tell.

Differences between the language of the older and younger generation occur at different linguistic levels, not only in the lexicon. As mentioned in Section 18.5.3, young people in Britain are more likely to say *innit?* than older people and the use of this tag is becoming more common amongst young people outside the Asian groups. Conversely, in Surinamese Dutch, [w] is used much more by older people than by younger speakers. In Chapter 19 we will come back to differences in language use between older and younger people, and address the question of young people introducing new variants that may, later on, come into general use in the language community as a whole. What is then their contribution to language change?

18.5.5 Gender

The last social factor we discuss here is that of gender. The speech of women and men may at times be different. Some general trends have been found:

- in pronunciation: women often speak slightly more 'correctly' than men;
- in vocabulary: some words in youth language are more used by boys than girls;
- in conversation or speaking behaviour: in contrast to men, women seem to be cooperative rather than interruptive.

In sociolinguistic research, the term 'gender' is used since it is a social variable, whereas sex is a biological variable. When women and men speak differently, this is often not because of biology but because of their different role and position in society. In a study of American male and female psychotherapists talking to clients, for example, the female clients were interrupted three times more often by both male and female therapists than the male clients. Women in the role of client seem to have a lower status than men in the same role.

In some languages there are clear gender differences in the lexicon and other areas of language. In Japanese, for example, the first person pronoun *watashi*

Table 18.2 Scores for the variable 'verbal morpheme *-ing* of men and women in Norwich (Britain). A higher score means a more frequent use of the non-standard variant

Class	Women	Men
Low 1	97	100
Low 2	81	91
Middle 1	68	81
Middle 2	3	27
High	0	4

is a polite form and also used far more by women. Men use the second person pronoun *kimi* far more than women do; women choose other forms. In general women use more polite forms than men in their language. In Koasati, a Muskogean language spoken in Louisiana, words ending in /s/ when pronounced by men are pronounced with an /l/ or /n/ by women. Such gender differences pose an interesting problem for young boys who are exposed mainly to the input of their mothers. How do they learn the 'men's speech'?

In western societies these differences in language use between men and women are usually of a gradual nature and not absolute. In the Norwich study of the *-ing* variable, which we mentioned in Section 18.5.2, the results from the various social classes have also been differentiated according to gender, as we see in Table 18.2.

What can Table 18.2 tell us about differences between men and women? First of all, we see in both groups a gradual decrease in the use of non-standard variants from the lower social class to the higher level. Secondly, we notice that in each social class, men realise the non-standard variant more frequently than women. In other words, men across all social classes adhere less to the norm than women. This has also been found in sociolinguistic research of other language communities. A possible explanation is the hypothesis that the social dialect of the working class is more often associated with being strongly masculine and that men desire this image.

A good example of a link between the use of a certain non-standard variant and a 'macho' image can be found in a study of language use among teenagers in Sydney (Australia). When the sociolinguistic researcher, who spoke a standard variant of Australian English, was present, both boys and girls would adapt their language use. In that situation, the boys moved towards the non-standard variant (marked in bold face) in (14).

Boys

(14) a. I didn't know what I did . . . what I **done**.

b. We were skating around . . . we **was** skating along.

Girls

(15) a. If you **was**. . .if you were just friends
b. And **me** and Kerry. . .or should I say, Kerry and I.

As (15) illustrates, the girls, unlike the boys, corrected their speech in the direction of the standard variant.

It is not always the case that men prefer the non-standard variant and women the standard variant or the prestige language of a certain community. Their choice of language may depend on the position and status of the two sexes in their community. For example, in South Africa, Thonga women more often speak Thonga than the prestige language, Zulu, and when they speak Zulu they deliberately speak it badly. The men in this society, on the other hand, more often use Zulu than Thonga. This difference in language use can be explained by looking at the different position of women and men in society. In Thonga society women have high status and a strong position, so for them, speaking Zulu is not of great importance. On the contrary, by deliberately speaking it badly, they are rebelling against Zulu domination. But the men do have a practical interest in speaking Zulu, because it may help them to get a job in the city or in the mines.

18.6 Other Factors: Situation and Linguistic Context

In Section 18.5 we briefly discussed five social factors that may influence language variation. These five are speaker related. But we have also noted that speakers, even in the same circumstances, do not always use the same variants. Speakers can choose what to say, depending on the situation. The way speakers express what group they belong to may be different from one conversation to the next. The Yorkshireman who usually says [kʊmɪn] may well say [kʌmɪŋ] when he is in the town hall. That is, in addition to the five speaker-related factors of the preceding section, we can identify a range of so-called **situational factors** that influence the choice of a particular variant of a linguistic variable. One of these situational factors is 'topic of conversation'. When a speaker relates how she quarrelled with a car driver who almost knocked her down, her use of language is likely to be different from that used to discuss an academic subject. Another important factor is the 'addressee' or more precisely the 'relationship between speaker and addressee'. You speak differently to a good friend than to a stranger, especially when this person has a higher social position.

In sociolinguistic research these situational factors are often taken together. But, as we saw in Section 5.4, we can distinguish a range of conversational situations, from highly informal to extremely formal. These situations are then linked up with a specific style, again ranging from informal to formal. Note that this sociolinguistic notion of style is different from that of literary studies.

Sociolinguistic style is not to do with the characteristic use of language of a particular person, but with a way of speaking that is appropriate to a certain situation. To determine which particular style is being used, you look at the frequency of occurrence of the various language variants: if *me and Anita* and other non-standard variants occur frequently, the style is labelled informal. Conversely, if *Anita and I* and other standard variants have a higher frequency, the style is formal.

The more formal the situation, the more frequent the use of standard variants, and this holds true for all language users from all social classes – as long as they have had an opportunity to learn these, of course, for example through education. That is, we are looking here at general differences of style. As we saw in the Norwich investigation of the *-ing* variable, in the most formal situation (reading out a text) the speakers of the lowest social group produced almost the same number of standard variants as the speakers from the highest social group did in the most informal situation (a casual conversation). A result like this emphasises again that the differences in language use between social groups is not absolute, but only gradual.

Sometimes a particular text can be 'placed' immediately; we can tell which context it would fit into. Consider the texts in (16).

(16) a. Gallas to Eduardo. He's got a chance. Eduardo. Yes! Yes! Hit the crossbar and bounced back.

b. First you need to peel, chop and core the apples. Rub together the flour and butter until they have a breadcrumb consistency, then mix in the granulated sugar. Put the apples in a dish and sprinkle the mixed fruit and dark brown sugar over them.

c. Whoever in interstate or foreign communications by means of a telecommunications device knowingly makes, creates, or solicits, and initiates the transmission of any comment, request, suggestion, proposal, image, or other communication which is obscene, lewd, lascivious, filthy, or indecent, with intent to annoy, abuse, threaten, or harass another person . . .

Most speakers of English will be able to say what sort of context the texts in (16) belong to. The syntax, the topic, the words used – and also the intonation if you hear the words spoken – all clearly mark (16a) as part of a soccer report on the radio. Example (16b) has a high usage of the imperative form and specialised vocabulary that indicates it is part of a cooking recipe. The last text (16c) has many variants that mark it as highly formal, probably in written form and probably legal. This kind of language use, where the language belongs to a certain situation and is often associated with a group of speakers, is called a **register**. We find registers in all sorts of professional groupings, such as lawyers, bricklayers, academics, as well as in many other kinds of groups, for example mountaineers, stamp collectors and cycling fanatics. A register is often marked by a terminology of its own, a jargon. When a journalist says that the newspaper is being *wrapped up*, he does not mean that it is being packaged, but only that the current shift will not accept further copy to print. When someone refers to the *pack* of cyclists, he means all the cyclists in the group.

Apart from the social and situational factors we have discussed above, there can also be more strictly linguistic factors that influence language variation. In the study of a Dutch dialect spoken in Leiden it was found that speakers often omit the final *-t* on words where it follows a consonant. However, this deletion is not consistent. The preceding consonant is important – *-t* reduction after /p/ or /f/ ([ko:p] instead of [ko:pt] 'buys', [ho:f] instead of [ho:ft] 'head') was five or six times more frequent than after an /l/ or /n/ ([spe:l] instead of [spe:lt] 'plays', *verwen* instead of *verwent* 'spoils'). These linguistic factors are called the **linguistic context** of a variable.

18.7 Language Variation and Social Meaning

Suppose a university lecturer in Britain addressed a class speaking in a Yorkshire dialect or a public relations manager in the United States addressed a press meeting in a Texan dialect. What would be the reaction of the audience? How would they view this speaker? Would they rate what he was saying just as highly as if his colleague had said the same thing but using a standard variety? This question brings us to the social evaluation of different varieties of language. In principle, variants are different ways of saying the same thing; in other words, variants have the same linguistic meaning. But there is a difference; they are not identical in every respect. It makes a great deal of difference whether a speaker uses a dialect or a standard variety.

People are assessed on the basis of their language use. Differences such as the one between *innit?* and *isn't it?* play an important role here, for they nearly always carry a different **social meaning**. The social meaning is the extra information carried by a particular language form when it is associated with the social status of the speaker. When a speaker says *Me 'n Anita workin' late*, the message is not only that the speaker and Anita are on late shift but also that the speaker comes from the lower social class, as we discussed in Section 18.5.2. Interestingly, the same feature can have two different values. In British English the pronunciation of /r/ after a vowel, as in /kar/ instead of /ka/, is considered non-standard. In American English it is the reverse.

Sometimes you hear people use forms such as *he gave the money to Anita and I*, instead of *to Anita and me.* Some people pronounce a word like *excuse* as *hexcuse*, inserting an initial /h/ where there is none in Standard English. What is behind this variation? This, too, has to do with the social meaning that is assigned to language forms by a particular language community. Why do people say *to Anita and I*? It is commonly known that conjoined forms involving a pronoun should, in subject position, be in subject case. Speakers of non-standard English often use the object form of the pronoun in this context, thus *Anita and me went to the pictures*. When speakers try to avoid seeming to be non-standard they often use the standard form but in all contexts, thus ending up being non-standard again. Dropping the phoneme /h/ in syllable initial position is also seen as non-standard, and is thus sometimes inserted when a word begins with a vowel. Language users are aware of these social meanings, and may not want to be seen as, in their own view, vulgar, or lower class, or uneducated. For this reason they sometimes wrongly exchange a vulgar form with a form that looks more standard, even though it actually is not. This is called **hypercorrection**. There are many examples of this hypercorrection from many languages. In modern Cantonese, for example, the /ŋ-/ sound is often dropped so that [ŋàa] 'tooth' is pronounced [àa]. This pronunciation is regarded as non-standard and so some speakers wrongly insert the [ŋ] where it should not be, as in [ŋǒi] for [ǒi] 'love'. In Bulgarian there is variation between /ja/ and /e/ in specific contexts whereas speakers of western dialects only use /e/. These speakers of western Bulgarian often wrongly use /ja/ when they are trying to be correct, as in *golyami* instead of *golemi* 'big'.

In general, variants in the standard language, that is, the language with the highest social prestige, have the highest status. This was discovered in an American research project where people had to assign certain character traits to speakers on the basis of their speech only. They could not see the speakers. Recordings of American English speech from people of Mexican descent were played. There were two subgroups, one with many non-standard variants in their speech, and another whose speech closely resembled the standard language. Participants in the study were selected from companies in the southern states of the USA. They were asked: how likely do you think it is that the speaker will get a job as a supervisor, a skilled worker or a half-skilled labourer? The results were very clear: the participants thought that the standard speakers were most likely to get the job of supervisor, and non-standard speakers that of half-skilled labourer. These findings are confirmed by many other investigations which show that people are assessed very quickly on the basis of their language use.

The attitude of language users towards a language variety is called a **language attitude**. This attitude is based on the social meaning of language forms associated with a particular social class or group. In the case just discussed, we saw that the attitude towards a particular variety is applied to every individual speaker using that variety. We have attitudes towards varieties of one language, but also towards different languages. Thus, for some people Russian sounds sad, Italian romantic, German authoritarian, American English vulgar, British English upper class, etc. Some languages in a particular community have a higher status than others. As we pointed out in Section 3.4, the attitude towards the language to be learned as a second language is an important predictor of success.

It is not the case that people always take a negative view of non-standard language and variants. How else could those varieties continue to survive? In fact, non-standard varieties often enjoy a **covert prestige**, as an expression of group identity which distinguishes 'us' from 'them' (Section 18.5.5). Speakers will adapt their choice of language variety according to their audience – a union leader addressing his members during a strike may choose different variants than when making a political statement to the media. In Britain a variety of English is emerging, so-called Estuary English, that is a mixture of features of Standard British English and Southern English. It is used by many, even in more formal situations, since it is considered more friendly than the standard variety.

In many countries there is pride in the regional and other varieties of the language that exist. Literature may be published in that variety with a spelling system that reflects the pronunciation of the variety. There is poetry written in Lancashire English, for example, pop songs in Swiss German, plays in the dialects of Southern Italy and so on.

Summary

Languages are not homogeneous entities; differences within a language are called **language variation**. This variation is the subject of the sub-discipline of linguistics known as **sociolinguistics**. An interesting difficulty in this field is how to define clearly what can count as a language and what as a **dialect**. Dialects are, in general terms, the forms of language use that occur in a certain area or community. A more general term for different forms of language use is **language variety**. In addition to dialects there are also, for example, **accents**: language varieties that are defined by pronunciation.

Language variation occurs at every linguistic level. Thus we find **phonological**, **morphological**, **syntactic**, **lexical**, **semantic** and **pragmatic variation**. At all these levels a certain linguistic unit (the **linguistic variable**) can be realised by a range of different **language variants** (or expressions).

Language variation is not arbitrary or unsystematic, but is related to social factors. The best known language varieties are the **regional dialects**, which are separated by **isoglosses**. A great deal of variation is, however, not determined by regional factors. For example, different social classes often use different forms of language; these social varieties are called **sociolects**. Alternatively, language users may speak an **ethnic variety** or **ethnolect** (such as African American Vernacular English), that is, they use variants that are characteristic for a specific ethnic group. A third factor is gender. Men and women sometimes use different varieties, with women often showing a preference for standard forms. A fourth factor is age.

The linguistic forms used by speakers are not only determined by the social factors mentioned above, but also by the speech situation. So, in addition to social factors, **situational factors** play an important role in language variation. Different **styles** and **registers** can be determined by the particular situation in which they are used. Style may depend on the more or less formal character of a speech situation. Registers correlate with specific situations and are used by all kinds of professional and other social groups; they are often characterised by a special jargon. The actual expression of a certain linguistic variable is not only dependent on situational factors, but also on the **linguistic context**.

Language varieties often have a **social meaning** because they are connected with certain groups in society. Because of this social meaning we sometimes find **hypercorrection**. Language varieties are the object of **language attitudes** which usually reflect non-standard forms having a lower status than standard forms. Non-standard forms can, however, enjoy a certain **covert prestige**.

ASSIGNMENTS

1. Take two languages or varieties that you know well. Should they be considered as separate languages or varieties of the same language? Justify your answer.
2. Give examples of variation at the level of phonology, morphology, syntax, lexicon, and pragmatics from a language you know well.
3. Give at least one example of a linguistic variable which has more than two different variants from a language that you know well.
4. Why would factors such as social class or age influence language use and the choice of certain language forms or variants? Consider also that young people continually produce new words or give new meanings to existing words. Why do they do this?
5. What consequences could the emancipation of women have for the linguistic differences between men and women?
6. An analysis of the British Queen's speech to the nation since 1952 has revealed substantial changes in her speech, moving towards the more modern standard variety of English. Which factors do you think have influenced this change?
7. What would you think of a television news presenter who was a heavy dialect speaker? What is the basis for your view?

TEST YOURSELF

1. Do linguistic features determine whether a certain form of language use is called a language?
2. Are dialects homogeneous?
3. What is a linguistic variety?
4. What is the difference between a dialect and an accent?

5. How do variants relate to a linguistic variable?
6. What is the difference between lexical and semantic variation?
7. Which social factors are connected to language variation?
8. Are differences between people from the lower and higher social classes in the realisation of a certain linguistic variant, for example replacing a /t/ with a glottal stop as in [bʌtə] versus [bʌʔə] for *butter*, gradual or absolute?
9. What is a register?
10. What is meant by the social meaning of a linguistic form?

Acknowledgments and Further Reading

Good introductory texts to language variation are Milroy (1987) and Chambers & Trudgill (1980). A more recent handbook contains more detail (Chambers, Trudgill & Schilling-Estes (2004), together with Hudson (1996) and Wardhaugh (1986)). Bergvall, Bing & Freed (1996) offer recent insights concerning language and sex/gender. The examples of correction (by boys and girls) towards, or away from, the standard language come from Eisikovits (1987). The neurolinguistic effects of properties of the speaker were studied by van Berkum *et al.* (2008). The examples from Italian come from D'Alessandro & Alexiadou (2006). The first English dialect map comes from Pietsch (2005), the second from Kortmann & Wagner (2010). The European Charter for Minority Languages (1992) is available on line. Harrington *et al.* (2005) discuss the changes in the British Queen's speech.

chapter 19

Language Change

19.1 Introduction

(1) a. Fæder ure thu the eart on heofonum, si thin nama gehalgod.
    b. Oure fadir that art in heuenes, halewid be thi name.
    c. Our father who art in heaven hallowed be thy name.
    d. Our Father in Heaven, may your name be honoured.

From these versions of the beginning of the Lord's Prayer it is quite clear that the variety of English in (1a) is very different from the modern English in (1d). Versions in (1b) and (1c) are from periods in between. Languages are not, of course, permanent entities. The English language of the twenty-first century is very different from that of four hundred years ago (1c), and even more different than Old English from the year AD 990 (1a) and Middle English from 1380 (1b). English will without any doubt be different again in the twenty-second century.

Language change is the topic of this chapter. In Section 19.2 we will discuss what sort of changes occur in language, and how such changes are analysed within historical linguistics. In the next section, Section 19.3, we discuss the process of change. New language variants do not just suddenly appear. They have a starting point; they may begin in certain social groups and then find their way into the language community at large, as we will explain in more detail in Section 19.4. New variants do not just spread among the language

Linguistics, First Edition. Edited by Anne E. Baker and Kees Hengeveld.

users and the community, but also across the language itself. First they may occur in a restricted number of linguistic contexts, but when the change takes hold, the number of contexts increases steadily. This embedding of changes into the language system is the central theme of Section 19.5. In the previous chapter we saw how different language variants may elicit very different social evaluations. In the same vein we will close this chapter with a discussion of how language change can give rise to very different value judgments (Section 19.6).

19.2 Historical Linguistics

Historical linguistics is the subfield of linguistics in which we aim to describe and analyse changes in language. This entails the registration of earlier stages of the language. What changes are actually possible in language? In example (1) above we already saw that speech sounds in words can change over time. The middle consonant in *fæder* changes from /d/ to /ð/ in *father*. Morphology can also change. The word meaning 'heaven' in (1a) has a suffix *-um* in *heofonum* that has the function of marking case. Such morphological case marking has disappeared in Middle English (1b). The lexicon can change too. For example, the verb *hallow* and its earlier forms meaning 'to make holy or 'to revere' has become restricted in use in Modern English. In fact, language change can occur on every individual linguistic level. Below, we discuss the various kinds of language change in more detail.

When studying language in a historical perspective, it turns out that sound change is not restricted to individual words or isolated forms. It operates across the sound system as a whole. In English the change from /d/ to /ð/ as in *fæder* to *father* was a change that spread through the whole language. It involved not only these consonants but other plosive consonants such that the plosive changed into the equivalent fricative sound: /p/→/f/, and /t/→/θ/. These changes happened not only in English but also in other early Germanic languages. The changes were investigated by Jakob Grimm in the nineteenth century and are known as Grimm's law, an example of a sound law as we discussed in Section 17.3. Dialects often retain older forms, which can partly explain dialect variation, as we saw in Section 18.5.1.

Some changes can cause contrasts between sounds to disappear either totally in the sound system or in certain positions. In some varieties of Russian, for example, the short vowel /e/ and the long /e:/ that were distinct in Old Russian merged to become /e/. In some Germanic languages, such as German, and in some Slavonic languages, such as Russian, Polish, and Czech, the consonant at the end of the word is always voiceless. Thus /d/ at the end of a word is pronounced as a [t], and the /b/ as a [p], etc.

(2) German / Russian

German	Russian
Hund [hunt] 'dog'	mig [mɪk] 'moment'
Polish	**Czech**
rod [rot] 'birth'	lahev [lɑhef] 'bottle'

This is a general process, known as final devoicing, which took place in the languages just mentioned hundreds of years ago. This change has also taken place more recently, for example, in Canadian French. The presence of this rule may influence the way in which speakers of these languages pronounce English words such as *mob* and *cub*, with a final [p] rather than [b], which can lead to misunderstandings. The rule of final devoicing can be formalised as follows (the symbol '#' indicates the end of a word) as in (3):

(3) C→ [-voice] /_______ #

This rule states that a consonant C becomes voiceless at the end of a word. This rule does not apply in all languages, clearly not in Standard English. In Yiddish, a Germanic language, it has in fact disappeared, so there the word *hund* is pronounced with [d] at the end. By adding and subtracting such rules over time, the sound system of a language can change; this is called **phonological change**.

Another form of language change takes place at the level of word formation. An example is the addition to the English language system of the *-able* rule, which creates adjectives by tagging the *-able* suffix onto verb stems, as in *washable* and *drinkable*. The *-able* suffix arrived in English as part of a large number of French loan words such as *acceptable* and *charitable*. Subsequently, the suffix was incorporated into English as a separate morpheme and began to be combined with non-French stems such *wash* and *drink*. This new English rule constitutes a **morphological change**.

In sentence construction, too, there have been all kinds of changes and some are ongoing. Modern French has traditionally a two-part negative construction, with *ne. . .pas*, as in (5a). The first part is now disappearing, so that (4b) is now common, particularly in spoken French. In the context of written advertisements the form in (4b) can now also be seen.

(4) a. *Je n'ai pas d'argent.*
b. *J'ai pas d'argent.*
'I don't have any money'

This is an example of an ongoing change and it is possible to see that this **syntactic change** is progressing relatively quickly.

Some changes take far longer and they can be quite radical, especially in word order patterns. Let us compare modern German and English, which both belong to the West Germanic language family. In examples (5) to (7) we will focus in particular on the position of the subject (S), the object (O), and the finite verb (Vf) and infinite verb (Vi) in these two languages in different structures.

(5) *Word order in the main clause:*

a. English	S	Vf	Vi	O
	Elena	will	buy	chicken.
b. German	S	Vf	O	Vi
	Elena	wird	Huhn	kaufen.

(6) *Word order in the main clause with non-subject in initial position:*

a. English	X	S	Vf	Vi	O
	Tomorrow	Elena	will	buy	chicken.
b. German	X	Vf	S	O	Vi
	Morgen	wird	Elena	Huhn	kaufen.

(7) *Word order in a dependent clause:*

a. English	Conj	S	Vf	Vi	O
	that	Elena	will	buy	chicken.
b. German	Conj	S	O	Vi	Vf
	dass	Elena	Huhn	kaufen	wird.

In all three different English sentence types (5a, 6a and 7a), the order S-Vf-Vi-O is obligatory. That is, Modern English is a true SVO language. Modern German, on the other hand, looks more like an SOV language in many respects, for in all three cases either the non-finite verb (Vi) or finite verb is in last position (see also Section 9.3). In the past English was more like German: the Old English sentence in example (8) resembles the pattern of (6a) above.

(8) *Word order in the main clause with non-subject in initial position:*
Old English

X	Vf	S		O	Vi
Da	gewilln-ode	he	his	wombe	gefyll-an.
Then	want-*past*	he	his	belly	fill-*infinitive*

'Then he wanted to fill his belly.'

From Old to Middle English there were many changes in the language, and the syntactic pattern of (8) is now no longer viable in English. The assumption is that the underlying Proto-Indo-European language (see Section 17.3) had a predominantly SOV order. This implies that English has moved further away from this original word order pattern than German.

For ordinary language users, these types of change are less noticeable since they take place over a protracted period of time. The most striking kind of change is the appearance of new words, usually in connection with new objects or phenomena that need to be named. The word *porcelain*, for example, appeared in the English language in the early sixteenth century to describe the particular quality of earthenware recently imported from China. It got this name because of a resemblance to the appearance of conch shells called *porcellana* in Italian. A word like *helicoptère* appeared in French for the first time having been coined by Gustave de Ponton d'Amecourt in 1861 as he was working on the development of the machine. Words can also disappear, as for example the medieval Dutch verb *folen*, which has completely vanished, unlike its English equivalent *to fool (around)*. But this kind of change is hardly noticed. A third option is that words can acquire new social meanings. The English word *madam* is used currently as a title or form of address in a formal style, whereas in earlier varieties of English it had the less formal meaning of 'wife'. Words can acquire a specialist meaning in certain registers (see Section 18.6). The terms *mail, spam* and *chat* had original meanings in English but have acquired related but specific meanings, or even completely new meanings, when used in the area of internet and computer technology. Interestingly, French has tended to invent new words for these terms: *courriel* 'e-mail' from *courier électronique* 'electronic post', *pourriel* 'spam' from *courriel poubelle* 'e-mail rubbish bin', and *clavarder* 'to chat' from *clavier bavarder* 'keyboard chat'. The preceding examples all illustrate the complex process of **lexical change**. Lexical change can also take place through borrowing. This will be discussed in more detail in Chapter 20.

Linguistic elements can also change their status within the linguistic system, for example when a lexical word changes into an element with a grammatical function (see Section 11.4 on content and function words). An interesting case is that of English *-ly*, German *-lich* and Dutch *-lijk*. Today, this is a suffix in each of these three languages, but around AD 400 in Gothic it was a full lexical noun, *leik*, meaning 'body'. It could occur on its own but also form part of a compound like *liubaleiks* 'having a lovely body'. This word ended up as *lovely* in English, *lieblich* in German and *liefelijk* in Dutch. The Gothic word *leik* must have had a relatively abstract meaning, as it could occur in a compound like *sildaleiks* 'having a rare body', that is, 'strange'. The process we have just described, of a lexical word changing into a grammatical element, is known as **grammaticalisation**. It is not a single change, but one with various different aspects: generalisation of the original meaning ('body' turns into 'in the way or manner of'), a change in syntactic status (from noun into suffix), and a reduction of the sound shape ([lɑɪk] turns into [li], [lɪk] or [lək]). There are many examples of this phenomenon from many different languages, spoken and signed. Even given the short period of time for which we have documentation of sign languages, it has been possible to establish that in ASL an old form of the noun *man* has become an affix in reduced phonological form to mark masculine gender as in *son*. Grammaticalisation obviously affects individual words, but at the same time it also affects the grammatical system. For example, the English pronoun *that* and related pronouns in other Germanic languages (German *dass*, Dutch *dat*) originally occurred in sentences such as *I saw that*. Subsequently, it acquired the function of a conjunction (see Section 8.3), as in sentences such as *I said that he would come*. This change then also made it possible to form a new type of embedded clause, as in (7a).

The last type of language change we will discuss here is that of **pragmatic change**, that is, a change in the rules of language use. In many languages the choice of personal pronouns involves the choice of the pragmatically appropriate form, as we discussed in Section 5.4. These rules have also been subject to change. In German, for example, the older polite form for the second person singular was the third person singular form *Er* (literally 'he'), but is now *Sie*, taken from the third person plural form. In Persian we also see that *u* as the third person singular 'he/she' is now restricted to informal situations and the plural form *išun* is no longer used for plural but has become the formal singular form. Change has taken place in the Dutch system in the use of *u* as second person singular form in formal situations and *jij* in informal situations. In the last quarter of the twentieth century this social status factor has become less influential in the Netherlands, but not in Belgian Flanders where Dutch is also spoken. There the form of *u* is used in almost all situations.

19.3 The Process of Change

In historical linguistics we make comparisons between different forms of language that reflect how that language has changed over the course of time. When we see that in period P_1 form X was used, and in period P_2 form Y, we can describe what has changed, but this is not to say we know how this change has come about. It is not the case that French speakers changed overnight from the double to the single negative construction in (4b). How does language change actually proceed? First of all there needs to be some trigger for starting off innovation. This means we have to look at variation in the language community in question, because that is where we can find the beginnings of change. In other words we say that language variation is the motor of language change. **Diachronic** study – that is, study over time – of language change can only be undertaken on the basis of **synchronic** analysis – that is, analysis at a particular moment – of language variation, as discussed in Chapter 18.

By way of illustration let us look at the use of the auxiliary verb *do* in English. In modern English this verb has to be used in a number of contexts, as illustrated in (9).

(9) a. Do you love him? *Yes-no question*
b. Who does he love? *Non-subject wh-question*
c. He does not love you. *Negative declarative*
d. Do not give up! *Negative imperative*
e. He really does need a wife. *Emphasis in positive declarative*

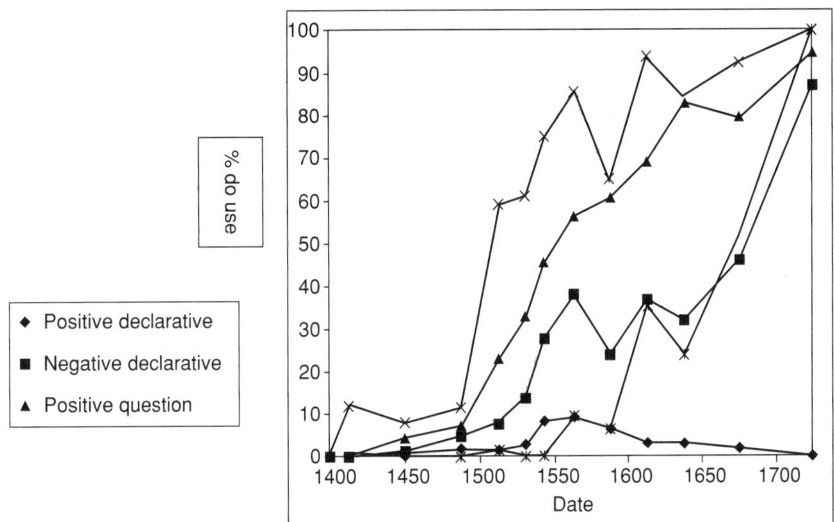

Figure 19.1 The development of *do* as an auxiliary in different sentence types between 1400 and 1700. Aitchison, J. (1991) *Language Change: Progress or Decay?* 3rd edn, Cambridge: Cambridge University Press.

In Old and Middle English the verb *do* was used as a lexical verb meaning 'to act' but there is hardly any evidence for *do* used in this grammatical way as an auxiliary, as we can see in the sentence in (10) dating from the fourteenth century.

(10) Believest thou this thing?

There is some evidence from the thirteenth century in dialects of South West Britain that *do* was used in positive declaratives. The other constructions with *do* are found from the end of the fourteenth century, as we can see from Figure 19.1.

They were, however, not used consistently. In the course of the fifteenth century there was a slight increase but the various uses of *do* increased rapidly in the next two hundred years, with some development taking place even later than that. In Shakespeare's texts, for example, there are many uses of *do* as an auxiliary but also many without. So we can divide the development of *do* as an auxiliary roughly into three stages as shown in (11).

(11) Stage I Form X e.g. *V not*
Stage II Form X and Y e.g. *V not* and *do not V*
Stage III Form Y e.g. *do not V*

In more technical terms we say that the rule or element involved in the change under consideration is **categorical** in stages I and III, that is, there is only one form possible, whatever it is, whereas at stage II it is **variable**, that is, there are two or more different forms possible at the same time. Note, however, that the schematic representation of the process in (11) does not always come out so neatly in practice. For example, stage III may never happen. In that case we are faced with a situation where a new form has been introduced alongside the older one, and the two continue to coexist. An example is the negative construction in French mentioned in (5). Both forms, one with *ne* and one without, exist alongside one another. In fact, in the history of French there has been change to and fro over many hundreds of years between one-word negative constructions and two-word negative constructions, so it is not clear where this current trend will lead. Will Stage III ever be reached?

Suppose now that we wanted to investigate step by step how exactly processes of change unfold over time. How can we do this? We have to trace in detail how a particular form is realised over the course of time and how a new form spreads through the language community. The information in Figure 19.1 shows how frequent the forms were on the basis of an analysis of many different kinds of written texts from different areas of Britain. But a reconstruction of the spoken language is, of course, impossible. Even for changes that are ongoing today this is often difficult enough. Take, as an example, the general use of the tag word *innit?* in some varieties of British English (12a) as opposed to the standard tag questions forms (12b).

(12) a. We gonna buy that car innit?
b. We're going to buy that car, aren't we?

In principle, recordings could be made of the language use of a representative sample of British English speakers and then analysed in order to establish how often the 'old' and the 'new' forms are being used, and by whom. Then, after twenty years or so, the same exercise could be repeated, and conclusions drawn about the way the change has spread. This poses a number of problems, however. To begin with, it is not easy to plan and implement a research project over such a long time span. Moreover, after twenty years, whose language use should be recorded – that of the original sample, or perhaps that of a new generation? And what if the language change in question is proceeding only very slowly, so that for example after twenty years nothing much has happened? Should we then do the whole exercise again after, say, fifty years? But which speakers should then be used for comparison with the original sample? And on top of it all researchers are expected to produce results in a relatively short period of time.

In view of these difficulties many sociolinguists study the processes of language change not only in 'real time' but often also in 'virtual time'. This simply means that they have different age groups in their research population and that differences between these age groups are taken as a basis for hypotheses on ongoing changes. The underlying assumption is that older informants are more likely to use the older language variant and the younger ones will more often use the new variant. A second assumption is that the use of the new variant by the younger generation is not a temporary or transitional phenomenon, and that they will not change to using the older variant when they themselves are older.

Let us consider an example of both the 'real time' and the 'virtual time' approach to the problem of language change. In English the verb *help* can be used either with a preposition *to* before the related infinitive, as in (13a), or without (13b).

(13) a. I will help you to wash up.
b. I will help you wash up.

This variable was studied using the citations database of the Oxford English Dictionary, that is, from the beginning of the seventeenth century to the present day. For twentieth-century usage, databases of British and American Standard English were also used.

The construction *help*+zero+infinitive is being used in modern times more frequently than the *help*+*to*+infinitive construction (see Figure 19.2). In more detailed analysis comparing American English and British English it appeared that speakers of American English started to increase their use of *help*+zero+infinitive earlier than the speakers of British English but that both

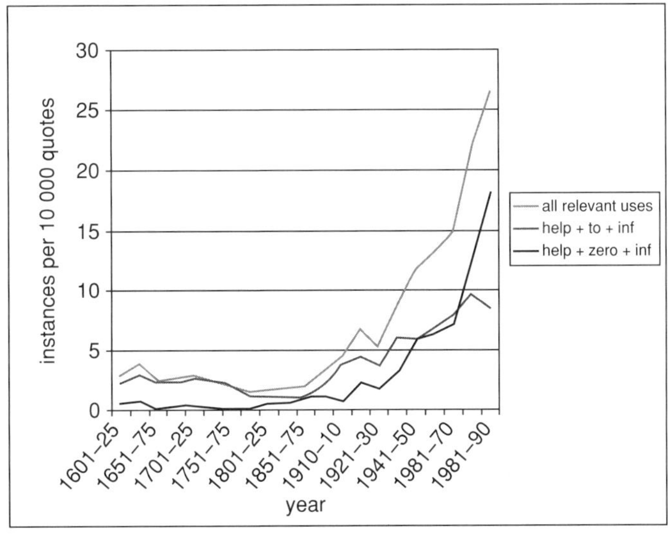

Figure 19.2 The frequency of the use of *help* with and without *to* + infinitive between 1600 and 1990. Mark Davies mark_davies@byu.edu

varieties are now using this variant more frequently than the *help+to+*infinitive construction.

In Hebrew, language change is taking place quite rapidly under the influence of the many second language learners of Hebrew. A study of modern spoken Hebrew in Israel showed various changes taking place, including regularisation of exceptional cases as illustrated in (14).

(14) Hebrew

a. bexar'tem	you (pl.) chose	Standard
b. ba'xarnu	we chose	Standard
c. ba'xartem	you (pl.) chose	new form

In the past tense the stress (marked with a ' before the stressed syllable) is placed on the penultimate syllable in all cases (14b and c) except the second person plural (14a). This leads to the reduction of the vowel in the first syllable in (14a). In the new variety the stress pattern for the second person plural has been regularised as in (14c). Younger speakers use this form far more than older speakers and are thus instrumental in bringing this change about. It seems obvious that we really have a language change here, and that the stress pattern is being regularised. Such a conclusion may, however, be premature. It could also be that this is a temporary phenomenon. It is entirely possible that, in twenty years time, the younger respondents will be using this variant less. In other words, it could well be that the regularised form is merely part of the street lingo of the young today, comparable to other words that happen to be popular and fashionable with their peer group (see Section 18.5.4). However, on closer scrutiny this conclusion appears less convincing, since in many areas of Hebrew regularisation is taking place and has been taking place for some time. Thus, additional historical information here allows us to equate virtual time with real time, and this in turn justifies drawing conclusions about ongoing language change from the comparison of the way language is used by different age groups.

19.4 The Role of Social Groups in Language Change

As we have seen, young people can introduce new variants into the language. But is age the only social factor that influences language change? As we already discussed in detail in Chapter 18, there are several factors connected to variation in the language and variation is the source of change. The third person plural pronoun currently used in spoken Swedish in subject position is *dom* 'they'. The earlier form was *de* and this form is still used in written Swedish. This replacement has also affected the article so that the article *de* in the phrase *de nya cyklarn* 'the new bicycles+*definite*' is also pronounced as *dom*. This change has come from the northern dialect forms and from the lower social classes. In Estuary English, the variety that is emerging in the South East of Britain, many features come from the dialect of East London. Glottalisation of /t/ as in [bʌʔɘ] 'butter' is now found in Estuary English as well as the fronting of /θ/ to /f/ as in [fiŋk] 'think'. The dialect of East London is strongly associated with the lowest socio-economic groups. However, Estuary English is not so restricted socially and the changes are moving from the lower groups into more middle-class speech. Such language changes in Swedish and English, starting from the lower social groups and then gradually spreading to middle and higher groups, is known as **bottom-up change**.

Our next examples are cases of the opposite type of language change, **top-down change**. In a sociolinguistic investigation of New York City, the realisation of the variable 'post-vocalic /r/' was studied in a range of different conversational situations and by speakers from different social classes. At issue was the pronunciation of /r/ at the end of a word or just before a consonant, that is, in words like *bar, more, star, Saturday, expert*, etc., as we mentioned in Section 18.7. In contrast to Standard British English, the /r/ is pronounced in most American varieties of English, giving American [bɑːr] against British [bɑː]. But up to 1940 New York City was the exception to this rule, and an r-less pronunciation was customary there. Since then, however, this has changed and the New Yorkers started producing the final /r/ sound. That is, /r/ was now pronounced, but not by everybody and not all the time. After all, as we said before, language changes take time and do not happen overnight. Table 19.1 summarises the results of the investigation carried out in 1964.

What conclusions can we draw from Table 19.1, especially with respect to the differences in language use between social groups and between styles? The table contains a large number of figures, but it does allow us to state the following:

- the higher the social class, the more often /r/ is pronounced; it clearly is a change that was introduced from above;

Table 19.1 Pronunciation of the variable /r/ in words such as *car* and *horse* in 6 social classes in New York City in 1964. Five styles are distinguished from the informal style to the most formal, that is, in words in minimal pairs like *guard* and *god*. The higher the score on the (r) index, the more often (r) is pronounced.

	Social class					
Style	**Low 1**	**Low 2**	**Middle 1**	**Middle 2**	**High 1**	**High 2**
Colloqu. speech	2	4	9	8	9	20
Formal style	3	8	16	18	24	36
Reading text	8	18	20	28	30	37
Word list	19	30	36	40	65	52
Minimal pairs	45	48	58	63	88	69

- the more formal the style, the more often /r/ is used; people evidently think that the /r/ has to be pronounced in formal language use, that this is 'proper language use'.

The pattern for the highest-but-one social class confirms this conclusion. This class has the highest score on the (r) index for the word list and for the minimal pairs, that is, 65 and 88 respectively. Note, however, that these figures do not indicate actual language use, but rather people's *views* as to how they ought to be talking. The highest-but-one social class obviously wants to speak more correctly and more in accordance with the new norm coming from above than they already do. They are in effect more conservative than the conservatives. Another way of looking at it would be to see this as a case of hypercorrection, a notion we discussed in Section 18.7.

These findings, plus what we know about the pronunciation of /r/ in the past, about the social evaluation of /r/, and about its distribution across age groups, lead to the following conclusion: the language change we are studying here is a case of top-down change, because it proceeds towards what is seen as the norm of the higher social classes. In Swedish we also find top-down change. The simple past tense ends in the written form in regular verbs with *-ade* as in *tackade* '(they) thanked' and the compound past in *-at* as in *har tackat* '(they) have thanked'. In spoken Swedish, however, both forms are often pronounced as *-/a/*. More educated and higher class speakers have started pronouncing the forms following the written forms, and so with a /d/ or /t/, and this change has spread to speakers from lower classes.

Table 19.1 also illustrates that in this type of sociolinguistic investigation we should take into account not just differences that may exist between social groups, but also other differences as discussed in Section 18.5. In the study of the variable 'post-vocalic /r/' younger speakers were shown to pronounce the /r/ more than older speakers but also to evaluate the pronunciation more positively. Gender as a social variable is also a relevant factor in language change, sometimes in combination with other variables. Earlier in this section we discussed Estuary English and the use of glottalisation of /t/. Women are apparently producing this more than men. In Section 18.6 we saw that the realisation of a linguistic variable can depend on the degree of formality of the conversation. The term 'style' was used to indicate this. The data in Table 19.1 demonstrate that style is definitely relevant here. In everyday language use, for example, there is no difference between the highest-but-one social group and the two middle groups: the three groups have an (r)-index score of 9 versus 8 and 9 respectively.

Large groups of second language learners in a community can have a considerable impact on language change. In the Hebrew example we discussed in Section 19.3 the regularisation of exceptional cases is seen as being due to the large number of second language learners of Hebrew. It is interesting to compare two languages such as Faroese and mainland Norwegian which had a common ancestor. Mainland Norwegian has been influenced by different groups of second language learners whereas Faroese has changed relatively little, since speakers are isolated on an island. It is possible, for example, that the use of the tag *innit* we have mentioned earlier is also related to the large number of Asian speakers in Britain, but we have to be careful with this interpretation since this form also occurred in other varieties of English.

It is important to realise that we need information from a range of different sources before we can be certain of the conclusions we draw. It could, after all, be that the class distribution in Table 19.1 represents an unchanging social pattern of language variation, where one class uses one language variant, and the other a different one. But the data which indicates more widespread use in younger speakers shows that there is likely to be a language change taking place. Some features remain stable as, for example, the pronunciation of *th* in words like *think* and *Thursday*. The pronunciation of *th* in the United States shows enormous variation, ranging from the standard pronunciation [θ] to [t] so that *think* and *Thursday* are pronounced *tink* and *tursday*. This pattern of variation is in fact quite stable, and there is no apparent language change.

From the examples given so far it should be clear that studying language change involves more than just looking at the standard language. It is not the case that 'English' changes, or 'Farsi' or 'Chinese'. Usually researchers focus on a particular dialect, and one of those dialects could be the standard variety. But the use of the standard variety may be spread out over a wide area, and the speakers of the standard language constitute a very heterogeneous group, which is hard to delimit geographically. This is why many researchers tend to concentrate on specific dialects, as for example in the project on the /r/ variation in New York City.

19.5 Embedding Changes into the Language System

From a social point of view, language change proceeds from one social group to the next, in a gradual way, in the sense that not all members of a particular group suddenly start to use the new variant. How does this work from a linguistic point of view? When a new variant is introduced, is it always realised in all cases where it would be possible? As we saw in the discussion of the *do* auxiliary in English (Section 19.3), the use of a form is variable. Even a single author such as Shakespeare will vary in his usage in the same play. The question in general here is: is there a pattern in the linguistic contexts in which the change takes place?

In the domain of phonological change, the gradual introduction and dissemination of new variants is known as **lexical diffusion**. The term refers to the slow spread of a new variant across the lexicon, as a kind of virus that affects more and more words. The pattern of lexical diffusion is often that of an S-curve. In the first stage a limited number of words change in

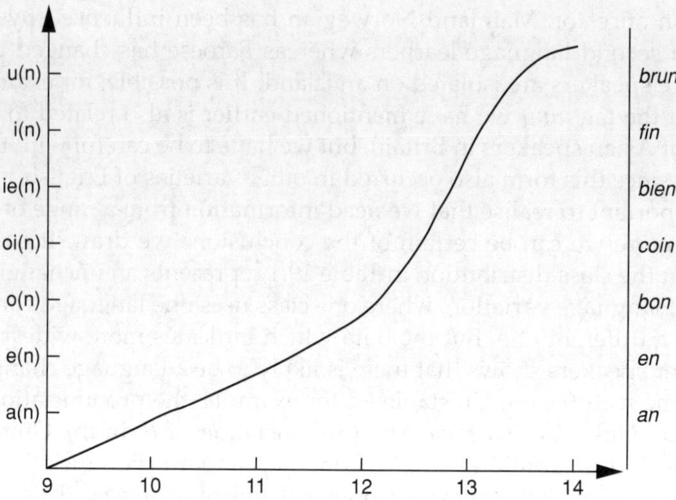

Figure 19.3 Phonological change in French words ending in /n/. The horizontal axis indicates time in centuries and the vertical axis the spread over the lexicon in terms of categories of words. Aitchison, J. (1991) *Language Change: Progress or Decay?* 3rd edn, Cambridge: Cambridge University Press.

pronunciation, in the second stage far more words are affected as the change speeds up, and in the final stage it may take a long time until the last words have also changed. In French the sound /n/ at the end of a syllable disappeared in pronunciation as in *an* 'year', from Latin *annus*, and *fin* 'end', from Latin *finis*. This change began in the tenth century with the nouns ending in *-an*. Later the words ending in *-en* and *-on* etc. started to lose their /n/. The change for the lexicon was completed by the fifteenth century. As we see from Figure 19.3, initially, the pace of change was slow, so the curve is rather flat, then in a short period of time many more words changed, as represented by the steep rise of the curve, and in the fourteenth century the last words were holding out against this change, so the curve flattens out again. On the vertical axis we can see that there is a systematic principle governing the vowel contexts in which the change occurs: /n/ is first deleted after /a/, and last deleted after /y/. The linguistic context here clearly influences the way in which the change proceeds. But lexical diffusion is not always such a neatly systematic process, affecting a sound change in one type of word, and only after that in another.

In ASL there is a tendency for two-handed signs to change so that they use identical handshapes on both hands. So we see that an old form of the handshapes for the sign depend-on in (15) involved two different handshapes and that the new form has symmetrical handshapes.

(15) ASL

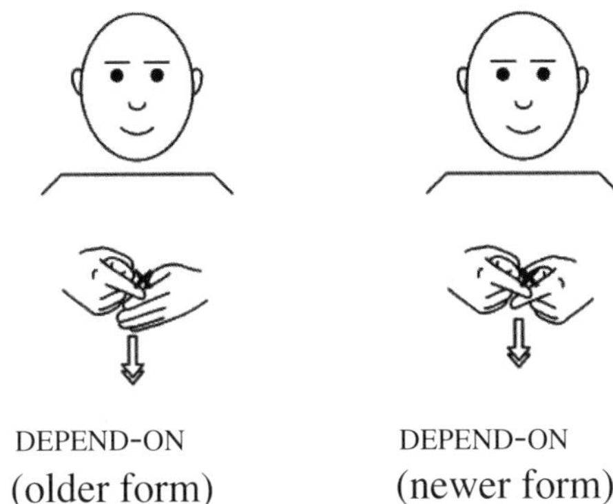

DEPEND-ON (older form) DEPEND-ON (newer form)

This change was first noted in a few specific signs but now seems to be spreading in the ASL lexicon. Similar changes have been noted, too, in British Sign Language and Sign Language of the Netherlands.

19.6 The Evaluation of Language Change

'You shouldn't say *with you and I* but *with you and me*.' It is quite usual to hear statements like this. As we discussed in Section 18.7, varieties of a language have a social meaning. In the same way changes in language have a social value. They are often viewed negatively, especially when they are bottom-up changes, that is from social groups with lower status. Many people believe that their language is going to degenerate when such non-standard forms come into general use. Linguistic history shows, however, that it is inaccurate to speak of 'degeneration' or 'decay'. Once a particular change is completed, the new form will have become the generally accepted norm for the whole language community. You would be hard put, for example, to find anyone in France who feels that their language has degenerated because the /n/ at the end of a word has disappeared. The change happened a long time ago and is complete, so this is just how it is, and no one knows any better.

A negative attitude with respect to new language forms is very often caused by the fact that those new forms are introduced by speakers with a relatively low social prestige. As we indicated in Section 18.7, attitudes towards a particular language or variety of language is determined in large part by the attitude towards the social group that uses this variety or variant. The handshape change in ASL is not clearly associated with any social group and people often do not notice it. The glottalisation of /t/ in Estuary English is far more accepted than the use of *innit?* or the omission of /h/. People who think nothing of using the first form will often hold forth in strongly negative terms about the last two. From a linguistic point of view there is no real difference between these cases – but from a social point of view there quite clearly is.

SUMMARY

In this chapter we have discussed the process and the possible causes of language change. Changes can happen at the various levels of language, and thus we have **phonological, morphological, syntactic, lexical, and pragmatic changes**. Sometimes a lexical element changes and takes on a grammatical function, in a process called **grammaticalisation**. Language change can be studied over time (**diachrony**) or at a particular moment (**synchrony**). In the latter case, coexisting varieties may reflect changes that are ongoing.

The process of language change often starts from a **categorical** situation (only the 'old' form), goes through a **variable** situation (both the 'old' and the 'new' form), and ends in a categorical situation (only the 'new' form).

Language variation forms the basis for language change. New forms gradually enter and spread through the language community, and change is linked to a range of social factors. Here we distinguish between change from below (**bottom-up**) and change from above (**top-down**), depending on where and in which social group a particular change originates. New language forms gradually enter the language system. New phonological variants spread slowly through the vocabulary of a language: this process is called **lexical diffusion**.

ASSIGNMENTS

1. Give two examples, from a language you know well, of variants which are increasingly being used. Choose an example of a lexical variant and one of a variant from a different linguistic area.
2. In English, speakers used to say *more people* and *more cheese* but *fewer people* and *less cheese.* Nowadays it is more common to say *less people.* Could this be a case of language change? What type of change could be involved here?
3. Language change is a process that may take decades. So how can a researcher, within a limited amount of time, determine what is going on? Take as an example the increasing use of *ask* as a noun as in *that is a big ask.* Devise a study to examine how this change has come about and how it is progressing.
4. Have young people got a special role in the process of language change? Does change always start with them? What is the role of the other social

groups in language change? What could be the function of the media (in particular TV, radio and internet) in language change?
5. Language change is often perceived as negative. Why is this?

Test Yourself

1. What is phonological change?
2. What relation is there between language change and language variation?
3. How can language change be studied synchronically if change is a process that unfolds over time?
4. What is the difference between 'top-down' change and 'bottom-up' change?
5. What is the role of hypercorrection in language change? What are certain groups of speakers doing in this case?
6. What is lexical diffusion?
7. When does the language community take a negative view of a language variant?

Acknowledgments and Further Reading

A very readable introduction to language change in English is that by Aitchison (1981), from which we have taken Figures 19.1 and 19.3. Figure 19.2 is from Mark Davies' web site corpus.byu.edu/historical-syntax.asp. Bynon (1977) and Hock (1986) are English-language handbooks. The example of historical change from ASL comes from Suppalla (2008). The English examples come from Ellegård (1953), Mair (1995), Warner (2006) and Ryfa (2003). Hebrew examples are taken from Ravid (1995). Table 19.1 is based on a study by Labov (1966).

chapter 20

Bilingualism

20.1 Introduction

In the head offices of many multinationals the working language is English. However, at home and with their family, employees will normally use their own language. In international schools, students are often taught part of their curriculum, for example geography and history, in one language and other subjects in a different language. In the Amazon area small groups of hunters need to know not just their own language but also those of their neighbours, and in addition some Portuguese or Spanish. All over the world, migrants try and find a balance between using their own language and that of the country they are living in. In these and other similar situations we have to do with **bilingualism**, or, where more than two languages are involved, **multilingualism**. In this chapter we will use the term 'bilingualism' to refer to the general situation of using more than one language. Members of bilingual communities often think nothing of using one language at home and a different one in the street or at work. At a conservative estimate half the world's population is bilingual, meaning that in their everyday life they constantly move between two or more languages. The numbers are rapidly rising, in particular through increasing international migration.

Linguistics, First Edition. Edited by Anne E. Baker and Kees Hengeveld.

When studying bilingualism we can focus on various different kinds of phenomena, depending on our perspective. First of all, we may be interested in the language community. What is the relative position of the various different languages in a bilingual society, and how is this position changing? Secondly, we may focus on the individual speaker who is bilingual. What effect does bilingualism have on language users, in particular on the way they use their languages? Finally, the language itself can become the object of study. What happens to languages that are 'in contact', that is, spoken in the same community? How do they influence each other? In this chapter we will take these three perspectives, discussing first the language community, then the language users, and finally the language itself.

In Section 20.2 we are concerned with the bilingual community. The position of languages in such a community is often highly dependent on the language policy of the relevant authorities. If this language policy aims at fostering bilingualism, then, for example schools may offer bilingual education. These two issues, language policy and bilingual education, are discussed in Section 20.3 and Section 20.4 respectively. In Section 20.5 we will take a closer look at bilingual language users, focussing in particular on their language abilities and on the influence of bilingualism on their (cognitive) development. In Section 20.6 we will discuss the consequences of language contact for the languages concerned. Finally, in Section 20.7, we will deal with the emergence of new languages in situations of language contact.

20.2 The Bilingual Community

As shown in Figure 20.1, there are in principle three different types of bilingual community. In Type I language A is spoken by one group of speakers, and language B by a different group. Contact between the two groups can be maintained by a relatively small group of bilinguals who serve more or less as interpreters and translators. Type I can only exist when there is a strong geographic or socio-cultural separation between the two groups. Such a separation can be found in Switzerland where the mountainous nature of the country aided the linguistic separation of the four regions using French, German, Italian, and Romansch. Canada is also an example of Type I, where English and French are relatively separate in the different provinces. In communities of Type II (almost) everybody speaks both language A and language B. This type of bilingualism can be found in many strongly bilingual countries in Africa. In Europe in western areas of the Czech Republic, the so-called Sudetenland, German and Czech were spoken by almost everyone up until the 1950s. In language communities of Type III part of the population speaks one language (A), while the rest of the population speaks both language A and their own language B. There are many examples of this type, especially in countries with large migrant populations. In the United States, for example, the large majority

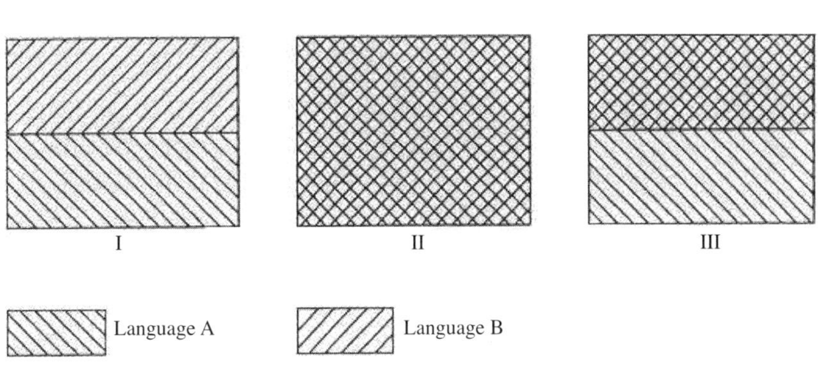

Figure 20.1 Model of the different types of bilingual community.

of the population uses only one language, English, while there are a number of sub-communities that, in addition to English, use a different language, for example Spanish, Russian or Chinese.

Some countries such as Switzerland and Canada are officially bilingual, and the different languages involved have – in principle at least – equal status. But this is by no means always the case. Usually, one language is the official language and other languages are considered to be minority languages. In Great Britain, for example, English is the official language but in addition a wide range of minority languages is used such as Punjabi, Gujarati (both from India), Italian, Greek, Welsh, Scottish Gaelic, etc. Sometimes, minority languages are indigenous, as with Basque in France and Spain, and most sign languages. Sometimes they have been imported, for example Turkish in Germany, Punjabi in Britain or Polish in Ireland.

In many bilingual communities the two languages serve different functions: one has high status (H), the other low (L). In a typical case, H is the official language and is used exclusively in formal situations, though hardly anyone learns it as their first language. L, on the other hand, is the language for everyday, informal situations, and most members of the community have this as their mother tongue. Such functional separation is known as **diglossia**. Haiti, for example, has French as its official language (H), even though hardly anyone learns this as their first language. French is the language of education, newspapers, official publications, etc. In contrast, the L-language is Haitian, a creole language (see Section 20.7). A similar diglossia exists between Modern Standard Arabic and the spoken varieties in the different Arab countries.

In a bilingual situation it is possible that people who want or have to communicate with each other do not speak each other's first language. In this case they may resort to a third language, which is then called a **lingua franca** in that situation. A lingua franca functions as a contact language between people with different mother tongues. In many parts of the world today English serves as the lingua franca. In large parts of East Africa, Swahili has this function; in South East Asia it is Malay.

Minority languages often have low status. They are not valued in society at large, and they cannot be used for communication outside the groups for whom they are the first language. For this reason it is often difficult for minority groups to continue to use their own language. As a result there may be a **language shift** towards the language of the majority, while the minority language is used by fewer speakers and in ever fewer situations. In the Breton-, Welsh- and Irish-speaking communities of the Celtic fringe in north-west Europe, there has been an ongoing language shift over the last centuries. French has been replacing Breton and English is dominating Gaelic and Welsh. The majority language is first used as the means of communication between children, making inroads into the position of the family as the key domain for the preservation of the minority language. In Turkish families in Germany, for instance, German is often used as the family language. Interestingly, Welsh has experienced some revival over the last twenty years, with many young people learning to speak it.

When the majority language becomes more important, the proficiency of individual speakers in their first language very often shows signs of decline. This can be seen clearly in the language of older Russian emigrants who have settled in Israel, where their ability in Russian decreases. This process is known as **language loss**. Similarly, German immigrants to Australia lose their command of German. They may have forgotten certain German words and only know their English equivalents, such as *screwdriver*, *elbow* or *ironing board*. They may also have problems choosing the right article (*der*, *die* or *das*) for German nouns, and speak, incorrectly, of **der Auto* instead of *das Auto* 'the car'.

When this process carries on over a few generations, the resulting decline in proficiency in the language community as a whole is known as **language erosion**. In Bretagne, France, for example, the Breton spoken by people in their thirties is worse than that of speakers in their fifties, and this in turn is worse than that of speakers in their seventies. The Breton language is clearly undergoing language erosion. Its vocabulary is being reduced and parts of it lost; inflectional endings and grammatical patterns are disappearing; stylistic options of old Breton are going out of fashion. In individual speakers such a decline in proficiency amounts to language loss; when this occurs in the whole community and continues down the generations the contrasting term is language erosion.

If language erosion continues unopposed, the language in question will one day cease to be used as a means of communication. When no one speaks the language any longer, then we speak of **language death**. In the past this has been the fate of languages all over the world, such as native languages in the United States, Canada, Australia, and South America and also of languages such as Cornish in Southern Britain. It has been predicted that by the end of the twentieth century between 75 and 90 per cent of the world's 6000 languages will have died out.

Language shift usually occurs in the direction of the majority language, but this is not necessarily the only option. Especially when minority groups begin to realise that they are losing their own language, and when this language is an essential part of their group identity, they may take steps towards **language preservation**, and try to obtain a stable position for their own minority language. Quite often this means that they will first have to try and recapture domains that have been lost to the majority language. The French-speaking minority in Canada, especially in the eastern province of Quebec, has waged a successful campaign for the position of French – helped along, no doubt, by the fact that French speakers are in the majority in Quebec. Similarly, in the Spanish region of Catalonia, around Barcelona, there has been a successful policy to stimulate the use of Catalan – facilitated also by the strong economic performance of this region. In Wales the policy of the British government has led to an increase in the number of Welsh speakers, especially among young people, over the last ten years. The recognition of minority languages as official languages is a support for language preservation (see Section 18.3).

20.3 Language Policy

The preceding section may seem to suggest that it is the individual language users who can choose to use a particular language or not, and so decide for themselves what happens to their language. But is this really the case? Are they autonomous in this respect? Can Moroccan or Ghanaian speakers in France use their own language in the post office? The answer to this is clearly no: they will normally have to speak French.

What happens to languages in a bilingual community depends not only on the behaviour of their speakers, but is to an important extent also determined by the **language policy** of the government. Language policy refers to the sum total of ideas, plans and measures taken by the government with respect to the languages and varieties of language in a society. The term can be used for both monolingual and bilingual situations. The domain of language policy is very wide; it can range from the standardisation or reform of the spelling of the national language to a decision to print explanations on the tax form in several minority languages. It is not only the government that needs to have a language policy. In a bilingual society individual institutions like a school, a business company, the coach of an international football team, or a bilingual family are all faced with the question: with whom do you speak in which language, and what (printed) information is made available in which languages?

Governments have different ways of reacting to bilingualism. In some cases several languages are recognised as official national languages, giving them the full rights of such a status. In South Africa, for example, English, Afrikaans,

Xhosa and Zulu are just four of the eleven official national languages. In other countries governments take the dominance of the one official language completely for granted. In some cases minority languages are seen as a threat to national unity, and so their use in public situations is not only discouraged but even forbidden. In France, for example, this has long been the official government position with respect to minority languages such as Basque, Occitan and Breton.

A common alternative is neglect and indifference. In this case the government does not actively pursue a language policy that is for or against minority languages, but just lets them be. This is often not very helpful for minority languages, as the majority language has all the advantages of power and prestige and will therefore win out easily. In Britain this was the case for many years with respect to Welsh, but more recently, as we have mentioned, Welsh people have started to fight for their rights and the number of Welsh speakers is increasing.

Finally, the government may decide to actively support both the majority and minority language in question, for example because it views minority languages as part of the culture of the community as a whole. Such support can take different forms in practice. It may lead to the institution of radio and TV broadcasts in the minority language, or to programmes for education in the language concerned. This has been the case for Welsh in Britain since the middle of the twentieth century, with Welsh becoming a compulsory subject in schools since 1990. We will discuss such programmes for bilingual education in more detail in the Section 20.4.

20.4 Bilingual Education

Zineb lives in Montpellier, France. At home, with her parents and her little brother, she speaks Arabic, and in the street she plays mostly with Arabic-speaking children. Then, one day, she has to go to primary school, the *école maternelle*, and is faced with a teacher who only speaks French, so all instructions are given in French, stories are told in French, etc. This is a common situation all over the world. Everywhere there are children who speak one language from birth but are confronted by another language when they go to school. Usually this is the official language of the country, which they then acquire as a second language. Often they already know a little bit of this new language, but this is certainly not always the case. Spanish-speaking children in the United States, Aboriginal children in Australia, and Turkish children in Germany do not automatically know the language they will encounter in school.

This gap between home language and school language may have all kinds of negative effects for the children in question. The most obvious of these is that they can only understand the lessons with difficulty, or perhaps not at all.

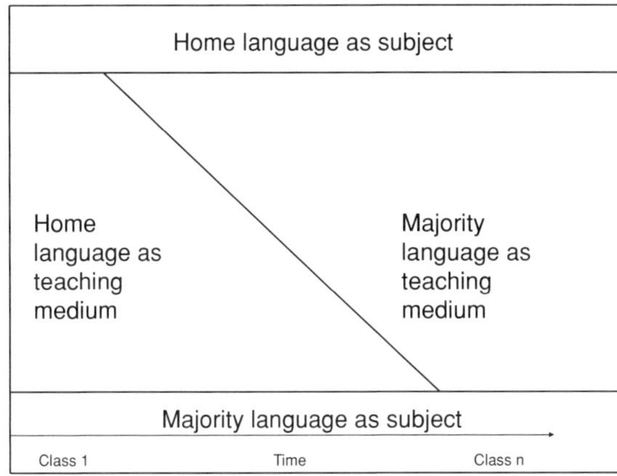

Figure 20.2 Model of a transitional bilingual programme.

At the same time, for the minority group as a whole, the effect is that further learning of their own language is not supported by the education system. This in turn may engender a negative attitude towards their first language as a language of little value and not relevant for literacy.

In order to address the educational problems of minority children, programmes have been developed for bilingual education. In most programmes a distinction is made between language as a subject to be studied (with emphasis on learning to read and write) versus language as a means of communication and instruction in other subjects, for example in arithmetic. In Canada, for example, some schools opt for an **immersion programme** in which all education is given in French. Other schools opt for partial immersion whereby fifty per cent of the curriculum is given in French. Another possibility is a programme whereby a transition is made from one language to the other. In the United States, for example, for the first few years of schooling children can be taught two languages, Spanish and English: English as a subject with the minority language, Spanish, as the overall medium of communication. This means that the children will learn to do sums in Spanish, their first language, which at the time they know best. At a later stage, when they have acquired a sufficient level of proficiency in their second language, English, the majority language will become the language used for communication and instruction. This transition is done gradually – first for part of the school week, and then increasingly for more time, until the minority language has been completely replaced, as Figure 20.2 indicates. In some countries only a very limited amount of time is spent on the minority language.

Such a model is known as a **transitional programme**. The model can be implemented in a number of different ways, depending on whether the second language is introduced sooner rather than later as the medium of instruction.

In the United States there are also transitional programmes for children whose mother tongue is Navaho or Chinese, in Great Britain for Italian-speaking children and in Australia for children of different Aboriginal communities speaking different first languages.

The outcomes of transitional programmes are generally positive. Especially in the first phase it is far easier for the children to master subjects presented in their own language. After all, they learn best in the language they know best. And, to the surprise of some people, such a bilingual education does not appear to have any negative effects for the acquisition of the second language, that is, the national or majority language. You might think that since there is less time for that second language, this would inevitably lead to a lower level of proficiency, but this is generally not the case.

Why is that so? There are at least two different explanations. The first is that the acquisition of a second language is strongly influenced by socio-emotional factors. In a transitional school the children are generally more at ease than in a school where only the majority language is used. And this in turn helps to stimulate the acquisition of that second language (see Section 3.4 where the factors of motivation and attitude were discussed). The second explanation has to do with the relationship between the two languages of a bilingual individual, and the way in which proficiency in the one language may influence proficiency in the other. This subject will be discussed in Section 20.5.

20.5 The Bilingual Individual

The first question is: when do we call someone bilingual? Two kinds of definition are possible here. Firstly it is possible to use a definition in which the key criterion is the individual's proficiency in each of the two languages. But how well should speakers have mastered both languages before we can call them bilingual? Must they also be able to read and write both languages? It is impossible to come up with a satisfactory answer to these questions. Here we will use a different definition that reflects the actual usage of the two languages. According to this second criterion, speakers that in their daily lives (have to) use two different languages are defined as bilingual. The level of proficiency is not relevant.

Many people have done research into the question of how those two languages are stored in the brain of the individual language user. Their focus has mostly been on the semantic systems of the languages concerned, and far less on their grammars. The issue often is whether the two languages are linked to one single semantic system or to two different ones. Do Italian – English bilinguals, for example, have two different notions for the words *cavallo* and *horse*, or are these two words linked with one conceptual notion HORSE that is language-neutral? In other words, do they have one mental lexicon or two? (see Section 2.2 for a discussion of the mental lexicon). The two languages are probably not completely separated; the semantic systems partially overlap. This conclusion is based, among other things, on the fact that in bilinguals with brain damage leading to aphasia (Section 2.3), it is usually both languages that are affected. Neurolinguistic testing has also shown that the terms for one concept are both activated – thus in Italian–English bilinguals, when a picture is shown of a horse, both *cavallo* and *horse* are activated and the word *cavallo* is activated when the speaker is presented with the English word *horse*.

In many Western countries the majority of people are monolingual, in the sense that they use only one language in their daily lives. This situation has led to a widespread notion that bilingualism is strange and abnormal, and must cause problems for the bilingual individual. But is this actually the case? A great deal of research has been done into the influence of bilingualism on the cognitive and intellectual development of the children concerned. Before the 1950s such investigations usually indicated negative effects, since bilingual children often achieved a lower score in IQ-tests than their monolingual peers. In those investigations, however, not enough attention was given to the fact that the bilingual children under investigation often came from socially disadvantaged backgrounds. This may have been the real reason why they did not do well in those tests. In later research, positive effects of bilingualism have been found. Bilingual children tend to show more awareness of language than monolingual children, also in terms of insight into writing systems. In addition, they can correct ungrammatical sentences better than monolingual children and there appears to be an advantage for bilingual adults in that symptoms of dementia appear later. Thus bilingualism can be an advantage rather than a disadvantage, as it can have a positive influence on development in both children and adults. But there are still questions about actual proficiency. Can bilinguals in fact learn to master both languages really well? In principle, bilinguals can be just as proficient in both languages as monolinguals in their single language, but in practice this does not happen very often. The reason for this is that the two languages involved are commonly used in different domains and in different situations, as we touched upon in Section 3.6. Take, for example, an English–German bilingual child in Germany, who speaks English at home but not German. This child is likely to know the English word *diaper* rather than the German word *Windel* 'diaper' from the home context. At school, on the other hand, the child will be likely to learn the word *Hecke* 'hedge' but will not necessarily learn the English *hedge* at home. A monolingual child would use just one single language in all domains, and so would more easily learn all the words of those domains in that one language.

Does more of one language necessarily mean less of the other? Is it the case that humans have only a limited 'language space' in their heads? Is there less space for another language if the first one has developed further? According to current insights into bilingualism this is definitely not the case. A greater proficiency in the one language is thought in fact to lead to a greater proficiency in the other. This view is based mostly on research findings into the effects of bilingual education. If the home language of a child is involved at least initially in education, then being bilingual usually does not have a negative effect – and sometimes has a positive effect – on the acquisition of the majority language, despite the fact that less time is available for this language. In Section 3.5 and again in Section 20.4 we looked at one possible explanation, namely the influence of socio-emotional factors on second language acquisition. A possible second explanation involves the fact that the two languages are inter-related.

The preceding discussion might seem to suggest that bilingualism is always beneficial, but this is not the case. Negative effects can and do occur, especially in minority groups with a low socio-economic status and a low appreciation of their own language and culture. Such effects can be linguistic, cognitive and socio-economic. If a child's first language has had too little opportunity to develop, so there is no sound basis for successful second-language acquisition, the overall result may well be that these children achieve only a low level of proficiency in both languages. This was in fact the case of Ahmed, who at thirty years of age made many mistakes in his German but knew only just enough Turkish to converse at a basic level (Section 3.5, example 16).

So far we have focused on the bilingual language community and the individual bilingual person. Now we will change tack and concentrate on the languages themselves. What happens to the languages that are used in a bilingual community, and what influence can this situation have on the languages involved?

20.6 Bilingualism and Interference

The bilingual speaker is continuously faced with the job of separating the two language systems in everyday usage. In general, bilinguals operate on a clear separation of functions and use the two languages in different situations. Various factors in a conversational situation – such as the topic of conversation, the addressee, and the location – may influence the way in which language is used. Arabic speakers in Egypt tend to use English, for example, for formal use in e-mail messages but Arabic in informal chat rooms. Thus, their **language choice** is influenced by situational factors, just as with the stylistic choices people make within one single language (see Section 5.4 and Section 18.6). More importantly, by their choice of a particular language people may shift and change the tone of a situation, from formal to informal for example, just as you might do in French by changing over from *vous* 'you.*polite*' to *tu* 'you.*familiar*'.

Bilinguals may change from one language to the other in the course of a single conversation. This is known as **code switching**. It can occur between sentences, as we can see in the e-mail text from a young Egyptian woman to her Egyptian girlfriend (1). In the text of the mail where Arabic is used, the words are glossed and translated in the usual way. Interestingly, the context also has an effect on spelling since numbers are used in e-mail and phone text messages to represent Arabic letters that do not occur on a Roman keyboard – here the numbers 3 and 7 represent the voiced and voiceless pharyngeal fricatives respectively (see Section 14.5.2).

Arabic/English

(1) Hello Dalia,

7amdellah	3ala	el-salama	ya	Gameel.
Praise.allah	for	the-safeness	oh	beautiful (one)

'Thank God for your safe return, my sweet.'

we	alf	mabrouk	3ala	el-shahada	el-kebeera.
and	thousand	blessed	for	the-certificate	the-great

'Congratulations on the big certificate.'

Keep in touch . . . I really hope to see you all Soooooooooooooon (Maybe in Ramadan).

Kol	Sana	Wentom	Tayyebeen.
Every	year	and.you.*plural*)	well.*plural*

'Happy Ramadan.'

Waiting to hear from you. . .
Laila

Some of these cases of code switching involve phrases like *Kol Sana Wentom Tayyebeen* and other ritual greetings in Arabic that are typically related to the Arabic context within which the conversation took place. But for a phrase like *keep in touch* it would have been equally possible to choose an Arabic phrase.

Code switching in between sentences may happen under the influence of situational factors, for example when there is more than one conversation partner. One sentence is addressed to the group for whom language A is the most obvious choice, and the next sentence is then spoken in language B, as this is the preferred choice of the other person.

Code switching may also occur in quite formal written language. In countries with bilingual populations where most readers can be expected to know both languages, such switching occurs quite often. It is a frequent phenomenon in the English language newspapers in the Philippines or in Hong Kong, where switches occur into Malay or Chinese. In (2) a phrase from English is inserted into a Spanish sentence.

Spanish/English

(2) Los amos del espectáculo – pues *the show must go on* siempre,
the directors of.the show – since *the show must go on* always,
pase lo que pase – han dado la pauta.
happens that which happens – have given the standard
'The directors of the show – since *the show must go on* always, whatever happens – have set the standard.'

This incorporation of English words into many contexts is very common today. It occurs in many languages and, as mentioned above, involves writing systems too. Thus, for example, English phrases in Russian advertisements are written in Cyrillic script. But code switching is by no means a modern phenomenon. It happened in texts from centuries ago, as in example (3) taken from a letter from an English merchant to another Englishman. This was written in 1548 and reproduced here in the original spelling. French was incorporated, being the language of the upper classes at that time.

English/French

(3) Off peas or warre I knowe not what to wryte,
'Of peace or war I do not know what to write,'
but we arre threatened by *Mons[ieu]r de Rochepot, Mareschal de France,*
'but we are threatened by Mr De Rochepot, Marshall of France,'
qu'il viendra voir devant le Sainct Jehan ses amis de Boulloigne et Messieurs de Callais.
'that he will come to see before St Jean his friends in Boulogne and Gentleman of Calais.'
I trust they shal be well entertaigned iff they cum, and thus the Lord be with you, in haest.
'I trust that they will be entertained well if they come, and so the Lord be with you, in haste.'

An interesting question is why bilingual speakers would want to mix their two languages. In the past it was thought that this was the result of a low level of proficiency in both languages, so that what the speaker did not know in the one language was said in the other. However, it turns out that such switches frequently occur in the conversations of people who are actually quite proficient. In some language communities, or within subgroups of those communities, such as young Puerto Ricans in the United States, it is quite common to mix the two languages in order to give expression to a 'mixed' identity. The speaker shows that he belongs both to the Spanish-speaking Puerto Ricans and, that as a speaker of the status language, English, he is also a citizen of the United States. In the urban communities of the Republic of Tartarstan it is common for speakers to be balanced bilinguals and code switching between Tatar and Russian is standard, and thus not an expression of mixed identity.

The examples we have seen so far of code switching have been at the level of whole sentences or phrases. A very common form of code switching is at the level of individual words. These words are often used because there is no apparent equivalent in the majority language. In example (4) the English word *bluff* is used in the French newspaper *Le Figaro*.

French/English

(4)	L'Australie	accuse	la	France	de	bluff.
	Australia	accuses	the	France	of	bluff

'Australia accuses France of bluffing.'

In (5) we see that an English expression *sweatshop*, meaning a workshop or small factory where many people work in cramped conditions and for little pay, is used in this newspaper text since there is no equivalent Spanish expression.

Spanish/English

(5)	No	fue	eso	lo.que	sucedió	en	los	paises	asiáticos
	not	was	that	which	happened	in	the	countries	asian
	que	empezaron		como	*sweatshops*				
	that	began		like	sweatshops				

'That was not what happened in Asian countries that started out as *sweatshops*.'

In examples (4) and (5) we see the insertion of an individual word from one language, here English, into a sentence in another language, here French and Spanish. This kind of code switching can be incidental. But if this occurs more often than randomly, the borrowed word can become established in the lexicon of the other language. Such words are then called **loan words** and the process is referred to as **borrowing**. Most languages borrow words and this borrowing is especially stimulated where there is interaction with another language community (see Section 11.10 and Section 17.3). Some languages are avid borrowers. Dutch has borrowed many words in the past from French (*bureau*, *cafe*, *niveau*), and more recently from English (*manager*, *weekend*, *part-time*, *loser*, *funky*). English also borrowed many words from French in the past. Speakers of languages such as French fight against such trends. Loan words often occur in specific sectors or domains of society. In Turkey, for example, the French played a big part in the development of the railways and so many words connected to this area, such as *peron* from French *perron* 'platform' or *bilet* from *billet* 'ticket', have been borrowed into Turkish. In computer and information technology many terms are being borrowed from English, such as *web site, attachment, screensaver, flow charts, power point, shift, delete* and *recycle bin*.

Loan words will often be adapted to the sound system of the recipient language, as we briefly mentioned in Section 16.2. Let us look at the examples of English loan words in Japanese (6).

Japanese
(6) a. biniiru
'vinyl'
b. shinaa
'thinner'
c. sutairo
'style'

Japanese does not have English sounds such as /v/ as in *vinyl* (8a), nor /θ/ as in *thinner* (8b) and substitutes other consonants for these sounds. Japanese also makes no distinction between /l/ and /r/ having an intermediate consonant, so the final /l/ in *vinyl* and *style* becomes /r/. These are adaptations in terms of individual sounds but adaptations also occur in the phonotactics of syllable structure. Japanese does not allow clusters such as /st/ and so inserts a vowel as in *sutairo* (8c). A vowel is inserted at the end of *sutairo* and *biniiru* since Japanese may not end a syllable with a consonant. These kinds of phonological adaptations of loan words are very common in languages that borrow.

In the same way, languages also adapt loan words to the morphological system of the recipient language. The example in (7) shows how the verb *chat* has been adapted into Italian, and (8) into German.

Italian

(7)	chattare	chatta	chattiamo	avete chattato?
	'to chat (e-mail)'	's/he chats'	'we chat'	'have you chatted?'

German

(8)	chatten	chattest	wir haben gechat
	'to chat (e-mail)'	'you.chat'	'we have chatted'

The borrowed verb *chat* is conjugated and declined according to the rules of the recipient language, Italian in (7) and German in (8). Thus we find the *-ato* suffix in the Italian past participle attached to the English verb *chat* in (9) and the *ge-* prefix of German past participles attached to the same English verb in (10). The other tenses are also conjugated with the usual suffixes from the respective languages.

A special case of adaptation of loan words can be found in the following compounds taken from Welsh (9).

Welsh

(9) a. maes rygbi
field rugby
'rugby ground'

b. lledr sgio
slope ski.*non-finite*
'ski(ing) slope'

c. car cebl
car cable
'cable car'

Loan compounds such as these consist of a combination of a loan word from language A (here English) and an original word from language B (here Welsh), as in (9a) and (9b). There are also loan compounds where both parts have been borrowed, as in (9c). In all these compounds the modifier obeys the rule of Welsh, namely that the modifier follows the noun to be modified (see Section 13.4), which is the reverse pattern of the donor language, English.

A different and more subtle form of influence from one language on another can be found in the use of expressions such as Spanish *tener un buen tempo* 'have a good time', which comes directly from English *to have a good time*. This is used in United States Spanish, but does not exist in European or Latin American Spanish. Such expressions are known as **loan translations**. What is borrowed here is not a word form or word combination, but a whole expression. The English compound *skyscraper*, first used in the United States in 1883, has been translated into many languages: French *gratte-ciel*, Spanish *rascacielos*, German *Wolkenkratzer*, etc. In a loan translation an expression from language A is directly and literally translated, almost word for word, into language B. A creative example is the French/English new formation *port-a-pet* 'carry a pet' for a foldable carton box in which to carry your pet to the vet.

Do bilinguals always manage to keep the two languages apart? For some bilinguals the answer is yes, for others it is no. When language A is spoken and elements of language B make their way into it, this is called **interference**. This linguistic phenomenon is best known from research into second language acquisition, as we saw in Section 3.5. In second language acquisition the direction of interference is almost always from the mother tongue to the second language; for this process the notion 'transfer' is generally used. In the case of bilinguals, such as children who acquire two languages simultaneously (Section 3.6), interference can take place in both directions. We can find interference at all levels of the linguistic system and it can take many different forms.

The phenomenon of borrowing as a type of language change first begins at the level of the individual speaker, in the form of interference. One or a few speakers begin to adopt foreign elements in their speech. When more speakers follow this example, and the process acquires a systematic character, the original language will have changed. We have then moved from interference to borrowing of an element from language A into language B. At a lexical level, this borrowing of words from another language usually has a cultural aspect, as we saw in the example of French railway terms being borrowed as loan words from French into Turkish. When a new notion or product is adopted, the word for it comes along as well. Beyond the word level, languages can also converge in grammar and in phonology if they are in contact over a long period of time (see Section 17.2 under *Sprachbund*). Large numbers of second language learners can be the source of this contact between two languages, and thus the source of language change (see Section 19.4).

In this section we have discussed how language contact may affect the languages concerned in many different ways. There is one further possibility, though, that we have not yet discussed, and that is the emergence of a new language. This will be the subject of Section 20.7.

20.7 The Emergence of New Languages

Many of the more than 6000 languages still in use in the world today have slowly developed from earlier languages. Thus, English has its origin in dialects of West Germanic, French in Vulgar Latin, etc. It is precisely such slow and gradual developments in the course of history that enable us to reconstruct language families such as Indo-European (see Section 17.2). Not every language came into being in this way, however: some have developed in a far shorter period of time, and do not have one single clear ancestor. These are the **creole languages**.

How many creole languages there are is not known; we simply do not have the necessary historical information. But we do know that since 1500, the beginning of European expansion and the slave trade, about a hundred new languages have come into being. These languages are mainly spoken in the Caribbean, on the coast of West Africa and the islands of the Indian Ocean and the Pacific, but there are others – Nubi, for example, is a creole language spoken in Uganda and Kenya and which is based on Arabic and several African languages.

Creole languages owe their existence to specific social circumstances. Imagine the following situation. In a market in Budapest, Hungary, a Vietnamese seller is trying to persuade a customer from Romania to buy. They do not have a language in common, but both know a little bit of Hungarian and German, and use these as best they can to try and convey their intentions. This is probably a one-off situation, but what happens when people who do not have a language in common need to communicate regularly with each other? It is quite possible that this will bring into existence a simplified linguistic system, a **pidgin** language. A pidgin can arise in a situation of incipient trade, when people use mostly body language together with a few words in order to explain something to each other. If this contact between groups of speakers continues, this improvised communication system may progress further and start to develop some basic rules. In this case a new form of language has arisen which, initially at least, is nobody's mother tongue.

Many pidgins disappear again, but others grow in importance and at some point in time there may be children who acquire a pidgin as their first language. In such circumstances a pidgin will develop into a fully fledged language, a creole. An example of this can be found in New Guinea, where Tok Pisin (literally 'Talk Pidgin') has become one of the national languages. Many other pidgins will function as a lingua franca.

Although creole languages are thought to be just as complex as all other human languages, their structure still reflects how they originated from a pidgin. The absence of verbal inflectional endings is a case in point. A typical example is the sentence in (10) from Sranan, a creole language of Surinam in South America.

Sranan

(10) mi ben sa wani aksi yu wan sani.
me *past future* want ask you one something
'I would like to ask you something.'

What linguistic features can we observe in this sentence? First of all that *mi* (from English *me*) is the unchanging form for the first person singular; there is no distinction as there is in English between *I* and *me*. Then, the past tense particle *ben* comes from English *been*, and the future particle *sa* from *shall*. The verb *aksi* comes from spoken English *aks* 'ask' with an extra vowel added at the end; the same goes for the modal verb *wani* 'want'. Finally, *sami* derives from *something*. As we can see, the majority of elements in Sranan come from English, but they have undergone all kinds of formal and semantic changes.

Pidgins never arise in a vacuum. Very often they are based on the vocabulary of the language of a dominant group such as slave traders and plantation owners. In the Sranan case (10), that language was the English of the eighteenth century. On the other hand, pidgins are also influenced by the structure of the language of the subordinate group, in this case the African slaves in Surinam. As a consequence, the structure of many Caribbean creole languages like Haitian and Sranan closely resembles that of the languages of West Africa, even though the vocabulary of those languages has not been adopted or retained. The situation we have here is one in which the vocabulary of one language, in this case a European colonial language, is matched with the grammar of a different language, in this case one from West Africa. The Sranan sentence in (11) shows constructions that you also find in a number of West African languages.

Sranan
(11) Na kon Roy ben tyari Sjori kon?
Is come Roy *past* carry George come?
'Did Roy carry George here?'

Within one sentence we find here a chain of verbs: *kon* 'come' ... *tyari* 'carry' ... *kon* 'come', which together mean something like 'to carry here'. This type of verb chain is well known in many languages both in West Africa and in the Caribbean. The same goes for the repetition of verbs. To emphasise a particular aspect of the action, the verb is mentioned both at the beginning of the sentence and again later in the sentence. To indicate that the direction of the action is towards the speaker, sentence (11) repeats the verb *kon*. The construction can be paraphrased as: 'Is it *coming* that Roy came to carry George?' or 'Is it *here* that Roy carried George?'

In the history of new languages an important role has been played by the process of **relexification**. The basic grammatical structure of the mother tongue is retained, but the vocabulary is replaced by that of another language. An example is the language Media Lengua, literally 'in-between language', which is a relexified form of Quechua with Spanish vocabulary spoken in Ecuador (12). It probably originated in the beginning of the twentieth century when young Quechuan workers came to work on the railways.

Media Lengua
(12) kuyi-buk yirba nu-wabi-shka.
cavia-*benefactive* grass *neg*-there.is-*tense*
'There is no grass for the cavias.'

Quechua
(13) kuyi-buk k'iwa illa-shka.
cavia-*benefactive* grass there.is.*neg-tense*
'There is no grass for the cavias.'

Spanish
(14) No hay hierba para los cuyes.
Neg there.is grass for the cavias
'There is no grass for the cavias.'

By comparing the sentences in (12), (13) and (14) we can see that in Media Lengua the content word *yirba* is taken from Spanish and an adapted form of the verb meaning 'there is' from the Spanish *haber.* The content word *kuyi* and the word order and grammatical suffixes are from Quechua.

Note that relexification can also occur outside the context of new languages and without pidginisation and creolisation, that is, when there is wholesale lexical borrowing, as for example when many languages today borrow computerese from American English.

Some new languages are not as completely new as creoles. These new languages appear to be a simplified version of a language that is used outside its original area. When such a new variety of language arises from the contact between different dialects of one and the same language, very often most of the original dialect differences will disappear, and the result is called a **koine** (from Greek *koinos* 'common'). Koines emerged in Northern China in the seventh to tenth centuries, for example, or in the United States in the seventeenth century in the large Spanish or Portuguese settlements when large groups speaking different dialects had to communicate with each other. Koine properties can be found in, for example, Afrikaans in South Africa, which had its origin in a range of different Dutch dialects that were simplified and amalgamated, although Nama, the language of the Khoekhoe, also played an important role in the formation of Afrikaans. Another example is Sarnami, the language of the Hindustani community in Surinam, which arose from a range of cognate languages from North India spoken by plantation labourers who were contracted by the Dutch after the abolition of slavery.

Summary

In many communities in the world people use more than one language in daily life. These communities are characterised by **bilingualism** or **multilingualism**. In bilingual communities we often find **diglossia**, when two languages, one more prestigious than the other, are used in different **circumstances**. A **lingua franca** can be used as a contact language between people who speak different mother tongues.

Language communities can undergo changes, which may lead to **language shift**, **language loss**, **language erosion** and finally **language death**, or its opposite, **language maintenance**. The final outcome often depends on the **language policy** of the relevant authorities, for example when schools offer bilingual education to children who speak a minority language at home. Bilingual education can consist of an **immersion programme** or of a **transitional programme**. In the latter initially the minority language is used, and this later changes to the national language or that of the dominant majority.

Bilingualism often comes particularly to the fore in everyday contact situations. Here an important issue is that of **language choice**. Sometimes both languages are used in the same conversation, which can lead to **code switching**. The basis for this sort of influence is **interference**: the incidental use of elements from one language while speaking the other. In situations of language contact we find more long-lasting influences of one language on another, often in the form of **loan words**, **loan compounds** and **loan translations** in the process of **borrowing**. Finally, new forms of language can emerge: **creole languages** which emerge from **pidgins** or from processes such as **relexification**. A creole language must be distinguished from a **koine**, that is a new variety of language that arises from contact between speakers of different dialects of a language outside the original language community.

Assignments

1. Take a large city you are familiar with. What are the three languages with the largest numbers of speakers in that city? How can you find this out?
2. Think of an example of a diglossic situation and a situation where there is no functional separation between varieties/languages. Why do you think that no functional separation has occurred in the latter case?
3. Many languages spoken by indigenous minorities are dying out and are being replaced by the dominant language of the majority group living in the area. Can you think of three advantages and three disadvantages of this process – for the speakers involved, and for mankind in general?
4. Compare two examples of governmental language policy from two different countries. Why have these policies been adopted?
5. Many children do not speak the same language at home and in school. Often these children are given a transitional programme of bilingual education. What are the arguments used to justify such a programme?
6. In many large cities where several languages are spoken young people use a mixed language amongst themselves. Is this mixed language a form of code switching, borrowing, an indication of lexical problems or the beginning of a creole?
7. Can loan words always be fitted into the grammatical and phonological system of the borrowing language? Think of three examples of loan words borrowed into a language you know well and analyse how they have been adapted (if at all).

Test Yourself

1. What is the difference between diglossia and bilingualism?
2. What is the difference between language shift and language loss?
3. What is a transitional programme of bilingual education?
4. What factors play a role in language choice?
5. What is the difference between a loan word and a loan translation?
6. When does a pidgin become a creole language?
7. What is relexification?
8. What is a lingua franca?

ACKNOWLEDGMENTS AND FURTHER READING

Useful introductions to bilingualism are by Romaine (1995), Arends *et al.* (1994), and Edwards (1994). A more advanced guide can be found in the handbook by Kroll and de Groot (2004). Bialystok (2001) and De Groot (2011) discuss the relationship between bilingualism and general development and cognition. Code switching is the subject of Milroy & Muysken (1995), which goes into more detail on many of the topics discussed in this chapter. Baker (2006) discusses the issues of bilingual education. Examples from Arabic come from Warschauer *et al.* (2002), early English from Nurmi & Pahta (2004). The Media Lengua example is taken from Muysken (1996).

References

This list of references includes all of the bibliographic sources which are found either in the main body of the text or in the Acknowledgments and Further Reading sections at the end of each chapter.

Abley, M. (2003) *Spoken Here: Travels Among Threatened Languages*, New York: Houghton Mifflin.

Aboh, E.O. (2004) *The Morphosyntax of Complement-Head Sequences: Clause structure and Word Order Patterns in Kwa*, New York: Oxford University Press.

Ahlsén, E. (2006) *Introduction to Neurolinguistics*. Göteborg: Göteborg University Press.

Aikhenvald, A.Y. (2007) Typological distinctions in word formation, in Shopen, T. (ed.), *Language Typology and Syntactic Description. Volume III: Grammatical Categories and the Lexicon*. Cambridge: Cambridge University Press, pp. 1–65.

Aitchison, J. (1976) *The Articulate Mammal*, London: Routledge.

Aitchison, J. (1981) *Language Change: Progress or Decay*? London: Fontana.

Aitchison, J. (1991) *Language Change: Progress or Decay?* 3rd edn, Cambridge: Cambridge University Press.

Anderson, S.R. (1985) Typological distinctions in word formation, in Shopen, T. (ed.), *Language Typology and Syntactic Description. Volume III: Grammatical Categories and the Lexicon*. Cambridge: Cambridge University Press, pp. 3–56.

Arends, J., Muysken, P. and Smith, N. (eds) (1994) *Pidgin and Creole Languages: An Introduction*, Amsterdam: Benjamins.

Arias, R. and Lakshmanan, U. (2005) Code switching in a Spanish-English bilingual child: a communication resource. In Cohen, J., McAlister, K.T., Rolstad, K. and MacSwan, J. (eds), ISB4: Proceedings of the 4th International Symposium on Bilingualism. Somerville, MA: Cascadilla Press, pp. 94–109.

Asher, R.E. (1982) *Tamil*, Amsterdam: North Holland.

Ashton, Ethel O. (1944) *Swahili Grammar (Including Intonation)*, London: Longman.

Atchley, R.A. *et al.* (2006) A comparison of semantic and syntactic event related potentials generated by children and adults. *Brain and Language* 99, 236–246.

Austin, J.L. (1962) *How to Do Things With Words*, Oxford: Clarendon Press.

Aydede, M. (2004) The Language of Thought Hypothesis, *Stanford Encyclopedia of Philosophy* (online), Stanford: Stanford University.

Baker, A.E., van den Bogaerde, B., Pfau, R. and Schermer, T. (in preparation), *Sign Linguistics: the Basics*, John Benjamins, Amsterdam.

Baker, C. (2006) *Foundations of Bilingual Education and Bilingualism*, Cleveland: Multilingual Matters.

Baker, M. (1988) *Incorporation: A Theory of Grammatical Function Changing*, Chicago: University of Chicago Press.

Basbøll, H. (2005) *The Phonology of Danish*, Oxford: Oxford University Press.

Linguistics, First Edition. Edited by Anne E. Baker and Kees Hengeveld.

Bat-El, Outi (1993) Parasitic metrification in the modern Hebrew stress system. *The Linguistic Review* 10, pp. 189–210.

Bauer, L. (1995) *Introducing Linguistic Morphology*, Edinburgh: Edinburgh University Press.

Beekes, R.S.P. (1995) *Comparative Indo-European Linguistics: An Introduction*, Amsterdam: Benjamins.

Bergvall, V.L., Bing, J.M. and Freed, A.F. (eds) (1996) *Rethinking Language and Gender Research: Theory and Practice*, London: Longman.

Berko Gleason, J. (1997) *The Development of Language*, 4th edn, Needham Heights, MA: Allyn & Bacon.

Berkum, J. van, Brink, D. van den, Tesink, C., *et al.* (2008) The neural integration of the speaker and the message. *Journal of Cognitive Neuroscience* 20 (4), 580–591.

Berlin, B. and Kay, P. (1969) *Basic Color Terms: Their Universality and Evolution*, Berkeley, CA: University of California Press.

Bialystok, E. (2001) *Bilingualism in Development: Language, Literacy, and Cognition*, Cambridge: Cambridge University Press.

Bickel, B. and Nichols, J. (2007) Inflectional morphology, in Shopen, T. (ed), *Language Typology and Syntactic Description. Volume III: Grammatical Categories and the Lexicon*, 2nd edn, Cambridge: Cambridge University Press, pp. 169–240.

Birdsong, D. (ed.) (1999) *Second Language Acquisition and the Critical Period Hypothesis*, Hillsdale, NJ: Lawrence Erlbaum.

Boersma, P. and Weenink, D. (2005) Praat: doing phonetics by computer, www.praat.org [accessed online April 2011].

Bogoras, W. (1917) *Koryak Texts*, Leyden: Brill.

Booij, G. (2007) *The Grammar of Words*, Oxford: Oxford University Press.

Bright, M. (1990) *The Dolittle Obsession*, London: BBC.

Brown, C.M., and Hagoort, P. (1999) The cognitive neuroscience of language: challenges and future directions, in Brown, C.M. and Hagoort, P. (eds), *Neurocognition of Language*, Oxford: Oxford University Press, pp. 3–15.

Brown, G. and Yule, G. (1983) *Discourse Analysis*, Cambridge: Cambridge University Press.

Bybee, J. (1985) *Morphology: A Study of the Relation Between Meaning and Form*, Amsterdam: John Benjamins.

Bybee, J., Perkins, R. and Pagliuca, W. (1994) *The Evolution of Grammar: Tense, Aspect and Modality in the Languages of the* World, Chicago: Chicago University Press.

Bynon, T. (1977) *Historical Linguistics*, Cambridge: Cambridge University Press.

Byrd, D.M. and Mintz, T.H. (2010) *Discovering Speech, Words, and Mind*. Oxford: Wiley-Blackwell.

Carroll, D.W. (1999) *Psychology of Language*, 3rd edn, Pacific Grove, CA: Brooks/Cole.

Chambers, J.K. and Trudgill, P. (1980) *Dialectology*, Cambridge: Cambridge University Press.

Chambers, J.K., Trudgill, P. and Schilling-Estes, N. (2004) *The Handbook of Language Variation and Change*, Oxford: Blackwell.

Chomsky, N. (1972) *Language and Mind*, expanded edition, New York: Harcourt, Brace Jovanovich.

Clark, E. (2003) *First Language Acquisition*, Cambridge: Cambridge University Press.

Comrie, B. (1976) *Aspect*, Cambridge: Cambridge University Press.

Comrie, B. (1985) *Tense*, Cambridge: Cambridge University Press.

Comrie, B. (1989) *Language Universals and Linguistic Typology*, 2nd edn, Oxford: Blackwell.

Cowan, W. and Rakušan, J. (1998) *Source Book for Linguistics*, Amsterdam: Benjamins.

Croft, W. (1993) *Language Typology*, Cambridge: Cambridge University Press.

Cruse, D.A. (1986) *Lexical Semantics*, Cambridge: Cambridge University Press.

Curtiss, S. (1977) *Genie: A Psycholinguistic Study of a Modern-Day "Wild Child"*, Boston: Academic Press.

D'Allesandro, R. and Alexiadou, A. (2006) The syntax of the indefinite pronoun *nome*. *Probus* 18.2, 189–218.

Damico, J.S., Müller, N. and Ball, M.J. (2010) *The Handbook of Language and Speech Disorders*, Oxford: Wiley-Blackwell.

De Bot, K., Lowie, W., and Verspoor, M. (2005) *Second Language Acquisition: An Advanced Resource Book*, London: Routledge.

De Groot, A.M.B. (2011) *Handbook of Bilingualism: Psycholinguistic Approaches*, New York: Oxford University Press.

Deacon, T.W. (1998) *The Symbolic Species: The Co-evolution of Language and the Brain*, New York and London: WW Norton and Company.

Deutscher, G. (2011) *Through the Language Glass. Why the World Looks Different in Other Languages*, London: Arrow Books.

Dik, S.C. (1997) *The Theory of Functional Grammar*, 2 volumes, Hengeveld, K. (ed.), Berlin: Mouton de Gruyter.

Dixon, R.W.M. (1972) *The Dyirbal Language of North Queensland*, Cambridge: Cambridge University Press.

Dixon, R.W.M. (1988) *A Grammar of Boumaa Fijian*, Chicago: University of Chicago Press.

Donzel, M. van (1999) *Prosodic Aspects of Information Structure in Discourse*, Utrecht: LOT.

Edwards, J. (1994) *Multilingualism*, London: Routledge.

Eisikovits, E. (1987) Sex differences in inter-group and intra-group interactions among adolescents, in Pauwels, A (ed.), *Women and Language in Australian and New Zealand Society*, Sydney: Australian Professional Publications, pp. 45–58.

Elbert, S.H. and Pukui, M.K. (1979) *Hawaiian Grammar*, Honolulu: The University Press of Hawaii.

Ellegård, A. (1953) *The Auxiliary "Do": The establishment and regulation of its use in English*, Gothenburg Studies in English, 2. Stockholm: Almqvist & Wiksell.

Ellis, R. (1994) *The Study of Second Language Acquisition*, Oxford: Oxford University Press.

Evans, N.D. (1995) *A Grammar of Kayardild: With Historical Comparative Notes on Tangkic*, Berlin: Mouton de Gruyter.

Evans, N.D. (2000) Word classes in the world's languages, in Booij, G., Lehmann, C. and Mugdan, J. (eds), *Morphology: A Handbook on Inflection and Word Formation*, Berlin: Mouton de Gruyter, pp. 708–732.

Evans, N.D. (2003) *Bininj Gun-Wok: A Pan-Dialectal Grammar of Mayali, Kunwinjku and Kune*, 2 volumes, Canberra: Australian National University.

Everaert, M. *et al.* (ed.) (1995) *Idioms: Structural and Psychological Perspectives*, Hillsdale, NJ: Lawrence Erlbaum.

Everett, D.L. (2008) *Don't Sleep, There Are Snakes. Life and Language in the Amazonian Jungle*, New York: Pantheon.

Fabb, N. (2005) *Sentence Structure*, 2nd edn, London: Routledge.

Fillmore, C.J. (1968) The case for case, in Bach, E. and Harms, R.T. (eds), *Universals in Linguistic Theory*, New York: Holt, Rinehart and Winston, pp. 1–88.

Fletcher, P. and MacWhinney, B. (eds) (1995) *The Handbook of Child Language*, Oxford: Blackwell.

Foley, W. (1997) *Anthropological Linguistics: An Introduction*, Oxford: Blackwell.

Frake, C.O. (1964) How to ask for a drink in Subanun. *American Anthropologist*, 66 (6), 127–132.

Freeborn, D., Langford, D. and French, P. (1993) *Varieties of English. An Introduction to the Study of English*, Basingstoke: Palgrave Macmillan.

Frisch, K. von (1923) *Über die 'Sprache' der Bienen*, Jena: Gustav Fischer Verlag.

Gaskell, M. G. (2007) *The Oxford Handbook of Psycholinguistics*, Oxford: Oxford University Press.

Gass, S.M. and Selinker, L. (1994) *Second Language Acquisition: An Introductory Course*, Hillsdale, NJ: Lawrence Erlbaum.

Goedemans, R.W.N. and van der Hulst, H.G. (2005) Fixed stress locations, in Haspelmath, M., Dryer, M., Gil, D. and Comrie, B. (eds), *World Atlas of Language Structures*, Oxford University Press: Oxford, pp. 62–65.

Greenberg, J.H. (1963) Some universals of grammar with particular reference to the order of meaningful elements, in Greenberg, J.H. (ed.), *Universals of Language*, Cambridge, MA: MIT Press.

Gudykunst, W.B. and Mody, B. (2002) *Handbook of International and Intercultural Communication*, London: Sage Publications.

Halliday, M.A.K. and Hasan, R. (1976) *Cohesion in English*, London: Longman.

Harrington, J., Palethorpe, S. and Watson, C. (2005) Deepening or lessening the divide between diphthongs: an analysis of the Queen's annual Christmas broadcasts, in Hardcastle, W.J. and Mackenzie Beck, J. (eds), *A Figure of Speech: A Festschrift for John Laver*, Hillsdale, NJ: Lawrence Erlbaum, pp. 227–261.

Haspelmath, M. (1995) The converb as a cross-linguistically valid category, in Haspelmath, M. and König, E. (eds), *Converbs in Cross-Linguistic Perspective*, Berlin: Mouton de Gruyter, pp. 1–55.

Haspelmath, M. (2002) *Understanding Morphology*, London: Arnold.

Haspelmath, M. (2007) Coordination, in Shopen, T. (ed.), *Language Typology and Syntactic Description. Volume II: Complex Constructions*, 2nd edn, Cambridge: Cambridge University Press, pp. 1–51.

Hawkins, J.A. (1983) *Word Order Universals*, New York: Academic Press.

Hock, H.H. (1986) *Principles of Historical Linguistics*, Berlin: Mouton de Gruyter.

Hovdhaugen, E. *et al.* (1989) *A Handbook of the Tokelau Language*, Oslo: Norwegian University Press.

Huang, Y. (2006) *Pragmatics*, Oxford: Oxford University Press.

Hudson, R.A. (1996) *Sociolinguistics*, 2nd edn, Cambridge: Cambridge University Press.

Johnston, T.A and Schembri, A. (2007) *Australian Sign Language (Auslan): An Introduction to Sign Language Linguistics*, Cambridge: Cambridge University Press.

Joseph, B. and Philippaki-Warburton, I. (1987) *Modern Greek*, London: Croom Helm.

Kortmann, B. and Wagner, S. (2010) Changes and Continuities in Dialect Grammar, in Hickey, R. (ed.), *Eighteenth-Century English: Ideology and Change*, Cambridge: Cambridge University Press, pp. 269–292.

Kroll, J. and de Groot, A. (eds) (2004) *Handbook of Bilingualism*, Oxford: Oxford University Press.

Kuiken, F. and Vedder, I. (2008) Cognitive task complexity and written output in Italian and French as a foreign language. *Journal of Second Language Writing* 17 (1), 48–60.

Labov, W. (1966) *The Social Stratification of English in New York City*, Washington, D.C: Center for Applied Linguistics.

Ladefoged, P. (2001) *Vowels and Consonants*, Oxford: Blackwell.

Ladefoged, P. and Maddieson, I. (1996) *The Sounds of the World's Languages*, Oxford: Blackwell.

Lakoff, G. and Johnson, M. (1980) *Metaphors We Live By*, Chicago: University of Chicago Press.

Lakshmanan, U. (1994) *Universal Grammar in Child Second Language Acquisition*, John Benjamins, Amsterdam.

Lardiere, D. (2008) Feature-Assembly in Second Language Acquisition, in Liceras, J., Zobl, H. and Goodluck, H. (eds), *The Role of Formal Features in Second Language Acquisition*, Hillsdale, NJ: Lawrence Erlbaum, pp. 106–140.

Larsen-Freeman, D. and Long, M.H. (1991) *An Introduction to Second Language Acquisition*, London/New York: Longman.

Laver, J. (1994) *Principles of Phonetics*, Cambridge: Cambridge University Press.

Leuninger, H., Hohenberger, A., Waleschkowski, E. *et al.* (2004) The impact of modality on language production: evidence from slips of the tongue and hand, in Pechmann, T. and Habel, C. (eds), *Multidisciplinary Approaches to Language Production*, Berlin: Mouton de Gruyter, pp. 219–277.

Levelt, W.J.M. (1989) *Speaking: From Intention to Articulation*, Cambridge, MA: The MIT Press.

Levinson, S.C. (1983) *Pragmatics*, Cambridge: Cambridge University Press.

Lewis, G.L. (1967) *Turkish Grammar*, Oxford: Clarendon Press.

Li, C. and Thompson, S. (1981) *Mandarin Chinese: A Functional Reference Grammar*, Berkeley, CA: University of California Press.

Lyons, J. (1968) *Introduction to Theoretical Linguistics*, Cambridge: Cambridge University Press.

Lyons, J. (1977) *Semantics*, 2 volumes, Cambridge: Cambridge University Press.

MacDonald, L. (1990) *A Grammar of Tauya*, Berlin: Mouton de Gruyter.

MacSweeney M., Woll. B., Campbell, R. *et al.* (2002) Neural systems underlying British Sign Language and audio-visual English processing in native users. *Brain* 125, 1583–93.

Mair, C. (1995) Changing patterns of complementation, and concomitant grammaticalization, of the verb *help* in present-day British English, in Aarts, B. and Meyer, C.F. (eds), *The Verb in Contemporary English: Theory and Description*. Cambridge: Cambridge University Press, pp. 258–272.

Mampe, B., Friederici, A.D., Christophe, A. and Wermke, K. (2009) Newborns' cry melody is shaped by their native language. *Current Biology*, 19 (23), 1994–1997.

Martínez I., Arsuaga J.L., Quam R. *et al.* (2008) Human hyoid bones from the middle Pleistocene site of the Sima de los Huesos (Sierra de Atapuerca, Spain), *Journal of Human Evolution*, 54 (1), 118–124.

Matthews, P.H. (1974) *Morphology: An Introduction to the Theory of Word Structure*, Cambridge: Cambridge University Press.

McNamara, D.W. and Kintsch, W. (1996) Learning from texts: effects of prior knowledge and text coherence. *Discourse Processes*, 22, 247–288.

Miller, G.A. (1991) *The Science of Words*, New York, Scientific American Library.

Mills, A.E. (1985) *The Acquisition of Gender*, Heidelberg: Springer Verlag.

Mills, A.E. (1985) The acquisition of German, in Slobin, D.I. (ed.), *The Crosslinguistic Study of Language Acquisition. Volume 1: The Data*, Hillsdale, NJ: Lawrence Erlbaum, pp. 141–254.

Milroy, L. (1987) *Language and Social Networks*, 2nd edn, Oxford: Blackwell.

Milroy, L. and Muysken, P. (eds) (1995) *One Speaker, Two Languages*, Cambridge: Cambridge University Press.

Mitchell, R. and Myles, F. (1998) *Second Language Learning Theories*, London: Arnold.

Mithun Williams, M. (1976) *A Grammar of Tuscarora*, New York: Garland Publishing.

Montrul, S. (2009) Incomplete acquisition of tense-aspect and mood in Spanish heritage speakers. *The International Journal of Bilingualism*, 13 (3), 239–269.

Montrul, S. (2010) Research methods in L2 acquisition and bilingualism. 6th EMLAR (Experimental Methods in Language Acquisition Research), Utrecht, The Netherlands, February 3–5.

Moravcsik, E. (2006) *An Introduction to Syntax*. New York: Continuum.

Mosel, U. and Hovdhaugen, E. (1992) *Samoan Reference Grammar*, Oslo: Scandinavian University Press.

Munro, P. and Gordon, L. (1982) Syntactic relations in Western Muskogean, *Language* 58, 81–115.

Muysken, P.C. (1996) Media Lengua in Ecuador, in Wurm, S.A., Mühlhäusler, P. and Tryon, D.T. (eds), *Atlas of Languages of Intercultural Communication in the Pacific, Asia, and the Americas*, Berlin: Mouton de Gruyter, pp. 1335–1337.

Nieuwland, M.S. and Van Berkum, J.J.A. (2008) The interplay between semantic and referential aspects of anaphoric noun phrase resolution: evidence from ERPs. *Brain and Language*, 106, 119–131.

Noonan, M. (2007) Complementation, in Shopen, T. (ed.) (2007) *Language Typology and Syntactic Description. Volume II: Complex constructions*, 2nd edn, Cambridge: Cambridge University Press, pp. 52–150.

Nurmi, A. and Pahta, P. (2004) Social stratification and patterns of code-switching in Early English letters. *Multilingua*, 23 (4), 417–456.

Olmsted, G.J. and Gamal-Eldin, S. (1982) *Cairene Egyptian Colloquial Arabic*, Amsterdam: North Holland.

Pandharipande, R.V. (1997) *Marathi*, London: Routledge.

Parr, S., Byng., S. and Gilpin, S. (1998) *Talking About Aphasia*, Buckingham: Open University Press.

Pietsch, L. (2005) Some do and some doesn't: verbal concord variation in the north of the British Isles, in Kortmann, B., Herrmann, T., Pietsch, L. and Wagner, S. (eds) *A Comparative Grammar of British English Dialects: Agreement, Gender, Relative Clauses* (Topics in English Linguistics, 50.1), Berlin & New York: Mouton de Gruyter, 125–209.

Pietsch, L. (2005) *Variable Grammars: Verbal Agreement in Northern Dialects of English*, Tübingen: Niemeyer.

Pinker, S. (1994) *The Language Instinct: The New Science of Language and Mind*, London: The Penguin Press.

Prins, R. (1987) *Afasie- classificatie, behandeling en herstelverloop*. Dissertation. University of Amsterdam.

Pullum, G.K. and Ladusaw, W.A. (1986) *Phonetic Symbol Guide*, Chicago: University of Chicago Press.

Pylkkänen, L. and Marantz, A. (2003) Tracking the time course of word recognition with MEG. *Trends in Cognitive Sciences*, 7 (5), 187–189.

Ramirez, H. (1997) *A fala Tukano dos Yepa-Masa. Tomo 1. Gramática*, Manaus: Inspetoria Salesiana.

Ravid, D. (1995) *Language Change in Child and Adult Hebrew: A Psycholinguistic Perspective*, Oxford: Oxford University Press.

Roberts, J.R. (1987) *Amele*, London: Croom Helm.

Romaine, S. (1995) *Bilingualism*, 2nd edn, Blackwell: Oxford.

Ryfa, J. (2003) *Estuary English: A Controversial Issue*? Masters thesis. University of Posnan.

Sacks, O. (1989) *Seeing voices*, Berkeley, CA: University of California Press.

Saeed, J.I. (1997) *Semantics*, Oxford/Cambridge, MA: Blackwell.

Sapir, E. (1921) *Language*, New York: Harcourt, Brace & World.

Sapir, E. (1929) The status of linguistics as a science. *Language*, 5, 207–214.

Sarno, M. T. (1998) *Aphasia*, San Diego, CA: Academic Press.

Saussure, F. de (1916) *Cours de Linguistique Générale*, Paris: Payot.

Savage-Rumbaugh, S. and Lewin, R. (1994) *Kanzi: The Ape at the Brink of the Human Mind*, New York: Wiley.

Scalise, S. (1984) *Generative Morphology*, Dordrecht: Foris.

Schegloff, E.A. (2000) Overlapping talk and the organization of turn-taking for conversation, *Language in Society*, 29 (1), 1–63.

Schiffrin, D. (1994) *Approaches to Discourse*, Oxford/Cambridge, MA: Blackwell.

Schuell, H. and Benson, L. (1972) *The Minnesota Test for Differential Diagnosis of Aphasia*, Minneapolis: University of Minnesota Press.

Searle, J.R. (1969) *Speech Acts*, Cambridge: Cambridge University Press.

Sebold, A. (2002) *The Lovely Bones*, Little Brown.

Shewan, C.M. (1988) The Shewan Spontaneous Language Analysis (SSLA) system for aphasic adults: description, reliability and validity. *Journal of Communication Disorders*, 21, 103–138.

Shopen, T. (ed.) (2007) *Language Typology and Syntactic Description*, 3 Volumes, 2nd edn, Cambridge: Cambridge University Press.

Siewierska, A. (1988) *Word Order Rules*, London: Croom Helm.

Simmons, N. and Johnston, J. (2007) Cross-cultural differences in beliefs and practices that affect the language spoken to children: mothers with Indian and Western heritage. *International Journal of Language and Communication Disorders*, 42 (4), 445–465.

Simpson, G.B. and Burgess, C. (1985) Activation and selection processes in the recognition of ambiguous words. *Journal of Experimental Psychology: Human Perception and Performance*, 11 (1), 28–39.

Slobin, D. (ed.) (1985) *The Crosslinguistic Study of Language Acquisition. Volumes I and II*, Hillsdale, NJ: Lawrence Erlbaum.

Slobin, D. (ed.) (1992) *The Crosslinguistic Study of Language Acquisition. Volume III*, Hillsdale, NJ: Lawrence Erlbaum.

Smith, C.S. (1991) *The Parameter of Aspect*, Dordrecht: Kluwer.

Smith, N. (2002) *Phonology: The Basics*, Oxford: Blackwell.

Smith, N. (in preparation) *Phonology: The Basics*, Oxford: Wiley-Blackwell.

Smoczyńska, M. (1985) The acquisition of Polish, in Slobin, D.I (ed.), *The Crosslinguistic Study of Language Acquisition. Volume 1: The Data*, Hillsdale, NJ: Lawrence Erlbaum, pp. 595–686.

Spencer, A. (1996) *Phonology*, Oxford: Blackwell.

Spruit, A. (1986) *Abkhaz studies*. Dissertation. Leiden University.

Steen, G. (1994) *Understanding Metaphor in Literature*, London: Longman.

Stross, B. (1974) Speaking of speaking: Tenejapa Tzeltal metalinguistics, in Bauman, R. and Sherzer, J. (eds), *Explorations in the Ethnography of Speaking*, Cambridge; Cambridge University Press, pp. 213–239.

Supalla, T. (2008) Sign language archaeology: integrating historical linguistics with fieldwork on young sign languages, in Quadros, R.M. *Sign Languages: Spinning and Unravelling the Past, Present and Future*, Petropolis: Editora Arara Azul.

Sutton-Spence, R. and Woll, B. (1999) *Linguistics of British Sign Language*, Cambridge: Cambridge University Press.

Thomas, J. (1995) *Meaning in Interaction: An Introduction to Pragmatics*, London/New York: Longman.

Thomason, S.G. and Kaufmann, T. (1988) *Language Contact, Creolization, and Genetic Linguistics*, Berkeley, CA: University of California Press.

Thompson, S., Longacre, R. and Hwang, S.J.J. (2007) Adverbial clauses, in Shopen, T. (ed), *Language Typology and Syntactic Description. Volume II: Complex Constructions*, 2nd edn, Cambridge: Cambridge University Press, pp. 237–300.

Tomasello, M. (2003) *Constructing a Language: A Usage Based Account of Language Acquisition*, Harvard, MA: Harvard University Press.

Tomlin, R.S. (1986) *Basic Word Order: Functional Principles*, London: Croom Helm.

Traxler, M. and Gernsbacher, M.A. (2006) *Handbook of Psycholinguistics*, 2nd edn, Oxford: Elsevier.

Van Valin, R.D. Jr and LaPolla, R. J. (1997) *Syntax: Structure, Meaning and Function*, Cambridge: Cambridge University Press.

VanPatten, B. and Williams, J. (2006) *Theories in Second Language Acquisition*, Routledge.

Waller, A., Black, R., O'Mara, D.A. *et al.* (2009) Evaluating the STANDUP pun generating software with children with cerebral palsy. *ACM Transactions on Accessible Computing*, 1 (3).

Wardhaugh, R. (1986) *An Introduction to Sociolinguistics*, Oxford: Blackwell.

Warner, A. (2006) Variation and the interpretation of change in periphrastic DO, in van Kemenade, A. and Los, B.J. (eds), *The Handbook of the History of English*, Oxford: Blackwell, pp. 45–67.

Warschauer, M., El Said, G.R. and Zohry, A. (2002) Language choice online: globalization and identity in Egypt. *Journal of Computer-Mediated Communication* 7.4.

Wilner, J. *et al.* (eds) (2007) *Wortubuku fu Sranan Tongo: Sranan Tongo–Nederlands Woordenboek*, 5th edn, Dallas: SIL International.

Wray, A. (2000) Review of apes, language and the human mind: Sue Savage-Rumbaugh, Stuart G. Shanker and Talbot J. Taylor. *Journal of Pragmatics*, 32, 827–830.

Zeshan, U. (2000) *Sign Language in Indo-Pakistan: A Description of a Signed Language*, Amsterdam: Benjamins.

Zwartjes, O. (2007) Agreement asymmetry in Arabic according to Spanish missionary grammarians from Damascus (18th century), in Zwartjes, O., James, G. and Ridruejo, E. (eds), *Missionary Linguistics III/Lingüística Misionera III. Morphology and Syntax* (Studies in the History of the Language Sciences volume 111), Amsterdam: John Benjamins, pp. 273–303.

Sources of Illustrations

Illustrations are the authors' own or in the public domain with the exception of those listed below:

Figure 1.1	Frisch, K. von (1923) Über die 'Sprache' der Bienen, Jena: Gustav Fischer Verlag.
Figure 2.4	MacSweeney, M., Woll, B., Campbell, R. *et al.* (2002) Neural systems underlying British Sign Language and audio-visual English processing in native users, *Brain* 125, 1583–93.
Figure 2.6	Illustration taken from Card Materials for the Minnesota Test for Differential Diagnosis of Aphasia (Pack One) by Hildred Schuell and Lawrence Benson, University of Minnesota Press © 1965 University of Minnesota.
Figure 4.1 (a and b)	Montrul, S. 'Research methods in L2 acquisition and bilingualism' 6th EMLAR (Experimental Methods in Language Acquisition Research), Utrecht, The Netherlands, February 3–5, 2010.
Figure 5.1	NOAA Photo Library, NOAA Central Library; Association of Commissioned Officers.
Figure 8.2	Montrul, S. (2010) Research methods in L2 acquisition and bilingualism. 6th EMLAR (Experimental Methods in Language Acquisition Research), Utrecht, The Netherlands, February 3–5.
Figure 10.5	Esther Parriger.
Figure 10.7	Montrul, S. (2010) Research methods in L2 acquisition and bilingualism. 6th EMLAR (Experimental Methods in Language Acquisition Research), Utrecht, The Netherlands, February 3–5.
Figure 17.1	Otto Zwartjes.
Figure 18.1	Pietsch, L. (2005) Some do and some doesn't: verbal concord variation in the north of the British Isles, in Kortmann, B., Herrmann, T., Pietsch, L. and Wagner, S. (eds) *A Comparative Grammar of British English Dialects: Agreement, Gender, Relative Clauses* (Topics in English Linguistics, 50.1), Berlin & New York: Mouton de Gruyter, pp. 125–209.

Figure 18.2	Laver, J., (1994) *Principles of Phonetics*, Cambridge: Cambridge University Press.
Figure 19.1	Aitchison, J. (1991) *Language Change: Progress or Decay?* 3rd edn, Cambridge: Cambridge University Press.
Figure 19.2	Mark Davies mark_davies@byu.edu
Figure 19.3	Aitchison, J. (1991) *Language Change: Progress or Decay?* 3rd edn, Cambridge: Cambridge University Press.

Index

Numbers in **boldface** refer to pages where a concept is defined in most detail.

Linguistics, First Edition. Edited by Anne E. Baker and Kees Hengeveld.